# fashion

## the key concepts

jennifer craik

Oxford · New York

English edition
First published in 2009 by
**Berg**
Editorial offices:
First Floor, Angel Court, 81 St Clements Street, Oxford OX4 1AW, UK
175 Fifth Avenue, New York, NY 10010, USA



Photo editor:
Shellaine Godbold



Berg is the imprint of Oxford International Publishers Ltd.

**Library of Congress Cataloging-in-Publication Data**
Craik, Jennifer.
Fashion : the key concepts / Jennifer Craik.
p. cm.
Includes bibliographical references and index.
ISBN-13: 978-1-84520-452-5 (pbk.)
ISBN-10: 1-84520-452-2 (pbk.)
ISBN-13: 978-1-84520-451-8 (cloth)
ISBN-10: 1-84520-451-4 (cloth)
1. Fashion design. 2. Fashion merchandising. 3. Fashion designers. 4. Clothing trade. 5. Fashion—Psychological aspects. 6. Clothing and dress—Symbolic aspects. 7. Clothing and dress—Erotic aspects. I. Title.
TT507.C834 2009
746.9'2—dc22
2009015293

**British Library Cataloguing-in-Publication Data**
A catalogue record for this book is available from the British Library.

ISBN 978-1-84520-451-8 (Cloth)
ISBN 978-1-84520-452-5 (Paper)

Typeset by Apex CoVantage, Madison, WI, USA.
Printed in Great Britain by the MPG Books Group, Bodmin and King's Lynn

**www.bergpublishers.com**

# contents

# acknowledgments

Fashion has always been a passion of mine, and I hope that this book will make it your passion too. The fashion revolution of the 1960s and 1970s, when youth culture and popular culture dominated media space and created a fashion system that challenged the authority of Paris, captured my attention and shaped my subsequent research interests. Questions about body, space, and identity have underpinned my investigations into the meaning of fashion. Hopefully, this book shares those questions with readers. The book is designed to introduce key concepts, issues, and debates in fashion studies and, as such, is not intended to be exhaustive. A list of further reading, indicative case studies, and a lengthy bibliography provide rich material for furthering your understanding of specific topics and themes.

My deepest thanks go to Tristan Palmer, who proposed the title and nurtured the book into existence with incredible patience. Once again, the fabulous team at Berg (especially Ken Bruce) and Julia Rosen has given the project its material form. Many thanks to anonymous reviewers whose feedback and comments on an earlier draft have hopefully helped improve the text. The writing of the book has been aided by the advice and support of a number of colleagues and friends: Margaret Maynard, Prudence Black, Anne Peirson-Smith, Alison Goodrum, Sharon Bell, Mary and Wilfred Brimblecombe, Lil Agerup and Peter Richards, Mark Peoples, Mary Hapel, Jean Neely, Margaret Paynter, Claire Marrison and Mark Arkell, Gabrielle Cameron, Kathryn Wynn and Geoffrey Warren, Rhonda Turner and family, and Wendy and Wayne Ralphe. My wonderful colleagues at the University of Canberra have provided extraordinary support and inspiration—especially Jordan Williams, Greg Battye, Tim Thomas, Michael Sergi, Craig Bremner, Paul Magee, Cath Raby, Sue Thomas and Stephen Parker. Margaret Gardner, Keith Cowlishaw, and Kate Kennedy and colleagues in the School of Fashion and Textiles at the RMIT University, Melbourne—and have supported me in an adjunct professorship that has provided enormous stimulation from the coalface of fashion.

The extraordinary support of Sharon Peoples, who not only helped type and edit the text but contributed many ideas and collaborated on numerous case studies, has enriched the resulting manuscript. Shellaine Godbold has done an incomparable job as photo editor of sourcing illustrations and securing permissions. One case study was kindly contributed by Amelia Groom. Kylie Janssens and Ella Cameron have provided physiotherapy and insights about fashion and handbags. Sincere thanks to you all. Above all, immeasurable gratitude is due to my long-suffering but ever-supportive family—Aidan, Sean, Erinn, and John Wanna—who have endured patiently another writing marathon. John, as usual, has attempted to improve the quality of the text. Hopefully, in the process, some of the content has rubbed off and improved his dress sense!

*Jennifer Craik*
*Canberra*

# illustrations

**Isabella Blow.** Photo: Donald McPherson

# introduction

## why study fashion?

### i. the purpose of this book

This book explores the phenomenon of fashion and how we can study it in accessible yet comprehensive ways. The topic of fashion raises ambivalent responses. People tend to be for it or against it. Those who like it and are followers of fashion see the way we style ourselves as a key aspect of our identity and how we appear to others. Those who decry fashion regard it as ephemeral, trivial, and a sign of an emphasis on style over substance. Fashionistas (slang for fashion devotees or patrons) are often regarded as airheads, as frivolous and easily influenced by fads and media hype. Even so, fashion and how it works are becoming an increasingly significant part of the study of **culture.** While we might be ambivalent about it, we are still fascinated with it—hooked perhaps on the polarizing effect of fashion itself.

*Fashion: The Key Concepts* introduces students to the key terms, issues, debates, and milestones in fashion theory and research. Because it is introductory, topics will be dealt with schematically, with suggestions for further reading listed at the end of the book. Fashion concepts appear in **bold typeface** when first used in the text and are defined in the glossary. Readers are also directed to fashion dictionaries such as Guido Vergani's *Fashion Dictionary* (2006) and Gavin Ambrose and Paul Harris's *The Visual Dictionary of Fashion Design* (2007). Throughout each chapter are boxes that illustrate points in the text, while longer case studies conclude each chapter. A list of fashion milestones is appended to give readers a quick overview of major moments in fashion history. Where fashion designers are mentioned in the text, brief biographical details are provided; however, no appendix of designer biographies is included because numerous other sources provide this information (Buxbaum 2005). For readers who are studying fashion, an indicative list of questions for essays and class discussion plus an annotated guide to further reading are included.

The bibliography includes many sources of academic fashion scholarship as well as material from fashion magazines, advertisements, diverse Web sites, and other popular sources. Most fashion theory and research emanates from Europe and North America, so it is high time that fashion be recognized as a phenomenon that occurs everywhere and touches the lives of everyone. This book is intended in part to redress this imbalance. The literature, illustrations, and case studies draw on many different sites of fashion, fashion cultures, and examples of fashion-in-action. Readers of this book and students of fashion should consider these reflections in relation to their own fashion context. Accordingly, I encourage students of fashion to draw on the popular resources on fashion that surround them, for fashion is not just confined to the catwalks, collections, and curators but exists everywhere, in multiple forms and experiences. Immerse yourself in *your* fashion universe as you read this book!

**Anna Piaggi.** Photo: Gabor Deri. Creative Commons Attribution 3.0 Unported

## ii. defining key terms

In this introduction, the ways in which the term *fashion* has been defined are presented briefly along with other fashion-related terms. More extensive definitions are provided in later chapters and the glossary. See box 0.1 for definitions of some key terms.

So what is fashion? Dictionaries define **fashion** as "a prevailing custom or style of **dress,** etiquette, procedure, etc."; "conventional usage in dress"; an established mode; and as a prevailing make, shape, style, pattern, or manner. These definitions convey both a sense of a consensus about a desired mode of behavior or appearance and a sense of successive change, movement, and redefinition. Fashion is a cultural practice that is bound up with the specification of our sense of self both as individuals and as members of groups. But as identity means creating distinctiveness, fashion always has to balance reflecting the contemporary consensus about fashion with the specific arrangement of signs and symbols that mark out an individual as appearing to be unique. At a broader level, the fashion industry is also a "cultural industry" that establishes the aesthetic and practical dimensions of our **clothing** habits as well as constituting a keynote global consumer industry.

Hence, unlike other cultural practices that define our sense of self, the essence of fashion is change and consensual trends, even though individuals believe that they make choices from

**Box 0.1 Definitions of Key Terms in Fashion Theory**

|  |  |
|---|---|
| **Dress** | Clothing, apparel, garb; ornaments or adornment of the body; everyday or functional modes of dress |
| **Clothing** | Garments collectively; raiment, clothes, apparel, covering |
| **Fashion** | A prevailing custom or style of dress, etiquette, procedure; a shared and internalized sense of the modish style of the time |
| **Style** | A combination of silhouette, construction, fabric, and details that make the performance of an outfit distinctive |
| **Fads** | Short-term styles that are fashionable for a moment but quickly discarded |
| **Classic** | A style that lasts for an indefinite period of time |
| **Trend** | The direction in which a fashion or style is heading |
| **Antifashion** | An outfit or style that is outside the fashion system, perhaps customary, traditional, or unchangingc |
| **Fashionable/Fashionability** | Conforming to fashion |
| **Culture** | Ways of living, traditions, and habits that are particular to a social group and transmitted from one generation to another; development or improvement by education or training; a particular stage or state of civilization; the act of cultivating or tending |
| **Subculture** | A distinctive network of behavior, beliefs, and attitudes existing within a wider culture |
| **Consumer culture** | A culture permeated by consumerism or the purchase of goods to acquire social value |

a range of options to create a certain style in a unique and distinctive way. In the act of making fashion choices, a person is animating (making alive, activating, performing) her or his body by imposing on it a social veneer that permits it to perform in specific desired ways and to be interpreted in the intended manner by others. In other words, *individuals perform their identities and social roles through their choice and mode of wearing clothes and accessories.* This is the act of **performativity,** or the ways in which the body assumes a sense of self by creating a recognizable identity through the way the body is clothed, gestures, expressions, and movement. As the chief curator of the Kyoto Costume Institute, Akiko Fukai, put it, “Fashion can be regarded as the story of the fictitious body as visible surface” (quoted by Hibbert 2004: 24). This means that although we know that bodies exist, the clothed body is an arbitrary manifestation of the individual in which the chosen identity is imagined and constructed through apparel and gesture.

The paradox of fashion is that in trying to look distinctive, we model ourselves on others and give off an impression of uniformity. Just look around a lecture room, a nightclub, or a sports

**Australian supporters.** Photo: Clayton Scott. Clayton Scott

arena, where you find an unstated commonality of dress among the majority offset by a few distinctive outriders! This consensus in fashion and dress is most keenly seen in old photographs and documentaries of other times and cultures, where a uniformity of dress and a codified range of styles are immediately apparent. Often, the "look" seems comical or absurd (especially when viewed retrospectively) and we ask why the subjects of the photograph or film allowed themselves to dress in such a silly and conformist way. So we have a play between the projection of (unique) individuality and conformity to (shared) group identity. This is overlaid by a tension between "now-ness" (adopting the latest fashion or trend) and habitual or **customary** dress (conforming to long-lasting dress codes and stylistic conventions). The constant change of fashion can only be intelligible against the backdrop of everyday clothing habits. So, ironically, change depends on simultaneous stability as the bedrock of the impetus to fashion. So there is a constant dynamic or tension between consensus and change.

This raises the question of how to understand or analyze the phenomenon of fashion. Fashion is made up of several social practices:

- **The selection of clothes or apparel—individual garments that go in and out of popularity**
- **Ways of wearing and combining an array of clothes**
- **Trends in accenting certain aspects of bodies and apparel through the use of decoration and accessories**

So clothes are not just neutral garments and apparel but rather are structured into social processes and meanings by the ways in which their details and rules about wearing them construct cultural symbols and messages. To summarize this discussion of the definition of fashion:

**In a fashion system, clothes function as symbols that indicate social markers such as status, gender, social group allegiance, personality, fashionability, and sexuality.**

The symbols are internalized or naturalized among a fashion culture so that they are understood almost automatically. Cultural symbols are culturally specific and historically variable. Groups or types of fashion symbols are organized into symbolic systems that are *specific to a culture or subculture and intelligible to us, but only among us (whoever the "us" might be in a particular fashion milieu).* Fashions change over time but nonetheless are intelligible at a particular moment in time, and their traces (e.g., in archival photographs, paintings, museum collections) can be retrospectively interpreted as revealing characteristics of individuals, groups, and cultures. In this sense, we can think of fashion as a system of communication almost like a language made up of a vocabulary (a collection of items of clothing typical of a culture), syntax (the rules about how clothes can be combined or organized), and grammar (the system of arranging and relating garments) and conventions of decoding and interpreting the meaning of a particular look (see also Barthes 1984, 2006; Lurie 1992).

## iii. key approaches to studying fashion

Although many students of fashion want to learn about it simply because they like dressing up or

**Sloane Rangers.** Photo: Giles Moss. Giles Moss

shopping for clothes, this doesn't happen in a vacuum. We need to understand why fashion fascinates us and acquire tools that help us make sense of fashion as a cultural phenomenon. This means that we have to understand how different writers have analyzed fashion from particular perspectives, that is, developed theories of fashion. You may not be interested in theory, but if you ignore it, your understanding of fashion will be limited and one dimensional because it will lack a critical perspective, which will make your attitude toward fashion shallow. This is not to say that what you like and don't like is not valid, but it does mean that these are just opinions that do not take account of the myriad of factors that shape why fashion is how it is and why you like certain

**Zoot suits.** Photo: Gordon Parks. Library of Congress, Prints and Photographs Division

fashions and not others. These factors include the history of clothes, the structure and economics of the industry, artistic influences on taste, the social organization of a culture (which, for example, determines status and cultures of gender), and factors that shape cultural continuity and change. Fashion theorists try to develop a model that takes account of these various factors.

Consequently, how we make sense of fashion depends on which intellectual or disciplinary approach we adopt to study fashion. Although we can all have reactions to, or make judgments about, the fashion sense of, say, our grandparents in family portraits, English dandies of the early nineteenth century, African potentates (autocratic and corrupt leaders) in customary dress, actors at the Oscars, a gaggle of black-clad Goths, housewives in the supermarket, or hippies in the 1960s, the study of fashion as a recognized academic discipline has been a relatively recent phenomenon.

Here, I will briefly introduce several different perspectives that have shaped contemporary fashion theory. These will be elaborated later in the book and reflected on in the conclusion, but this introduction should give you some preliminary tools to see how analysts have tried to make sense of fashion.

### Dress History: The What and the When

Traditionally, understanding fashion was the province of dress curators and historians, who were interested in describing and categorizing the particular features of apparel and changing forms of dress. This instrumental approach to the study of fashion was called "dress history." These analysts interpreted dress as the genre of objects that reflected aspects of design, construction, fabric, and **aesthetics.** This systematic collection and analysis of apparel created historical records of changing modes of dress and extensive museum collections of examples of dress in the past, thus contributing to the classification of different kinds of clothing and successive dress styles.

Examples might include collections of the fans, hats, or gloves of a culture or period; aristocratic dress or working people's dress; sporting outfits and uniforms; and the costumes and dress of preindustrial societies (e.g., the beaded outfits of North American First Peoples, Chinese mourning dress, Moravian folk costume, Indonesian batik, or the contemporary adaptation of the Korean *hanbok*). These collections were classified as material culture and often not regarded as very important by museums and galleries—sometimes relegated to storage and rarely put on display. Items of apparel are expensive to restore and preserve, leading some institutions to collect other kinds of artifacts that could be curated more easily and cheaply. Nonetheless, these collections of clothing artifacts have been essential resources for the development of contemporary fashion theory and research—and the basis for fashion exhibitions.

In Britain, one of the founding figures in fashion research was James Laver, a print curator at the Victoria and Albert Museum in London from 1922 to 1959. He began to study fashion simply to date the pictures in the collection, since clothes were often the most obvious indicator of the time depicted. This accidental approach to the study of fashion was called "the What and the When" (quoted by Carter 2003: 121). Dress collections consisting of an array of items from a particular period (e.g., London pop fashions of the 1960s, **Edwardian** men's suits, Victorian women's underwear) and static displays of models dressed in garments typical of a period in museums and galleries reflected this approach.

In a more reflective and historical vein, the Textile Society of Hong Kong conducts regular visits to specialist dress collections and artisans to explore such topics as ornamental Chinese button fastenings; decorative edgings on **cheongsam** (*qipao*); and lotus shoes, socks, ankle covers, and leggings associated with the custom of foot binding (see www.textilesocietyofhk.org). These collections not only emphasize the historic specificity of these items but illustrate their contextual variability, imaginative and superb use of color and texture in design, exquisite manufacture, and individual variability. In short, such collections are not just demonstrations of customary dress but vivid examples of earlier Chinese fashion impulses.

These are examples of the what and the when. Other displays exhibited examples from a (notable) benefactor's wardrobe, so we can add "the who" to this type of dress history, where the who was usually a member of the social elite (e.g., royalty, aristocracy, or what we would now call a high-profile **celebrity**). Nordiska Museet in Stockholm staged an exhibition of the stage clothes of the pop group Abba in 2000, while the Arts Centre in Melbourne curated a touring exhibition of Kylie Minogue's costumes in 2004. These exhibitions focused on particular entertainers, but they also encapsulated fashion trends of the time and shifting definitions of celebrity.

Meanwhile, museums and galleries worldwide have been curating exhibitions on fashion and dress in growing numbers for the past three decades, not just exhibiting items of apparel but contextualizing the design, the role of designers, textiles, connections with other cultural forms (e.g., art movements or architecture), promotion, **consumption,** and the cultural milieu in which fashion circulates. Exhibitions have been so numerous that it was not possible to include a list of major fashion exhibitions in this volume. Increasingly, then, attention in museum exhibits has turned from fashion as collections of representative objects to the dynamic interpretation of fashion-in-action.

### What About the How and the Why?

Valuable though these histories and exhibitions have been, the dating and classificatory approach to explaining the significance of dress did not address issues such as the following:

- **What made certain styles fashionable at one time?**
- **How and why did fashions change over time?**
- **How and why have cycles of fashion sped up with cycles of consumer behavior (market economies and times in history when individuals have had more means to purchase clothes of their choice)?**
- **How have changing gender codes and norms of sexual behavior influenced fashion systems?**
- **What have been the effects of transforming political regimes on the fashions of civil society?**

Because traditional dress history could not answer these questions (and often such questions were never posed), Laver tired of the what-and-when approach and started asking about the how and the why. He questioned accounts of the history of fashion in Europe as well as considering types of dress that were regarded as nonfashion, for example, school uniforms, children's dress, military uniforms, theatrical costume, and athletic clothes (Carter 2003: 121).

Laver became one of the first English dress historians who sought to contextualize fashion trends in social, cultural, aesthetic, and political terms. Of his many writings (see the bibliography), the best known were *Taste and Fashion: From the French Revolution to the Present Day* (1937), *Modesty in Dress: An Inquiry into the Fundamentals of Fashion* (1969), and *A Concise History of Costume* (1969, republished as *Costume and Fashion*). He also wrote on British military uniforms, fashion plates, theatrical costume, dandies, and fashion in the Jazz Age. Inevitably, Laver's influence on fashion scholarship has been immense, although subsequent scholars have challenged some of his interpretations.

### Anthropologists, Ethnologists, and Social Scientists

While dress historians were formally associated with the study of fashion, arguably richer veins were to be found in the work of anthropologists, ethnologists, and the precursors of social scientists such as Herbert Spencer, Thorstein Veblen, Georg Simmel, Alfred Kroeber, J. C. Flügel, Ernest Crawley, Alfred Radcliffe-Brown, and Ruth Benedict (see Carter 2003; Johnson, Torntore, and Eicher 2003). However, these writings were often addenda to primary investigations and often did not receive close attention until long after they were written. These theorists were interested in developing so-called grand theories of society and culture as a whole and used the example of dress and fashion as an instance of their general principles.

In particular, such theorists wanted to explain why humans were distinctive and how they differed from animals. Factors like language, collective modes of living, forms of social exchange, and the use of symbolic systems were part of the answer. Among the most important symbolic forms were modes of dress—that is, the fact that humans have always adorned the body with skins, fabrics, ornaments, pigments, and so on. Clothing, therefore, was seen as a key clue to understanding humanity.

Accordingly, the hallmark of anthropological accounts of fashion was the emphasis on explaining fashion (as well as customary dress, everyday dress, and costume) in terms of its role in culture as a whole. These studies were concerned with how dress and decoration formed part of the cultural practices and communicative codes embedded in cultures that were studied by ethnographers and anthropologists—usually preindustrial and colonial societies.

Early anthropologists were interested in defining fashion or clothing behavior in relation to protection, concealment or modesty, and decoration, that is to say, the purposes for which humans clothed and adorned their bodies (e.g., Crawley 1912; see Johnson et al. 2003: 8–11). While Crawley recognized the communicative role of clothing in social display and as social currency, Alfred Radcliffe-Brown (1922) was more interested in the relationship between clothes as a means of situating an individual in the social context. Ruth Benedict took this approach further by making a distinction between clothes from earlier cultures and those in contemporary cultures, arguing that while the former were differentiated geographically, the latter were differentiated in time "as a swift succession of styles" (Johnson et al. 2003: 11). This focus on social change has been a recurring theme in subsequent fashion theory. Benedict (1931: 237) was one of the first to reject the idea that fashion was a feature of earlier civilizations, arguing that it was specific to modern mass-production societies.

One of the most enduring definitions of fashion was provided by Edward Sapir in the 1931 edition of the *Encyclopedia of Social Sciences,* where he defined fashion as "custom in the guise of departure from custom" (140). Sapir distinguishes fashion from fads, taste, and custom where "the very essence of fashion is that it be valued as a variation in an understood sequence, as a departure from the immediately preceding mode" (141), which is adopted by the majority (or significant minority of tastemakers or trendsetters):

**Particular people or coteries have their fads, while fashions are the property of larger or more representative groups. A taste which asserts itself in spite of fashion and which may therefore be suspected of having something obsessive about it may be referred to as an individual fad. (Sapir 1931: 139)**

So a fad is usually a short-term trend that is adopted by a limited group and deemed bizarre by the majority, while a custom "is the element of permanence which makes fashion possible" (Sapir 1931: 139). He argued that while most fashions are succeeded by other fashions, "occasionally a fashion crystallizes into permanent habit, taking on the character of custom" (Sapir 1931: 139). *Taste* is a broader term that refers to the conscious expression of the ideal of style by a dominant group within a fashion system, where that ideal is recognized as superior and imitated by people in their quest to define their individual sense of self and identity. As Stephen Bayley (1991: 71) puts it in his iconic book on the subject,

**if good taste means anything, it is pleasing your peers; bad taste is offending them. But cultivated bad taste, or kitsch, can achieve either result.**

**Taste is more to do with manners than appearances. Taste is both myth and reality; it is not a style.**

So "a new fashion becomes psychologically necessary, and thus the cycle of fashion is endlessly repeated" (Sapir 1931: 140). The key to this approach to fashion is the link between individual expression or uses of symbolic and communicative codes and the role of these codes in maintaining social organization and consensus on collective behavior. While fashion might seem to be just about clothes, how we clothe ourselves has important implications for society as a whole and as a key mode of cultural expression.

A competing approach was adopted by economists, who were primarily interested in theorizing economic behavior as a whole. They examined changes in the textile trade and clothing markets as signs of economic cycles and trends in a mechanical manner. Exponents included Alfred Kroeber (1919), Jane Richardson (see Kroeber and Richardson 1940), and Ingrid Brenninkmeyer (1963). Kroeber, although an anthropologist by training, rejected anthropological explanations of imitation, emulation, and competition and sought scientific measurements of the relationship between trends in fashion and economic trends accompanying the development of modern societies.

He analyzed certain details of women's dress from 1844 to 1919 (evening dress depicted in fashion plates)—depth of décolletage and width across the shoulders, waist height and length, skirt length and width—to show there were "waves" of change (also called cycles or rhythms) that systematically recurred in a pattern reflecting social and economic developments. Although few analysts have repeated (or expanded on) these studies, Kroeber's work is still cited as a turning point and seminal classic in the emergence of fashion studies.

### Social Psychologists and Sociologists

As the twentieth century progressed, fashion attracted other disciplinary perspectives that focused on the fashion phenomenon as a specific social system itself rather than just seeing it as an example of general social principles. These accounts emanated primarily from

- **Social psychologists, who were interested in accounting for individual motivations and needs that underpinned dress behavior and fashion trends**
- **Sociologists, who were more interested in understanding the "lemming-like" (unthinking, indiscriminate) way in which groups of people adopt dress codes,**

**Bai Ling.** Photo by Jason LaVeris/FilmMagic. Credit: FilmMagic. 2007 Jason LaVeris

**especially in a consumer culture, where one acquires social value by buying the attributes one desires**

Questions about how clothes denote social status (hierarchies, **class** position and differentiation, age, gender, and ethnicity) were central to such approaches. This was in the context of how clothes interacted with symbols of economic wealth and power, measured through characteristics of role play, social authority, and regulation. Some attention was also given to explaining the aesthetic impulses and psychological dimensions that underpinned fashion behavior. These contrasting approaches have spawned an array of new disciplinary and interdisciplinary approaches

**Queen Elizabeth II.** Photo: NASA/Bill Ingalls

in the late twentieth and early twenty-first centuries with possibilities that are touched on in chapter 1 and reflected on in the concluding chapter.

### Interdisciplinary Approaches

As you can see from the brief descriptions above, each of these approaches focuses on a specific model of culture and society and postulates a particular way of relating the individual to the social whole—for example, explaining fashion in term of human distinctiveness or the psychological needs of individuals, or as a reflection of the economic state of a society. From the 1960s, critiques of cultural theory began to question these compartmentalized and one-dimensional approaches to understanding social and cultural phenomena, and approaches that were more inclusive and less prescriptive were developed. These approaches have been called variously structuralist, semiotic, postmodern, and poststructuralist.

While these approaches will be discussed in subsequent chapters, for our purposes here it is sufficient to say that recent and contemporary approaches to fashion theory are distinctive in two ways. First, they tend to draw on more than one disciplinary focus; that is, they are inter- or multidisciplinary. Second, they are interested in explaining the minutiae or details of fashion behavior as a cultural code for creating meaning for particular individuals or groups rather than just seeing fashion as exemplifying general principles.

## iv. how is this book organized?

This book introduces a range of issue, topics, and debates that have been central to fashion theory. However, it is only an introduction, and readers will find it necessary to use the material here as a starting point for deeper investigations of particular topics. The aim is to summarize and evaluate specific approaches, findings, and case studies to show how the field of fashion studies has matured and changed over time as the global reach of fashion has hastened and evolved. The book is divided into eight chapters that can be read separately or sequentially, although some themes (such as issues of gender and sexuality) recur across chapters. Introductions and summaries of each chapter will help to orient the reader. The central preoccupations of the study of fashion form the basis of subsequent chapters.

In chapter 1, "The Fashion Impulse," we deviate from the usual format of introductory texts by challenging one of the key features of fashion theory, namely, its ethnocentric point of view. Fashion is often defined as a feature specific only to modern European societies and is seen as different from the clothing habits of other societies and other times; terms such as *costume, dress,* and *customary clothing* are used to reinforce their purported difference. I have questioned this ethnocentric approach in my book *The Face of Fashion* (Craik 1994), arguing that while the modern system of fashion is certainly distinctive, it is not unique, and that other systems of fashion should be seen as competing with, or parallel to, the dominant consumer-based system of fashion with which we are all familiar. The use of color in fashion is central to this chapter. Case studies illustrating the emergence of key themes in fashion and its analysis are:

1. **The regulation of fashion**
2. **Black mourning dress**
3. **Fashions in New Guinea headdresses**
4. **The sailor suit: from function to fashion**

Chapter 2, "The Eurocentric Fashion System," provides an overview of the development of modern consumer culture and the Eurocentric fashion system. The shift of preeminent fashion capitals from centers like London and Vienna to Paris is explored, as well as the role of fashion in America in confirming the iconic status of Paris fashion. The recent diversification of Eurocentric fashion into contemporary forms is traced. The emergence of the designer system as the heart of fashion creation, the development of designer collections, couture clientele, diffusion lines, licensing, and the blurring between couture and luxury fashion are covered. The argument is advanced that because Paris has dominated academic and popular accounts and images of fashion, the status of Paris as synonymous with fashion has become accepted folklore. Yet there are numerous reasons why we might question the assumption that what happens on the catwalks of Paris determines how people dress in everyday life far away from this European hub. For example, there are now other cities that are proclaimed fashion capitals, such as New York, Milan, London, Shanghai, and Tokyo. Yet their respective influences are generally assumed to be local rather than global. This paradox is explored in this chapter and illustrated by case studies of:

5. **Beau Brummell**
6. **The influence of Coco Chanel**
7. **Yves Saint Laurent as style muse**
8. **Daslu luxury retailing**

In chapter 3, "Fashion Cycles, Symbols, and Flows," we explore how fashion is theorized by social scientists and cultural analysts from a variety of disciplinary perspectives. The chapter traces the shift from systemic analyses to theories that see fashion as self-referential systems or regimes of meaning-making through the use of specific codes and combinations of the elements and connotations of items of apparel. The disciplines of semiotics, structuralism, and **postmodernism** treat fashion as a domain of symbols that can be likened to a visual language of communication that structures how dress and decoration function as a body technique and cultural practice. Fashion enables the body to perform identities appropriate to specific roles, statuses, and contexts. The effectiveness of these symbolic regimes depends on how definitively communicative codes are shared. Examples include:

9. **The meaning of men's ties**
10. **Jeans as über fashion**
11. **Sexuality and stilettos**
12. **The magic of cosmetics**

Following the focus on symbolic communication, chapter 4, "Fashion, Body Techniques, and Identity," develops issues associated with the role of fashion in actively creating and re-creating identity, whether individual, collective, social, or subcultural. Fashion creates, on the one hand, the appearance of uniqueness and distinctiveness, as well as, on the other, the appearance of the uniformity upon which the former depends. Dress and decoration, then, are key techniques of diverse aspects of identity: gender and sexuality, race and ethnicity, subcultures, and consumer cultures. Case studies provide examples of specific modes of identity construction, particularly:

13. **Fashion and identity in Harajuku**
14. **Acquiring the techniques of royalty**
15. **The metrosexual man**
16. **The cult of thinness**

The focus of chapter 5, "Fashion, Aesthetics, and Art," is how fashion is intrinsically located in an aesthetic realm and hence has particular connections with art and culture. This chapter explores the relationship between art and culture and whether or not fashion is a form of art or just a reflection of aesthetic trends. Specifically, fashion has been related to the development of **modernity** and its preoccupations, such as spectacle, spectatorship, museology, and representation. More recently, the postmodernist movement has produced new themes in fashion, triggering debates on the subjects of art as fashion and the legitimacy of artwear, the relationship between fashion and space, and the fragmenting relationship between couture and cult fashion. Case studies are:

17. **Fashion photography and heroin chic**
18. **Exhibiting Vivienne Westwood**

19. **Wearable art**
20. **Fashion and the wristwatch**

In chapter 6, "Fashion as a Business and Cultural Industry," we attempt to unravel some of the aspects of the organization of fashion as an industry that consists of a vast interconnected web of enterprises—some multinational, many very small—that traverse competing fashion systems from the local to the global. While there has been some interest in the economics of fashion, there has been less in the characterization of the fashion industry as an interdependent series of loops that encompass all aspects of design, production, marketing, and consumption. Because of the complexity of the fashion industry—and the textile, clothing, and footwear industry sector more generally—detailed information and industry data about many components of the sector are difficult to obtain. Not only are there different levels of the industry (from exclusive haute couture to mass-market fashion to cult and niche fashions), but there are serious debates concerning aspects of the fashion industry system concerning the ethics of exploitative conditions of production (sweatshops), hypnotic hoodwinking of consumers (fashion slaves), environmental impacts and sustainability of fashion, and extraordinary nonrational extremes of excess and waste (in a boom-and-bust industry). The relationship between fashion consumers, fashion forecasting, and the emergence of the luxury fashion niche market is also discussed. These industry dynamics are the subject of case studies concerning:

21. **Celebrity models**
22. **Louis Vuitton as luxury accessory**
23. **The Gap as global fashion**
24. **Secondhand clothing**

Chapter 7, "Popular Culture and Fashion," interrogates the imperative to make clothes visual in ways that appeal to viewers and turn them into voracious consumers dying to get their hands on the latest fashion "must." Here we examine the connection between the rise of popular culture and the contemporary fashion industry. As well as examining how fashion is interpreted in the media, the chapter also explores how media is involved in the fashion system, how fashion relates to star systems, the role of style setters and gatekeepers, and the relationship between fashion and sports. Case studies explore:

25. **Sports clothing for everyman**
26. **Australian bush wear as urban chic**
27. **Retailing erotic lingerie**
28. **Oliviero Toscani's advertisements for Benetton**

In the concluding chapter, "The Politics of Fashion," fashion is dissected as a political and politicized phenomenon. Although students of fashion may not be interested in mainstream politics, readers will realize that fashion is a highly political cultural practice that creates diverse controversies and moral panics. The pressures to regulate fashion practices, as well as the role of fashion in establishing a sense of place and national identity (especially through colonial and postcolonial movements), are examined. The chapter concludes with a discussion of the impact of globalization and transnationalism on the fashion industry and on fashion as a cultural practice. Case studies cover:

29. **The politics of veiling**
30. **Renegotiating Chinese identity in fashion**

31. **Indian fashion: from diasporas to designers**
32. **Burberry's brand of Britishness**

This introduction has explored definitions of key concepts as well as signposting early theories of fashion that have influenced contemporary ways of analyzing fashion concepts. So, having introduced some key definitions and approaches to fashion, we need to pose the question—what is the fashion impulse? We take this up in the next chapter.

# chapter 1

# the fashion impulse

**CHAPTER OUTLINE**

I. Investigating the fashion impulse
II. Color and fashion through time
III. The color black in fashion
Case study 1: The regulation of fashion
Case study 2: Black mourning dress
Case study 3: Fashions in new guinea headdresses
Case study 4: The sailor suit: from function to fashion

**WHAT DOES THIS CHAPTER COVER?**

In this chapter, we set the scene for the study of fashion by exploring whether the concept of fashion is confined to contemporary consumer culture. To illustrate this, the use of color in fashion, especially the prevalence of black, is explored. Three case studies on the regulation of fashion, fashions in New Guinea headdresses, and the shifting symbolism of the sailor suit from function to fashion conclude the chapter.

## i. investigating the fashion impulse

In the introduction, three early approaches to studying fashion were outlined. The significance of these is not only that they shaped subsequent fashion theory but that they recognized the significance of clothing, dress, and ornamentation as a complex system of cultural communication that not only articulated the collective **identity** of a culture but also exhibited enormous individual variability, creativity, innovation, and experimentation. While sometimes classified as customary, much of this behavior conformed to the characteristics we identify with fashion behavior. For this reason, I have argued that fashion should not be defined as exclusively the preserve of the culture of modernity but that other systems of fashion should be recognized and examined in their own terms.

Many theorists have argued that fashion is a modern cultural practice that coincided with the emergence of **capitalism** and consumer culture, but I have argued elsewhere that fashion is *not* exclusively the domain of modern culture and its preoccupations with individualism, class, civilization, and consumerism (Craik 1994: 3). Fashionable impulses (constantly changing clothing codes and stylistic registers) occur in non-Western and non-modern societies too. Yet the perception (and the myth) has been that non-Western cultures have stable and unchanging clothing codes (called costume or customary dress), a perception perhaps driven by the "snapshot" (or synchronic) approach to ethnographic case studies as well as the desire to emphasize the difference between "us" (civilized individuals) and "them" (pre-civilized groups). In fact, where longitudinal studies have been conducted, successive changes in the details and decoration (if not the basic garments) can be found.

Indeed, many early theorists used the term *fashion* to describe the dress performances of preindustrial cultures. Not only is it ethnocentric to insist that fashion in contemporary culture is fundamentally different from that of other societies, but it is elitist, shallow, and plainly wrong. Often this view has stemmed from superficial attention to other clothing customs or lack of understanding of the specific variations and distinctions created by individuals. To assign a form of clothing as customary obviates the need to investigate below the surface manifestations to elicit the significance of particular outfits—rather, as a whole, a group designated as wearing customary dress is merely assumed to represent and embody the essence of the whole.

A contemporary comparison would be that men in business suits wear the customary dress of adult male sedentary workers in contemporary culture. Suits may then be classified in terms of

**Men's fashion.** Photo: Paul Goyette, flickr.com/photos/pgoyette. 

color (black, blue, brown, pinstripe, **plaid**), cut (single breasted, double breasted, etc.), and **fabric** (**wool,** polyester, **silk,** velvet, linen, etc.) and perhaps related through these distinctions to formal properties of status, role, and ethnicity. But to do so ignores the minutiae of variability in terms of how individuals make choices about suits and manipulate the details of wearing them—for example, the choice of **tie** (or bow tie), shirt, cuff links, belt, and so on. So we can classify the business **suit** as customary dress, but to understand how it is worn, we need to examine the performance of the individual in using the suit to project a sense of identity within the wider suit-wearing group. Similar arguments could be made about so-called power dressing for career women who wish to maximize their potential by adopting a form of dress that commands respect and minimizes perceptions of femininity. At a wider level, fashions in suits change over time, so individuals balance their habits and preferences with some incorporation of the trends of the time.

We could make the same argument about the little black dress, purportedly an item in every fashionable woman's wardrobe. This is infinitely variable in type and individualized in many ways, for example, by the choice of **accessories.** Consequently, I am arguing that the clothing behavior of many cultures and societies exhibits fashion in how clothes become part of social performance. While we can argue that contemporary fashion is a distinctive system (hooked onto consumerism and **globalization**), my contention is that it is not fundamentally different from other fashion behaviors in other fashion systems.

It is true, however, that the term *fashion* is specific to European culture, although just as fashions change, so too has the concept of fashion. The term *fashion* has been used since the fourteenth century to refer to a particular mode or manner of dress or **style,** deriving from the Latin *facio* or *factio* (meaning "making" or "doing"), which then referred to political acts but gained an association with mode or custom. The spelling and meaning further changed (Old French, *fazon*; Middle French, *facon*; modern French, *façon*) to become *fashion* in English. The French adopted the term *la mode*. The word always had connotations of appearance in accordance with prevailing norms and customs. By the late fifteenth century, fashion had acquired its modern meaning of the modes prescribed by the elite. Unlike the word *dress,* with its implications of stability and banality, *fashion* denotes change and prestigious imitation, while other terms—*style*, *mode*, *taste*, *vogue*, *fad*, *craze*—are subsets of fashion.

However, as I have argued above, fashion is not a phenomenon that has only existed since the fourteenth century. Nor has it been confined to Europe. For example, Cannon (1998: 29–34) has traced changing demands of Canadian Native customers for the goods sold by traders in northeast and western Canada after European settlement in 1497. The formation of the Hudson Bay Company in 1670 signaled the start of the lucrative fur trade and opening up of new settlements across Canada where Natives exchanged fur for goods, a trade that continued up until the late nineteenth century. Customers were very specific in demanding certain types of cloth, colors, materials, and shapes of beads and other items of clothing and adornment. For example, at different times, there were fashions for agate beads, glass beads, blue beads, colored metal. In fact, Native tastes "were highly volatile and subject to change at any time" even between the ordering of certain items and their delivery. One trader remarked that "fashion reigned [in North Saskatchewan] as imperiously

**Audrey Hepburn, lunch on Fifth Avenue.** Photo by Keystone Features/Getty Images. 2007 Getty Images

as in 'more civilized lands,'" forcing traders "to respond to the changing demands of Native fashion throughout the course of the North American fur trade" (Cannon 1998: 31). He concludes:

**The fur trade is just one example of the *fashion-driven* demand for goods that can develop among small-scale, non-industrial societies. ... Native demand for beads, cloth and other items of apparel *exhibits all the criteria of fashion.* Consumption of these goods was substantial and clearly subject to the tastes and desires of consumers rather than suppliers. (Cannon 1998: 34; my italics)**

This example shows that the trade in apparel among the Canadian First People shared the same characteristics as, say, the contemporary demand for handbags. Consumers were willing to pay for goods, their tastes were very specific, and tastes changed at both the individual level and the collective level, as is evident in the

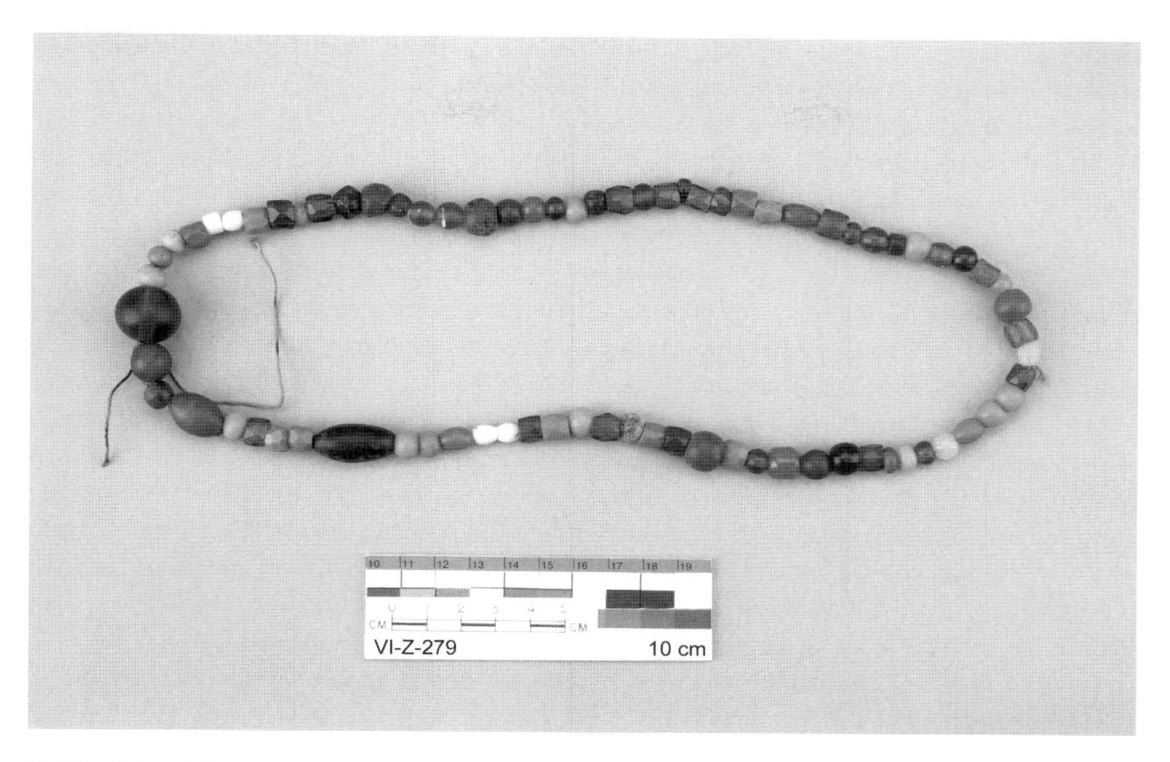


**Trade bead strand.** Canadian Museum of Civilization.
Canadian Museum of Civilization

demand for new colors, shapes, sizes, and types of beads and trinkets. Traders changed their supplies to cater to changing demands, and individual consumers combined and utilized their purchases in specific and distinctive ways that emphasized their individuality. Cannon (1998) argues that tastes sometimes changed once or twice a year, triggered by influential tastemakers shifting their choice of apparel, to which traders responded—evidence of fashion behavior, namely, "the expression of individual identity, shaped and modified through social comparison." The First People set the terms of demand, and European traders employed modern **marketing** strategies to satisfy the fashion impulse.

Other examples where tastes in non-Western dress and decoration have changed are the headdresses of New Guinea highlanders (see case study 3), Polynesian and Japanese fashions in tattooing, Yoruban forms of dress (Drewal and Drewal 1990), variations in Moravian folk costume (Bogatyrev 1971), Sumbanese textiles (Adams 1973), and variability in South American fashion and dress (Schwarz 1979), as well as well-documented examples of historical and contemporary fashions in kimonos, saris, Chinese ceremonial robes, and veils (Craik 1994: 19–23; Dalby 1993; Garrett 2007; McCracken 1988: 58–59; Rutherford and Menzies 2004; Wilson 1986). In their study of the masks made for and used in the Gẹlẹdẹ masquerades and performance spectacles of the west Yoruban people of Nigeria and Benin, Drewal and Drewal (1990) document the multiple influences on the design of the elaborate headpieces that complement the colorful and splendid robes. In many ways, the headpieces are reminiscent of the headpieces (or poufs) commissioned by France's Queen Marie Antoinette as her signature look, which "allowed her to play at politics and look fashionable at the same time" (Weber 2006: 104–5). Shortly after Louis XV's death, she wore the *coiffure à l'Iphigénie,* "a lyrical confection wound with black mourning ribbons, trimmed with a black veil, and topped with a crescent moon," thus paying tribute to the deceased king as well as to Gluck's opera *Iphigénie en Aulide* (Weber 2006: 105). Many of her poufs combined social commentary and satire with fashion, though whether these aided the queen's aim to become a political force is unclear. The public was scandalized by her infamous *coiffure à l'Independance ou le Triomphe de la Liberté,* which she wore to celebrate the victory of a French frigate against the British in 1778, and she became a cause for concern because of her fashion excesses. Oddly enough, however, there are parallels between the poufs of Marie Antoinette and those of the Yoruba. The latter incorporated models reflecting all aspects of Yoruban society—deities, spirits, animals, plants, antisocial behaviors, important figures—as well as elements of Western culture, such as a man on a motorbike. Satire and ridicule were often part of the message, just as it was with the poufs of Marie Antoinette. As Drewal and Drewal (1990: 220) observe,

**thus by simply depicting coiffures, fashions, and body arts, or by creating complicated tableaux on these carved heads, the artist comments on the individual's essence, which is then carried into the midst of the assembled community for evaluation. In this way, the visual arts contribute to the shaping of culture as they express the attitudes of the owners of the world.**

In this sense, it is absurd to view the fashion impulses of preindustrial societies as fundamentally different from those of contemporary societies.

Such examples suggest that achieving distinctiveness in dress and decoration has been a universal process of the construction of social identity. Preindustrial, industrial, colonial, and modern societies have *all* engaged in a play between customary, fashionable, and assertive forms of clothing the body such that different clothing systems are dynamic, constantly changing, forming and reforming, and in competition with specific cultural allegiances.

One curious example is the Bolivian bowler hat favored by the Aymara women since the 1920s. There are numerous stories as to how this happened. According to one story, a consignment of bowler hats mistakenly ended up in Bolivia and the enterprising entrepreneur decided to off-load them by spreading the rumor that they aided fertility, prompting a rush of women who, once converted, retained this distinctive—yet exotic—form of hat, which is regarded as customary but exhibits features consistent with high fashion (see box 1.1).

This example demonstrates how an arbitrary item of apparel can become incorporated as a fashion item then elaborated on in terms of how it is worn (at an angle) and its variants. The care to which Cholas go to keep their hats in good condition, the price of the hats, and the theft of hats all suggest that this is a highly valued item of fashion that is set off by the wearer's choice of skirts (*polleras*) and underskirts (*centros*) as well as by the number that are worn and how they are evaluated by bystanders. This is clearly an individual choice

**Bubble-up fashion.** Photo: Agnieszka Los. Agnieszka Los

motivated by knowledge of the fashion code and performance intent of the wearer, not a collectively determined one—although it can be interpreted by the community of Cholas.

Since European colonial excursions into the "exotic" lands of "other" people, fashion systems have both changed internally and collided. In an article called "Why Do the Natives Wear Adidas?" Arnould and Wilk (1984: 748) explored the prevalence of the consumption of Western goods in non-industrial societies and related the **trend** to "the concepts of socially distant reference groups and emerging elites" (see box 1.2).

Even in non-primitive societies, the desire for certain Western goods can become a mania when free access is denied—take the example of the black market for denim jeans (Levi's in particular) in Eastern Europe before the collapse of the Soviet Union. That demand persisted despite the fact that "crimes 'in favor of private property' [were] punished [and] underscore[d] the difficulty of policing the flow" (Arnould and Wilk 1984: 748).

## Box 1.1 Cholas in Bowlers

One of the things that sticks in the mind of most visitors to La Paz is the traditional dress of many of the local women—a bowler hat worn slanted on the head and a long decorative skirt called a pollera or often 2, 3 or more of them! These distinctive looking residents of the capital city are known as cholas or cholitas and have been wearing this traditional dress for many years.

The bowler hat (or derby hat as it is also known) always seems too small for the owner and for some unknown reason is usually perched on top of the head tilted to one side (if any one knows the reason why they tilt it please let me know). These hats are a source of pride for the cholas and theft of these hats straight from the wearers head has been a problem in La Paz. At a cost ranging from US$50 to US$200 it is not so surprising as US$50 is about what an average Bolivian earns each month. The hats always seem sparkling clean and brand new and its not uncommon to see cholas covering their hats with plastic wrap when it rains to keep them that way.

The wearing of the hat originates from the times when they were in fashion in Europe and were also worn by the upper class Spaniard settlers in La Paz. For a long time people of mixed Spanish and indigenous blood were not respected by either the Spanish or the indigenous population, as pure blood was seen as the ideal by both sides. The Spanish thought the indigenous to be simple and savage people whilst the indigenous despised the Spanish for the invasion of their homelands and maltreatment of them. Due to there being less Spanish women than Spanish men it was inevitable that some would take wives from the indigenous population and as time went on the mestizo population (mixed Spanish and indigenous blood) started to increase. The mixed race women became known as Cholas and the traditional dress was most likely adapted from a mix of the Spanish fashion of the time and the indigenous traditional dresses in order to give themselves a sense of identity. Originally the men were known as cholos but today this is seen as a derogatory term and is not often heard.

The long flowing skirt that is worn by the cholas is known as a pollera and is often covered in sequins with decorative seams. Beneath the pollera is usually a layer of underskirts called centros. As many as 20 polleras and centros can be worn together (not an uncommon amount in festivals) although a combination totalling 3 or 4 is more likely. This can make these tough looking women seem extremely wide and definitely makes them hard to pass on the narrow streets!

To the unknowing tourist it seems like many of the cholas wear very similar clothing and that fashion must be an unknown entity to them but in fact each year there are new styles of pollera, different fabrics in season and even chola fashion shows. The style of the hat pretty much stays the same from year to year, possibly due to the cost.

Whilst the chola style of dress is still very much in evidence in La Paz, like so many places, things are changing. More and more the young girls are turning to western style dress and forsaking the traditional costume of their mothers, at least in their day to day lives. This is to be expected really as more indigenous are entering higher education and pursuing professional careers. Culturally it is expected that they wear more business like attire to become successful. You will find many indigenous girls in the universities of La Paz these days but are unlikely to find any wearing a pollera and hat.

Maybe for the first time since the chola traditional dress was adopted a difference of opinion regarding fashion has developed between daughters and mothers but there doesn't seem to be a danger of the traditional costume disappearing altogether. It still features strongly in festivals and formal celebrations for both young and old alike.

Source: Bolivia Blog. 2007. "Bolivia Facts—La Paz Cholas—Bowler Hats in Boliva." http://www.boliviablog.net/2007/02/la-paz-cholas-bowler-hats-in-bolivia.html

**Chola.** Photo: Wilson Dias/Agência Brasil. Creative Commons Attribution 2.5 Brazil License

The conundrum is to explain why Western goods become so attractive—and moreover, why only certain goods become highly desirable; in other words, "the flow is highly selective" (Arnould and Wilk 1984: 748). Arnould and Wilk identify the difference of "gift economies" of primitive societies as the source of the phenomenon. In such economies, the importance of the gift was less the object than the act of exchange, which in turn was valued in terms of the ranking of the goods gifted. In other words, objects are "evaluated in terms of their worth, not their value" (Arnould and Wilk 1984: 749). Worth referred to aspects of social organization and esteem, and while some

**Box 1.2 The Phenomenon of Consumption of Western Goods by Primitive People**

Peruvian Indians carry around small, rectangular rocks painted to look like transistor radios. San Blas Cuna hoard boxes of dolls, safety pins, children's hats and shoes, marbles, enamelware kettles, and bedsheets and pillowcases in their original wrappings. Japanese newly-weds cut inedible three-tiered wedding cakes topped with plastic figures in Western dress. ... Tibetans, bitterly opposed to Chinese rule, sport Mao caps. ... When a Swazi princess weds a Zulu king, she wears red touraco wing feathers around her forehead and a cape of windowbird feathers and oxtail. He wears a leopard skin cloak. Yet all is recorded with a Kodak movie camera, and the band plays "The Sound of Music." In Niger, pastoral Bororo nomads race to market on camelback carrying beach umbrellas. Veiled noble Tuareg men carry swords modeled after Crusaders' weapons and sport mirrored sunglasses with tiny hearts etched into the lenses.

Source: Arnould and Wilk 1984: 748.

Western goods could not be accommodated in these regimes of value, others (like cowrie shells, beads, blankets, and bottled beer) were, because they were "dissimilar to those already preallocated in the complicated calculus of gift obligation" (Arnould and Wilk 1984: 749). Young people were particularly important in this process since they wanted to escape the dictates of traditional culture and/or sought to identify with distant reference groups that were associated with particular consumer goods (such as baseball caps or athletic shoes). Goods that became popular were incorporated into the calculus and bestowed with a certain social worth:

**Since a model for differentiated haute cuisine, couture and architecture is lacking within their own culture, what these groups have done, Jack Goody ... argues is to borrow the "gear of western codes of consumption." (Arnould and Wilk 1984: 751)**

This borrowing can be quite sophisticated, with different groups identifying with different products of brands—for example, **Adidas** over **Nike**—depending on their fit in the worth and social ranking of goods. The circulation of goods was thus controlled through regulation of access to and the value of certain goods (similar to sumptuary laws, discussed below). In short, "the eros-related exchange of gifts [in primitive society] differs from the logos-inspired commerce of goods [in Western society], and the passage from one to the other engenders unique forms of consumer behavior" (Arnould and Wilk 1984: 751).

This account of the uptake of consumerism and fashion-related behavior in non-industrial societies provides a link to accounts of the emergence of modern consumerism in European-derived societies. The expanding universe of fashion coincided with the rise of mercantilism and consumerism as the acquisition and trade of material goods expanded, and thus the possibility of literally fashioning an identity and way of life out of consumer objects. In turn, these material possessions became **symbols** of well-being and of social status. In an effort to control the multiplication of material culture, political regimes enacted laws known as

**sumptuary laws** across Europe to regulate the ownership and display of material goods, for example, luxury items, certain colors, garments, and accessories (see case study 1).

In 1294, Philippe passed a sumptuary law in France relating the number of robes one could have to one's income and status (Heller 2004: 320). Thus a duke, count, and baron (and their wives) could have four robes per year, and a knight and banneret had three, while prelates, squires, dames, chatelaines, and knights were permitted only two. The cost of cloth was also prescribed for each group. While a sliding scale of fines was prescribed for infractions, there was the possibility of renouncement too. Enforcement seems to have relied on top-down directives to heads of households and informers, who could report transgressions. Public shaming and ridicule may also have been powerful incentives to persuade people to adhere to the laws. Subsequent laws proscribed gifts of robes too as the quest for visible demonstration of social status and role drove the tension between enforcement and flouting of dress regulations. According to Heller (2004: 333), "Sumptuary laws testify to the anxiety as well as the innovations engendered by this increased competition for visibility." She concludes that these regulations were not just about enforcing customary dress but about fashion:

**Rather, it should be clear that fashion for any man of wealth or position was well developed, accepted by the society, and even expected. The causes of tension were the bulges and wrinkles in the hierarchy: when decisions were designated to be made by a single person for others, but those others wanted to make decisions for themselves. This is fashion in its essence: the desire to make decisions about personal display for oneself, seeing them as a means of personal expression. (Heller 2004: 339)**

While many of the laws were directed at members of court society, the burgeoning bourgeoisie was also targeted because it was "acquiring symbols in its quest for greater status and wealth, which the high nobles and the royalty found threatening" (Heller 2004: 343). By controlling the value of cloth and number of robes one could possess, the king was responding to increased visible consumption, which was challenging traditional courtly display, and the vestmental evidence of income (in the form of ignoring the regulations) suggested that hierarchical categories "seemed to be constantly shifting, and income did not always correspond either to status or consumption" (Heller 2004: 348).

Such sensitivities to escalating social upheaval were also apparent in **Elizabethan** England, where Queen Elizabeth I enacted the Statutes of Apparel in 1574, prescribing the types of fabrics, colors, and garments that women of different status could wear (see box 1.3).

These statutes related to the cost of materials and status accorded to different colors and garments. A similar set of edicts related to men's clothing. Such laws created visible systems of social distinction and cultural roles—a practical aim, but one often thwarted by the drive by individuals to create distinctiveness or seek higher status by emulating the elite. Sumptuary laws repeatedly failed due to transgressions that flaunted a world turned upside down. Dress regulation was often the product of political control; for example, the 1746 Dress Act banned the wearing of Highland dress (including the **tartan** or **kilt**) in Scotland in an effort to quell the quest for independence by

**Box 1.3 Elizabethan Clothing Allowed for Women**

| Status | Fabric | Color | Garment |
|---|---|---|---|
| Queen, Queen Mother, children, sisters, aunts | Silk | Purple | |
| Duchesses, marquises, countesses | **Sable**<br>Gold fabric | | Gowns, **kirtles, partlets,** sleeves |
| Viscountesses and baronesses | Tinselled satin, silk, or cloth embellished with gold | Gold | Cowls, partlets, kirtles, sleeves |
| Wives of knights of the Garter/Privy Council, etc. | Velvet Fur | Crimson Black | |
| Wives of barons' sons or of knights | Velvet Leopard fur Silk embroidery Spangles or pearls of gold, silver, or pearl | | Gowns Cowls, sleeves, partlets, or linings |
| | Enamelled chains, buttons, **aglets**, and borders | | |
| | Satin, damask, or tufted taffeta | | Gowns, kirtles, or velvet in kirtles |
| | Fur | Grey | |
| Daughters of knights | Silk **grosgrain**, doubled **sarcenet**, **camlet**, or taffeta, satin, or **damask** | | Gowns<br>Kirtles |
| Gentlewomen attendants | Liveries given by their mistresses | | Liveries |
| Lesser order gentlewomen | Velvet, tufted taffeta, satin | | |
| | Gold or silver | Gold or silver | Petticoats |
| Knights' daughters | Damask, taffeta, or other silk | | Petticoats and cloaks |
| Lower-class women | Wool, linen, and sheepskin | Brown, beige, yellow, orange, russet, green, gray, blue (from woad, not indigo) | |
| | Silk, taffeta, and velvet trimmings | | Buttons and coat facings, hats, and caps |

Source: Elizabethan Sumptuary Laws. n.d. "Elizabethan Clothing Law for Women." http://www.elizabethan-era.org.uk/elizabethan-clothing-allowed.htm

Scottish clans. Although such dress quickly disappeared as everyday dress, Highland clubs adopted the outlawed dress, and by the time the act was repealed in 1782, the kilt had become acknowledged national dress. Thus, the desire to eliminate a mode of dress resulted in its elevation to the symbolic costume of nationalist politics.

The other aim of dress regulation was moral; thus prostitutes and courtesans were often the target of prescriptions and proscriptions. In ancient Rome, prostitutes wore flame-colored togas. In sixteenth-century Italy, prostitutes and courtesans, who were banned from donning respectable forms of dress, often were so well dressed that they could not be distinguished from noblewomen (Storey 2004: 96). Gowns made of expensive cloth such as velvet and silk, a preference for bright colors, and the conspicuous display of precious jewelry created tensions relating to concerns about status, morality, and—just perhaps—envy among the lower classes that had no chance of ever wearing such finery. Not only did they flaunt clothes inconsistent with their social status, but they seem to have acquired a **taste** for wearing men's clothes by the end of the century. Although this has been explained as a lure for homoerotic sexual practices, it may have been simply to flout a nighttime curfew on prostitutes. Evidence of growing concern about the activities of these "dishonest" women was the edicts passed in the seventeenth century designed to evict prostitutes from the city, as well as others prohibiting the wearing of masks and Carnevale costumes, dressing as men, and wearing nun's habits (Storey 2004: 99).

Concern seems to have stemmed more from moral concerns than from the existence of a large group of wealthy courtesans.

**What was really causing concern was that a great many prostitutes were dressing in a manner inappropriate for their status, in clothes which they would only have been able to dream of wearing had they remained in a hierarchical society in which just wearing the trappings of social mobility constituted a threat to the established order and could cause resentment in the city. (Storey 2004: 101)**

In effect, and perhaps inadvertently, prostitutes were cocking a snoot at the honest citizens around them.

Europe was not alone in officially regulating fashion. Many—if not most—societies have at some stage attempted to prescribe who can—and cannot—wear what and when. During the Qing dynasty in China, for example, there were highly codified regulations concerning what members of the royal court could wear in terms of color, design, and fabric (box 1.4).

While only the royal family could wear dragon symbols, civic officials were also codified by animal symbols in the Qing dynasty: first rank wore the crane, second the golden peasant, third the peacock, fourth the goose, fifth the silver pheasant, sixth the egret, seventh the mandarin duck, eighth the quail, and ninth the paradise flycatcher (Cammann 1952: 196). These symbols ensured instant identification as to rank and role. Decoratively, they were the basis on which gowns were designed. They could have infinite variations on embellishments as long as the rules about motif, cloth, color, and adornment were followed. The resulting gowns were magnificent individually and collectively but in no way could be seen as a **uniform**; each gown was highly distinctive and individual.

**Kimono.** Photo: Shellaine Godbold

**Dragon robe (modern).** Sherrie Thai of ShaireProductions. Creative Commons Attribution 2.0 Generic

**Box 1.4 Early Qing Conventions for Dragon Robes (Before 1759)**

| | | |
|---|---|---|
| Emperor | Bright yellow, tawny yellow, blue | 5-clawed or 3-clawed dragons |
| Heir apparent (1676–1712) | Tawny yellow | 5-clawed or 3-clawed dragons |
| First degree prince and their sons, second degree princes | Any colors except yellow | 5-clawed dragons |
| Third and fourth degree princes, imperial dukes, and Chinese nobles, officials (1st–4th rank), Officers of the Imperial Guards | Any colors except yellow | 4-clawed dragons |
| Empress | Bright yellow, tawny yellow | 5-clawed dragons |
| Imperial consorts | Any colors except yellow | 5-clawed dragons |

Source: Schuyler Cammann. 1952. *China's Dragon Robes.* New York: Ronald Press. 191.

Although sumptuary laws disappeared during the seventeenth and eighteenth centuries, either by repeal or because they lapsed, elements lingered and there are still examples today—for instance, the ban on head scarves in French schools, the compulsory blue **burka** for women in Afghanistan, bans on **nudity** on public beaches, dress codes in pubs and sports venues, school uniform regulations, and the lifting of the ban on head scarves in Turkish universities.

By the nineteenth century, fashion had become annexed to the project of self-actualization, expanding the project of the dandies in constructing and managing the minutiae of chosen personae. Status, role, occupation, and gender—even nationality—became leitmotifs of fashionable display. However, many of these automatic readings of fashion systems were undermined during the twentieth century as mass media, popular culture, world wars, mass migration, and globalization resulted in the proliferation of fashion systems that now competed with each other and subverted one another.

Usually, at this point in a book on fashion, there is a discussion of theories of fashion. Here, I've decided to start with something in which students of fashion may be more interested and then use this example to show how contemporary fashion theory can be used to analyze the phenomenon of color in fashion.

## ii. color and fashion through time

As we can see from the examples above, the use of color has been a key aspect of how people have clothed themselves as a group and how individuals have created unique identities in the quest to both belong and stand out in parallel fashion systems (Fukai 2004). But color has also been used by authorities as a visible marker to regulate clothing habits. As Dominique Cardon (2004: 229), research director of the Centre National de la Recherche Scientifique, wrote in the catalog for the "Fashion in Colors" exhibition,

**even before the invention of the first artificial and synthetic dyes, which signaled the start of a new type of intellectual and technological adventure, all civilizations in the world had managed to live in colors—they dyed human and animal skins, hair, teeth, bones, and all sorts of vegetable fibers and woods, in the whole range of colors of the rainbow.**

The colorful basis of fashion is a fascinating place to start our exploration of fashion. At the heart of the modern fashion phenomenon is the belief that fashion trickles down from the self-appointed fashion elite to wider society unless there are regulations (and adequate disincentives) to stop this imitation. However, as the example of sumptuary laws shows, in the case of prostitutes and courtesans, some styles and fashions are emulated *by* the elite. However, if we stick to the **trickle-down theory** for the moment, we can see that this assumes a *vertical* model of consumption, where the system of production determines the practices of consumption (Fine and Leopold 1993; cf. Miller 2004: 116). In this model of production, the designer or tastemaker is accorded a godlike position of influence on how fashions are set in motion and how they change. Yet is this so?

Let's take the example of color—what determines what color clothes you buy? **Yarn** and textile manufacturers, retail groups, and trade

**Trickle-down fashion.** Image: Shellaine Godbold

associations claim that "the first response to a **garment** by the consumer is color" (Grove-White 2001: 195–96). A key question is, then, who determines what colors individuals prefer—is it designers, individual psychology, one's color clothing history, or what? There is no doubt that fashion designers are acutely aware of the connotations of colors (e.g., **white** for purity or neutrality, **red** for sexiness, **black** for power or evil, etc.) and use the **color wheel** to select combinations of primary, secondary, and tertiary colors in their collections. Apart from the choice of a **monochrome** (use of a single color), a designer might select complementary (opposite) colors, triads (three equally spaced colors), or analogous (adjacent) colors—or variations of these.

Despite the importance of color, oddly enough, there has been little written about the relationship between fashion and color. There have, however, been a few exhibitions on the subject, including "The Right Chemistry: Colors in Fashion, 1704–1918" (Highbee Gallery, Kent State

University Museum, Kent, Ohio, December 16, 2004–February 19, 2006) and "Fashion in Colors" (Cooper-Hewitt National Design Museum, New York, December 9, 2005–March 26, 2006). Let's review the literature that does exist (e.g., Fukai 2005). First, we need to understand the history of dyes in the manufacture of textiles and clothing, and how breakthroughs in dye technologies sparked a fashion for the new shades that could be produced more easily using industrial techniques.

Historically, dyes were made from natural ingredients (plants, animals, and minerals) such as **woad** (blue); **indigo** (blue-violet); chamomile, barberry, and marigold (yellow); henna, ocher, iron, and walnut (brown); lac, cochineal, brazilwood, and madder (red); logwood (purple and black); and acacia, chestnut, and eucalyptus (neutrals). King Tutankhamen's tomb contained red fabric made from madder, while some Mediterranean cultures made purple from the fluid of the trumpet shell or purple fish, which, at 8,500 mollusks per gram, made it more expensive than gold. Clearly there was a connection between color and social elites. In Europe, it was not until the fifteenth century that dyeing cloth became more common and consequently clothes became more colorful.

Grant McCracken (1982: 61) examined the clothing of two groups at the court of Elizabeth I "to show how clothing served as an agent of history by giving cultural form and order to a highly innovative, dynamic historical moment." He wondered why young men wore white and older men wore black, a choice that he related back to the connotations of light and dark colors and their relationship to the respective characteristics of youth and age. He suggested that the radical distinction between the two groups stemmed from the fact that each group "defined itself in precisely the terms the other group rejected, and refused as utterly inappropriate the terms the other group adopted," resulting in a stark contrast between the color codes of clothing adopted by each group as a visible code for the distinctiveness of each group. McCracken mapped the logic of the color code that shaped the dress of young men and old men, as shown in box 1.5.

McCracken suggests that this distinction in dress created two warring factions at court, with the young men in brightly colored dress becoming political opponents of the old guard and actively aligning themselves with the new policies of Elizabeth. Meanwhile, the older men, through their more severe dress, gave off qualities of gravity, stability, and mental acuity. Dress was used as "a cultural operator" where the contrast between white and black created "the dazzling spectacle with which so much of the Elizabethan world was constituted" but could only end "in the eclipse of one group by the other" (McCracken 1985a: 526):

**Dress as operator created structure that would give rise to structure. It had narrowed the range of possibility and set the stage for transition. (McCracken 1985a: 527)**

Through ill-fated military incursions and squandering of wealth, the young men of Elizabeth's court were thwarted in their ambitions and found themselves defeated, eschewing their "light-reflecting ornaments" and "brilliant dress" and exchanging it for the black dress of melancholic men and the old, using the color of the new garb to signal their previously rejected qualities.

**Dress as an operator capable of signifying new structural relationships served them now even in their failure. Their new place at court**

**Box 1.5 The Color-Coded Dress of Men at Elizabeth I's Court**

| | |
|---|---|
| **Youth** | |
| Light (preferred) | (1) because reflective of the light of Elizabeth<br>(2) because suggestive of<br>(a) lightness of wit and movement<br>(b) humoural balance<br>(c) mental order<br>(d) positive political virtue |
| Dark (avoided) | (1) because contrary to light<br>(2) because suggestive of<br>(a) heaviness<br>(b) humoral imbalance<br>(c) mental distress<br>(d) negative political inclination |
| **Age** | |
| Light (avoided) | (1) because suggestive of light, unstable emotion |
| Dark (preferred) | (1) because suggestive of gravity, stability and mental acuity |

Source: McCracken 1985a: 524.

**was made manifest by the color of their dress. (McCracken 1985a: 528)**

This example shows how transparently color can be annexed to social, cultural, and political agendas as a visible marker of innovation, change, victory, and defeat as well as hierarchical and psychological states of mind. The use of color in clothing and dress thus appears to have a universal role in human endeavors.

In other cultures (Africa, Asia, South America, North America), the use of dyes appears to have been more common and more sophisticated much earlier. Arthur Wolf (1970) explored the use of color symbolism in Chinese mourning rituals. Taking the example of funerals in Sanshia in northern Taiwan, he discovered a complex interplay of mourning dress relating to the relationship of a mourner to the deceased and signaled by choice of cloth (from rough to fine hemp, flax, or muslin) and color (neutral, blue, yellow, or red).

**Yellow, the imperial color, is of a higher order than red, and red in turn is of a higher order than blue. The overall order is from mua:-po [rough] gowns, at one end of the scale, through gowns of te-a-po [fine], blue, and red, to yellow gowns at the opposite end of the scale. (Wolf 1970: 191)**

The important point is that these gowns and colors do not stand in opposition to each other, but as a continuum from "sorrow and mourning to joy and renewal," where blue is in the middle between the extremes of joy (red) and sorrow (yellow) (Wolf 1970: 191). Mourning dress thus conveys multiple and changing meanings. This is in contrast to the Western meaning of black for sorrow and sympathy (Taylor 1983; Whitfield 2008)—although in recent years, Western funerals have introduced colored mourning dress—especially for children—to reflect or symbolize the celebration of the life of the deceased rather than dwell on her or his passing.

In traditional Chinese mourning dress, these color and cloth contrasts are counterpoints and sometimes connote different meanings. For example, while red is an expression of joy, it is also a prophylactic and is used as a means of warding off evil. So red has two meanings and two functions and thus might be worn at a funeral but signify different things. White, on the other hand, is worn as a mark of courtesy (not obligation). Wolf (1970: 206) concludes:

**The use of textures and colors to spell out social statuses in visual detail also gives us an invaluable opportunity to study Chinese symbolism. We see that textures and colors are not isolated signs, but rather points on a scale. ... The scale is not simple: although the items at either end remain positive and negative in all contexts, the meaning of the items towards the middle varies with context. Contrasted with red, blue carries negative connotations; compared with white, it is a positive color. The meaning of a color depends on its place in the Chinese spectrum and the use of color in a particular context.**

This example of the dynamics of color symbolism in China illustrates the variable connotations of colors as well as their very significant social role as markers of distinction, difference, genealogy, emotion, desires, psychology, and gender. Once the technological challenges of dyeing were appreciated in Europe, many of the advances made in European dyeing practices were the result of contact with other cultures. The Byzantine Empire in the Middle Ages was the center of cosmopolitan culture and intellectual and aesthetic tastes that influenced the rest of Europe. It was also the center of the manufacture of finely woven cloth that was often embroidered with gold and silver as well as exquisitely dyed in **purple** (largely reserved for royalty), violet, yellow, and greens. According to Schneider (1978: 416),

**Constantinople was known to Europeans as the richest and most magnificent city in the world. ... Certain monochrome colors permitted it to become a cosmopolitan center of fashion as its courtiers abandoned the plain Roman toga for Mandarin-style coats of stiff, embroidered brocade.**

Schneider suggests that the trade imbalance between the Byzantine Empire and the rest of Europe partially triggered a desire among states in Europe to redress the situation and establish their own manufacturing and export industries. Cloth, she argues, was one key symbol of national liberation, and a convoluted tussle between clothing manufacture in Flanders, England, Italy, and Spain ensued through to the Renaissance. Such was the ostentatious display of luxury clothing and goods amid the growing influence of morally sensitive religious orders (typically clad in black), that cities and nations began to introduce sumptuary laws to curb conspicuous display and "frivolous fashion [that] had led to envy, greed, and sexual license":

**Among the frivolities they condemned were bright colors, whose use was limited by establishing the proper number of variegated borders on petticoats and sleeves according to a person's rank and marital status. (Schneider 1978: 432)**

Unmarried women were permitted to wear more colors than wives and widows, while higher-ranking people also could wear colors more boldly. The ban on colors not only was driven moral concerns but was due to the fact that "they were obtained with dyes that were too precious" (Schneider 1978: 432).

The reliance on naturally occurring substances (sometimes imported at exorbitant prices) made dyeing a cumbersome and expensive proposition that relied on the skill and specialist knowledge of dyers (who were highly regarded)—not to mention a smelly one. Elizabeth I banned the processing of woad within five miles of her residences because the smell was so disgusting (Schneider 1978: 419)! The breakthrough in transforming dyeing from a complicated and unpleasant process to an efficient factory industry came with the ability to use chemical substitutes, one of the earliest of which was Prussian blue manufactured from potash and iron salt in 1702. This was followed by the discovery of **mauveine** (from quinine) in 1856. Both became fashion colors and were highly sought in the 1850s and 1860s. Other aniline colors followed, including fuchsia, magenta, and violet.

Subsequent advances in chemistry revolutionized the production of dyes in the later part of the nineteenth century, and by the end of the First World War, textile dyeing was a highly industrialized process using chemicals—a long way from the pounding of plant roots with a mortar and pestle. The manufacture of fluorescent colors and metallics transformed color possibilities in the 1980s. Nonetheless, use of natural ingredients has persisted in artisanal fashion and design and has been revived in movements such as artwear and ecological dress pressure groups.

Despite the importance of color in fashion, much of the theory behind the process stems from social psychology, on the one hand, and art theory, on the other. For example, there is now an industry of color consultants, who match colors to personality traits and advocate that consumers select clothes on the basis of their ideal swatch palette. Companies like Color Me Beautiful advise clients on the colors that best complement their skin tone, hair color, and personality type. This schema is based on Johannes Itten's color theory, which matched colors with seasons and subsequently imbued colors with personal attributes. For example, violet is associated with inspiration, indigo with love, blue with tranquility, green with balance, yellow with intellect, orange with controlled vitality, and red with physical energy. Consumers are codified in terms of seasonal types, as shown in box 1.6.

So we might assume that a person in a bright floral shirt is outgoing and strong minded, while a person in a pale beige shirt is shy and introverted. Armed with a swatch patch, a consumer should be able to shop for color, confidently knowing what messages she or he will be sending in a fuchsia, forest green, charcoal, or apricot outfit. And yet it seems that only a minority shop in this way—most stick to a much more limited palette, with dark colors to the fore.

Why, then, does the textile industry put so much emphasis on color, forecasting at least two years in advance (Grove-White 2001: 196)? According to the International Trade Centre (2001), "colors change twice or three times a year" in

**Box 1.6 Colors in the Seasonal Typology**

Winter types: Dark hair and fair complexion with cool undertones; varying skin tones; cool and clear saturated colors with blue undertone recommended

Summer types: Blonde, brunette, or ash-brown hair; pink skin tone; soft colors with blue undertones recommended

Spring types: blonde, red, or gold-brown hair; ivory, peach, or beige skin, sometimes with freckles; clear warm colors with yellow undertones recommended

Autumn types: dark brown with red or honey tones in hair; peach to golden-yellow skin tones, often with freckles; rust brown, warm red, and earth tones (e.g., greens, orange, brown, red) recommended

the fashion and accessories export market, and changes are "planned three to five years ahead." In fact, the choice of color for a new season is regarded as of paramount importance by the chairman of International Textiles: "It is color which dictates the mood or ambience of a season and it is color which supports the whole towering edifice of fashion" (quoted by Grove-White 2001: 195). The thirty or so colors recommended for a season are described in terms of looks, lifestyle, and age (Grove-White 2001: 196), as in the forecast for colors and fabrics for home interior and fashion published by the International Color Authority for autumn/winter 2008/09, shown in box 1.7.

This forecast uses the names describing the colors (e.g., peppermint green, pansy purple, dark steel) to convey the attributes ascribed to particular shades (freshness, intensity, romance, classicism, etc.). For women, colors are also associated with the style and shape of the clothes (sculptured, draped, etc.), while men's colors are associated with well-known stereotypes of masculinity (poet, college boy, etc.). By such denotations, a fashion designer can match the theme of a collection to appropriate colors while a consumer can match her or his sense of identity or personality with a suitable garment.

Thus it would seem that fashion consumers are overwhelmingly conservative in their selection of new clothes and in the combination of items in their wardrobes. Although clients of color consultants may take their swatch of thirty colors on shopping expeditions, most consumers narrow their choice down to just a few. This is very different from the approach of non-Europeans to color in dress (see box 1.8).

This example has provided an overview of the role of color in fashion and the technological advances that have enabled the production of new colors and hues, including fluorescent and metallic shades. This seems to support the logic of the contemporary fashion system. However, although color has been a key part of designer collections and exemplary items that have become retrospectively anointed as a symbol of their time, one aspect of the story of color and fashion defies this logic: namely, the preference for black as the iconic fashion color. Miller (2004: 117) notes:

**I have not met anyone as yet who would disagree with the general qualitative assessment that styles and colors being worn as one goes to work each day, or looks around the street, or even goes out in the evening are far more**

### Box 1.7 Fashion Color Forecast for 2008/9

The home decoration reflects the personalities, temperaments and likes of a person or a family. Each person or family is stating themselves through the choice of color, fabric and pattern …

**Trend forecast for women and men fashion**

For women, there will be four major themes:

- **Sheer**: layering of chalky white, peppermint green, gray, sage and dusty pink and blue, pale lemon and lime for freshness;
- **Sculptured**: colors such as magenta, tangerine orange, caramel brown and camel are used for a vibrant and intense touch;
- **Tailored**: a sophisticated sense created by using slate gray pebble, inky blue ad indigo with lilac, pansy purple and deep damson;
- **Draped**: green is the new black, and olive, jungle green, moss and indigo is matched with mint and light gray, bronze and gold shades.

For menswear, there will be another four major themes:

- **The poet**: pink-tinged pastels, with snowflake, dark steel and blue-gray as accent, and also romantic and pure, clean colors;
- **The eccentric**: fun and elegant, with pink being key;
- **The traditionalist**: a classic sense created by dark rich colors, emphasis on brown, with navy and green;
- **The college boy**: burgundy, gold, orange and basalt, inspired by the club blazers, scarves and regimental ties.

Source: 2456.com. 2007. "Colors and Fabrics for Home Interior in 2008/09" http://textile.2456.com/eng/feature/printed.asp?fsid=2363

### Box 1.8 Tswana Coats of Many Colors

In a chapter on the attempts by missionaries to clothe the naked natives of Tswana in South Africa, anthropologist Jean Comaroff (2003) discusses missionary Mary Moffat's efforts to introduce secondhand clothes from England and to teach needlecraft to the locals, who experimented with their own sartorial codes—much to the discomfort of the missionaries. In 1842, Moffat recorded that:

> A man might be seen in a jacket with but one sleeve, because the other was not finished, or he lacked material to complete it. Another in a leathern or duffel jacket, with the sleeves of different colors, or of fine printed cotton. Gowns were seen like Joseph's coat of many colors, and dresses of such fantastic shapes, as were calculated to excite a smile in the gravest of us. (Quoted by Comaroff 2003: 103)

Like the modern consumer, the Tswana were reinterpreting sartorial conventions in their usage of the components of garments, choice of fabric, use of color, and recombination to create new items by **bricoleur** tailors. But whereas the contemporary everyday consumer seeks restraint and self-discipline in the fashion impulse, the Tswana sought experimentation and diversification.

**homogenized than what is available in the shops. The shops have become far more homogenized over the years. ... But this seems to follow rather than force the trends in what people wear. It is simply that attempts to create distinction in color and print do not sell sufficiently over the long term.**

In short, "the logic of modern women's clothing ... seems to imply that the driving force has been the customer not the couturier" (Miller 2004: 117). This certainly seems to be true of the history of color in fashion. For despite the kaleidoscopic range of colors and polychromatic possibilities, the symbolic connotations of colors, the purported psychological matching of colors to personalities, and individual preferences for a small number of colors in clothes, how can we explain the dominance of just one color in fashion—black?

## iii. the color black in fashion

> *Black is a uniquely powerful, mysterious and seductive color. The little black dress attributed to Coco Chanel plays only a very small part in the history of fashionable black. To understand why "that special black dress ... is both chic and armor," we need to go much deeper into the history of the symbolism of black. (Steele 2007: np).*

So begins Valerie Steele's essay in the catalog for "The Little Black Dress" exhibition. While children learn that the primary colors are red, yellow, and blue, color analysts argue that the colors white (light), red (the most saturated color), and black (dark) are the basis of color systems. These predominate in ethnographic contexts such as body painting and acquire strong and contradictory meanings across cultures—red blooded, red flag, red skin, red shirt, red dress, red carpet, red light district, red triangle (a sign of danger), redneck, a red (communist sympathizer). Red—the color of blood—is diametrically associated with fertility and life by some cultures, and with sterility and death by others (Lévi-Strauss 2004: 21).

White is the color of mourning in some societies while black is used in others. On the other hand, white is often associated with goodness, purity, and cleanliness in positive ways (e.g., white wedding, white witch, white stocking, white knight, white sale, white collar, white wash) or badness, emptiness, or uselessness in negative ways (e.g., white elephant, white slaver, white ant, white livered). Black has multiple connotations: death (black plague, black hole), oppositional politics (Blackshirts, black power, blackmouth), **eroticism** (black magic, black lace), elegance and luxury (little black dress, black tie, black label), respectability (black letter), madness (black dog), secrecy and the illicit (black market, blacklist, blackmail, Black Jack, black arts).

Let's now turn to the fashion for black. According to one industry analyst, 70 percent of all fashion apparel sold in Britain is black (Colour Affects 2007). We might want to question this percentage but we would probably agree that there is a dominance of black in fashion-related consumer transactions when a myriad of colors are available (Di Trocchio 2008). As fashion writer Corrie Perkin (2008: 17) wrote, reviewing the National Gallery of Victoria's exhibition "Black in Fashion: From Mourning to Night,"

**black has been a fashion constant since the early 20th century, when women started to**

**identify it as chic, glamorous and stylish. It has also been an enormous industry success. Put simply, black sells. (See also National Gallery of Victoria 2008)**

But why, when so many other colors and shades are available, is black so popular? Partly it relates to black's connotations as a fashion color of sophistication, drama, and safety (National Gallery of Victoria 2008). So, instead of choosing a color that makes a statement, consumers typically select something that does *not* stand out, that blends in with the surrounding clothing habits. In other words, rather than using clothes to project a strong sense of identity, consumers choose a color that is *absorbed* into the collective and thus reassures them that they do not look different (Clarke and Miller 2002; Grove-White 2001: 197; cf. Miller 2004: 116–27).

**Ethnographic** research into how consumers shop for clothes suggests that the experience is filled with anxiety about finding something suitable that fits, feelings of pressure created by the available range of clothes and by salespeople, and the fear of social embarrassment should one choose something that significant others might judge inappropriate or unflattering. Because of these mixed emotions, rather than taking advantage of the "combinatorial freedom" of color, consumers tend to censor their shopping behavior by narrowing down their choice of colors to two or three, usually "in favor of black or darker colors" (Grove-White 2001: 197). It is possible that by doing so, a consumer takes the question of color out of the shopping decision-making process, since Grove-White found that her respondents "did not particularly refer to the role of color in fashion spreads and highlighted style and cut as being more important outward 'signs' of 'not being out of fashion' ":

**Style was seen as an indicator of subjective taste and self-image: "to sort of define the type of person you are or categorize you from the rest of society at large."**

Combining the emphasis on style and cut with a restricted color palette, a consumer can maximize the mix-and-match (combinatorial) potential of her or his wardrobe, using an item in a contrasting color to offset the monochromatic look of the main elements. As one respondent put it, "So if you bought lots of black things they all went together and they all looked more or less okay and you know. ... So if you got it in black it was safe, you couldn't really go far wrong" (quoted by Grove-White 2001: 199). In other words, black is "safe and controllable."

As a result, black has become the fashion color par excellence as the "iconic ... backdrop to modern dress," according to Miller (2004: 115). He goes on:

**If by chance any other color tries to get a look in, the fashion magazines will say "brown is the new black" or "green is the new black," though it has now become pretty clear that for most of the time black is the new black.**

While we are all familiar with this convention and at least tacitly accept the connotations that black as a fashion color is deemed to signal, why has it become so entrenched when other facets of fashion behavior would suggest that a plethora of color choices would better suit the industry?

Generally, common descriptors for black include *qualities of darkness, funereal, raven, gloomy,* and *unknowable.* In her brilliant exposition of the meaning of black in fashion, Hollander (1978) argues that it is the most powerful color in fashion because of its connotations of the sinister. By the end of the eighth century, "black was considered the monastic color par excellence" (Schneider 1978: 423). Yet black was first incorporated in clothing in Europe as "the straightforward color of death, appropriate for mourning but nothing else" (Hollander 1978: 365). It was not until the fourteenth century that black was used as a "foil for color" in clothing and to enhance facial features (Hollander 1978: 365–66). Hollander argues that it was not until clothing choices became imbued with aesthetic principles that black spread from mourners and monks to the ranks of the fashionable. Courtiers remained fixated by colorful garb, so when adventurous individuals chose black, they posed a striking contrast to the normative mode.

While this account of the trend of wearing black cites moral and religious concerns about asceticism, renouncement of ostentation and wordly goods sparked "a generalized distrust of color in European culture":

**Medieval Christians abhorred purple and turned it from a color of royalty, as under Byzantium, to a symbol, like black, of penitence, melancholy, and death. They associated red with the tempting devil, while yellow, the color of state robes in Imperial China, signified sensuality and cowardice, and was selected for Judas' dress [and later the Nazi insignia for Jews]. (Schneider 1978: 422)**

Schneider argues that this use of black as a symbol of pious self-restraint had some economic reasons, namely, the development of a European industry of textile production and dyeing that rejected the **polychrome** (multicolor) textiles of the East in favor of monochromes.

The first general uptake of black seems to have occurred in the fifteenth and sixteenth centuries, when black with white neck ornamentation (e.g., a ruff or collar) or headwear gained currency. In Holland, black was widely adopted as evidence of Calvinist religious and moral beliefs. Dutch portraiture of the seventeenth century, for example, reflects this habit. As a reviewer of "Dutch Portraits: The Age of Rembrandt and Frans Hals" at the National Gallery in London observed,

**most people in most of these paintings wear black from head to toe, except for a flash of white around their neck from a collar or ruff. It's true of the women as it is of the men. And, while not the full burka, it is a religious look that makes the painter's task much more difficult. (Januszczak 2007: 8)**

While this blackness could have made for very dull paintings, Januszczak argues that the Dutch artists excelled in using the "dramatic possibilities of black and white" to highlight expressions, gestures, play of light, and depiction of moods. Over time, black spread from the confines of the clergy and devout followers to the upper bourgeois classes of professionals, which established a trickle-down pattern.

Between the Middle Ages and the Renaissance, the preference for black became entrenched, although also elaborated. In courts such as those of Philip the Good in Burgundy and Philip II of Spain, fashionable black was the order of the day and this trend spread northwards. But the allure of black was to unravel during the Renaissance, when trade with the East brought new textiles and dyeing technologies to Italy and Spain, leading to the production of magnificent polychrome woolen and silk fabrics:

**Portrait of the artist Marten Pepijn, Sir Anthony van Dyck (1599–1641).** Koninklijk Museum Voor Schone Kunsten Zntwerpen. Lukas—Art in Flanders VZW

**Renaissance Italy virtually exploded with color. Among its peacock themes were parti-colored garments in which the sleeves were of contrasting colors, the pants legs also, and the body of still another color. Garments, now intricately tailored, were slashed with hundreds of cuts to reveal a different color underneath. Variations in color made it possible for individuals to design their own clothes, and court fashion "changed with a rapidity which had been unknown before." For the first time since the fall of Rome, reds and purples surfaced to mark off not only courtiers and royalty from the less prestigious ranks, but the merchant elite as well. (Schneider 1978: 427)**

Despite this parade of peacocks, black persisted in some quarters (for example, among nobles in Florence and Venice) as a symbol of modesty and sobriety, while clothes in mid-sixteenth-century England were made of "uniformly undyed or 'sadly' dyed cloth of wool" (Schneider 1978: 428). This cloth was so rough that exports to India were used only as blankets for elephants and horses! So, we find a mixed palette of color and black throughout Europe, and a tension between polychrome and monochrome was set in place.

Debates about Renaissance fashion were both moral and economic, resulting in sumptuary laws to regulate **conspicuous consumption** of luxury and exotic goods and apparel. In this quest, "black clothing, symbolic of pious sacrifice and advocacy of indigenous development, served well to 'catalyze feelings' and to communicate goals" and to help people deal with ambivalent feelings about consumer goods that they "both coveted and repelled" (Schneider 1978: 433). By the eighteenth century, even Italy had second thoughts about color, with one observer describing an evening at the opera as like being at a funeral ceremony. Black was the color of Italy's establishment, the only relief being the garish multicolored decorations of Carnevale, a parodic response to the status quo. Black also had a political and economic function:

**Black dress, one of the chief means of communicating asceticism, also had a practical dimension; unlike polychrome clothing, it could be elaborated and perfected by indigenous craftsmen using indigenous raw materials. As such, it participated directly in the revolutionary transformation of European society that took place in the Middle Ages and began to redress the relationship of Europe to the outside world. (Schneider 1978: 439)**

This account of the history of black in European clothing emphasized the ambiguous and contradictory impulses that underpinned the fashion for black among different societies, economies, classes, and events. It is this multivalent set of symbols that surrounds black that has underpinned its diverse manifestations in contemporary fashion.

Thereafter, black went in and out of fashion, and with it a mixed set of symbols that were both positive and aesthetic ("piquant and arresting") and negative and moral ("godliness, professionalism, bourgeois solidity, or mourning") (Hollander 1978: 373). Black, then, had a place in customary dress (for mourning and among monks), in occupational dress (professions), in aesthetic and dramatic costume (e.g., artists and actors), and increasingly in **antifashion** (e.g., among clerks, maids, and shopgirls).

These multiple syntagmas associated with wearing black were at the core of the popularization of black as fashion in the twentieth century. Black (suits) became the look for men by default, while fashion history cites Coco Chanel's little black dress as the "new chic antifashion" for women in the 1920s and 1930s (Hollander 1978: 385). The ambivalent connotations of black persisted, but it was not until the 1960s that black became a dominant fashion color that paraded its countercultural and rebellious stripes, epitomized by the black turtleneck sweater worn by the Beat generation. **Leisure wear** and **sportswear**, which had traditionally eschewed black, began to prefer it, sometimes borrowing from its prominence in dance wear and the new fabrics developed for exercise clothes.

While Hollander (1978: 388) argues that black had "lost most of its symbolic significance" by the late twentieth century, it is possible to argue that its historical and highly charged meanings and messages are recuperated in new appropriations of black in contemporary fashion. This is clearly so in the case of the use of black in a **subculture** concerned with darkness and death, for example, among **Goths** or Satanists; the preference for black among (male) actors, poets, and cultural workers; and the use of black as a default color for formal wear and outfits designed to make a point.

Among consumers in general, colors are often used to offset the dominant choice of black. Here is a classic chicken-and-egg situation. Because black is so often on the racks, consumers buy black, and because black is the best-selling color, manufacturers keep making black clothes. And so black continues to dominate fashion.

But is this logical from an industry point of view? Miller (2004) argues that it is not. The fashion industry rests on its ability to offer something new. It is a complex global network of highly competitive elements whose survival depends on difference rather than homogeneity. Yet black persists and proliferates despite this and the best efforts of up-and-coming entrants to innovate and offer something different. Miller explores whether this is because of the historical connotations of black, the modernist aesthetic of black, or consumer tendency to reject color. He concludes that it is the "burden of freedom," the fear of risk, and the insecurity that accompanies the fashion shopping experience (or ordeal) that drive the rapacious consumption of black in the quest for sophisticated distinction and rejection of all the colors of the rainbow, which are embraced and celebrated in clothing genres such as the **sari** and **kimono**.

We may be no closer to understanding the predilection for black in fashion, but it is clear that this convention defies logic within the fashion system itself, as well as our common belief that the modern individual can wear whatever she or he wants, unfettered by expectations and habits. This example illustrates that although fashion theory elevates the importance of designer (especially Parisian) fashion in shaping the industry globally, other forces may play a more significant role in the fashion choices and clothing habits of most people. And although most attention is paid to fashion, it seems likely that everyday dress habits in fact drive the industry.

Although particular designers, celebrities, and outfits have been credited with creating the fashion for black—such as Coco Chanel, Juliette Greco, Audrey Hepburn, and Giorgio Armani—it seems more likely that they have come to retrospectively embody the shared connotations of black as a fashion statement rather than having single-handedly set the scene. Such an assumption must underpin the study of fashion and the organization of this book.

## iv. conclusion

This chapter has introduced the study of fashion through the example of color in fashion. First, we discussed whether fashion should adopt an ethnocentric approach, which distinguishes clothing habits in preindustrial societies from those in industrialized consumer cultures. We have argued that similar impulses can be identified in all cultures and that we need to think of fashion systems as parallel and competing rather than thinking of Western culture as having the only true fashion phenomenon. The twists and turns of how color—and particularly black—have featured in fashion demonstrate the complexities of fashion as cultural history that fashion theories have tried to model and analyze. Those are the subject of the next chapter.

The following case studies exemplify the impulse across societies to regulate fashion; the institutionalization of black mourning dress; the fashion impulse in the context of headdresses of New Guinea highlanders; and the transformation of the symbolism of a practical garment or uniform—the **sailor suit**—into a global fashion icon spanning all cultures.

## CHAPTER SUMMARY

- Fashion is not just the province of the modern Western fashion system.
- The fashion impulse is the achievement of distinctiveness in dress through clothing codes and symbols that balance the impulse to belong to a group and the individual desire to stand out and assert the attributes of the self or persona.
- The regulation of clothing codes and habits accompanies the fashion impulse in all cultures as part of the project to internalize status and distinction through a combination of proscriptions and prescriptions.
- Western or European fashion cultures are distinctive in that the objects of fashion are valued as objects from which exchange value is deemed to emanate or in which it is deemed to reside, as opposed to clothing and fashion impulses in gift economies, where clothing habits are driven by the social worth of clothes and the complex social exchanges that take place around them.
- Just as Western fashion systems appropriate the fashion impulse of other cultures, so too other cultures appropriate elements of Western fashion.
- The use of color in fashion demonstrates the universal importance of color codes and symbols to designate social meanings; however, the connotations of colors are context specific and variable.

## CASE STUDY 1: The Regulation of Fashion

The most comprehensive study of sumptuary laws (legislation designed to control the conspicuous consumption of clothes and apparel) is Alan Hunt's *Governance of the Consuming Passions: A History of Sumptuary Laws* (1996), and the following case study is largely drawn from this work. As we have seen, rules about how people should dress are so fundamental to human society that they are frequently encoded in legislation or codes of conduct (e.g., by professional bodies, schools). Of particular importance in European society was the existence of sumptuary laws, which regulated civil conduct concerning, among other things, who could wear what under what circumstances. Sumptuary laws were legislated rules designed to limit conspicuous consumption, in particular, that of clothing and modes of dress. They were passed in a number of European countries between the twelfth and eighteenth centuries—and were flirted with in North America in the eighteenth century.

Restrictions might be placed on the type of garment that certain groups or people could and could not wear. Gold and silver fabric, jewelry, and ornamentations were often restricted, and expensive fabrics (e.g., silk, lace, velvet) might be restricted. While sumptuary laws also existed in antiquity—for example, in ancient Greece (600 BC) and ancient Rome (300 BC–AD 300), and during the T'ang period in China (AD 618–906) and the Tokugawa period in Japan (1600–1868)—their longevity in European countries between 1100 and 1700 coincided with the emergence of modernity.

European sumptuary laws existed in numerous places, including Italian cities, France, Spain, Swiss cantons, England, German provinces, and Scotland, and accompanied Europe's transition from premodernity to modernity. Rather than waning, sumptuary laws and dress codes were fundamentally tied up with the mercantile revolution that fanned conspicuous consumption and the consequent need to preserve social hierarchies. As a result, sumptuary laws proliferated at this time. They became increasingly concerned with dress codes, formal codification, the preservation of class distinctions, and the denouncement of extravagance and luxury. Alongside this codification was the emergence of dynamic sartorial sensibilities that became known as fashion. Dress became a means to subvert the social order and negotiate the neophyte consumer culture.

Sumptuary laws were therefore of two types: on the one hand, the imposition of expenditure limits and, on the other, the reservation of particular kinds of cloth or styles for certain groups—either as a privilege or as a negative prohibition. Yet the nature of these laws suggests that they were a response to challenges to existing hierarchies, that is, to the elite's social anxieties about changing social realities.

The legislation of sumptuary laws was partly intended to enforce the moral regulation of popular pastimes associated with emerging forms of popular culture. Sumptuary laws were not just about the arbitrary imposition of idiosyncratic laws from above, but a contested response to wider social changes and political challenges from below. The discourse of this moral regulation was centered on ideas of idleness and luxury, both of which were perceived as problems to be managed. This involved two related issues. As wage labor grew, workers were exercising their right to behave as they pleased. Furthermore, they had the capacity to purchase goods and the leisure time to enjoy them. Previously, the ability to buy luxuries was restricted to the elite.

However, pastimes were also regulated. The medieval regulation of games was replaced by the specific regulation of dangerous and idle activities like drinking and gambling in the late Middle Ages. Games that provided opportunities for gambling were especially despised, as were popular festivals, sports, and recreations of the working class, especially those that occurred in and around the alehouse. As people became more mobile, the problem of the vagrant became a major concern, resulting in strategies like the issuing of licenses and passbooks, the use of badges, and attempts to monitor behavior through restrictions on movement. Consumerism and leisure went hand in hand. But this was troublesome to the elite, who wanted to preserve their status through exclusivity, while aspirant classes resisted attempts at regulation.

Increasingly important, too, were sartorial devices used to allude to distinction, role, and place. Some of these were sanctioned, others a deliberate form of fraud. In the late fifteenth century, beggars evaded vagrancy legislation by dressing as pilgrims or discharged soldiers or sailors, leading to legislation requiring ex-military personnel to carry discharge papers or the equivalent. The adoption of a recognized dress code was a—reasonably successful—strategy that allowed people to project certain attributes of persona and that fooled enough people to necessitate remedial legislation. Yet there is little evidence that such legislation worked. Prescriptions and proscriptions fuelled a desire for the prohibited or illicit items. Economic changes meant that increasing numbers of people had the ability to acquire prohibited items, leading to waves of panic as prohibited items became fashionable and imitated by the lower classes. Instead of removing status differences, sumptuary laws provoked competition and imitation and put a high price on evidence of symbolic distinction.

Because they made social distinction visible, the regulations were resented and resisted. The proliferation and longevity of sumptuary laws across Europe reflected successive transformations of the economy, gender relations, urbanization, and politics. Clothing the body became a key element of the project of modernity. Of all forms of clothing, those with instantly recognizable codes and signifiers became a convenient form of shorthand.

Modern fashion systems have created similar informal mechanisms of instilling conformity and limiting transgression or alternative clothing codes. In contemporary culture, brand names epitomize this process. Known brands create a specialist clientele and knowledge of their deemed attributes and associated status. Those in the know are prepared to pay more for the cachet of association. While this conspicuous display of accumulated cultural capital works for a niche market, should a brand become too popular, the trendsetters move on to a new style or fashion, thus repeating the **fashion cycle**.

In short, the attempts of governments and authorities to regulate clothing behavior reflected primary moral and status concerns in societies that highlighted divisions between classes, because people subverted the intended visible markers of distinction and difference. Clothing regulation survived only when coupled with draconian penalties. Otherwise, such regulations spurred the transformation of cultures of clothing to new fashion cycles of modernity.

## CASE STUDY 2: Black Mourning Dress

**Mourning dress.** Photo: Robert Lawton. Creative Commons Attribution ShareAlike 2.5 License

Often we regard black as synonymous with death, but in fact it was only during the **Victorian** period (1840–1900) that black became entrenched as the color of mourning dress. As we have already seen, this stemmed from a mixture of the uptake of black by religious orders as normative, connotations of piety, and renunciation of conspicuous consumption by Protestants, as well as its growing popularity as high fashion among aristocrats and upwardly mobile classes. The reason that black became so entrenched as the color of mourning stems from the impact of the deaths of her mother and then husband, Prince Albert, on Queen Victoria. She went into deep mourning and remained clothed in black for the rest of her life. Most of her court, as well as many in wider society, emulated this dress code.

The adoption of black as normative dress for mourning posed new challenges, one of which was cost. At a time when families of the bereaved were financially stressed, the cost of the obligatory appropriate garb was crippling. This led to the development of extensive sources of advice (columns in popular publications, specialist mourning stores, mourning **fashion illustrations**, and etiquette guides). Mourning dress became a specialist form of fashion with seasonal changes and individual interpretations that required constant monitoring and accreditation by the self-appointed arbiters of mourning etiquette.

Mourning dress was not confined to the immediate stages of the funeral and burial but was worn during a series of stages over time: first mourning, second mourning, ordinary mourning, and half mourning. Each stage required a different form of dress for different members of the family—parents, grandparents, siblings, aunts and uncles, cousins, spouses, and so on. Over time the period required for mourning extended from a maximum of six months in the 1765 French court to a maximum of two-and-a-half years in a British family between 1876 and 1897 (Taylor 1983: 304).

This highly elaborated system was an attempt to order "emotions into a meaningful form" in order to deal with the death of a loved one (Whitfield 2008: 26), although as box 1.9 shows, the onus of this graduated demonstration of grief was laid on women, who "had to master knowing the correct combination of materials, trimmings and colors appropriate to the occasion" and wear "these for the correct periods of time" (Whitfield 2008: 29). Although there were copious sources of advice, this suggests that infractions were common and that, like sumptuary laws, advice on mourning dress was an attempt to rein in behavior.

Perhaps more important was the pressure for the bereaved (woman) to remain in seclusion—while widowers were pressured to seek a new wife (often a sister or relative of the deceased) after a short period of mourning. Particularly in the period of ordinary mourning, women could play with the advice on fabrics, finishings, and trimmings in order to "subvert their grave appearance" (Whitfield 2008: 34), and there are many examples of highly fashionable mourning outfits that succeeded in combining regulations with style. Often, new models in mourning dress were merely modified versions of mainstream fashion featured in black. In the later stages of mourning, other colors were permitted—gray, white, ivory, cream, mauve, or purple.

**Box 1.9 Recommended Lengths of Family Mourning, 1876-97**

| | First mourning | Second mourning | Ordinary mourning | Half-mourning | Total |
|---|---|---|---|---|---|
| Widow for husband | 1 year 1 day in bombazine and heavy plain crape | 9 months with less crape | 3 months in black silk with ribbon and jet black watch | 6 months min. in half-mourning colors | 2½ years |
| Widower for wife | 3 months in black suit, with black watch chain, buttons and tie | | | None | 3 months |
| Mother for child | 6 months in bombazine and crape | | 3 months in black silk | 3 months in half-mourning | 1 year |
| Child for parent | 6 months in black or white crape | | 3 months | 3 months | 1 year |
| Wife for her parents/mother-in-law | 18 months mantle in paramatta and crape | | 3 months | 3 months | 2 years |
| Grand-daughter | 6 months in crape | | 2 to 3 months | 1 to 3 months | 6 to 9 months |
| Second wife for husband's first wife's parents | | | 3 months | | 3 months |
| Servants | Same as their employers but in cheap, tougher fabrics, and black and white only for half-mourning | | | | |

Source: Adapted from Lou Taylor. 1983. *Mourning Dress: A Costume and Social History.* London: George Allen and Unwin. 4

But this was not always easy, and public approbation played a large role in monitoring the codes of mourning dress. When Victoria died in 1901, the sixteen-year-old daughter of a nonconformist minister went to watch the funeral procession. She recalled:

> I had no black clothes. My mother lent me a black hat and gloves, and, of course, one had black shoes and stockings those days; but I had a rich violet costume, and as I descended the stairs the family in the Hall looked horrified. "She will be mobbed" declared my brothers. It rather spoilt my day—I was the only bit of color in all London. (Quoted by Taylor 1983: 252)

From this time on, black mourning dress receded as mandatory wear and was publicly renounced after the death of King Edward VII in 1910, when race goers at Ascot wore highly fashionable dresses and extravagant hats in black and white so striking that the event became called "Black Ascot." This seemed to mark the start of a new attitude toward mourning dress.

Nonetheless, black for mourning has persisted. Taylor (1983: 280) cites examples of the funeral of a scrap-metal dealer in Sussex in 1971, when hundreds turned out to watch an elaborate procession led by an all-black horse-drawn hearse with top-hatted drivers leading twenty black limousines. It is likely that he was a Romany and that the funeral was following Eastern European Romany mourning codes. Taylor also cites the death of the Festival Pearly Queen of London in 1976, when the procession of mourners in their pearly finery, draped in black sashes, recalled the earlier funeral of the founder of the Pearly Kings and Queens in 1930, showing that in the case of this subculture, tradition remained at the fore (Taylor 1983: 279–80).

Black has remained common, and when important mourners dress differently, observers comment, as was the situation when Prince Charles wore a white naval uniform to the funeral of the Egyptian president, Anwar Sadat, in 1981—while an American woman raised eyebrows with her white mourning suit, gold belt, and gold-heeled stilettos:

> It was not the choice of white, nor even the trousers that broke the rules. Gold, however, is still not acceptable as an accessory of mourning. (Taylor 1983: 250)

However, many of these rules are not written down, and it is only in transgressions that the unstated assumptions that underlie the conventions of mourning dress are revealed. The fact that such conventions are highly localized and internalized among a particular group or within a culture is evident when other customs of mourning are examined. White has been and is commonly also used as the color of mourning—for example, in China, India, Japan, and Hungary as well as among the Lodagaa of Ghana, the Ibo of Nigeria, and the Asaro mud men of Papua New Guinea (Taylor 1983: 248–51). White was also worn for the death of a child in Victorian times. Other colors used for mourning include gray (also sometimes used for wedding dresses by women still in partial mourning), red (for example, in sixteenth-century Italy), and purple (for the mourning dress of royalty in numerous cultures).

Increasingly, funerals are being redefined as a celebration of the life of the deceased rather than as a sorrowful outpouring, and mourners are encouraged to wear colorful clothes that reflect the joyful memories of the deceased. At a funeral in 2007 for the unexpected death of a much-loved neighbor, each of his grandchildren was allowed to buy a special outfit for the event. The most memorable of these was eight-year-old Tilly's shiny red patent leather shoes and bright red dress. It seems that mourning dress had come full circle.

## CASE STUDY 3: Fashions in New Guinea Highland Headdresses

It might seem a long way from headdresses in New Guinea to the catwalks of fashion cities, but there are many parallels. I explored the headdresses worn by Papua New Guinea highlanders in my book *The Face of Fashion* (Craik 1994: 19–23, 25–26, 154–55, 157), where I argued two points: first, that the modes of constructing and decorating the headdresses of the Hageners have many similarities with contemporary fashion practice, and second, that the Hagen use of body decoration illuminates our understanding of contemporary cosmetic practice as much as it reveals its significance among Hageners.

In the western highlands of Papua New Guinea is the market town of Mount Hagen, which has traditionally been and remains a commercial hub and meeting place for the numerous surrounding tribes. The area has become widely known by anthropologists, filmmakers, travelers, and museum curators largely because of its residents' colorful and diverse dress, adornment, and body decoration. A beneficiary of wealth from coffee and tea plantations, Mount Hagen has had to accommodate multiple and often conflicting customs and mores, which has given it a reputation for being a bit like America's Wild West. Tradition and modernity, belonging and mobility, tribal customs and consumer culture, and past and present rub shoulders sometimes uncomfortably. It is this tension between then and now, and them and us, that makes Mount Hagen so fascinating and relevant to this study of fashion.

In August and September, before the tropical wet sets in, many communities in the highlands stage festivals, including the Mount Hagen Show in August and the Goroka Show in September. Participating

**A mudman from Asaro with his unique clay mask.** Photo: Jialiang Gao, peace-on-earth.org. Creative Commons Attribution ShareAlike 3.0 License

tribes include the Melpa, Mendi, Gimi, Umeda, Wiru, Huli, Kauil, Komblo, Chimbu, Benbena, Okapa, Asaro, Roro, and Samo. At these shows, local communities dress up, parade, and dance as part of a festival of food, wealth, and matchmaking. Central to these festivities is the display of elaborate headdresses, body decoration, and costume using local materials combined in spectacular and colorful designs. Materials include shells, bones, tusks, feathers, wings, birds, twines, leaves, beads, animal teeth, flowers, vegetation, human hair, and possum fur. This might sound a bit bland, but the ingenuity and imagination with which these materials are used defy belief. This is artistic creation of the finest order.

As this list of materials suggests, there is an enormous array of possibilities from which any dancer can chose. The diversity of designs in any anthropological text (e.g., Gröning 2001; Kirk and Strathern 1987)—or any of many online photographic collections—attests to the extraordinary degree of individual manipulation of aesthetic codes and incorporation of materials to achieve desired effects in the designs. Yet, as Malcolm Kirk comments,

> unfortunately, a photograph cannot adequately convey the spectacle of such an event. One's senses are overwhelmed by the military precision of the massed columns, the almost mesmerizing effect of a forest of plumes flexing in unison, the rhythmic stamp of feet so that the very earth shakes as they pass by, and the stirring chants of a thousand voices rolling majestically down the valley. (Kirk and Strathern 1987: 18)

Let's just take one description of the costumes of Huli dancers:

> The men wear wigs of human hair, often impregnated with powdered ocher pigment and fringed with dried ever-lasting daisies. These everyday wigs curve downwards over the head, but occasionally one sees the upturned crescent-shaped ocher wigs that were once worn by bachelors participating in the now-defunct *haroli* cult.
>
> The iridescent blue fan-shaped plumage [called *yagama*] worn on the wig just above the forehead comes from the breast shield of the Superb Bird of Paradise. ... The black oval-shaped plumage worn immediately behind the *yagama* also comes from the Super Bird of Paradise. ... The red-and-yellow feathers radiating out from this blue/black combination come from the tail of a lorikeet. The sprays of orange plumage atop the wigs are the flank feathers of the Raggiana Bird of Paradise; the black sprays are cassowary feathers. The speckled blue, yellow, and black forehead bands, or head, are the skins from a type of ground snake the Huli call *lepage.* (Kirk and Strathern 1987: 18–19)

There is no doubt that such radiant displays are not just the uniform of custom but exhibit individual interpretations, innovations, and adaptations. Highlanders have incorporated many new materials—cowie shells used as currency in the 1930s; mother-of-pearl shells traded by coastal communities; pigs' tail fringes; lids from sardine cans, which serve as mirrors; enameled metal used to replace bailer shells; coins with a hole drilled through (jewelry); combs; paper labels; crocheted beanies in national colors; and so on. At the 1967 Mount Hagen Show, one Melpa man "aroused considerable amusement" by wearing "coconut-shell breasts" over brightly colored designs "usually worn only by Melpa women," playing a transvestite role even though "transvestism does not ... have any formal part in traditional Melpa ceremonies" (Kirk and Strathern 1987: 20). This was clearly an individual parody.

So, while drawing on recognized aesthetic codes, each dancer makes considerable individual interpretations and embellishments in the details of body decoration and headdress. Dancers go to

**Huli Wigman from the Southern Highlands of Papua New Guinea.** Photo: Nomadtales. Creative Commons Attribution 2.1 Australia License

enormous lengths to create spectacular effects and a new look each year. There is fierce competition among dancers to achieve the most effective display so that spectators are drawn to the decorations first and then decipher who is wearing them. As Marilyn Strathern (1979: 243) concluded,

> they are not dressing up in costumes taking animal or spirit form; they are not masks, enacting myths or working out dramas. They are pretending to be no one but themselves, yet themselves decorated to the point of disguise. This idea is incorporated specifically into aesthetics: a dancer recognized at once has decorated himself poorly.

The dancer is then conveying multiple messages—about the decorations, about himself, and about the community he represents such that attributes of the self (those belonging to the individual) and his social status and wealth are "inextricably bound together" in the social presentation offered by the decorations (Ebin 1979: 71). This conflated set of messages is often misinterpreted by Western observers, who see decoration as a mask or disguise of the "real" self, as expressed in the following observations:

> The corrupting influence of an alien culture. ... Note the fragments of broken comb suspended from the finely decorated wig. This man is a dandy: he uses tiny pieces of yellow ground vine, seed pods and even a feather-adorned nose-stick to enhance his undeniably striking appearance. (Sinclair 1973: n.p.)

This reaction wants it both ways: it recognizes similarities with Western fashion behavior by the use of the term for a stylish man, "a dandy," yet insists that this behavior is intrinsically different but has been infected by Western ("alien") culture.

But how can we make sense of these designs and practices of highlander costume? Andrew Strathern (1987: 10) has criticized accounts that insist on differences and similarities between the highlander costume and Western costume and decoration but says that although his extensive fieldwork over more than twenty years enables him "to spot obvious ethnographic errors or gaps," it does not necessarily help him appreciate "the people's own aesthetics and symbolism." The accounts he refers to—whether by anthropologists, ethnographers, ethnologists, missionaries, museologists, journalists, or administrators—tend to interpret dress and decorative behavior as exemplary of a holistic social or cultural essence. In this frame, the individual appears merely as a cog in a wheel of a social system that unwittingly reproduces itself through "traditional," unchanging, and almost mindless collective emanations.

Even Andrew Strathern and Marilyn Strathern have struggled to develop a model that explains the costuming practices of individuals that balances particular choices with social meanings. Above all, there is a continuum rather than an opposition between the individual and the social. Although local informants say, "It is just decoration" (Strathern 1987: 13), and sometimes deny what appears to observers to be overt mimicry (for example, of courting or mating behavior), there are parallels between highland and Western decorative practices. As Andrew Strathern (1987: 12) observes,

> in contemporary European usage, the entire potency of makeup is dedicated to enhancing the individual sexual attractiveness of its wearer. The style of makeup certainly also reflects social class, but its relationship to collective values and aspirations has become submerged in an emphasis on the individual. Correlatively, skin ceases to be something that is affected by social relationships with others. It becomes instead an artifact to be managed by social relationships with others: beauty salons replace sacrifices to the mother's brother. This is not to say that beauty magic or beauty technology is an exclusive possession of industrialized society. Evidence from Trobriand Islands (on the southeastern tip of New Guinea) convincingly refutes any such notion. It does mean that in western society there is an individualistic ideology specifying the connections between skin and the person that excludes social relationships as cause and sees them only as a result of individual qualities or manipulation.

Western accounts of highland practices equally fail to see the individuals in the group, so decorations are definitively correlated with social standing and their value is deemed to be social worth or exchange value (in terms of status or power). Indicatively, components of decoration are read as having overt and incontestable symbolic meaning. This is an explanation of the symbolism of color in Oceania:

> Red, the color of blood, has a special position and is regarded as especially potent and magical. The Mount Hagen communities … believe that the red coloring can help a man become prosperous, and in many parts of Oceania the sick are rubbed with red ochre, which is believed to have medicinal powers. The Mendi … interpret certain face patterns like an oracle. They paint a young girl's face part black and part red—the black half symbolizing the spiritual future of her clan, the red the future economic prosperity of her group. If the colors blur during the dancing, this is seen as a bad omen. (Gröning 2001: 76)

And so colors are interpreted in a strict symbolic economy that "reads off" the attributes that colors are deemed to represent. Yet on the same page of Gröning's account, eight examples of very "different types of face-painting from various parts of New Guinea … from … 1967 and 1973 at various ceremonies in the Mount Hagen area" suggest that there is enormous variation in the use of color, types and placement of markings, incorporated materials, and so on. If this were just a traditional society engaging in non-changing costume, this kind of variation in just a few years would surely not occur.

This brief account emphasizes that highlander costume practices are not just fixed traditional forms of dress where each sign, symbol, and use of color can be interpreted as having some fixed and unchangeable meaning. Instead, there is synchronic (at any one time) and diachronic (over time) variation as well as considerable individual creations that ad lib and embellish any shared code or symbolism. In this sense, highlander dancing costume and body decoration conform to the notion of fashion. It is also sensitive to consumer concerns concerning the value of materials, introduction of new materials, and the value of money (currency), which constitutes a parallel system of value to that of traditional wealth (pigs and cowie shells). It is often difficult, time consuming, and expensive to acquire the materials for costumes, so just the process of creating headdresses and accessories is a major part of highlander life. The fact that materials like exotic feathers became a major export industry for Western fashion—especially millinery—has deprived highlanders of important raw materials to the point that many bird species are endangered or extinct. This situation has necessarily prompted the incorporation of other items to replace them.

So, if we accept that highlander costume and body decoration bear many similarities to Western fashion, these similarities have increased in recent years as contact with Westerners and consumer culture has increased. In particular, highland festivals have become part of the tourist circuit, with specialist companies offering cultural tours to visit such events. Dignitaries and celebrities have also joined the spectacular circus. Inevitably, costuming and body decoration have been modified for these occasions, along with the rules about who is eligible to dance and decorate. Under such provocation, such events will almost inevitably become just a publicity stunt and morph into something else. Costumes, too, have been modified to meet the demands of regular performances.

One such example is the spectacle of the mud men of Asaro (near Goroko). Legend has it that this scary spectacle happened inadvertently after the Asaro hid in a river after being defeated by rivals. Emerging later to escape, they were covered in mud (or whitish clay), which terrified their opponents, who thought they were spirits of the dead. The fear of the spirit world has guaranteed the mud men a special place in highlander culture and Western romanticism of primitive people and the spirits of the dead.

The mud men have come to stand for the exoticism of New Guinea and appear in many Western images of the highlands as well as in films, television shows, and advertisements. As Otto and Verloop (1996) note, Asaro mud men have been used in Australian television advertisements for orange soft drinks as well as a 1993 Benetton advertisement for Tribū perfume, an evocative name that was illustrated by a collection of cultural symbols of each "tribe." Another advertisement in 1995 for a four-wheel drive vehicle featured mud men above the caption "Mudmen from Papua New Guinea get their first glimpse of a Frontera, thanks to its powerful new engine and anti-clog brakes" (Otto and Verloop 1996: 349).

As a result, mud men are widely regarded as a product of tourism and certainly capture the imagination of tourists and Westerners. Even their costumes—bodies in white and huge headdresses of a whitened round sphere with eerie holes for eyes and ears and dogs' teeth in their mouths—have accommodated the new age. Their features have become much more differentiated with nostrils, carved ears, brows, cheekbones, scars, and the like, making each highly individualized and rather more like *Star Wars* characters like Yoda than mud men. And of course, highlanders are conversant on films like *Star Wars* due to the ubiquitous DVD. Instead of using white clay to achieve a cracked and dried skin covering, they have found that acrylic body paints have proved highly successful. The mud men—plus mud children and women—appear at any important public event.

This example shows that although the history of Western fashion is a history of asserting difference from premodernity, in fact, it is simply another—albeit seemingly more sophisticated—fashion system among many.

## CASE STUDY 4: The Sailor Suit: From Function to Fashion

In contrast to the attempts to enforce clothing behavior by regulation, the case of the sailor suit illustrates the informal channels by which a fashion becomes established then proliferated as a global style icon. It has had various overlapping incarnations—as work wear, a uniform, a fashion, and a dramatic prop (in diverse contexts). The sailor suit also has some connections with Queen Victoria, who starred in the case study on mourning dress. But while that fashion involved the institutionalization of black, the sailor suit revolved around the popularization of blue and white as iconic symbols of the sea (and the beach).

The sailor suit began life haphazardly in the early 1800s, developing out of the informal dress code of sailors as a practical outfit for deck work. This evolved into a recognizable suit typically consisting of a white or blue middy blouse with a large v-shaped collar at the front and low flap at the back, bell-bottom trousers, a dark-colored necktie, a wide-brimmed hat, and a lanyard (O'Hara Callan 2002: 205–6). Legend has it that the flared pants allowed sailors to roll up their trousers to their knees for deck work, while the necktie could be used as a sweat band and tar kerchief.

This practical garb makes sense, but why did it become a universal icon of fashion? The answer is shrouded in mystery, but two factors seemed to play a role. First, the sailor suit was adopted as a naval uniform initially by the United States Navy in 1813—in fact, it was only abandoned in 1998! The United Kingdom adopted the sailor suit in 1857. However, by then, the second factor had already come into play. In 1846, Queen Victoria had a sailor suit made for the four-year-old Prince of Wales, Albert Edward (later King Edward VII, whose death signaled the end of black mourning dress). The image of the prince in smart blue and white entranced the public and sailor suits became popular wear for boys and later girls.

By the late nineteenth century, sailor suits had become the most common outfit for well-dressed young boys. As a fashion columnist writing in 1887 observed, "A boy before he rises to the dignity of trousers and jackets is never as happy as in a Middy suit or Jack Tar, and these suits are now selling in thousands" (quoted by Wagner 2006). Because of their practicality, ease of construction, and loose fit, sailor suits were very suitable for early mass production of clothing, which further enhanced their popularity.

A pictorial representation of a walking-out costume in 1894, for example, showed a boy "dressed in the popular [white] sailor suit, dark stockings and ankle-boots. On his head is the round 'tam-o'-shanter' " (Cassin-Scott 1997: 154).

It was, perhaps, the first example of a global fashion for children by the 1870s. The bell-bottom trousers were sometimes exchanged for short pants or skirts for girls, and various details modified, but the overall look of the oversized v-shaped collar and loosely fitting shirt remained. Meanwhile, most navies adopted a version of the sailor suit too, so there were parallel histories of the suit as a uniform and as a fashion item.

For a humble uniform designed to unify navies and provide a practical form of uniform, the sailor suit has had a remarkably rich and varied history. An exhibition in 2004 called "Sailor Style: Art, Fashion, Film," held at the Australian Maritime Museum in Sydney, traced the journey of the sailor suit "from gangplank to catwalk" and its diverse manifestations in "art, fashion, film, fetish or cult" (Nice, quoted by Meacham 2004). The instantly recognizable elements of the sailor suit are the use of blue and white with dark-colored contrasts. Stripes; arrows; anchor, sea creature, and ship motifs (often embroidered); buttons; braid; and even lace embellished these uniforms. These decorative touches have been translated into instantly recognizable nautical themes in fashion and decoration, including

**Child dressed in sailor suit.** Photo: Sidney Arthur Mounteer, c. 1898, Library of Congress, Prints and Photographs Division

interior design. Sailor suits also became a type of school uniform, initially in naval academies but later in other schools in Europe, America, Asia, and Australasia.

The naval battles that formed part of nationalist struggles and the two world wars saw the proliferation of sailor suits in navies around the world and sustained the attention to, and attraction of, these striking forms of military attire. However, they began to decline in popularity during the 1940s and had disappeared as an everyday mode of dress for children by the 1950s. Nonetheless they persisted in popular iconography, for example, in musicals, vaudeville, drag shows, pantomime, Hollywood films, and children's dress-ups and as costumes for cartoon characters. They had by this time attracted a certain ambivalence due perhaps to the prevalence of queens, gays, and cross-dressers in the navy and the custom of nautical drag shows, which, in turn, influenced the naval themes of musicals such as *HMS Pinafore* and *South Pacific* (Garber 1992: 57–59).

Despite these ambivalent connotations and diverse uses, the sailor suit remained a form of "best" wear for children—as ceremonial outfits for the children of royalty, for ring bearers and ushers at weddings, as a uniform for choristers, as school uniforms, and so on. In such contexts, the sailor suit almost constitutes a form of customary wear. In other contexts, however, the sailor suit acquired sexual connotations, especially due to its popularity as the basis of Japanese school uniforms. The extracurricular activities of school girls and young women dressed as school girls (*kou-gyaru*, or kogal girls) prompted a mania (and associated moral panic) for the fetishization (*buru-sera* or sailor-bloomer fetish) of the sailor suit (or *sailor fuku* in Japanese) and the frequent appearance of cartoon characters in sailor suits in anime and manga (Craik 2005: 224–27; Kinsella 2002; McVeigh 2000; Richie 2003).

Throughout the twentieth century, sailor suits had cyclical revivals in many fashion collections. One of the first designers to appropriate naval references was Coco Chanel, who in 1914 designed sailor blouses made in **jersey** fabric. In the 1920s and 1930s, she made flared button-front trousers (yachting pants) in soft fabrics for women and used nautical motifs (boatnecks, gold buttons and braid, etc.) in her suits (Charles-Roux 1995: 134; Meacham 2004; see chapter 2). These designs became the prototype of the resort wear and leisure wear that dominated the fashions of the 1930s and beyond. A subsequent revival of the sailor suit occurred in the late 1960s and 1970s with flares and **disco** pants, in the 1980s among ravers, and in the mid-1990s revival of **bell-bottoms** (Meacham 2004).

International designers such as Claire McCardell, Calvin Klein, Michael Kors, John Bartlett, and David and Elizabeth Emanuel and the recent collection of Valentino Garavani attest to the attraction of the sailor suit as a resilient part of the grammar of contemporary fashion collections and customary wear. According to cultural researcher Fiona Allon, "the whole history of sailors is about the camp. It's about display, about preening oneself, about being flamboyant" (quoted by Meacham 2004). Accordingly, sailor suits have been repeatedly appropriated as the ultimate symbol of practicality, freedom, sexuality, and hedonism: something simultaneously nice but naughty.

**Japanese winter school uniform.** Photo: Masami. H. Creative Commons Attribution 3.0 Unported

So sailor suits have had a long and mixed history not simply as uniforms for sailors but as "best" wear for children; shorthand for characters; inspiration for fashions, architecture, and interior decor; and props for sexual innuendo and popular culture, with their longstanding connotations of ambivalence between discipline and punishment, freedom and licentiousness. The sailor suit epitomizes the diverse meanings of fashion and interpretive strategies to explain it. It is an interesting case study that demonstrates how a particular outfit can simultaneously straddle genres of work wear (occupational dress), uniform, fashion, and subcultural dress in cross-cultural contexts as a part of the global reach of fashion.

# chapter 2

# the eurocentric fashion system

**CHAPTER OUTLINE**



**WHAT DOES THIS CHAPTER COVER?**

This chapter provides an overview of the development of modern consumer culture and the Eurocentric fashion system. We trace the shift from centers like London and Vienna to Paris as the preeminent fashion capital, as well as the development of American fashion. Topics covered include the designer system, couture, prêt-à-porter, diffusion lines, and licensing. Although Paris has been seen as synonymous with fashion, other centers such as New York, Milan, London, Shanghai, and Tokyo are competing as fashion cities.

## i. consumer culture and fashion

> *Fashion is the costume of European culture. (Von Falke 1881, quoted by Foley 1893: 461n)*

In this section, we introduce the development of the modern Eurocentric fashion system. We have already discussed the idea that there are parallel fashion systems at different times and in different cultures, but European fashion beginning in the mid-nineteenth century is usually taken as the preeminent fashion system for two reasons: first, it is interconnected with consumer culture and, second, its phases of fashion are arguably shorter than those of other fashion systems. But to understand how this occurred, it is necessary to go back before the Industrial Revolution and urbanization.

In the previous chapter we discussed the role of sumptuary laws in attempts to regulate conspicuous consumption by imposing rules about who could wear what items of clothing, as well as the colors and fabrics they used. The aim was to produce a visible register of status difference.

However, numerous studies suggest that these efforts were flawed and that rather than contain the desire to display oneself through clothes, such laws in fact created a demand for "a taste and feeling for consumer goods [that] caught on among other social classes besides the upper"; thus the correspondence between "dress and social hierarchy in early modern Europe was highly complex and varied" (Belfanti and Giusberti 2000: 359). There was a huge focus on appearance and apparel's symbolization of social role and place amid major upheavals in society across Europe:

**In social, economic, political and religious terms, the years 1350–1650 were ones of enormous change. Nevertheless, although the precise nature of sumptuary preoccupations altered, there remained an enduring interest in the significance of what people wore which often seems to have bordered on obsession. (Richardson 2004: 1–2)**

Such an interest in fashion was epitomized by the popularity of the "'jointed baby,' 'Mademoiselle,' or fashion doll [that] seems to have been in vogue in the fourteenth century, if not earlier" (Foley 1893: 464n). These dolls were taken through Europe to "stimulate taste" (Stearns 2001: 17) and promulgate the latest modes, which were copied by seamstresses and tailors for elite clients.

As early as the 1500s, especially during the reign of Elizabeth I in England (1558–1603), there were declamations about the display of finery and invisibility of class differences, including denunciations of the number of French and Italian luxury goods available in England (Foley 1893: 459; Stearns 2001). At stake was not just the flouting of regulations but the cycle of changing tastes and thus imbalances of supply and demand, which created a problem for the economy. Demand for fabrics (e.g., silk and feathers) meant variously unmet demand (e.g., not enough ostrich feathers), oversupply (e.g., unsalable fabric, which put mills and workers out of business), and either escalating or plummeting prices. As early as 1380, a chronicler in Limburg in the Netherlands reported that "the fashion in raiment was so changed, that he who last year was a master-tailor, became in a twelvemonth a laborer" (Foley 1893: 465).

Where, for example, local entrepreneurs attempted to meet demand by establishing ostrich farms, their fortunes were dependent on feathered hats remaining in fashion. Foley (1893: 470n) reported that in the 1880s, the price of quality ostrich feathers fell from £250 to £25. Fashion cycles also necessitated versatility among workers so they could change from feather trimming to "fringe, fur-sewing, and artificial flower-making"; meanwhile the effects of a "slowly waning taste" led to "degradation in skill and wages" (Foley 1893: 473–74). Feather curlers, meanwhile, lost their jobs or went half time (Foley 1893: 473n). In Paisley in Scotland, the producers of "pseudo-Indian shawls" switched to engineering and shipbuilding after 1850, since these were regarded as more secure industries (Foley 1893: 472). A moral poem written in 1566 noted the consequence of fashion cycles:

**Fashions in all our gesturings fashions in our attire,**
**Which (as the wyse have thoughts) do cum,**
**and goe in circled gyre. (Drant, "A Medicinall Morall," quoted by Foley 1893: 465n)**

There was also a sizable industry in Europe producing cloth, and it contributed significantly

**Ostrich feather hat**

to domestic economies and exports. In 1500, for instance, two-thirds of English exports were of woolen cloth (Richardson 2004: 3). Some argue that the expanding system of "putting out" (outsourcing or piecework) in the late fifteenth century was "the seeds which would blossom into a capitalist-organized, market-orientated economy" (Richardson 2004: 3). Indeed, during Elizabeth's reign, domestic cloth was traded for the exotic luxury textiles from the empire.

By the seventeenth century, there were significant patterns in consumer trends. For example, clothes were not longer produced within the household but purchased in the marketplace. But in towns there was a huge division between the wealthy elite and the urban poor. Among the latter, clothes were rarely changed and one individual might have two outfits—one for work and one for "best." For the former, inventories of wardrobes were extensive. For servants and domestic staff, clothes became an important issue. In the late fourteenth century, some employers used clothes as partial payment of wages, because they were so valuable and expensive. Where **livery** was not provided by patrons, the families of the workers were expected to provide a suitable set of clothing since the presentation of staff reflected on the status of the employers (Crawford 2004: 158–60).

Indeed, public denunciation of such practices was couched in the complaint that "laborers and servants were earning too much" and "gaining access to and wearing clothes that were too good for them" (Crawford 2004: 161). There was a booming secondhand clothing market in towns and cities from the sixteenth century, while ready-made clothes were also being sold, enabling wider social groups to access a relatively huge range of clothing (Belfanti and Giusberti 2000: 361). Clothing was a visible sign of self and status, but it was exploited as a flexible means of creating and manipulating appearance.

**Within the hyper-visibility of urban space, participation in a shared rhetoric of domestic, leisure and clothing cultures could be displayed, judged and refined. (Richardson 2004: 13)**

**Even by 1650, however, there remains a fundamental distinction between elite and non-elite clothing—its nature, its function, its relation to the market and to a wider notion of aesthetics and artistic production. (Richardson 2004: 18)**

Nonetheless, from now on, it was fashion itself, not sumptuary legislation, that was setting the codes and rules of the "hierarchy of appearances" not only in a process of emulation or imitation of elite fashion but also in an "inversion" based on fashion being modeled on the attire of the popular classes (Belfanti and Giusberti 2000: 361–62). With these dialectical clothing practices, fashions in clothing effected a shift from "a crude to a subtle method of expressing social superiority" (McKendrick quoted by Belfanti and Giusberti 2000: 362). This change was symbolically linked to the French Revolution, the democratic motives of which popularized the idea of individual choice, where fashion was the most visible shorthand orchestration of the "expression of personal choice and taste" (Belfanti and Giusberti 2000: 362). Rapid change in fashionable styles was institutionalized, and industries were increasingly forced to adjust to the consequences of shifting tastes. Exemplifying this, in the late nineteenth century, a Yorkshire mill owner wrote:

**In the crinoline days Bradford dress goods from English wools were in great demand. When the ladies preferred clinging fabrics (cashmeres, &c) the advantage went to the soft goods of France (which are now largely made in Bradford). When mohairs and alpacas were in fashion, Bradford by its yarns got the advantage. When braids are fashionable, Bradford benefits. When calico prints were much in fashion, Bradford suffered; on the other hand it obtained advantage from the demand for *mousseline de laine.* (Foley 1893: 472n)**

These industry and economic upturns and downturns henceforth characterized the fashion industry. Taste became increasingly determined by promotions in the early media and outlets of fashion. In 1893, Foley (1893: 472) wrote:

**Now the sovereign people's tastes are besieged simultaneously and en bloc by shop windows, advertisement, fashion paper, and pattern.**

So we can see that fluctuations in fashion and cycles of fashion were entrenched in Europe well before the **Industrial Revolution.** Roche (2000: 198) argues that it is a moot point whether a "sartorial Ancient Regime" existed, since there was a relationship between clothing and appearance determined by scarcity and limited exchange as well as clothing codes. There was a huge difference between the wealthy and the poor—even during the reign of Louis XVI, the poor were dressed in rags and went barefoot (Roche 2000: 199), while those at court lounged in luxurious excess. In cities and towns, clothing codes were becoming more complex and variable, while even the "sartorial consumption of country-folk was never totally frozen" (Roche 20000: 204). By the end of the seventeenth century, Paris had established itself as the leader in consumer fashion, with other places lagging behind. Consumption of linen and clothing also varied with occupational status, with the nobility spending 13 percent or their income, while artisans and shopkeepers spent 28 percent; officials and professionals 13 percent; wage earners, casual workers, and laborers 8 percent; and servants 20 percent (Roche 2000: 206). During the eighteenth century, the relative amount spent on apparel steadily increased, although class differences remained, with male nobility owning an average of eighty items of apparel and female nobility fifty-five, while lower-class men owned five, and women ten each (Roche 2000: 214).

However, the fashion machine sped up in Europe with the coming of industrialization and urbanization. Factories and techniques of mass production replaced putting out and outsourcing. Once there were means of producing and distributing goods that could be purchased by other people, the trade in goods created an economy of value alongside consumer markets. People could buy a cultural identity and thus social credentials. Mass production accelerated the process, and with mass-produced goods came mass markets for clothing and fashion. At this point, fashion became as much a consumer culture as it was a culture of identity, status, and role. Not only could one display one's standing through one's choice of apparel and adornment, but one could purchase a desired identity and exhibit it in a process of conspicuous consumption. According to Roche (2000: 215), this period witnessed considerable upheavals, for while the "civilization of manners" increased, conflicts about appropriate modes of appearance and behavior disrupted consensual patterns of the past. The value of clothing consumerism was indicated by the increasing theft of clothes and the growth of the secondhand clothing market, "which enabled a person to appropriate the appearance of someone else" (Roche 2000: 218–19). This instability and flux became the basis of the modern fashion system by instilling new values:

> **Instead of obligation to redistribute, the power of accumulation and enrichment. Instead of the weight of custom and tradition, the force of individual choice and renewal. ... Thereafter, fashion inserted itself between constraint and freedom. (Roche 2000: 220)**

The development of modern fashion tastemakers replaced the vestiges of decline of the European courts as the tastemakers and trendsetters. As civil society grew in economic, political, and social importance as democratic regimes replaced aristocratic ones and states consolidated under the banner of nationalism, the so-called trickle-down system of taste making was challenged by "trickle-up" **fads** and fashions set by the newly wealthy and influential classes. Meanwhile, the Industrial Revolution spawned new mechanized techniques of production that enabled mass production to replace artisan labor, while colonial expansion brought new fabrics and fibers such as silk and cotton and new design influences from the exotic cultures of "other" places such as the East and Far East. Urbanization created new centers of production, distribution, and consumption and new markets for the expanding consumer society. Photography constituted a major change in the reproduction and representation of fashion and style and, along with illustrative techniques, formed the basis of the emerging popularity of fashion plates and **fashion magazines** in the late eighteenth century.

## iii. paris fashion

> *It is in Paris or nowhere. (Luien Lelong, quoted by Veillon 2002: 86)*

With all these changes converging, the processes of designing and producing fashion also changed. *Couturières* still determined the main design styles, but they were annexed to the **marchandes de modes,** who increasingly held sway over fashionability. The most famous *marchande* in Paris was **Rose Bertin,** who dominated ancien régime fashion in the 1770s through her incomparable client Marie Antoinette, consort of Louis XVI. Bertin's skill as a tastemaker stemmed from her ability to anticipate trends while appealing to the tastes and proclivities of her elite clientele, blending the familiar and the new to seduce them to experiment with new fashions and fads. Arguably, her approach became the model for the emerging generation of self-styled designers after the French Revolution and installation of the republic and, ultimately, the shape of the Paris fashion industry, which began to take form in the 1850s and 1860s.

The distinctive characteristics of the Eurocentric fashion system included an enhanced emphasis on planned obsolescence, a focus on newness and now-ness, and a correspondence between symbolic value and economic value, to which consumer behavior is central. In the last half of the nineteenth century, the stage was set for the birth of modern fashion:

- **Disposable income was increasing for all classes, and a desire for consumer goods was increasing.**
- **Ready-made clothes were available in draperies and clothing stores.**
- **There was a secondhand market for apparel.**
- **The fashion magazine (and fashion print and illustration) industry was developing.**

This was also the period when the new department stores were opened, such as **Bon Marché** in Paris (1838), the Marble Palace in New York (1848), Macy in New York (1858, new building 1902), Marshall Field in Chicago (1865), Bloomingdale's (1872), Harrods in London (1874), Wanamaker's in Philadelphia (1876), David Jones in Sydney (1877), Woolworth in Lancaster (1879), Wertheim in Berlin (1896–99), Samaritaine in Paris (1905), and Selfridges in London (1909). These offered grand temples for consumerism and safe and respectable environments for ladies, with restaurants, chapels, toilets, theaters, exhibitions, and of course an unimagined array of goods for sale. By providing diverse activities, the department stores were akin to the entertainment and leisure centers of today. These new ways of selling and buying appealed enormously to the middle classes and newly waged, as well as offering respectable employment for men—and women—as sales assistants. Consumer culture was markedly enhanced by the advent of this new approach to shopping. The cycle of fashion was one of the beneficiaries.

The birth date of the Eurocentric fashion system is sometimes given as 1858, when Englishman Charles Worth established a fashion house in Paris. It is perhaps ironic that the first acknowledged **designer** of Parisian **couture** was an Englishman who learned the clothing business in London and exploited the **retailing** possibilities before moving to Paris in 1845 and applying his **tailoring** skills to this expanding market (see box 2.1).

The influence of Charles Worth on Paris fashion led to the establishment of the business model that became the cornerstone of its success. This model combined catering to the elite with the production of second-tier fashions for elite aspirants. In using shop **models** to show his clothes and courting what we now call media promotion, he broke the aristocracy's exclusive hold on fashion. Fashion could be desired by anyone who craved fashionability. The distinctiveness

### Box 2.1 Charles Worth: The Father of Haute Couture

Born in 1825 in Lincolnshire, England, Charles Worth was apprenticed to London textile merchants, from whom he learned the essentials of the textile industry and developed an interest in the design of clothes. After arriving in Paris in 1945, he first worked for the textile firm Gagelin, selling textiles, shawls, and ready-made clothing and setting up a dressmaking department. Building on the success of the latter, in 1858 Worth established his own design studio, which became the model of subsequent design and couture houses. Worth's star rose with the Napoleonic regime (1808–73), which reinstated Paris as a center of luxury and modernization. Napoleon III's marriage to Empress Eugénie brought him her patronage and ensured his success among wealthy clients. His high profile among aspiring trendsetters made Worth a wealthy and sought-after icon of fashionability.

Worth was an innovator in several ways. First, he combined his knowledge of historic costume with new design elements and meticulous attention to the fit of the garment, complemented by the highest standards of tailoring and craftsmanship. Second, he favored the use of luxurious and exotic textiles and trimming. Third, although primarily designing one-off outfits for his elite clients, he also presented a collection of designs on models for a wider clientele, who then commissioned individual modes. Fourth, he was the first male dressmaker to challenge the role of tailors and artists as clothes designers/producers for the elite. His success in exhibitions and in attracting coverage in fashion magazines ensured that he was widely known as perhaps the first designer celebrity, the "supreme arbiter of taste" (De Marly 1980: 23).

Worth's significance as a designer was his ability to apply tailoring and what might now be called body sculpting to the design of dresses in new shapes and with unusual lines, thus producing a succession of new lines for women's dress and establishing the habit of constant change in fashion. By 1971, he had a staff of 1,200 and was far and away the largest couturier in Paris (De Marly 1980: 23). On his death, he was praised as

> the first to take female costume away from routine and bourgeois pettiness; the first to place Parisiennes upon the triumphant road of art, and to teach them not just to clothe themselves, but to adorn themselves. (*L'Illustration,* quoted by De Marly 1980: 40)

After Worth's death in 1895, the courturier's house continued under the management of his sons and Paul Poiret, who was employed as designer in 1901. The House of Worth continued to be run by family members until 1952.

**Worth dress.** Photo: St Edmundsbury Borough Council. Creative Commons Attribution 2.5 License

of the Parisian approach to fashion became the combination of tailoring fit to the body and drawing on the legacy of extravagance and imagination in design.

If Worth was the father of Paris fashion, Paul Poiret became its impresario. When Poiret set up his own business in 1903, he injected a new energy and innovation into both the design of clothes and the milieu in which his fashion was promoted through the illustrations of Paul Iribe, a theatrical approach to promotion, involvement in interior design, modern methods of production and promotion, and modern ideas about sexuality. He was a cultural impresario whose influence on the nature of Paris fashion was long lasting.

Paris fashion can arguably be divided into periods or eras (for detailed accounts of the development of the French fashion industry, see De Marly 1980; English 2007; Mendes and de la Haye 1999; Palmer 2001; Steele 1988; Troy 2003; Wilcox 2007). Despite the decade-by-decade time line and characterization that we are using here, it is important to remember that this is a convenience that obscures the broader history of Paris fashion and accords too much importance to some designers at the expense of others and

**Paul Poiret suit.** Photo: Bain News Services. N.Y.C.George Grantham Bain Collection (Library of Congress)

fashion trends more generally. As Steele (1988: 245) has argued,

**the literature of fashion has emphasized the creative "genius" of certain couturiers in a way that distorts the real history of fashion. Ironically, it can even obscure the actual achievements of individual designers by inflating their alleged "influence."**

Nonetheless, as a heuristic device, we can categorize twentieth-century Paris fashion as follows:

- **The Belle Epoque (1895–1914)**
- **The era of expansion (First World War, 1914–18)**
- **The effervescence of the Roaring Twenties (1918–29)**
- **The era of leisure, pleasure, and sport (1930–39)**
- **Restraint, realism, and pent-up desire (1939–45)**
- **New looks for a new world (1947–50s)**
- **The premature death of haute couture (1960s)**
- **Reinvention for popular culture (1970s)**
- **Reinvigoration and restructuring (1980s and 1990s)**
- **Global competiveness (2000s)**

During the Belle Epoque (1895–1914), the emergence of competing couture houses and infiltration of fashion's elite by wealthy "commoners" created a problem for the **House of Worth** that persisted through the twentieth century:

**The grandest orders came to it almost automatically, but the taste of young people was moving away from such splendor. (De Marly 1980: 41)**

No longer were the clients of couture exclusively members of the aristocracy as opera singers, actresses, and heiresses joined the crowd and traveling shows to London and America created new client bases that couturiers like Poiret, Madame Paquin, the Callot Sœurs, and Jacques Doucet exploited. Despite challenges to the moral basis of couture by campaigned by medical professions; pre-Raphaelite artists; the Rational Dress Society; and the advocate of trousers for women, Amelia Bloomer, the desire for couture persisted.

During the twentieth century, Paris fashion was the centerpiece of the Eurocentric fashion system or industry. It was known as the home of **haute couture**, although there are many French designers who have never been involved in haute couture and show ready-to-wear collections. Moreover, as the always tiny client base of haute couture has shrunk (and now arguably is largely made up of Hollywood stars and aspirant social climbers of newly consumerist societies), even elite couturiers have turned their attention to ready-to-wear lines, accessories, and **licensing** to supplement (in fact cross-subsidize) their elite one-off designs.

The word *haute couture,* which comes from the French words for "high" or "elegant" (*haute*) and sewing (*couture*), is a term for high-quality fashion design and construction of one-off garments for individual clients. The term developed in France in the late nineteenth century to refer to the body of dress designers called the Chambre Syndicale de la Confection et de la Couture pour Dames et Fillettes in their effort to register designs in order to stop other designers from copying them. In other words, this was a method of professional control of entry to an exclusive club, an extremely effective way to provide the imprimatur of excellence and elitism and perhaps the main reason for the success of Paris's bid to be the preeminent fashion city of the twentieth century. To qualify for membership as an haute couture house, designers must employ at least fifteen workers and stage two collections of at least thirty-five outfits a year. A couturier makes up a **toile**, a model or pattern of a garment in muslin or linen that is used as a pattern for making clothes either for individual clients or in batches for retailing. This was the first collective attempt to "brand" a group of designers in a distinctive way. Previously, dressmakers and tailors worked independently for individual clients through a vendeuse (see box 2.2).

In 1910, a rival organization, the Chambre Syndicale de la Couture Parisienne, was formed to promote French designs overseas. This organization and marketing propelled Paris into global prominence as *the* center of fashion design, a position cemented by the frequent use of French designers to make costumes for the leading ladies of Hollywood movies. The Chambre operated as a closed shop for designers who met certain criteria: they had to employ at least twenty people, show at least fifty designs to biannual seasonal collections, and either service an elite clientele or sell their patterns under license.

Despite the vicissitudes of the First World War (1914–18), this was an era of expansion for Paris fashion. Women became involved in the war effort and thus required clothes suitable for employment in factories, shops, and offices. Designers like Chanel were important because they offered new fashions in less structured fabrics like jersey, including trousers and jackets for women. Chanel credited the First World War with making her famous, but Steele (1988: 246) warns that much that has been written about Chanel is "closer to hagiography than historiography," and that Chanel's real legacy was not that she redressed all fashionable women but that she redressed the rich (her clothes were expensive) to "look young and casual" in a contrived manner that created the modernist ideal of the boyish body shape (Steele 1988: 247). This became a classic look that established a new mode of dressing for women.

The Chanel influence also seemed to capitalize on the wartime gains made by women and acted as a precursor to the 1920s popularity of sports (such as tennis and swimming). Leisure pastimes like dancing were epitomized by the advent of the **flapper** and the effervescence of the Roaring

**Box 2.2 Definitions of Paris Fashion**

| | |
|---|---|
| **Haute Couture** | From the French words *haute*, meaning "high," and *couture,* meaning "sewing." Refers to high-quality fashion design produced by a designer or couturier, usually for a specific client. Traditionally associated with the Paris fashion industry and the peak designer body, La Chambre Syndicale de la Couture. |
| **Prêt-à-Porter** | French for "ready-to-wear." Clothes carrying a designer label that are produced for a diffusion (modified) collection that is produced in volumes for "off-the-rack" purchase. |
| **Marchandes de Modes** | French term for sellers of fashion, usually in salons or studios, the forerunner of couture houses. |

Twenties (1918–29). Although formal fashions remained important for the elite female class, an increasing number of women adopted casual and informal clothes as their default wardrobe. This trend persisted throughout the 1930s in an era of leisure, pleasure, and sport. Nonetheless, Chanel was not the only designer with influence. Her lifelong rival, Elsa Schiaparelli, incorporated artistic inspirations such as **surrealism** and **cubism** in her clothes, which "were characterized by bold lines and a disciplined fit—sophisticated and hard-edged **chic** that was immediately recognizable" (Steele 1988: 250).

Other influences were Hollywood film couture, the growing manufacture of sports and leisure clothes for the mass market, and fascination with "colonial," Asian, and ethnic art and symbolism. Paris was a magnet for the rich, the artistic, the sexually promiscuous and homosexual, black culture, and the "menace Yankee" (the influx of Americans hungry for Parisian sophistication and excess as well as the impact of American culture on European mores). Such a mix of sensibilities produced instabilities and tensions as a modernist **zeitgeist** transformed behavior and attitudes in what was perceived as vulgarity and a slap in the face to French taste and sophistication. Clearly, a number of parallel trends in fashion occurred in which Paris played a key but overemphasized role.

The Second World War brought these developments to a halt as wartime privations including rationing (especially of non-essential clothes) and women's involvement in the war plus the German occupation of France led most of the couture houses to suspend operations (Bartlett 2004; Steele 1988: 266–74; Veillon 2002). Nonetheless, the couture business persisted throughout the war at least for a rich coterie of 20,000 French women and 200 customers of the German occupiers (Bartlett 2004: 119; Veillon 2002). These people continued to enjoy parties, balls, and theater excursions. Paris offered extravagant fashions for this group—fashions that shocked ordinary French men and women and were condemned by English and American commentators.

The rest of occupied France faced another reality—severe rationing of goods and fabrics and the imposition of the German campaign to persuade women to wear austere clothing and eschew the "shamelessly eroticized" and "whore-led" fashions of Paris (Bartlett 2004: 118; see also Guenther 2004). While women resisted the new German edict and struggled to remain fashionable and feminine, the war period highlighted the distinction between the fashion elite of Paris and the aspiring fashionable majority, for whom couture was out of reach. Their needs were increasingly being met by other developments, particularly in America, which was cut off from French wartime fashion trends and began to come into its own as a fashion and ready-to-wear producer. England, meanwhile, was subjected to extreme rationing and the campaign to promote the utility look, a plain and unadorned look that arguably stunted English fashion and couture for some time, as desirable. Stylistically, the period was one of restraint, realism, and pent-up desire (1939–45).

At the end of the war, the fashion industry was suffused by a new feeling of optimism perhaps best captured by Christian Dior's New Look collection in 1947, which presaged new looks for a new world (1947–50s). Although Steele (1988: 273) argues that the "look was there, in embryo, in 1939, and began to spread once Paris was liberated," in the postwar revival of fashion, major social and cultural changes challenged the stranglehold of Paris couture on fashion trends and consumer clothing habits, with new markets like America expanding the availability of affordable everyday fashion and using **advertising** and cinema to promote new trends and products.

If Chanel was seen as synonymous with prewar fashion, Christian Dior became the epitome of the postwar era. America, in particular, became hungry for French fashion—to read about it, wear it, and copy it (Palmer 2001). French fashions were eagerly sought after by wealthy North American matrons who valued the clothes and cared for them meticulously (in contrast to the impression that is often held about couture clients). With Dior's sudden death in 1957, the domination of Paris fashion shifted to Yves Saint Laurent and, to a lesser extent, André Courrèges, both of whom picked up on the embryonic popular culture that celebrated young people.

By the 1960s, with the youth culture revolution in full swing, considerable debate concerned the premature death of haute couture (1960s), which seemed unable to compete and whose client base was rapidly declining. Designers like Yves Saint Laurent responded by sensing new stylistic trends associated with popular culture and developing a ready-to-wear (**diffusion**) line for less wealthy women. Licensing the use of his name for global marketing of products like accessories allowed him to cross-subsidize the couture part of the business. This model was quickly adopted by other couture houses and led to a revival of Paris fashion through its reinvention for popular culture (1970s). Such strategies, however, depended on canny business models and efficient financial management, and while some houses prospered, other faced difficulties.

The business of couture was changing—old designers were being replaced by new young and often non-French designers, with popular culture and counterculture to the fore. Companies needed to position themselves in the tough global market, which led to a fury of reinvigoration and restructuring (1980s and 1990s). By the new millennium, the ability of Paris fashion houses to achieve global competiveness increasingly depended on integration into multinational conglomerates like **LVMH** (2000s). Paris fashion had survived a century but has been transformed into a well-oiled machine where design and artistry increasingly take a backseat to business acumen.

## iv. the paris legacy

The legacy of Paris has largely been written in terms of key designers who have posthumously been accorded iconic status and viewed as expressing the stylistic signifiers of successive eras. It is true that the names of individual designers, including Charles Frederick Worth, Paul Poiret, Mariano Fortuny, Coco Chanel, Jean Patou, Sonia Delaunay, Elsa Schiaparelli, Christian Dior, Pierre Balmain, Cristóbal Balenciaga, Yves Saint Laurent, André Courrèges, Christian Lacroix, and Jean Paul Gaultier, became household names. Designers such as Coco Chanel, Elsa Schiaparelli, Madeleine Vionnet, and Balenciaga had a profound influence on fashion from the 1920s to the 1950s, while Christian Dior's New Look was credited with setting the style of postwar fashion following World War II.

Within the designer world, however, there are distinct hierarchies of status and **brand** or label recognition. Without question, Paris established itself as the center of the fashion system of modernity (Rocamora 2006). The iconic houses of Parisian haute couture (e.g., Worth, Poiret, Chanel, Schiaparelli, Dior, Givenchy, Balenciaga) became the symbols of both the fashion designers (as an archetype of the profession) and their collections (or sometimes just one outfit), which epitomized the mood or a moment. These designers have been commemorated in typically florid hagiographies celebrating their genius and the uniqueness of the influence of each. This mode of biography has influenced accounts of subsequent generations of designers, who typically are accorded over-the-top retrospectives of their innate aesthetic brilliance to see or feel a trend or invent something entirely new. Paradoxically, it is this tradition of excessive hagiography (uncritical biographies that treat the subject as a genius) that has contributed to the mixed reputation of fashion designers as professionals.

As noted earlier, the elite Chambre was a self-constituted and self-referential guild and exclusive professional "club" whose power was invested in the rules of membership and codes of behavior. Like any private club or professional organization, this contributed to the mystique of special status, despite the fact that success really depended on the public reaction to the products developed by its members. Often, once the mystique was created, success was a self-fulfilling prophecy.

However, the elite status of the Chambre was diluted in the second half of the twentieth century by the infiltration of new designers, the death of original members, and changing winds of the everyday clothing culture that enveloped fashion cultures (see chapter 4). New couturiers were accepted into the Chambre, notably Yves Saint Laurent, Emanuel Ungaro, Christian Lacroix, Valentino, and Versace. When Kenzo Takada relocated to Paris in 1964 and found success (by selling designs to Louis Féraud, then launching his own collections and in 1970 opening Jungle Jap, which achieved huge success during the 1970s), the Chambre was obliged to establish a new membership criterion that recognized demi-couture. The admittance of Kenzo was a sign of a major change of the guard and new conditions even for haute couture. Following Kenzo, other Japanese designers including Issey Miyake, Yohji Yamamoto, and Rei Kawakubo were admitted in the 1980s.

Many of the newer designers were less interested in preserving the "closed shop" of the Chambre than in exploiting the possibilities of reaching new markets and developing a range of lifestyle accoutrements of fashion to expand consumer bases well beyond Paris and New York. Even so, the Chambre, "still all powerful today, has carefully guarded standards, controlling who can practice and how, and fiercely protecting the standards of the trade" (Cosic 2001: 23). Similar quality control is maintained by sister guilds like the Chambre Syndicale des Paruriers, which

**set similarly stringent standards for manufacturers of belts, buttons and buttons, hats and umbrellas. The standard of craftsmanship allows designers to let their imagination rip. French fashion is complicated, colourful, embellished, yet always sophisticated, and relies on master cutters and skilful sewers and embroiderers and all the other magicians who can solve any decorative problem a designer cares to invent. (Cosic 2001: 23)**

Alongside haute couture, designers modified designs to appeal to wider markets through **prêt-à-porter** and ready-to-wear collections. The inclusion of these new designers and their new approaches to marketing fashion legitimated their status as designers and their elevation into the pantheon of elite fashion stars (see Kawamura

**Issey Miyake.** Photo: FRANCOIS GUILLOT/AFP/Getty Images. 2008 AFP

2006: 60). A parallel version of this was the copies made of Parisian designs by designer copyists and department stores, whose representatives increasingly flocked to the fashion shows in Paris (and later other fashion capitals), including the main women's wear trade show, the Salon du Prêt-à-Porter, where over 1,000 companies exhibit to over 50,000 **buyers** and trendsetters. There are also the highly profitable spin-off industries of cosmetics and perfume, which are worth half the value of the French clothing industry alone.

This rise of the designer was an important development in the fashion machine. Already industrialization, urbanization, and nascent consumerism had created a demand for new goods, and mass-production techniques could produce sufficient supplies. The phenomenon of department stores and mail order extended the availability of goods and fuelled the desire for luxury and the latest styles. Fashionable products were sought after, and cities like London, Paris, New York, and Vienna became hubs for consumption. The rise of the designer epitomized this process and gave individuals a godlike status as predictors and shapers of consumer taste.

Fashion was not the only sphere in which one could experience the genius of the designer: architecture, interior design, and similar fields also were dominated by individual designer hero worship. This cult propelled but also disguised the emergence of industries actively producing mass culture. Much of the repetitive, poorly paid, highly specialized labor that went into haute couture was invisible—the beaders, embroiderers, screen printers, seamstresses, button makers, milliners, and the like, who produced the superbly crafted garments. Clients who could afford couture developed an interdependent relationship with a designer, both as an advertisement of the designer's work and as proof of fashionability. Designers and clients were in a symbiotic relationship. The success of Paris has been attributed to its use of highly skilled craftspeople and ambition to achieve perfection in design and manufacture.

Designers could set a new trend in shape, form, fabric, detail, and cultural references, which were eagerly adopted by a voracious clientele and public. Mass manufacturers of clothing quickly adapted design features and made new trends available to wider markets. Between haute couture and mass marketing were the custom tailor and dressmaker, who could copy couture designs for well-heeled customers. Sewing machines (first patented in 1846) and the spread of home sewing and pattern making further expanded the desire for the latest fashions into ordinary homes and the lower classes. Despite the two world wars in the twentieth century, Paris maintained its preeminent place, and French designers were the cream of the crop.

Despite the hype, however, haute couture was a fickle fashion system subject to the whims of the elite clientele of popular couturiers, who increasingly were located not in Europe but in America and, from the 1970s, the Middle East, and from the 1990s, Asia. Satisfying these customers was central to their survival, since clients were the living proof of a designer's status—modern-day advertising placards. However, their custom was not enough to guarantee profitability or viability of a couture label. Initially reluctantly, designers turned to other ways of making money through the production of diffusion ready-to-wear or prêt-à-porter lines (based on the key trends in haute couture fashion but modified for a less well-heeled market) and the production of designer perfumes as well as licensing arrangements for sunglasses, watches, handbags, footwear, jewelry and interior design objets d'art. In 1997, it was estimated that haute couture accounted for only 6 percent of fashion sales; the remainder was earned from licensing and ready-to-wear.

Although the number of fashion designers has mushroomed and the number of new cities vying to become fashion capitals has proliferated, the number of Paris couture houses has declined steadily during the postwar period (see box 2.3).

In 2004, there were just nine couture houses—Chanel, Dior, Givenchy, Gaultier, Lacroix, Mori, Sirop, Scherrer, and Torrente—with "correspondent second rank" members and a gaggle of "guest members" (Weston-Thomas, nd). These figures suggest that despite the persisting status of Paris couture, other pressures are influencing the business strategies of couture houses. The importance of shows has clearly been questioned, with a minority of the Chambre members choosing to show and a number of high-profile houses leaving the Chambre altogether (such as Yves Saint Laurent in 2002). Of the early members, only Chanel (with Karl Lagerfeld as designer) and Valentino still belong (Jackson 2006: 33–35). Emanuel Ungaro left in 2004. Reflecting this trend, the number of clients of couture houses has also declined. In the late 1980s, Nicholas Coleridge (1989: 170) estimated that there were only about 3,000 clients for the major Paris houses, of whom fewer than 700 were regulars. They came from Europe (250), North America (250), the Middle East (90), South America (50), and the Far East (30). About two-thirds of sales came from North America. Assuming that there were between fifteen and about twenty couture houses at this time, these figures suggest that on average each house might have just 150 to 200 clients for its made-to-measure lines. More recent figures suggest there may be 2,000 customers, of whom just 200 are regulars and 60 percent American.

Of these clients, only fifteen to eighteen were regarded as trendsetters who could successfully promote new designs to wider markets by modifying the design and distributing through diffusion lines. The changing nature of the market was reflected in the formation in 1975 of the Chambre Syndicale du Prêt-à-Porter des Couturiers et des Créateurs de la Mode (by Yves Saint Laurent's then–business partner Pierre Bergé) to promote the increasingly important ready-to-wear labels. Of its forty-four members, twenty-four are *créateurs,* while the other twenty produce both haute couture and prêt-à-porter (Costantino 1998: 50).

**Box 2.3 Number of Paris Couture Houses, 1958–2004**

| | |
|---|---|
| 1946 | 106 |
| 1952 | 60 |
| 1958 | 36 |
| 1967 | 19 |
| 1997 | 18 |
| 2000 | 18 |
| 2002 | 12 |
| 2003 | 8* |
| 2004 | 10* |

Source: Jackson 2006: 33–35.

* These numbers refer to the designers who held shows; another thirteen and eight designers who showed were either guest members or correspondent members

Additionally, designs are copied by designers and reproduced by department stores and fashion chains. The economics of this process is complex. A designer must build the mark of exclusivity into the price tag for house clients while betting on the exposure and free publicity value of a client seen wearing an outfit. A sliding scale of prices determined by the ability of specific markets to pay is also attached to the various diffusion lines. Designers are also lobbied by clients and celebrities to "lend" outfits for special occasions such as the Oscars, which creates a potentially tense symbiotic relationship between designers and elite clients.

We can assume that these numbers have further declined and that the customer base has shifted in accordance with economic trends in growing markets such as Asia. Both couture houses and less prestigious fashion houses are subject to economic fluctuations, and many have been to the financial brink at some stage.

**Couture parade Toni Maticevski:** Photo: Peter Duhon. Peter Duhon

Takeovers and restructurings are part of the elite fashion scene as fashion houses and labels become part of international conglomerates with global tentacles. Designers are also being incorporated in global design superstores (such as Emporio Armani, Versace, Chanel, Gucci, Burberry, Vivienne Westwood, and Guess?), which still aim to sell exclusivity, but to well-heeled customers in far-flung places, rather than corralled clients of couture houses.

Other designers (e.g., **Gap,** Diesel, Tommy Hilfiger, Emporio Armani, **Benetton, Zara**) have been more concerned with creating brand recognition through a range of products and selling these to mainstream markets. Sports houses (e.g., Nike, Adidas, Converse, Puma) have especially exploited this strategy. Even respectable Paris labels began to imitate the pitch to this wider mass market. As Mayer has observed, Louis Vuitton's distinctive geometric flower-patterned bags were among the first fashion items to gain global recognition among fashion-conscious wannabes and sparked copyists and fakes (cited in Buxbaum 2005: 158). Chanel also splashed its interlocking

**Versace Medusa logo.** Photo: Daniel di Palma. Creative Commons Attribution ShareAlike 2.5 License

*C*s onto handbags and apparel, and Gucci successfully marketed its men's loafers worldwide in the 1970s, while others followed the trend of simply adding their moniker to apparel (Hermes's *H*, Gucci's *G*, Ralph Lauren's Polo, Christian Dior's DIOR, Versace's Medusa head, Saint Laurent's YSL, etc.). The success of Nike's tick has come to symbolize the success of this shorthand label marketing strategy in the global consumer village.

Nonetheless, a star system among designers has dominated the arena, with reputation for apparel vying with media visibility and marketing success. Very often, designers cross-subsidize their "elite" or couture, artwear or **avant-garde**, or experimental collections through certain lines (perfumes, T-shirts, handbags) that proclaim the label and keep it in the public's consciousness. Hence there is a tradeoff between the profit margins of sales, critical acclaim (of reviews and uptake of collections), iconic or must-have items that secure public attention, and the popular media profile of the designer as celebrity (see Jackson 2006: 39).

In this hierarchy of fashion sites, Paris was the peak throughout the twentieth century, even though rival cities staked out claims for the title. Paris's position was maintained not only by its already mentioned guilds but by its stamina and success. While rival bodies nibbled away at Paris's preeminence at the edges, they also forced the Paris Chambre to modernize and restructure the public face of the industry. Over the century, more and more designers realized that success had less to do with design brilliance than with the ability to be seen and remain in the limelight, attract attention and controversy, even be bad. Designer success then became more a matter of media manipulation and a canny sense of marketing than the apparel itself.

The designer star system is an artificial construction that projects an image of the mood of the fashion of the moment and of the character of the designer. As Lipovetsky (1994: 182) puts it,

**the star system is based on the same values as fashion, on the sacralisation of individuality and appearances. Just as fashion is the apparent personalization of ordinary human beings, so the star is the personalization of the actor; just as fashion is the sophisticated staging of the human body, so the star is the media staging of a personality.**

The star system relies on perpetual reinforcement of its existence and elite status, thus prompting the fashion system to stage spectacular events such as catwalk shows, fashion weeks, media briefings, magazine spreads, celebrity endorsements, and glittering parties. These are investments in self-worth and the imaginary system. The biggest Parisian designer stars include Worth, Poiret, Chanel, Schiaparelli, Dior, and Saint Laurent. The upper stratum of designers distinguish themselves by adopting the label "couturier," while the second tier is called the "creators" (Kawamura 2005: 70). Outside this system, there are of course other ranks of designers working in ready-to-wear, for diffusion labels for retail labels and copyists. Despite their affected elitism, the stars in reality depend on the existence of the lower ranks to maintain their elevated position. However, another challenge to Paris was gathering pace in the form of new fashion capitals that were stealing the limelight and creating new customer bases.

## v. new fashion capitals

What does it take for fashion hubs to be regarded as fashion capitals (Gilbert 2006)? According to Kawamura (2005: 52), it is the structural organization of the many actors and agencies involved in the design, manufacture, promotion, and distribution of fashion that characterizes a fashion capital. Central to this is the role of **gatekeepers** and promoters, who continuously sing the praises of the industry as unique and distinctive. The Paris fashion industry was helped from the outset by the direct involvement of the French government in assisting the industry and underwriting its promotion, aided by the industry bodies of couture and their efforts to maintain exclusivity of membership (as well as mechanisms such as sponsorship of apprenticeships, start-up loans, funding of fashion shows and promotions, and pricing regimes).

Fashion was, in this sense, a national cultural business rather than just another industry, which is how many other governments have viewed fashion. As Kawamura (2005: 53–54) argues, the French government has played an active role "in maintaining the French hegemony of fashion." She attributes the success of this arrangement to the alignment of economic (money and resource availability), social (networks of influence and support), and cultural (hierarchical regimes of taste and aesthetic value) capital, which is expressed in consumer choices that actualize identity and the performance of self:

> **The French fashion system first provides designers the symbolic capital and then allows them to convert that symbolic capital into economic capital. Recognition that groups participate in social arrangements that put them at an advantage suggests the importance of the domination of some groups of designers in Paris. Therefore, acceptance by the system places the designer within the system of stratification. (Kawamura 2005: 55)**

As economic restructuring and global trends in industry and consumerism have happened, fashion has been recognized as a value-adding industry that can assist governments to open up new economic opportunities, and a growing number of hubs have begun to establish fashion capitals (Gilbert 2000).

### New York as Fashion Capital

Although the Parisian grip on high fashion persisted through the twentieth century, the fashion industry in America was developing rapidly and arguably was a major factor in Paris's achievement of its iconic status. Designers such as Charles James, Claire McCardell, and Mainbocher and collections designed for stores such as Wanamakers created new looks for a more relaxed, modern, and leisure-oriented consumer culture in the early decades of the twentieth century. New York was the center of the fashion industry from the outset (Rantisi 2006; Stanfill 2006, 2007). Although commentators lamented that American fashion would never be taken seriously as a "world style centre" in the 1920s (Steele 1988: 282), developments in French and American fashion in fact went hand in hand as American design took its lead from Paris collections and adapted these for homegrown couture and ready-to-wear collections while Americans steadily came to dominate the Paris designers' lists of clients.

Other style arbiters (including Adrian, Travis Banton, Howard Greer, and Edith Head) were employed by Hollywood to create individual and emulated wardrobes for leading ladies such as Marlene Dietrich, Joan Crawford, Jean Harlow, Veronica Lake, Rita Hayworth, and Gloria Swanson (Keenan 1977). These designers recognized that films stars were America's fashion role models. Despite the mystique of Hollywood and its stylishness, Paris fashion was still coveted as the fashion center. Even Jackie Kennedy, as the United States' First Lady, mixed Paris fashion with the designs of American designers such as Oleg Cassini.

This was not just some pale imitation of French stylistic capital; over time, American fashion gained its own direction and strength, especially in the casual and leisure wear spectrum (Hall 2002; Welters and Cunningham 2005). For example, Hall (2002: 9) argues that although fashion history has adopted the perspective that "Paris designers decided *la mode,*" which trickled down (and across the Atlantic), in fact,

> **for decades California has been the most important fashion influence of the twentieth century. How odd that almost no one admitted it—certainly not the French, certainly not New York's Seventh Avenue. But the fact remains that more people dress in styles rooted in California than styles born almost anywhere else.**

These "casual, comfortable, lightweight clothing" styles came to dominate everyday dress and inform couture collections as well. The most successful clothes were blue **jeans** and swimsuits, which were adopted worldwide—but we can add other American items to the list, such as T-shirts, athletic shoes, and caps. Meanwhile, America was developing its own group of designers, whose clothes may not have been purchased far beyond the borders of North America, but whose more relaxed lines and cultural references resonated with fashion trends elsewhere. Hollywood films, popular music, fashion modeling and photography, television programs, and new sports (such as surfing, skateboarding, baseball, and windsurfing) made American-style fashions suitable for the postmodern era.

In the 1970s, American designers, including Ralph Lauren, Calvin Klein, Ann Klein, Geoffrey

**Vera Wang.** Photo: Daniella Zalcman. Daniella Zalcman

Beene, Halston, Liz Claiborne, Tommy Hilfiger, Tom Ford, Norma Kamali, and Donna Karan, began to gain international recognition. American fashion had come of age (Welters and Cunningham 2005). In sum:

**Americans developed their own quintessential style that features practical, well-made ready-to-wear looks. These looks were inspired by American life, particularly sports, but also music, movies, and television. The importance of subcultures in creating new styles that represented changing values is underscored … . These changes are reflected in the "bricolage of fashion" that began to appear in the 1960s. (Welters and Cunningham 2005: 7).**

New York has now attained acknowledgement as a fashion capital (Rantisi 2006; Stanfill 2006), although Los Angeles, especially Hollywood's celebrity culture, is the glitz fashion world capital.

### London as Fashion Capital

Although Paris fashion may be regarded as the epitome of couture, and American fashion as the heart of everyday fashion, the English fashion industry has a longer history than either. It has also had a close relationship with the development of both in a pattern that ebbed and flowed in terms of influence and visibility. This was traced earlier in this chapter. England's greatest contribution to fashion has been its tradition of tailoring, which, De la Haye (1997: 12) has argued, epitomizes "the British love of understatement" (see Breward 2004; Breward, Conekin, and Cox 2002; Hume 1997). The Industrial Revolution spurred English clothing manufacture and retailing, although a significant fashion industry seems to date from the late eighteenth century, when consumer goods became more widely available and affordable. This trend has been related to the concurrent emergence of a sense of Englishness, of which a distinctive sense of dress became an instantly visible symbol (see Breward et al. 2002). On the one hand, then, Britain was among the first nations to innovate forms of mass production and textile manufacture as large-scale industries, especially in the north of England. The ability to produce garments on a large scale was an enormous fillip to the escalating consumer society and could meet the needs of the burgeoning cities. On the other hand, Britain also relied on its distinctive tailoring tradition in custom tailoring, dressmaking, and retailing as well as its expertise in finishes and trims. Over the next century, English fashion exhibited a number of competing features: aristocratic and (what we would now call) nouveau riche–driven elite fashion, a strong tradition of men's restrained tailoring of suits and other garments derived from the rural elite, flurries into short-term and cheap fads and fashions by the newly employed, and a coterie of self-appointed fashion cognoscenti who lived for dressing to be seen and admired.

London was the acknowledged center of British fashion, although the importance of rural and regional influences and deviations cannot be underestimated. Significantly, it was Charles Worth, an English tailor, who crossed the English Chanel and established what is now deemed to be the model of the Parisian couture house. With Paris increasingly regarded as the epicenter of fashion, London became the poor cousin whose influences were acknowledged and incorporated but paled under the relentless spotlight that was turned on Paris. On another front, the American development of fashionable but affordable ready-to-wear and leisure wear designed for a more democratic view of the demographics of fashion consumers was a challenge (and affront) to the traditional and conservative legacy of a class-based Britain.

Meanwhile, fashion in Britain has largely revolved around quintessentially British brands and clothes—many associated, appropriately enough, with rainwear in dull gray, browns, and blacks (De la Haye 1997: 12). Some couture persisted, especially and most visibly in serving the needs of royalty and the aristocracy. Designers such as Norman Hartnell, Victor Stiebel (De la Haye 2002), Digby Morton, and Hardy Amies (Ehrman 2002) became household names associated with the rareified end of British society. Some English designers such as Edward Molyneux relocated to Paris, and Paris fashion often borrowed from English traditions. But generally, the first half of the twentieth century saw Paris in the ascendancy and English fashion lost visibility.

London fashion regained its status after World War II (De la Haye 1997; Wilcox 2007). Throughout, London had retained its tailoring tradition, most visible in Saville Row, the mecca of custom tailoring. Wilcox (2007) argues that the decade after the war, 1947–57, saw a major revival of London high fashion, following on from the success of Dior's New Look, but much more than just a pale imitation of developments in Paris. Nonetheless, as the catalog of the Victoria and Albert exhibition of "The Golden Age of Couture: Paris and London, 1947–57" shows, Paris produced the lion's share of memorable couture moments, while London's contribution seemed to be in promoting and representing developments in high fashion through fashion photographers such as Cecil Beaton, new fashion magazines (such as *Harper's*), and fashion models and aristocratic consumers who popularized new looks. The town planning approach to rebuilding London's West End and retailing sectors also produced particular kinds of shopping precincts and consumer habits that may have suppressed the development of couture consumption but created a framework for the emergence of broader-based fashion consumption (Edwards 2006).

English fashion as such receded into the background of fashionability, although its legendary tailoring remained sought after (mostly for menswear) and classic labels such as Burberry, Jaeger, Harvey Nichols, Norman Hartnell, and Hardy Amies were still revered by the aristocracy and the so-called **Sloane Ranger** (aspirant elite) class. Some English designers made a mark, for example, Jean Muir and Laura Ashley. Generally, however, English fashion remained in the doldrums until the 1960s and 1970s, when English designers such as Mary Quant, Ossie Clark, **Biba** (Barbara Hulanicki), Vivienne Westwood, Zandra Rhodes, and Laura Ashley began to attract international acclaim amid the image of **Swinging London** and the fascination with youth culture, rebellion, and popular music. Fashion-wise, this was the time of the street designer; the niche fashion **boutique**; and youthful fashion models as celebrities and role models (including Jean Shrimpton, Twiggy, Penelope Tree, Lisa Taylor, and Veruschka) and their Svengalis, the new generation of fashion photographers such as Lord Lichfield, David Bailey, Terence Donovan, Horst, and Helmut Newton.

London had regained its place as a fashion capital, although there was some debate in the 1980s as to whether it maintained this title. As part of the revived recognition of the contribution of culture to the economy and social vitality of British life, London Fashion Week was established in 1984. But it has always struggled to gain the spotlight it has coveted. As the fashion infrastructure of manufacturing and production has waned in Britain, British fashion has largely rested on the laurels of its contribution to a distinctive sense of

**Mary Quant.** Time & Life Pictures/Getty Images. Terry Smith

design. Indicatively, the strength of English fashion has emanated from art schools, not "couture" apprenticeships, and up-and-coming designers have often gone offshore in order to make it in established fashion centers such as Paris and New York. By the 1990s and 2000s, however, London fashion exhibited a greater confidence and flamboyance that confirmed its status as a global source of fashion trends. Moreover, English fashion designers such as Alexander McQueen, John Galliano, Rifat Ozbek, Vivienne Westwood, Stella McCartney, and Phoebe Philo continued to feed the global couture industry by working in other fashion capitals.

### Milan and Italian Fashion

While Paris, London, and New York still dominated fashion, Italian fashion was steadily developing its own distinctiveness. Italians were heavily influenced by Paris fashion (and Parisian designers gave Italian style short shrift), but Italians developed their own interpretations of Paris collections and a home-grown industry to produce couture (Steele 2003). Although the birth of the Italian fashion industry is dated as post–World War II and related to the implementation of the U.S. Marshall Plan (designed to stimulate postwar reconstruction and boost economic growth), Italian states had a long tradition of fine textile production and manufacture, which had, to some extent, been aided by the German suppression of the Paris fashion industry during the war. So the promotion of Italian fashion was closely linked to the promotion of Italian textiles, for example, as advocated by the Centro Italiano della Moda (founded in 1948 to promote rayon and other artificial fibers through a number of fashion shows that attracted foreign buyers, including the 1950 Venice Film Festival) (White 2000: 40). From 1951, fashion parades showcasing key Italian designers were staged to promote Italian fashion internationally, which was received with great acclaim. As early as 1952, American *Vogue* identified three distinctive characteristics of Italian fashion: the production of leisure and resort wear that suited the American market, superb fabrics and outstanding textiles designs, and affordable but exquisite evening gowns (Steele 2003: 23–24). Florence was the first Italian fashion capital, but Rome soon challenged this preeminence. The Florence Palazzo Pitti fashion shows were, beginning in 1954, coordinated by the Centro di Firenze per la Moda Italiana, while in Rome in 1958, the Camera Nazionale della Moda Italiana was established as a nonprofit body to represent diverse industry sectors in the promotion of the profile and value of the Italian fashion industry.

A number of designers made their names through these shows, including Alberto Fabiani (1910–87), Emilio Schuberth (1904–72), Emilio Pucci (1914–92), and Valentino (1933–). The popularity of Italian films and culture in the 1950s and 1960s made Italy the new center of fashionability. It provided a more relaxed style that suited new lifestyles but also possessed "greater sophistication and cultural cachet" than ready-to-wear clothing elsewhere (Steele 2003: 27; White 2000). A new generation of designers such as Nino Cerruti (1930–), and the brands Krizia (1957–) and Missoni (established 1953), confirmed Italy as a hub of haute couture and a source of ready-to-wear high fashion. An Italian look was already evolving, especially in men's suits, which had classic tailoring but a softer and slimmer modern **silhouette** and used new fabrics and colors. Beautifully tailored shirts were also an Italian specialty. These styles fitted the youth fashion revolution of the late 1960s, and Milan's status as a fashion center developed from this time. Meanwhile, the quality production of accessories such as handbags and shoes—for example, by Gucci (established 1921–), Bottega Veneta (established 1967), Fendi (established 1930s), and Salvatore Ferragamo (Fiamma Ferragamo, 1941–98)—quickly established an international reputation for fine craftsmanship.

Despite its drab architecture and layout, Milan had a long tradition in design (especially in interior design, graphic design, and architecture) and fashion later followed (Reinach 2006). Successes included Mila Schön (1919–1998), Roberta di Camerino handbags (established 1920), the "bad boy" youth culture fashions of Fiorucci (established 1967), Walter Albini (1941–83), and the distinctive **knitwear** of Missoni. By the late 1960s, designers were turning their backs on showing at the Pitti Palace in Florence to show in Milan, by now "the centre of production for the new ready-to-wear" (Steele 2003: 55). Fashion was innovative and future oriented and targeted to "real" people and promoted by a well-established production base.

While Milanese couture was still aimed at the rich and priced accordingly, Milan had the capacity to produce high-quality ready-to-wear for an in-between market that liked new fashion and popular culture trends. Of all the Milanese-born or -based designers—including Krizia, Moschino, Fiorucci, Gianfranco Ferré (1944–2007), and Max Mara (established 1951)—four fashion brands have dominated international perceptions of Milanese fashion: Giorgio Armani (1934–), Versace (Gianni, 1946–97, succeeded by sister Donatella), Prada (established 1913), and Dolce & Gabbana (established 1985).

Armani was arguably the first to develop "luxury ready-to-wear" that appealed to the nouveau riche fashionistas (Steele 2003: 60). It entailed a softer and more casual Italian look featuring less structured suits for men and women that "signified casual, expensive, sexy elegance" (Steele 2003: 63). This look was quickly adopted by celebrities, especially in Hollywood on film and television, and came to set the look of the late twentieth century.

By contrast, Versace poured the symbolism of the prostitute and streetwalker into explicitly sexualized baroque extravaganzas that contained echoes of Moschino's radical fashion excesses as well as complementing the new Armani studied casual attitude to fashion (Steele 2003: 71–77). Numerous Milanese brands established global distribution for affordable high fashion and cheaper ready-to-wear: Ermenegildo Zegna (woolen suits), La Perla (lingerie), Laura Biagiotti (knitwear and cashmere), Diesel (leisure wear), Benetton (global fashion), and Max Mara (suits and coats).

Milan's success as a fashion capital stems from the unique combination of "traditional craftsmanship, innovative design, and modern industrial technology" using a decentralized, artisan-based model of production in concert with design practice, on the one hand, and modern methods of export and marketing, on the other: "'that fine Italian hand'—the place where art and technology unite" (Steele 2003: 117). Notwithstanding this, Milan's preeminence in the 1980s and 1990s was challenged in the 2000s with the entry of Chinese textiles into Italy and the delayed investment in new infrastructure in Milan as a fashion city (Reinach 2006: 130–34).

### New Fashion Capitals

While Paris continues to glitter in the firmament of fashion capitals, a number of new centers, especially outside Europe, are claiming to be or wish to become fashion capitals (see Breward and Gilbert 2006). In Asia, cities like Shanghai, Beijing, Tokyo, Singapore, Bombay, and Hong Kong vie to be crowned fashion capitals. Case study 8 at the end of this chapter examines São Paulo's

Daslu store and its place in (cosmopolitan) Brazil's burgeoning love affair with fashion and luxury, case study 22 explores the global luxury market through the example of Louis Vuitton, and case study 30 gives an overview of China's changing ideas about fashion and the development of contemporary fashion trends.

Broadly speaking, there are two trajectories for non-European fashion capitals: on the one hand, places where local (customary or traditional) fashions and dress cultures have been supplanted or embellished by Western fashion and dress (such as China, India, Dakar in Senegal, Eastern Europe), and on the other, places that have been settled by Europeans who have imposed a largely European culture upon the country or city (such as Australia, North America, Brazil). In some cases, there has been a mixture of both or resurgences of "local" fashion amid Western fashion. One of the issues is how quickly some hubs have been transformed by Western fashion influences. Valery Garrett (2007: 240), in a book tracing the transformation of Chinese dress, recalls how when she went to Hong Kong in 1973, villagers in the northern New Territories wore traditional *shan ku* (black pajamas), while their Chinese cousins in Guangzhou

**Festival Mall, Hong Kong.** Photo: Jennifer Craik

(in southern China) wore the uniform of the Cultural Revolution, blue or green **Mao suits**.

**It was impossible to imagine that only seventy years earlier [in the early 1900s], mandarins clad in sumptuous dragon robes ... swept along in sedan chairs while their womenfolk, in richly embroidered gowns, tottered about on tiny bound feet.**

**Today, except in remote regions and areas populated by the minority groups, the dress of the vast majority of Chinese is indistinguishable from that of any other community around the world. Western dress has become the norm, ranging from top French and Italian designer labels purchased in up-market boutiques in Shanghai or Beijing to market stalls selling mass-produced goods, including designer imitations. (Garrett 2007: 240)**

Such a dramatic change has occurred in other fashion capitals too—such as Moscow since the fall of **communism;** Dakar, with its wealth and opening up of trade and travel; Tokyo, with its economic boom of the 1970s and 1980s; and Bombay, with its economic transformation of the 2000s. The pattern seems to be that Western fashion becomes popular, initially being bought elsewhere and imported into a new center, with distribution outlets and specialist boutiques opening up locally. Simultaneously, the desire for and fascination with Paris and global designer labels triggers development of a local fashion design and manufacture industry that sits alongside the Euro-based fashions with varying degrees of success and impact (successful in Brazil, Antwerp, Tokyo, and Singapore, but less so in Shanghai, Hong Kong, Melbourne, and Moscow). Fashion capitals, then, need to be seen as both sites of fashion invention and fashion consumption of global and local clothes and accessories.

A city like Tokyo also has a vibrant street culture fashion that confounds usual fashion theories and runs autonomously of mainstream fashion and dress cultures; see case study 13 (see also Kawamura 2006). In China, Western fashion spread from Hong Kong to Shenzhen (China's fashion capital in the 1980s) to Guangzhou and Beijing (in the 1990s) and north to Shanghai (in the 2000s) (Finnane 2007). Shanghai has invested heavily in reviving its reputation as a site of fashionability—indeed, it was known as the Paris of the East in the 1920s and 1930s. Centering largely on the Bund, the fashionable shopping precinct, Shanghai offers many exclusive fashion labels and reaps the benefit of establishing fashion design courses with designers such as Yang Liu, Mark Cheung, Wu Haiyan, and Wang Xinyuan, producing impressive couture although struggling to achieve commercial success (Mingxin and Lijun 2008: 107). The 2008 Beijing Olympic Games gave currency to Chinese fashion, with observers identifying an emerging Beijing look—"part flowing and layered, part boho and a touch tribal" (Kitchen 2008: 95).

By the 2000s, Italian, Japanese, and British fashion rivaled the preeminence of Paris, while Madrid, Tokyo, Antwerp, Berlin, Singapore, Shanghai, Hong Kong, and other cities now competed successfully on the stage of international couture.

## vi. conclusion

This chapter has linked the development of the modern fashion system to the emergence of a capitalist economy and consumer-based culture in which the value of goods played a role in the performance of a modern identity. Fashion has been a key sector concerned with creating symbolic value and identity, above all, in the development of the Paris fashion industry as the apex of Western fashion systems. This chapter has provided an overview of Paris fashion and explored its legacy for contemporary fashion before considering the rise of rival fashion capitals (London, New York, and Milan) as well as new fashion centers such as Tokyo, Shanghai, and Moscow that have emerged in the new millennium.

The following case studies illustrate some key aspects of these trends: the role of the English **dandy** Beau Brummell in establishing an iconic look for men that set the scene for contemporary masculine dress; the legacy of French designer Coco Chanel, whose fashions (many inspired by English dress but interpreted in a very French manner) have been argued to have revolutionized women's clothes and spurred the growth of leisure wear; the profound influence of Parisian couturier Yves Saint Laurent on fashions of the late twentieth century as well as in introducing licensing as the cross-subsidizing savior of Paris couture; and the establishment of luxury retailer Daslu in São Paulo, Brazil, as a one-stop shop for global luxury and lifestyle goods and services and a meeting place for the world's fashion glitterati.

## CHAPTER SUMMARY

- In the late nineteenth century, European fashion developed into a modern fashion system whose characteristic features were its integration with consumer culture and short fashion cycles that depended on a rapid succession of styles.
- Although the modern fashion system is relatively new there are numerous examples of earlier fashion systems and obsessions with fashionability amid proto-consumer cultures that can be identified in Europe and the East.
- Royalty across Europe but especially in France under the Bourbons was the conduit of trends in fashion that were adopted by (at least) the aristocracy and wealthier classes.
- The Paris fashion industry began to develop in the mid-nineteenth century but really took shape at the end of the century with the rise of fashion designers and fashion houses producing haute couture which dominated the twentieth century.
- Paris's positioning as the preeminent fashion capital was aided by the establishment of a protectionist industry body La Chambre Syndicale.
- From the 1960s on Paris fashion was under threat from youth culture and new fashion influences derived from popular culture with new kinds of designer labels and brands achieving global success.
- The industry of Paris fashion has been substantially transformed to meet the challenges posed by new competition and compete on the global fashion stage.
- New fashion capitals and centers such as London, New York and Milan are now competing as hubs offering a combination of design, production, marketing and retailing.

## CASE STUDY 5: Beau Brummell

**Beau Brummell.** Getty Images. 2007 Getty Images

Beau Brummell has a reputation based on leadership in fashion in the late eighteenth and early nineteenth centuries. However, his fastidious attention to clothes was only part of the story. He was devoted to the management of impressions, and his behavior was a device for evoking and controlling the effects he had on others, as well as benefiting from them. Brummell is an excellent example of the trickle-down/bubble-up theory put forward by Ted Polhemus in 1994, although in Brummell's case, it was a case of bubble up/trickle down.

Beau Brummell was born George Brummell in 1778 in London. His grandfather was a valet, and his father, Billy Brummell, was secretary and right-hand man to Lord North. Billy Brummell, as one of the rising civil servants, had grown prosperous and managed to send his sons to Eton. There, George acquired the initial nickname of "Buck" Brummell. Ian Kelly (2006: 80) suggests that this was due to either his habit of taking uncommon care of his sports gear on rainy days or the combination of his personality and background.

After the death of both of his parents by 1794, George, at fifteen, went to Oxford University. He only stayed a few months. He managed to convince the chief executor of his father's will to allow him to use his inheritance to buy an army commission. At seventeen, he took up the rank of **cornet** in the glamorous 10th Light Dragoons, the Prince of Wales's own regiment.

In the army, Brummell not only met the heir to the throne, Prince George, who was in his early thirties, but, as a member of the military, began to circulate within the same aristocratic social circle. The English aristocracy was a tight elite, and their numbers were small, consisting of no more than 1,200 ultrafashionable people, who closely controlled their image and access to their social circle.

Brummell was required to purchase the alarmingly expensive uniform of the 10th Light Dragoons uniform. It was dark blue with pale yellow facings and silver thread braiding. It also consisted of a blue sleeveless upper jacket, or shell, with braided epaulettes, cut long on the body and worn over a sleeved under jacket. Both items were "frogged and looped," and embroidered with horizontal braiding in white satin, and decorated with real silver tassels and fabric balls. The upper and under jackets were lined in silk. The headdress was a large Tarleton helmet, a peaked leather skull with leopard skin fastened with a silver clasp and the three Prince of Wales feathers. This was Brummell's passport to the elite class.

Full-length trousers, or pantaloons, as they were called, had been adopted by the highly fashionable Dragoons. Long pants were a new concept to both the middle and the upper classes. Although the French set the standards for court and military fashion, it was English tailoring that was much admired. The French, in their Anglomania passion for tailored British riding clothes, added full-length pants. European gentlemen had, prior to the French Revolution, indicated their class by wearing knee-length breeches. The revolution had seen the adoption of the pants of the workers, the *sans culottes.* The full-length trouser was exported back to Britain and absorbed into the military uniforms as pantaloons.

Subsequently, the full-length trouser became de rigeur for all but those required to dress as regulated when attending court.

The 10th Light Dragoons were a cavalry regiment and horses were a part of that uniform. As dress is also a technology, the relationship between the horse and the rider came into play. The British style of riding had developed into a riding system of controlling the horse with one's legs. These pants, knitted on stocking frames, enabled close contact between the horse and the rider, and the absence of **underwear** increased the rider's sensitivity (Kelly 2006: 126).

These close-fit pants also reflected the neoclassical fashions of the day. The white or cream pants showed every fold and bump of the genitals, like the classical white marble statues that were being brought to England from Greece and Italy. The fashion for women at the time was sheer white muslin tunics that revealed the anatomy beneath.

Brummell continued to wear this style of trousers after leaving the 10th Dragoons in 1799. Leather stirrups ensured that Brummell's pants stretched from braces to feet. He employed tailors experienced in military dress, who willingly complied with his exacting demands. He wore plain, lightly starched shirts with the collar high enough to almost touch his ears. This was followed by a triangle of fine Irish muslin neck cloth that was perfectly tied and became the trademark of the dandies who followed his lead. His somber-colored jackets were padded between the lining and the outer fabric, sculpting the appearance of a muscular body beneath.

Brummell's body beneath his clothes was subjected to constant attention to weight and a strict regime of cleanliness. His performed a daily levee (a ritual of dressing before an audience) for his coterie to observe how he dressed, to learn the exactitude of the wardrobe, to care for the body, and to display the understated chic that became his hallmark. Even the Prince of Wales attended these morning routines, which is curious, as a levee was considered a practice of the monarchy that was viewed by his subjects. These events were stage managed with the complicity of his servant and valet, Robinson, who made a point of passing the room containing the audience of male members of the *haut ton,* with a "quantity of tumbled neckcloths under one arm," which were "the failures" (Kelly 2006: 164).

Dressed as such, he set his sights on continuing to mix in the same tight social world of the Prince of Wales, under whom Brummell had served. After resigning his commission, he entered full-time into London society, where he was in growing demand. Here he acquired the nickname "Beau" Brummell.

He used his inheritance to establish a modest London address, from which he sortied out every day into society. He had no occupation. He relied on situations, scenes, and encounters. His daily routine consisted of his famous entrances and exits at exclusive clubs, private balls and entertainments, soirees, fashionable promenades, racetracks, private gambling clubs, and elegant salons. These activities did not give him, or others from wealthy mercantilist families, access to all of the English elite. He perceived that the ceremony of style was what separated the aristocracy from other classes.

Military life is full of ceremony, from the individual saluting an officer to the collective changing of the guard, acknowledging the presence of the monarch. These acts were carried out coldly without regard for personal interaction. Brummell's cold demeanor and malicious personality created distance, formality, and ceremony. He built a protective space bridged only by taste and refinement.

Just as in the military, Brummell was on show at all times. Uniforms contributed to a regime of discipline and a **masculinity** that was well defined in the eighteenth century. Continuing this practice, it was not only the meticulous self-surveillance he learned in the military, but also his awareness of having an audience. His conspicuousness was a source of continuous fascination in gossip, reportage, and anecdotes by diarists, chroniclers, and biographers.

When entertaining, Brummell positioned himself to be seen. At one of his exclusive clubs, Whites, Brummell would arrange his place to be in the bow of the windows at the front, where he would spend hours in conversation with his circle of acquaintances. Gambling at other clubs, such as Brooks's or Watier's, was also a spectacle in which Brummell's daring addiction and (declining) wealth could be displayed.

His extravagant lifestyle and gambling debts mounted to such an extent that he was forced to leave England for France in 1816. He slipped away quietly, as he could no longer maintain the position he had constructed for himself in London society. He lived in Calais, where he did not require a passport. In 1822, while in Calais, Brummell wrote *Male and Female Costume.* It was a history and aesthetic study of Greek, Roman and British costume. However, it was not published until 1932.

Unfortunately, Brummell contracted syphilis. There is no record of when this occurred. He has been described as asexual and never formed a conventional sexual relationship. Brummell lived on the surface of experience. His life was regulated by surfaces. His inner moral life appeared to be irrelevant to his life lived out in front of his audience (Smith 1974: 723). It was his management of impressions, the perfection of every aspect of his behavior and dress, and his manipulation of social settings with ultimate subtlety and with sublimity for which he is remembered. Rising up to a life of high aestheticism and decadence from the upper middle class, he created the concept or cult of the dandy, which continues today.

Sharon Peoples

## CASE STUDY 6: The Influence of Coco Chanel

**Coco Chanel.** Photo by George Hoyningen-Huene/ RDA/Getty Images. Getty Images

The name Chanel and the history of the label epitomize the changing phases of the history of Parisian haute couture (de la Haye and Tobin 2001). Initially centered on the work of designer Coco Chanel (1883–1971), the brand is now a global luxury brand that resonates with consumers wanting a brush with elite fashion through Chanel apparel and boutiques located in Europe, America, and Asia. The marketing of Chanel as a brand illustrates many key features of designer fashion, such as Chanel-branded accessories (e.g., sunglasses and handbags); Chanel-franchised designers such as Karl Lagerfeld; the unmistakable, globally recognized double-*C* **logo**; the iconic Chanel No. 5 perfume; Chanel fakes flooding the market, especially in Asia; and the myth of Coco Chanel's definitive role in reshaping twentieth-century women's fashion.

She established her **atelier**, later known as the House of Chanel, in 1910; retired in 1939 (at the outbreak of World War II); and did not reopen until 1954. She reputedly ruled the company with an iron fist until her death in 1971; since then it has been in the hands of the Wertheimer brothers. Chanel was a canny businesswoman employing in 1935 alone 4,000 workers and selling 28,000 designs internationally (Breward 2003: 45). When she reopened her business, she capitalized on the popularity of the New Look associated with Christian Dior (despite her dislike of him) and sought to expand her tentacles by capturing the expanding market in North America (Breward 2003: 47).

Described by her successor, Karl Lagerfeld, as rebellious and capricious, Chanel defied many of the conventions of her time, rejecting the structured fashions of the 1920s and engaging in numerous, perhaps unwise, liaisons with unsuitable lovers. Her unconventional personal life attracted public attention and ambivalent reactions yet fueled the demand for her clothes and kept her name in the public spotlight.

The Chanel brand is now marketed as audacious, perfectionist, unique, passionate, and visionary. Chanel's genius was in challenging stereotypes of women and their fashions by experimenting with fabrics then only used for undergarments (knitted jersey and simple cotton twills) as well as adapting English rural wear for men (including cardigans, twinsets, tweed jackets, jodhpurs, and pleated skirts). These have become the basis of contemporary leisure wear and signaled major changes in women's lives as they took up energetic sports and leisure activities and embraced the choices offered by popular media and culture.

While Chanel's trademark clothes, including bell-bottom trousers (or yachting pants) and pajamas for women, were unstructured and boyish (she borrowed the then-fashionable term *la* **garçonne** to describe them), she also produced elegant and opulent costume jewelry, suits, and gowns that became synonymous with her name.

**Box 2.4 Coco Chanel Time Line**

| | |
|---|---|
| 1909 | establishes hat workshop |
| 1910 | opens boutique on Rue Cambon |
| 1913 | opens boutique in Deauville—first sells jersey clothing (jackets, sweaters, skirts, shirts) |
| 1915 | opens boutique in Biarritz |
| 1918 | pyjamas for women |
| 1924 | costume jewellery collection applauded |
| 1925 | signature cardigan jacket |
| 1926 | introduces the little black dress and tweed suits inspired by the Duke of Westminster |
| 1939 | retired |
| 1954 | re-opened business |
| 1957 | introduced the quilted handbag |
| 1978 | introduced prêt-a-porter |
| 1983 | Karl Lagerfeld becomes Chanel designer |
| 1987 | first Chanel watch |
| 1993 | Chanel jewellery |
| 1999 | introduces Précision skincare range; a travel collection; licenses sunglasses and eyeglass frames |
| 2000 | unisex watch |
| 2002 | establishes Paraffection (group of specialist ateliers—ornamentation, feathers, embroidery, shoe maker, millinery) who work for Chanel) |
| 2003 | introduces Coco Mademoiselle range for younger market |
| 2006 | introduces The Luxury Line and the handbag with chain logo |

Her introduction of the little black dress in 1926 (promoted as a must-have in the fashionable woman's wardrobe) secured her place in the pantheon of Parisian designers. Her Chanel bag of quilted leather and its interlocking-*C* logo also became a staple Chanel product. Of all her garments, arguably it is the Chanel suit—a collarless, central-buttoning, straight-skirt affair originally in tweed and worn with a string of pearls—that has become her best-known legacy.

Chanel's ventures into perfume secured financial success for her name and the House of Chanel. Not only would her first perfume become one of the best-selling perfumes of all time, but it was also the first to be produced industrially using chemical substitutes rather than extracts from plants. First marketed in 1921, it was followed by other fragrances for women—and later men (see box 2.5). But Chanel No. 5 has remained the best-known Parisian perfume and the most recognized icon of the Chanel brand. Just as she recognized that new fragrances were necessary to keep the brand name popular, so too she recognized the value of using high-profile celebrities and models to promote her perfume, including Catherine Deneuve, Carole Bouquet, Suzy Parker, Stella Tenant, and Nicole Kidman.

**Box 2.5 Release of Chanel Perfumes**

| | |
|---|---|
| 1921 | Chanel No. 5 |
| 1922 | Chanel No. 22 |
| 1925 | Gardenia |
| 1926 | Bois des Iles |
| 1927 | Cuir de Russie |
| 1955 | Chanel Pour Monsieur |
| 1970 | Chanel No. 19 |
| 1974 | Cristalle |
| 1975 | Noir et Or |
| 1981 | Antaeus |
| 1984 | Coco |
| 1990 | Égoïste |
| 1996 | Allure |
| 1999 | Allure Homme |
| 2001 | Coco Mademoiselle |
| 2003 | Chance |
| 2005 | Allure Sensuelle |
| 2007 | 28 La Pausa |
| 2007 | 31 rue Cambon |
| 2007 | Bel Respiro |
| 2007 | Coromandel |
| 2007 | Eau de Cologne |
| 2007 | Chanel No. 18 |
| 2009 | Allure Homme Édition Blanche |

After her death, the Chanel brand lost its direction until the appointment of Karl Lagerfeld as designer in 1983. Unlikely as it seemed at the time, Lagerfeld had a knack for retaining enough classic elements of Chanel's moniker while taking design in a new direction and appealing to a new and younger clientele (Drake 2007). He has played with designs such as the Chanel suit by using new fabrics and patterns yet retaining the classic styling. In fact, no longer just worn by respectable high-profile women such as Jackie Kennedy and the Princess of Wales, the Chanel suit has become the preferred outfit for female celebrities who find themselves in court. Examples include models Jerry Hall and Naomi Campbell, Barbara Black (wife of media tycoon Conrad Black), and celebrity Paris Hilton. The choice of Chanel is a sign of preference for traditional haute couture, while the suit conveys that the wearer is well dressed and presented, classic yet stylish, adventurous yet demure, and just possibly apologetic.

Lagerfeld has shamelessly exploited the celebrity of supermodels, actors, and high-profile public figures to take the brand from the exclusivity of Parisian couture to global markets. This has fanned the desirability of the Chanel brand to such an extent that Chanel is one of the most copied brands in the now-huge fakes trade. While a genuine Chanel handbag may cost $1,500, a fake costs a mere $100 and exhibits almost as good craftsmanship. Designers are ambivalent about this trend because although they want to preserve copyright and ownership of trademark products and designs, the circulation of fakes popularizes the brand name and ironically spawns a new desire for the real thing.

**Lagerfeld.** Photo by FRANCOIS GUILLOT/AFP/Getty Images. 2008 AFP

According to Breward (2003: 42), "the history and myth of Chanel epitomize the limits and potential of modern couture as monstrous publicity machine." He concludes that her outstanding success was attributable to:

> her fundamental understanding of the value attached to celebrity in contemporary society, and the potential for applying the creative mystique of the couture designer to a much broader swathe of the fashion market. (Breward 2003: 47)

In this, Chanel demonstrates the factors that have shaped the development of Paris as the epicenter of the modern European-centered fashion system.

## CASE STUDY 7: Yves Saint Laurent as Style Muse

**YSL boutique**

> I had just blown out the candles of the cake for my ninth birthday when, with a second gulp of breath, I hurled my secret wish across a table surrounded by my loving relatives: "My name will be written in fiery letters on the Champs Elysées." (Yves Saint Laurent in the Metropolitan Museum of Art 1983: 15)

In 2008, French fashion designer Yves Saint Laurent died at the age of seventy-one. While some commentators remarked that this was a relatively young age to die, the surprise was that he lived so long. Behind the wealth and his fame as perhaps the most influential designer of the late twentieth century, Saint Laurent had a flawed and complex personality—chronically shy and repressed yet totally self-centered and egotistical. In an interview with Bianca Jagger, he was asked about the qualities he looked for in people, to which he replied:

> The qualities I see in people are what I perceive them to be. It is my vision of people that counts. It's all projection. If I am deceived it's my own doing. What interests me is my vision of others. (Quoted in Drake 2007: 141–42)

This view was confirmed by his business partner (and sometime lover), Pierre Bergé, who described him as "someone who can only live wrapped up in himself. The outside world does not interest him… . He could not care less." This combination of self-absorption, detachment, and personal vision was, on the one hand, the source of his immense creativity and ability to process trends in the world swirling about him and distill these into his fashion collections. On the other hand, it was the source of self-destructive behavior and mental instability that made him begin to withdraw from the outside world as early as 1972, when he was just thirty-six and his couture house was only ten years old. From then on, Saint Laurent's life and public image were deftly manipulated by Bergé and his retainers, who protected him when he was at his worst and propped him up for increasingly occasional public appearances.

This was a sad life for someone who had grown up in the French colonial town of Oran in Algeria, which at the time was, as Saint Laurent later said, "a glittering city in a patchwork of a thousand colours under the sedate sun of North Africa" (quoted in Metropolitan Museum of Art 1983: 15). A magnet for many cultures, Oran had a rich, lively, and colorful cosmopolitan and stylish lifestyle—at least for the expatriates, known as the *pieds-noirs,* a reference to their shiny black shoes. Born in 1936 before the horrors of World War II, and idolized by his family and reveling in this mesmeric tropical backdrop, Saint

Laurent showed a talent for drawing and making dolls' clothes as a child, which endeared him to his family but added to his ostracism at school, which "traumatized me for life" (quoted in Metropolitan Museum of Art 1983: 15). He was tall, skinny, bespectacled, and effeminate, qualities that did not sit well in macho culture.

Escaping as soon as he could to Paris in 1953 after winning a student fashion award (alongside Karl Lagerfeld—who became first a friend then a rival), he was confident that he would make it in the fashion capital and enrolled in the couture school of the Chambre Syndicale, where his talent already stood out. But he quickly became bored and quit, manifesting the first sign of the depression that was to plague him throughout his life. In 1955, he became an assistant in the house of Christian Dior—then the leading postwar Parisian couturier—where his legendary shyness and isolation set him apart yet hinted at his capacity to dominate through silence and passivity (Drake 2007: 14). His designs were already turning heads, and he quickly became assistant designer to Dior himself. On Dior's sudden death in 1957, though only twenty-one years old, Saint Laurent was chosen to be the Dior couturier.

With only nine weeks to design a collection, Saint Laurent returned to Oran—always his prime source of inspiration—and produced a flurry of sketches that were whittled down into the theme of the collection, the Trapèze dress. It was a sensation, and Saint Laurent was labeled *le nouvel enfant triste* (the new sad child) of the fashion world. Saint Laurent was launched, and a new silhouette overshadowed the much-touted Dior New Look. The world of couture was entering a new phase. For Saint Laurent, that was both a blessing and a curse. He later wrote of the

> anguish of not being up to the expectations of the critics, and, more important, not being equal to the task itself, not being able to create, waiting for three weeks out of four for the click that sets my fantasies in motion toward their appointment with the physical world. (Quoted in Metropolitan Museum of Art 1983: 15–16)

He gradually began to distance himself from fashion—the relentless pressure to "reinvent and reinvent"—saying he had "grown wary of fashion, more and more engrossed by style" (quoted in Metropolitan Museum of Art 1983: 17):

> Fashions pass quickly, and nothing is more pathetic than those puppets of fashion outrageously made up one day, pale the next, pleated or ironed stiff, libertine or ascetic. Playing with fashion is an art. The first rule is don't burn your own wings. (Quoted in Metropolitan Museum of Art 1983: 18)

The sureness of style was to become his leitmotif as he strove to combine "the essential nobility of a couturier's craft" of "dress[ing] women 'with the greatest perfection' " (quoted in Metropolitan Museum of Art 1983: 18) with the inspiration of the street, especially in his Rive Gauche prêt-à-porter collections designed for "interesting women who could not afford couture" (Metropolitan Museum of Art 1983: 20). He was the first to recognize that couture activities had to be subsidized by other activities, such as ready-to-wear collections. He identified his last Dior collection in 1960 as the first important definition of his style, inspired by the street but alienating "a lot of people sitting on the gilt chairs of a couture salon" (quoted in Metropolitan Museum of Art 1983: 20). This collection showed black "motorcycle jackets in alligator, mink coats with sweater sleeves, turtleneck collars under finely cut flannel suits" (quoted in Metropolitan Museum of Art 1983:20), themes that presaged the youth fashions of the 1960s.

While this moment catapulted his fashions into the stratosphere of elite couture, it simultaneously signaled strains in his personal life that would gradually overwhelm him. He was called up for military service—despite his obvious unsuitability—and, although discharged within weeks with severe mental illness, found that he had been replaced at Dior (by Marc Bohan). Successfully suing Dior, he used the settlement to establish the house of Yves Saint Laurent with Bergé as business manager. This proved to be a brilliant arrangement and the house went from strength to strength, with Yves' creativity at its peak and Bergé's financial talents finely honed.

Energized by youth culture, radical political unrest, the psychedelic drugs and counterculture of Marrakech, and free-love trends of the time, Yves Saint Laurent's fashions stole the headlines collection after collection, inspired by flea-market secondhand clothes, theatrical and ballet costumes, art styles (Mondrian, Picasso, and **pop art**), and naval dress and ethnic dress (African, Gypsy, Russian, Far Eastern). While experimenting with new themes, however, Saint Laurent retained an unparalleled grasp of classicism, cut, and finish. His collections could be dated, but the clothes themselves did not date.

He also revolutionized what women could wear, introducing Le Smoking (an evening jacket for women), elegant pantsuits for women, tuxedos, the **safari suit** as fashion—clothes that changed the way that women lived (Buxbaum 2004: 104). Ironically, though, Saint Laurent had an oft-repeated regret that he had not

> invented blue jeans: the most spectacular, the most practical, the most relaxed and nonchalant. They have expression, modesty, sex appeal, simplicity—all I hope for in my clothes. (Quoted in Metropolitan Museum of Art 1983: 23–24)

Saint Laurent also launched a perfume range, including Y (1963), Rive Gauche (1970), YSL pour Homme (1971), Kouros (1981), and Paris (1983). His nude appearance in the advertisement for his men's perfume sparked controversy but added to his fame, especially in America, always a strong advocate of his work and key source of inspiration for him. In 1983, the Metropolitan Museum of Art celebrated his career in "Yves Saint Laurent: 25 Years of Design," an exhibition that traveled to numerous countries and heralded a demand for fashion exhibitions globally.

In 1998, YSL stopped designing ready-to-wear, and the following year the house was sold to Gucci, who compensated Saint Laurent and Bergé but hired brash American Tom Ford as designer. This arrangement riled Saint Laurent, who retired in 2002, declaring: "In many ways I feel I that I have created the wardrobe of the contemporary woman and that I have participated in the transformation of my era" (quoted by Drake 2007: 366–67).

Saint Laurent's death signals, perhaps, the dawning of another age of fashion, namely of fast fashion and global reach. Designers come and go, and perhaps the age when a single name can dominate a generation of fashion has also passed.

## CASE STUDY 8: Daslu Luxury Retailing

While the epicenter of Eurocentric fashion may remain based in Europe and America, one enterprise shows that location can be transcended by a one-stop venue providing exposure to the major global luxury brands far from Paris. This is the Daslu phenomenon—a department store in São Paolo, Brazil, frequented by the well-heeled fashionistas of Rio de Janeiro, Salvador, Argentina, and Peru as well as rich visitors from elsewhere, such as supermodels and sports stars. In fact, it is now a major tourist attraction in São Paolo (Thomas 2007).

The store began in 1958 as a modest home shopping outlet. Brazilians are very fashion conscious, but at the time Brazil had a ban on imported goods and the aspiring fashionistas were frustrated by the lack of access to designer clothes. Two enterprising women, Lucia Piva de Albuquerque and Lourdes Aranha, began to buy high-fashion clothes in Rio and sell to friends in Lucia's home in São Paolo. Although this was initially an informal arrangement—a bit like Tupperware parties—demand quickly escalated. The house became known as Daslu (a contraction of the Portuguese for "In Lu's house") and gradually expanded into neighboring houses until it filled an entire block. Taken over by Lucia's daughter Eliana Tranchesi in 1983, the business began to stock Paris labels such as Claude Montana, Valentino, and Moschino before setting up its first in-store designer boutique, Chanel, in the mid-1990s. Success was immediate and other designer labels joined—Gucci, Prada, Zegna, and Dolce & Gabbana.

Daslu built up a client base of 70,000 clients, many of whom shop at least weekly—a phenomenal achievement in itself. When space ran out, Daslu relocated to a purpose-built Italian-style palace in 2005. With its cream marble floor and garden atrium, carpeted staircases, and an army of assistants, this is no ordinary department store. The store now stocks (through franchises) 110 international brand boutiques (including Louis Vuitton, Balenciaga, Jimmy Choo, Sergio Rossi, Chloé, Pucci, Yves Saint Laurent, the Gap, Banana Republic, Cartier, Giorgio Armani, and Manolo Blahnik) and ninety-three national brands that reflect the vibrant fashion culture of Brazil. It has also developed a house label, Daslu, which accounts for 60 percent of its sales and is also exported overseas.

**Daslu.** Photo: Elliot Carvalho. Elliot Carvalho

Described variously as a "temple of luxury," a "fashion designers' mecca," "an oasis of indulgence," and "Disneyland for the rich," Daslu is also a "shopping bunker." Disparities in wealth and the danger of carjacking on the streets mean that Daslu has been designed as a fortified enclave with secure underground parking and a rooftop helipad to secure the safety of its clients. There is no pedestrian access. (Approved) clients enter through security gates in vehicles or via helicopter.

Once inside, clients are allocated a personal assistant, a Dasluzette, who guides them through the labyrinth of boutiques, departments, restaurants, bars, and other facilities while they make their purchases. It is a world where the rich can spend hours in anonymity and security with others of their kind—a one-stop shop-and-play for the ultra elite.

Daslu has engineered a novel approach to luxury brands and retailing in this extravagant refuge. As in a department store, everything (including luxury cars, real estate, and beauty treatments) is under one roof. The emphasis is unashamedly on quality and elitism. Clients are pampered and closely monitored—unlike the anonymous designer brand boutiques that pride themselves on superciliousness and the ring of the cash register. While Daslu has encountered disputes with the Brazilian government over alleged tax evasion and social critics about the hedonistic conspicuous display of luxury amid grinding poverty of the surrounding favelas, Daslu has dazzled the luxury consumer. The development of luxury brand shopping malls globally suggests that the Daslu model is gaining favor in other safe ports of consumerism.

# chapter 3

# fashion cycles, symbols, and flows

**CHAPTER OUTLINE**



**WHAT DOES THIS CHAPTER COVER?**

This chapter introduces different approaches to understanding fashion, starting with three theories that see fashion as a cyclical process that repeats itself: the trickle-down theory, the collective behavior theory, and the six-stage general theory. The chapter then goes on to explore semiotic theories, which see fashion as symbolic systems of signs and codes. Following this, a number of interdisciplinary theories that have combined different disciplinary or analytic perspectives to explain the phenomenon of fashion are summarized. Finally, the chapter concludes by introducing the idea of fashion flows to illustrate how a fashion style becomes popularized and spreads from fashion centers to peripheral fashion hubs through a range of cultural practices and forms. Four case studies illustrate these arguments: the symbolic codes of men's ties, the global popularization of jeans, the eroticization of stiletto shoes, and the language of cosmetics and social identity.

## i. fashion as cycles and structures

One of the most difficult things to explain about fashion is how and why different styles become popular and then fall out of favor. In the introduction, we covered some examples of fashion theories that try to explain fashion as a form of communication and as a cultural practice and system. As we have seen, fashion theory explores a number of fashion's different roles: a symbol of essential humanness, a chronology of human development, an organic process of civility, descriptive shorthand for the features of a culture or subculture, and a cog in the wheel of social structure. In this sense, fashion needs to be seen as an organized set of codes, meanings, and practices that are organized into a complex system of social exchange.

Fashion systems consist of the combination of a number of elements:

- **Codified types of apparel**
- **Rules of wearing and combining garments**
- **Economic and symbolic exchange values**
- **Social meanings and statuses attached to apparel**
- **Codified modes of attaching identities to apparel**

So, how have fashion theorists made sense of this? Rather than surveying the myriad of theories here, we introduce the three most commonly cited fashion theories that have developed in the social sciences. These are:

- **The trickle-down theory associated with Thorstein Veblen (1899), Georg Simmel (1904), and Grant McCracken (1985)**
- **The collective behavior model of Herbert Blumer (1969)**
- **The six-stage general fashion theory of George Sproles (1985)**

Each of these theories explores fashion as part of a wider system in which cycles of fashion (how certain styles come around again and again) fit into the broader social structure and underpin the way in which individuals locate themselves as social beings within their cultural context. Common to the three theories is the investigation of how fashions move from the trendsetters to arbiters of fashion and then are taken up by wider sections of the population. Trickle-down theory explores how a style adopted by the elite is emulated by those who revere the style setters. The collective behavior model proposes that there is an unconscious consensus that emerges within a group to adopt a certain look, which is then adopted more generally, while the six-stage theory identifies a general theory of invention, popularization, obsolescence, and renewal that occurs on a cyclical basis.

### The Trickle-Down Theory Of Fashion

The trickle-down theory (box 3.1) emerged with debates about the nature of class society. Initially associated with the spread of fashion from royalty to the aristocracy and middle classes, trickle-down theory came to epitomize the development of capitalist society. Fashion became a mechanism to display class difference through the adoption of new styles of dress that differentiated the elite from the mass. However, as new styles were popularized and copied by the masses in a trickle-down process, the elite felt impelled to conjure up a new style that maintained their distinctiveness.

Whereas Veblen characterized this process in terms of the desire of the elite to look visibly different by way of extravagant purchases (conspicuous consumption), and to equally visibly reject outdated fashions in a display of conspicuous waste, Simmel was more concerned with the power of fashion to reconcile conflicting pressures on individuals. Fashion "allowed persons to express their individuality and afforded them the security of conformity with numerous similarly disposed peers" (Davis 1992: 111). Fashion, then, enabled people to visibly demarcate their social position and differentiate themselves from those

**Box 3.1 The Trickle-Down Theory of Fashion**

**Trickle Down**

Georg Simmel theorized that the elites set the fashions, which are copied by the lower classes or masses, producing a cycle of creation and innovation followed by imitation and modification. As a fashion ceases to be distinctive because of its dissemination to wider groups, the elite adopt new fashions in order to remain different. The cycle of fashion speeds up in periods of rapid social change as the elite seek to maintain their aloof status.

**Trickle Up, Bubble Up, or Street Style**

This theory reverses the trickle-down thesis and argues that more often, especially in recent decades, fashion impulses come from everyday, subcultural, or street influences and, once adopted by an influential set of fashion aspirants, get taken up by the fashion industry proper. While the street style embodied a badge of identity and difference, the designer version is oriented around stylishness and now-ness.

both above and below them in the social hierarchy. However,

> **just as soon as the lower classes begin to copy [upper class] style, thereby crossing the line of demarcation the upper classes have drawn and destroying the uniformity of their coherence, the upper classes turn away from this style and adopt a new one, which in its turn differentiates them from the masses; and thus the game goes merrily on. (Simmel 1904: 136)**

Not surprisingly, the trickle-down theory has proved very attractive to fashion commentators, partly because it accounts for the cyclical and relentless turn of the fashion wheel. However, critics argue that the theory is much too rooted in a notion of class differentiation, which is only one impulse toward fashionable behavior and cannot explain how the manifestation of class difference translates into the symbolic meaning of new fashions and styles to the individual (Davis 1992: 110–15).

Nor can it explain fashions that emerge from below and are adopted by the elite (the bubble-up or **trickle-up theory**—see Polhemus 2007: 327–31). In this reversal of the theory, it is argued that some fashions and styles originate among the non-elite or subcultures but are adopted by the elite. The case of blue jeans (explored in case study 10) is exemplary here. A garment marketed to miners and other blue-collar workers as durable and practical was adopted by rebel youths and popular musicians. In turn, jeans became the uniform of young people and gradually were adopted by older people too. Travel on any international airline, and you will see that jeans (of diverse kinds and brands) are ubiquitous—they have trickled up from the worker to the leisure traveler.

### The Collective Behavior Model of Fashion

In contrast to the top-down theory, Herbert Blumer argued that, rather than the elite setting fashion trends, fashion emerged from a collective desire to be "in fashion" through the articulation of a sense of taste at a given moment and endorsement of certain styles and looks over others. In this way, a fashion emerges from the collective unconscious of a culture rather than being imposed from above in a process of collective selection. Blumer (1968: 281) proposes that fashions are abandoned because they are overtaken by a new model of taste:

**The fashion mechanism appears not in response to a need of class differentiation and class emulation but in response to a wish to be in fashion, to be abreast of what has good standing, to express new tastes which are emerging in a changing world.**

According to Blumer (1968: 344), there are three features of fashion custom (see box 3.2).

While Blumer acknowledged the difficulty of explaining how this collective mood and sense of taste are actualized, his theory placed fashion in the hands of the masses rather than the elite as a visible reference to other changing dynamics of social life. It reconciled the fashion impulses of continual change, shifting cultural moods or zeitgeist, and the project of creating individual identity (see Kunz 1996: 319). However, while it may explain general popularization of fashion trends, Davis (1992: 120) emphasizes

**the failure of collective selection theory (along with trickle-down) to adequately consider the palpable influence of the elaborate institutional apparatus surrounding the propagation of fashion in the domain of dress.**

Nonetheless, it has continued to attract supporters, such as Grant McCracken (1988), who views fashion as a prefabricated set of codes rather than as a language. For McCracken, fashion is a shorthand way of signaling place and identity as well as performing social roles and interacting with the people around us. Clothes make up an outfit, which can be interpreted as reflecting a "social type" (e.g., role or occupation) or a certain look (e.g., avant-garde, leisurely, professional). While an onlooker takes in the individual garments that a person wears, it is their combination as a whole that is "read" and responded to. In this way, clothes come in prefabricated sets of meanings and messages that have been internalized by the wearer and onlooker alike (see image 4).

The uniforms of police are an example. The development of a police force went hand in hand with the development of an occupational uniform (adapted from military dress) that was designed to signify authority, discipline, status, and trustworthiness. The act of donning a police uniform conveys attributes to the wearer, who internalizes

**Box 3.2 The Collective Behavior Model of Fashion**

- Uniformity through consensus about a prevailing mode or trend and its connotations or associations with propriety (conformity to established standards of behavior or manners)
- An orderly and regulated way to monitor and mark the shifting underpinnings of social norms (e.g., from a religious basis to a civil one or from one aesthetic sensibility to another)
- The distillation or actualization of a common sensitivity and taste that sanctioned (endorsed and celebrated) new ways of acting and rejected (or ridiculed) ones that had become outmoded and old fashioned (thought of in this way, fashion operates as a conservative barometer of body-space relations within the social milieu that is shaped by changing cultural conventions)

those qualities. Although there are some variations, a police uniform is commonly thought of as blue with insignia of status and belonging, with a peaked cap, pleated shirt, dark navy military-style jacket, tailored trousers, and sensible shoes—and complemented by weapons of restraint and law enforcement. This has become the unconscious consensus about how the police should dress and what they should wear. Studies show that when police forces adopt more casual uniforms (perhaps khaki uniforms, like those of park rangers), the public loses respect for police, and the occupation in turn loses status.

This theory is useful as a broad-brush theory that can explain societal trends in fashion but is less useful for explaining why some fashions take off and others don't—or why some fashions are long lasting but others fizzle out as short-term fads.

### The Six-Stage General Fashion Theory

By contrast, a number of sociologists of fashion have adopted (and adapted) George Sproles's six-stage general fashion theory (see box 3.3), which accounts for the various points of the fashion system, including the development, popularization, decline, and replacement of a particular fashion or style.

Davis (1992: 123–58) collapses these stages into five stages: invention, introduction, fashion leadership, increasing social visibility, and waning. This dynamic model emphasizes that "fashion is an evolving process that involves sociological, economic and psychological factors," although it is also important to add ideological changes, especially "when the pendulum of change swings from on extreme to another, e.g. from asceticism to materialism," as happened when the Chinese Cultural Revolution gave way to policies of economic reform (see Kunz 1996: 320). Again, it is a broad theory that explains general trends and cycles of fashionability, but not deviations from fashion norms or new stylistic inventions that usher in a new fashion era or sensibility.

Yet even despite this century of the individual and conspicuous consumption, fashion has remained a sign of successive collective consensual designations of the zeitgeist, or spirit of the moment.

## ii. fashion symbols and codes

As we have seen, fashion is not just a covering for the body but a means of communicating about the body and can thus be considered a symbolic

**Box 3.3 George Sproles's Six-Stage Fashion Process Integrating Sociological, Economic, and Psychological Factors**

1. Invention of fashion through market or social norms
2. Endorsement and adoption by elites and celebrities
3. Diffusion of the fashion through the fashion conscious
4. Take-up of fashions by non-fashionable groups
5. Transformation of fashion from novelty to symbol of the times; simultaneous experimentation with new fashions
6. Obsolescence of existing style and start of new phase (Sproles 1985; see also Kunz 1996: 320)

Source: Sproles 1985.

system where clothes and the rules that govern how they can be worn can be seen as a type of language or set of signs. The theories discussed above have focused on theories that posit fashion as a system in relation to external factors such as class differentiation, economic development, psychological needs, or the civilizing process. We now turn to fashion theories that attempt to explain how fashion can be seen as an internal system of signs and symbols that create a (quasi) language.

To understand this, we need to apply semiotic and linguistic models to the elements of apparel and adornment and the codes and rules concerning them. To do this, we analyze not only the clothes themselves but how clothes relate to the body and how clothes enable or equip the body to perform as a social body through gesture and performance.

The theorist most strongly associated with this approach is Roland Barthes, who wrote the now-classic book *The Fashion System* (1984). Barthes was influenced by the theory of structuralism in postwar French anthropology and linguistics, which examined social phenomena as a set of interrelated components making up a complex whole. In the case of fashion, this meant examining the garments and elements of an outfit or a look that composed a vocabulary and a grammar (rather than reading off their external meanings).

Barthes' book has profoundly shaped recent fashion theory, although the book itself is often referred to rather than read since it is "monumental but indigestible" (Louis-Jean Calvet quoted by Stafford 2006: 119) or, as Stafford (2006: 120) says, "turgid, heavy, long, too methodological, even rebarbative [repellent]" (see also Carter 2003: 144).

Nonetheless, Barthes' book and his theory of the **semiology of fashion** have had a profound impact on the field. Fashion, he argues, is the product of the social relations and activities that are involved in putting an outfit together. Fashion is actualized through the way the garments are worn. Barthes makes a distinction between three kinds of garments—the real garment, the represented garment, and the used garment—corresponding to the processes of production, distribution, and consumption. According to Barthes,

**clothing seems to resemble a language in that it displays a synchronic density, but at the same time also has a diachronic dimension—a history—so that it (clothing) exhibits the dual aspects of system and process, structure and becoming. (Carter 2003: 155)**

To develop this analysis, Barthes drew on the discipline of semiotics. Semiology is the science of forms or signs, and in the case of fashion, the forms relate to the garments, details, accessories, and modes of wearing clothes. If we conceive of the elements as signs, we can see how they compose a language of clothes (or *langue*) and the clothed body of an individual constitutes a specific statement by way of the choice and arrangement of clothing (*parole*). To understand this, we need to break down the idea of a sign into two components: the signifier and the signified. The signifier is the physical referent, while the signified is the mental concept implied by the signifier.

A pair of sunglasses signifies protective eyewear; however, sunglasses worn by a known criminal convey a special type of meaning; that is, they evoke images of gangsters and gangland warfare. Sunglasses worn by a celebrity are typically very large and very dressy, indicating both top-of-the-range tastes (conspicuous consumption) and a desire for anonymity (invisibility in the

**Box 3.4 Terms Used in Semiology and Their Definitions**

| | |
|---|---|
| **Semiology of Fashion** | The meaning of the formal properties and signs of garments, decorations, and accessories and the rules of combining items of apparel |
| ***Langue*** | The formal or abstract language of clothes |
| **Parole** | The specific arrangement of clothing by a person |
| **Sign** | = the signifier + the signified<br>The signifier is the physical referent (e.g., a hat). The signified refers to the meanings and associations implied by the hat.<br>Examples include the following and their specific associated meanings.<br>• A baseball cap worn backwards by a hip-hop musician<br>• A bowler hat worn by a London banker<br>• A sombrero worn by a Mexican woman |
| **Syntagma** | The combination of garments that make up an outfit.<br>An example is a businessman's outfit of a Trilby hat; black, navy, or pinstripe business suit; white shirt; tie and tie pin; dark socks; and black lace-up polished shoes |
| **Paradigm** | Systems for differentiating the different components of each array<br>Examples include the paradigm of different types of hats—fedora, bowler, sun hat, sombrero, boater hat, baseball cap. |
| **Denotation** | The apparent or basic meaning of a garment<br>For example, a striped tie indicates formality, status, and possibly military service. A leather jacket indicates youth rebellion or a motorcycle rider. |
| **Connotation** | The symbolic embedded meanings of an item of apparel or how it is worn<br>Examples include the connotations (shared meanings) read into the following:<br>• A person wearing a hard hat<br>• A person wearing a high-profile soccer star jersey<br>• A high-profile female wearing a demure Chanel outfit for a court appearance<br>• A person in a khaki military-style shirt and **cargo pants**<br>• A person in houndstooth check black-and-white pants<br>• A woman in a long white gown and veil<br>• The peaked cap of a golfer |

everyday world). A pair of boots may signify hard-wearing footwear, but worn by a cowboy, they also indicate hard-living, adventurous, conservative masculinity. So we apparently instinctively read a contextual grammar into our clothing encounters.

This contextual reading is a code or set of shared rules that enables us to connect the signifier with the signified. Contextual codes might include primness, authority, formality, practicality, relaxation, and hostility. Some codes may be localized (e.g., a badge worn at school by a prefect), embedded in a subculture (e.g., kohl eye shadow worn by Goths), adopted as national dress (e.g., an Akubra bush hat, indicating a true-blue Aussie; see case study 26) or worn across the globe (e.g., the latest athletic shoes; see case study 25).

Thus we need to think of another level of signification: denotation and connotation. Denotation refers to the straightforward meanings that we attach to clothing. A man wearing trousers is simply read as wearing normative masculine dress. A woman in a pair of trousers might be interpreted very differently—especially in cultures where women do not or only rarely wear trousers. Moreover, a woman wearing trousers might invite a reading in terms of the features and symbolism of ladies' trousers (concerning the cut, length, details such as pockets or pleats, fabric, method of opening—fly or side zip—or width of cuffs) in a denotative way. A further level of reading identifies the type or style of trousers (jeans, dress pants,

**Doc Martens boots**

uniform trousers, leggings, track pants). A further layer of meaning concerns the overall outfit and the context in which it is worn or the wearer's way of life (e.g., that of a tomboy, of a female soldier, of an executive, of a female retiree).

In practice, it can be difficult to distinguish these layers of meaning and signification, but generally the last layer of interpreting the whole outfit is regarded as the connotation, or contextualized meaning and symbolism. These are culturally specific, so that the color white in Western culture symbolizes purity and being a bride, while white symbolizes aspects of death and mourning in other cultures. We internalize dominant fashion and dress codes in our milieu and make almost automatic readings and interpretations of events based on that knowledge. We might automatically take a female politician in a business suit seriously while dismissing one in a voile dress with a plunging neckline as frivolous. An immigrant wearing Western clothes might be more readily assimilated than one in customary dress. A little girl dressed in pink for a party is likely to be more readily accepted by all the other pink-dressed partygoers than a girl dressed in brown or puce.

One of the features of considering clothing as a signification system is that the allocation of meaning to a particular item or outfit is arbitrary, in the

**Goths.** Photo: Grant Mitchell. Creative Commons attribution 2.0

sense that it is a convention adopted and maintained within a particular cultural milieu—"for us, among us." Different cultures have different signifying systems. For example, black signifies death in Western culture, but not in all others. Skirts may indicate a liberated women to some, but an exhibitionist or seducer to others. Most Australian Aboriginal women still only wear skirts or dresses (except for those who have become successful in urban contexts). Women are advised to wear skirts for job interviews, and many professions (e.g., lawyers, politicians) and occupations (e.g., beauty industry, nursing) formally or informally prescribe (or prefer) skirts for female employees.

A further level of signification occurs in how we make sense of groups and sequences of signs. Signs that differentiate the array of garments that make up an outfit (e.g., top, bottom, footwear) are called syntagmas, while the differentiation of different components of each array (e.g., the types of possible tops—shirt, singlet, sweater, jacket) is called a paradigm. Of course, within a paradigm there are sub-paradigms (e.g., different types of jackets or belts). In interpreting a look, we simultaneously process the syntagmas (e.g., woman in shirt, skirt, stockings, and shoes) and then the paradigmatic particularities of the outfit (e.g., silk shirt with **cowl** neck, tailored skirt with knife pleats, thick black stockings, medium-heeled shoes) to gain an impression of both the type of outfit and the attributes of the wearer (e.g., female lawyer).

**Criminal clothing.** Photo: MagicTuscan. Creative Commons Attribution ShareAlike 3.0

The details of garments and outfits—for example, the type of color or cuffs, tailoring of jackets or pants, the type of buttons or braid decorating an outfit, or the choice of jewelry (pearls versus wide gold chain)—are often as important as the clothes themselves. Fabrics and patterns, such as black velvet, **houndstooth** check, denim, fur, brocade, and **Lycra,** also have specific connotations. Our systems of denotation and connotation collide in the act of interpreting an outfit or a look so that we strip away the knowledge that allows us to make connections and derive meanings. Instead, we naturalize our interpretation and connotation system. Our readings appear to be natural, and we sublimate our learned and structured building blocks of the significatory codes.

One way to unpick our symbolic fashion systems is to examine fashion writings since these both rely on naturalized significations and connotations and create new ones and remind us of other ones. So, an article about a designer's reworking of the little black dress both draws on shared denotations and connotations of this garment and suggests new elements or elaborations of the connotations (or embedded meanings and symbolism) of it and how it might be reinterpreted. Accordingly, the fashion system is at once established and dynamic, since it draws on what is naturalized but seeks to create new signifiers and signifieds in each new fashion phase.

This semiotic approach to fashion has the advantage of being able to analyze examples of fashion successes, phases, and trends and to make interpretations of particular garments, looks, and individual ways of composing a certain stylistic effect. Once regarded as a radical and controversial approach, semiotics or the language of clothes was the dominant fashion theory of the late twentieth century. Authors like Alison Lurie (1992) popularized this approach by proposing different symbolic codes that are employed in fashion to denote characteristics such as sex, status, subculture, and authority. Although there has been some debate as to whether there is a language of fashion, based on people's attempts to interpret photographs of subjects wearing a range of outfits, there is no doubt that there is a general literacy of fashion codes among fashion designers, fashion writers, fashion consumers, and media commentators.

## iii. interdisciplinary fashion theory

As noted in the introduction, the study of fashion and dress has been approached from a number of disciplinary frameworks (including anthropology, sociology, psychology, sexology, art history, and economics). Many of the earlier approaches used a general theory perspective. As illustrated in the previous section, semiotics and structuralism offer a more specific understanding of the meanings of particular fashions and modes of wearing fashion.

The impact of these approaches has been enormous and shaped late twentieth-century trends in cultural theory. Called postmodernism, contemporary theory has been more concerned with specific phenomena and its **deconstruction** in order to understand how cultural practices develop, circulate, and are maintained. This has resulted in a trend of interdisciplinary and cross-disciplinary approaches that draw on a number of aspects of a range of theories. Such developments have informed recent theorizations of the fashion phenomenon, which can be grouped as follows.

*Historical Approaches*

- Dress-and-textile history approaches to the study of dress and decoration focus on the formal properties and curatorial provenance of apparel as objects that typify a period or fashion era (e.g., Lou Taylor, Phillis and C. W. Cunnington).
- A social history approach locates clothing in its social context of economic, status, gender, ethnic, symbolic, and structural factors (e.g., Margaret Maynard, Christopher Breward).

*Consumer Culture Approaches*

- A material culture approach explores clothing as material objects that must be located in their cultural milieu and viewed as the building blocks of a specific cultural formation (e.g., Daniel Miller).
- Analysis of fashion using a history of consumption extends the material culture approach to explain the role of clothing in trade and the buying and selling of social status and identity (e.g., Susan Porter Benson, Grant McCracken).
- Marketing, management studies, advertising, and merchandizing studies consider fashion as an industry and commercial business.
- Industrial relations and political science focus on employment conditions of workers in the fashion industry and effects of outsourcing and subcontracting on the industry.

*Cultural Forces*

- A cultural history of fashion is an approach that is related is consumer culture history and that privileges cultural minutiae over institutional, political, economic, and "grand figure" accounts of cultural development (e.g., Daniel Roche, Liza Dalby).
- A sociology of culture theory is similar to cultural history but tends to divide the phenomenon under investigation into discrete aspects, such as language, identity, gender, status, sexuality, and system (e.g., Herbert Blumer, Mary Ellen Roach-Higgins, Joanne Eicher, Fred Davis, Diana Crane, Joanne Finkelstein).
- Diasporic and ethnic studies of fashion explore fashions that become a communicative strategy in order to situate diasporic communities and identities in the global village (e.g., Eicher and Roach).

*Communicative Relationships*

- The field of cultural and media studies treats culture as made up of discrete communicative components that interact to create cultural patterning that is distinctive to particular cultures (e.g., Jennifer Craik, Yuniya Kawamura, Roland Barthes, Malcolm Barnard).
- Subfields of cultural and media studies include textual analysis (e.g., Roland Barthes, Pierre Bourdieu, Patrizia Calefato), social marginalization, and subcultural analysis (e.g., Angela McRobbie, Dick Hebdige, Carol Tulloch, Ted Polhemus).
- Art history and visual culture studies of fashion treat apparel as aesthetic artifacts that are explored as the basis of cultural literacy and as tangible symbols of the essence of an aesthetic genre or

era (e.g., Valerie Steele, Rebecca Arnold, Beverly Lemire, Anne Hollander).

*Gender-Related and -Dependent Practices*

- Feminist approaches privilege the specific gendered implications of the manipulation of fashion systems to construct desired images of femininity (e.g., Elizabeth Wilson, Jane Gaines, Caroline Evans, Kathy Peiss).
- Psychoanalytic approaches explain fashion behavior in terms of unconscious sexual desires and erotic tendencies related to the formation of the ego and the id (e.g., Joanne Finkelstein, René König, J.C. Flügel).
- Masculinity and queer studies explore the particularities of men's relationship with fashion and the construction of masculinity and other sexualized identities (e.g., Christopher Breward, Farid Chenoune, Colin McDowell, Frank Mort, Shaun Cole).

Fashion is increasingly being studied from interdisciplinary approaches that combine two or more of the above approaches (Taylor 2002). For example, Christopher Breward (1998: 305) charts cultural studies as the defining framework for contemporary fashion theory. Cultural studies offers an interdisciplinary approach that adopts an engaged analysis that explores fashion-in-action, that is, how fashion enables the performance of the clothed body to produce a social self that occupies different roles in a person's cultural milieu. These can be summarized as four main variants of cultural studies that focus on different but related aspects of the fashion phenomenon:

- Textual analysis (semiotics and visual culture)
- Audience and consumption studies (ethnography, history, sociology)
- Ideology (hegemony, subcultures, pleasure)
- Pleasure and political identity (race, gender, sexuality) (Breward 1998: 305)

According to Breward (1998: 311), these interdisciplinary perspectives have converged in productive ways, enabling us "to understand cultural phenomena and social relationships that were not accessible through other disciplines, thus enriching our knowledge of an object category (fashion) that has clearly always played a central role in cultural/social processes."

## iv. fashion flows

So far in this chapter, we have introduced a range of different approaches to theorizing fashion and understanding fashion behavior. As we have seen, this entails understanding how fashion works or constitutes a system by examining the phenomenon internally and externally. Internal examination of fashion involves looking at clothing behavior as a system of selection, composition, and presentation where items of apparel and adornment constitute signs and symbols that are organized like a language. An external examination of fashion involves looking at fashion cycles, where a longitudinal perspective explores the rise and fall of certain styles of dress and decoration.

Fashion cycles are constructed and maintained by style trendsetters, who determine what counts as fashionable at any moment. The fashion elites may overlap with other social elites (the aristocracy, political leaders, and cultural arbiters) or be specific to the culture of style (fashion editors, popular culture celebrities, and cultural icons). Thus, the determination of who wears what relates to the establishment of codes of social status and maintenance of the position of social and cultural elites. The established argument has been that fashion involves a trickle-down phenomenon where the elite decide the latest fashions, and that these gradually percolate down to the middle and working classes in a process of diffusion.

Of course, once a particular fashion of the elite becomes popularized (for example, copied and sold by department stores and online), there is an impetus for the style setters to abandon that fashion and create a new look (obsolescence and reinvention). And so the fashion cycle is perpetuated. However, there is also evidence that fashion is as much a trickle-up phenomenon, particularly since popular culture and popular media enable the rapid proliferation of new ideas in dress and adornment.

This trickle-up process is often seen as originating in the twentieth century, but cultural histories are littered with examples where trickle-up fashion occurred prior to that time. Even Beau Brummell, the arbiter of the dandies' movement in the early nineteenth century, was a self-made court follower who in turn became the role model for the Prince of Wales and his entourage (see case study 5).

Popular theatrical figures, performers, entertainers, athletes, and socialites have also had a significant trickle-up influence on fashion throughout modernity. There is no doubt that the advent of mass media such as photography, film, popular music, video, and the Internet has created new means for the transmission of new trends and styles, which can be disseminated quickly and widely. Ironically signaled by the choice of blue jeans for James Dean and Marlon Brando in the films *Rebel without a Cause* (1955) and *The Wild One* (1954), respectively, the imprimatur of youth culture was confirmed as the new engine of fashion impulses. Popular musicians, fashion **models** and fashion photographers, Hollywood actors, and television stars joined the trendsetters' club. Subcultures that spun out of youth culture (such as mods, Goths, **Rastas**, **hippies,** rappers, disco devotees, and **ravers**) were quick to follow. The fashion industry has had to accommodate these external intrusions into its modus operandi.

Such changes complicate the way in which fashion operates as a system internally and externally. Design influences trickle both down and up. Celebrities, for example, at film openings and awards ceremonies and other events, are rated for their choice of designer outfit and how well (or not) it suits them. The reputation of a designer can be made or broken on such occasions. A successful gown can generate sales and copycat versions appear overnight and become available in clothing stores. This is an example of trickle-down fashion. However, fashion is also influenced by street fashions, subcultural fads, and the habits of popular culture role models, such as models, popular musicians, film and television actors, and athletes. Here a trickle-up phenomenon can be seen at work as a designer borrows an idea or motif and creates a high-fashion collection around it. The work of Vivienne Westwood is an example of this process (see case study 18).

So fashion flows have become more complex as fashion references have multiplied. Social status is also less important than before, as the celebrity machine can turn anyone into a star and role model to emulate. Changing gender roles and more accepting attitudes toward non-heterosexual

**James Dean.** Photo by John Kobal Foundation/Hulton Archive/Getty Images. 2005 Getty Images

proclivities have revolutionized the fashion system into competing and multifarious systems operating simultaneously. Moreover, place is not longer a constraining factor in fashion, as greater mobility and global marketing make fashion available everywhere, albeit with local interpretations or embellishments to create signs of distinctiveness. In this sense, fashion has become a highly diversified and interlocking set of systems pushed and pulled both by exclusivity and diffusion.

Whereas the modern fashion system (associated with the twentieth century) emanated from Europe and spread its tentacles to the periphery (America, Africa, Asia, and the Pacific), the contemporary fashion system can be depicted as a nodal system with fashion centers in different continents that span the places between and are mutually influential. No longer can the claim that Europe is the true center of fashion be sustained, as European fashion can be sourced in other fashion centers and it competes with other fashion systems. Nor, too, can some dress modes be excluded from the realm of fashion and cast as simply customary dress. Places such as India, Spain, and New Zealand have established vibrant fashion cultures that both rival and are interdependent with the dominant European fashion centers and brands. One of the key factors

**Marlon Brando.** Photo by Carl Van Vechten, Library of Congress, Prints and Photographs Division, Van Vechten Collection

in this shift has been the belated recognition of North America as a distinctive fashion subsystem and as a competitive creative generator of fashion trends (see Welters and Cunningham 2005). Thus, we can speak of fashion flows that simultaneously go up, down, across, and back again right across the globe.

## v. conclusion

In this chapter, we introduced dominant social science fashion theories that have explored fashion as cycles in a wider social structure and system. Newer semiotic and structuralist approaches to fashion that consider fashion as a symbolic communicative system constituting a language that makes up fashion codes were also discussed. The chapter then considered a range of recent interdisciplinary approaches to fashion that draw on diverse perspectives to explain the specific meanings of fashion apparel and behavior. Finally, the idea that fashion cycles need to be placed in a context that considers fashion flows from designers and manufacturers to promoters and consumers from a local to a global level was considered.

## CHAPTER SUMMARY

- Fashion systems are codified rules about garments, accessories, and combining these to create particular looks.
- There are three dominant social science theories:
    1. The trickle-down theory of fashion proposes that fashion innovations are spread from the elite to the non-elite by a process of emulation.
    2. The collective behavior model of fashion argues that fashion impulses are formed in the collective unconscious to become manifested as new trends and styles.
    3. The six-stage general theory of fashion locates different phases of the fashion system within a model of social invention, diffusion, popularization, obsolescence, and renewal.
- A semiotic theory of fashion explains fashion as a system of signs, symbols, and communicative meaning-making that sees items of apparel as a language with a grammar that is composed of symbolic codes.
- Key terms of a semiotic theory of fashion are *langue,* parole, sign, syntagm, paradigm, denotation, and connotation.
- Interdisciplinary approaches to understanding fashion include historical approaches, consumer culture approaches, cultural force theories, communicative relationships, and gender-related theories.
- Understanding internal and external fashion flows is central to the understanding of fashion cycles and systems.

## CASE STUDY 9: The Meaning of Men's Ties

**Necktie.** Photo: Shellaine Godbold

"A man and his tie are one and the same," claimed Beau Brummell. So what do ties signify—and what can we discern about different kinds of ties? How do we read the meaning of the choice of a necktie, **cravat,** or bow tie? What do striped ties convey? Who wears monochromatic ties (e.g., in red, blue, yellow, or lavender), and why? Who wears ties with colorful hibiscus flowers? Why does one man chose a tie with embroidered horseshoes, another a tie with polka dots, and another a tie featuring designer logos? Are ties with abstract Australian Aboriginal designs or Mondrian-like **geometric** patterns an artistic expression or a marker of cultural capital? Is the tie the only male garment that allows a man to express a softer expressive essence or harsh collective identity?

Our starting point is the assertion that the tie is an indelibly *masculine* form of dress (even though ties are sometimes worn by girls and women). It evolved as a significant marker of political elites and as the epitome of the cultural expression and symbols of taste of different regimes.

The tie has generally had an association with state leaders, their military entourages, and fellow travelers (family and relatives, household retainers, aristocrats, etc.). The earliest-known ties were those depicted on the life-sized Chinese terracotta-entombed army buried with the first emperor of Qin in 221 BC outside the ancient capital of China, Xi'an. Trajan's Column in Rome shows soldiers wearing neckties in a variety of styles. The bare neck was a sign of virility in ancient Rome.

In 1660 a group of mercenary Croatian soldiers recruited by France in the Thirty Years' War was distinctive for their neckwear, a string made of muslin or silk knotted around the neck to indicate their rank, the ends hanging loose on the chest and finished in a ribbon, tassel, or rosette. This item, called a *croatta*, became the cravat. So impressed was Louis XV with this neckwear that he created the post of cravat bearer. By this period, the cravat had become more elaborated into an embroidered napkin edged with lace that draped over the chest.

In the eighteenth century, the decline of aristocratic influence was reflected in changing fashions in neckwear, which were now established by the military, which preferred a black cravat, a fashion emulated by the rising bourgeoisie. The rising fortunes of the cravat were interrupted by the French Revolution, whose proponents favored a napkin-shaped cravat with flapping ends, while the counter-revolutionaries wore white cravats on waistcoats decorated with white fleur-de-lis. They also wore red ribbons around their necks. The fleur-de-lis and the ribbon were overt political symbols of aristocratic decadence and the guillotine, respectively.

In post-revolutionary France there was almost a mania for the cravat, which spread across the English Channel and was epitomized by Beau Brummell's elaboration of the cravat and his invention of his own knot. Nineteenth-century neckwear was very complex, with a multitude of rules concerning the many kinds of fabric, knots, and colors that could be used. In the mid-nineteenth century, however, the tie began to become more uniform in appearance and size. Thereafter, neckties came with a premade knot, until Edward VII invented the "free knot," which is still used today. A variant of this knot is the Windsor Knot, invented by Edward VIII before his abdication.

Twentieth-century ties were largely fads that only superficially altered the classic tie. Permitted changes in tie fashions included fads in fabric design (e.g., regimental stripes, plain, floral, or patterned). Ties can also vary in width and length. Despite this limited range of possibilities, ties have become a staple of most designers' collections and of licensing arrangements, as they offer an affordable trophy that signifies the qualities attributed to the designer and aspired to by the wearer of the tie.

From this history, it becomes clear that there is a clear symbolic register attached to the tie; it can be a sign of normative masculinity, authority and discipline, and sexual prowess and proclivities. For example, traditionally, so-called confirmed bachelors (code for homosexuals) and men of "artistic persuasion" wore bow ties or cravats rather than a tie, which connoted heterosexuality.

The choice of ties is related to occupation and lifestyle, so while former military men often wear regimental ties long after their demobilization, high-profile criminals are often seen in wide white ties over black shirts, mimicking Hollywood gangsters, while up-and-coming ebullient business men are stereotyped in bold, colorful, in-your-face designs. School ties are usually striped, reflecting their military origins. Contemporary politicians select a tie from a carefully devised wardrobe, matching colors with the colors associated with their parties. With academic gowns reserved for formal occasions, official ties—often bearing the crest of the university—have become a quasi uniform of university officials as well as the most common official gift for visiting dignitaries. (A scarf serves as the female equivalent.)

An underexplored element of the evolution of ties is the development of the horse-racing industry in modern Europe, when royalty and the aristocracy began to breed the new varieties of nimble and agile horses that had been brought from the East. Not only did these prove useful in military contexts, but they opened up a new leisure pursuit in the form of equestrian sports. Inevitably, this produced its own specialist clothing, in which ties became a shorthand symbol for the sport. Horse-related motifs, such as horseshoes, whips, riding caps, jockey colors, and club logos—as well as the horses themselves—became a replacement for the regimental symbol.

Freud regarded ties as a symbol of the phallus, and Flügel regarded all items of clothing as mechanisms for denoting sexuality. Joanne Finkelstein (1994: 220) suggests that the tie links the two symbols of male virility—namely, the male larynx and the male genitalia—thus turning a seemingly innocent and conventional habit of dress into a neon advertisement of male sexual prowess. In this sense the tie is the male equivalent of stiletto heels as the vestmental sign par excellence of sexuality, while for senior women executives, a scarf draped around the neck with ends hanging down the jacket has become a quasi tie indicating parity with powerful men.

Jennifer Craik and Sharon Peoples

## CASE STUDY 10: Jeans as Über Fashion

Jeans have become über fashion—a ubiquitous item of everyday dress as well as a global style icon. Jeans are the most common variety of long pants worn today. They are worn for everyday domestic activities, for leisure, for travel, to work, and even on social occasions. Jeans are the universal genre of pants that can be worn anywhere and found everywhere (Marsh and Trynka 2002; Sullivan 2006). They are distinctive because they seem, as Umberto Eco (2007: 315) has observed, to cling to the hips rather than "clutching the waist," almost like "a sheath around the lower half of [the] body," encasing the body and controlling its movements by imposing a "demeanor" on how the body performs and assumes exterior behavior. Eco (2007: 316) reflects:

> It's strange that the traditionally most informal and anti-etiquette garment should be the one that so strongly imposes an etiquette. As a rule I am boisterous, I sprawl in a chair, I slump wherever I please, with no claim to elegance: my blue jeans checked these actions, made me more polite and mature.

He concludes that jeans, "in imposing an exterior demeanor," are "semiotic devices, machines for communication," and influence "our view of the world in a demonstrably 'physical way' via the control of jeans on the groin" (Eco 2007: 317). So we have a paradox: jeans are, on the one hand, a ubiquitous form of clothing that is instantly recognizable and redolent with diverse meanings, and, on the other hand, a form of clothing that imposes itself on the body in quite rigid and distinctive ways. How has it come about that humanity in general has so readily come to accept the discipline imposed by a pair of blue jeans?

Jeans seem to have originated in seventeenth-century Europe as pantaloons, although they didn't really become popular until the nineteenth century. Gradually trousers evolved as preferred work clothes because of their practicality. Jeans had two precursors. One was the pants made of **denim,** a cotton-wool blend manufactured in Nîmes, in the south of France. The other was a fustian fabric of cotton, wool, and/or silk produced in Genoa, Italy, around the same time. The word *denim* came from Nîmes, while *jeans* came from Genoa. The popularity of these trousers for French rural workers and Genovese sailors was exported to England with the expansion of pan-European trade.

Jeans traveled with migrants from Europe to America with New World expansion, since their practicality and durability suited the frontier lifestyle. With the mid-nineteenth century and the expansion of the goldfields in California, jeans really came into their own. The figure usually credited with the rise of jeans is Levi Strauss (1829–1902), who started up a dry-goods supply house in the early 1850s. From the start, he retailed durable denim work pants. Around this time, the term *jeans* shifted from a descriptor for the fabric to the name of the style of pants: jeans were born!

The difficulty of finding sufficiently robust jeans able to withstand the rigors of manual labor and strong sales of the lines of jeans carried by Strauss prompted him to manufacture his own brand beginning in 1873. The special quality he introduced was copper rivets to reinforce the five pockets, a technique that was immediately adopted by the miners and soon copied by competitors. Levi Strauss's jeans were advertised for their suitability for "farmers, mechanics, miners and working men in general" (Sullivan 2006: 31).

Levi Strauss added the leather tag bearing his name to the rear in 1886, created the signature 501 style in 1890, and added the red tab to the seat in 1936. These have remained key brand symbols. Over time, overalls made of denim became popular for play clothes for children and for manual workers in the form of bib overalls.

Levi Strauss's main competitor, the Lee brand, was developed in the early 1900s, manufacturing work clothes and jeans under the slogan "The jeans that built America." This implied synchronicity between the jeans and American cultural history.

The next phase in the development of jeans was the association with the American cowboy culture of the Wild West from the late 1800s. This image was subsequently reinforced with the advent of Hollywood Westerns in the 1940s and 1950s. The jean-clad cowboy was an essential part of the plot. This was typified by actors John Wayne, Gene Autry, and Roy Rogers, whose macho images were reflected in the advertising campaigns of the third main jeans brand, Wrangler.

Although jeans were largely identified with male culture, women's involvement in the workforce in World War II saw the adoption of denim in their factory work clothes (such as overalls and jackets), as depicted in the film *Rosie the Riveter* (1944). Postwar, most respectable girls eschewed jeans for skirts or tailored trousers. Most American universities banned jeans on campus well into the 1960s and 1970s, especially for women.

Jeans, however, were adopted by artistic communities as a statement of an alternative lifestyle. Jack Kerouac's classic book *On the Road* (1957) was reportedly responsible for selling a million pairs of jeans. The 1950s ushered in the most major transformation, as Hollywood heroes and emerging cult figures in popular music such as Robert Mitchum, Marlon Brando, James Dean, and Elvis Presley chose jeans and denim jackets. The three films most commonly associated with establishing the iconic status of jeans in popular youth culture were *A Streetcar Named Desire* (1951), *The Wild One* (1953), and *Rebel without a Cause* (1955). As a result of these films, a quasi uniform of jeans, T-shirts, and leather jackets became irrevocably associated with youth rebellion.

Jeans dominated all genres of popular music and became the default uniforms of popular musicians from Gene Vincent, Eddie Cochran, Bob Dylan, rappers, and Bruce Springsteen to the Beatles (in their pre-**mod** Hamburg days), the Rolling Stones, mod bands, and Madonna. In fact, there are few pop music bands that have not ever adopted denim.

By the 1960s, jeans were de rigueur for young people, who were now relabeled teenagers. This created its own moral panic as respectable manufacturers of jeans resented the connotations of delinquency that denim had acquired. They were selling more but, in their eyes, to the wrong people. For example, between 1963 and 1966 Levi Strauss doubled its annual sales. When, they wondered, would the bubble burst?

Another phase of the story of jeans was in the making. Increasingly, consumers were looking for more stylish jeans than the standard workingman's jeans, and the main brands (Levi Strauss, Lee, Wrangler, and Cooper) were being pushed to develop new denim looks that complemented new youth fashions. Innovations included bell-bottom legs; a variety of colors instead of the traditional indigo; and stone-washed, faded, marbled, torn, distressed, patched, and embroidered jeans. Most key designers, including Paris couturiers, began to include jeans within their ranges, often as a keynote or best-selling line that cross-subsidized their more esoteric ranges.

Three hundred and fifty million pairs of jeans were sold in America in 1971, while Levi Strauss's sales increased tenfold between 1964 and 1975. But success also became a liability as numerous new brands flooded the market and new designers saw jeans as the entry-level passport to the industry. In the 1970s, pop culture's role models increasingly turned to other looks, such as the disco look. Unlike the jeans of workers, designer jeans were transient and fashions came and went. Increasingly, new gimmicks were used to maintain jeans sales, such as Calvin Klein's famous suggestive 1980

**Jeans.** Photo: judgmentalist. Creative commons attribution sharealike 2.0

advertising campaigns using Brooke Shields proclaiming that nothing could come between her and her Calvins.

Subcultures adopted specific variants of the jean to make sartorial statements in keeping with their values—such as the gay clone look epitomized by the band the Village People, the baggy jeans of **rap** dancers and the torn jeans of punks. In places where jeans were banned or unavailable, such as Eastern Europe, Africa, and China, jeans became a valuable **commodity** on the black market.

With all the new entrants into the jean market, the traditional brands came under threat and were forced to continually reinvent their classic designs alongside contemporary reworkings of the now-classic styles. Denim continues to play a major role in fashion collections, designer lines, and new twists by up-and-coming brands. The irony of contemporary jeans is that consumers can pay less than $50 for a basic brand or chain-store line, while others happily pay over $1,000 for an exclusive designer pair. The future of jeans seems secure in a global fashion village.

Jennifer Craik and Sharon Peoples

## CASE STUDY 11: Sexuality and Stilettos

There is no item of clothing in the modern fashion systems for men or women imbued with more sexuality than the stiletto high heeled shoe (Steele 1998, 2006). Women in stilettos are commonly portrayed as sexual predators and as a threat to the social order, but at the same time, women are encouraged to wear stilettos as a symbol of their essential **femininity** and fashionability. Despite these connotations, stilettos have been condemned as a health problem and medical issue responsible for fractured bones, deformation of the feet, and sprained ankles, and the source of back and muscular problems. Yet the image of stiletto heels remains one of glamour and the ultimate in femininity.

How is it that the stiletto has achieved this image? Designers of stilettos are usually men who extol the power of the stiletto to transform the body of the wearer and enhance her sexual appeal. Women themselves report feeling different and sexy in high heels. Actress Brit Ekland (1984: 142) wrote in her etiquette guide:

> If I come home alone my shoes are always the first thing to come off, but with a man around they are the last thing to go. Men love to see women in high heels.

Up until the late eighteenth century, men also wore heels. The most famous example of a man wearing heels was Louis XIV, who introduced shoes with red heels in 1673, ostensibly to confirm the elevation of his court. They were complemented by a red ribbon lacing the top of the shoe. These were immediately copied by his courtiers. Only the nobility were permitted to wear them, but only if they could demonstrate that they did not dirty their shoes! The custom was continued by French monarchs until the French Revolution. Red shoes were also worn by the Austrian chancellor Prince von Kaunitz, prince of Bavaria and Saxony, in the 1760s. They are depicted in portraits of the coronations of King George II, III, and IV in England. Today, red heels are still worn every year at the state opening of Parliament at Westminster and the Garter Ceremony at Windsor by the pages of Queen Elizabeth II of the United Kingdom (Mansel 2005: 15). Generally, however, the custom of high heels for men has disappeared, although occasionally a fashion for Cuban heels, platform shoes, and elevated shoes for short men reappears. And men rarely opt for red shoes!

Steele (1998: 60, 63) reports research that suggests that people categorize shoes into four types: feminine and sexy (high heels, strappy sandals, and high boots), masculine and practical (loafers, running shoes, and cowboy boots), asexual or dowdy (nurses shoes, pumps), and young and casual (thongs/flip-flops, clogs, and desert boots). This categorization shows a clear gender differentiation as well as a sexual-asexual distinction.

The history of the stiletto heel dates from the 1950s with the production of high heels that could be attached to a shoe (Wright 2007). The term *stiletto* seems to have come from its similarity to the thin and tapered stiletto knife, over time becoming the name for the ultra-high-heeled shoes. The shoe was the result of experimentation with the construction of high tapering heels, which required the insertion of a metal core in the wood to provide the necessary strength to carry the body. After research into the ergonomics of the stiletto heel in 1956, a model that incorporated a plastic heel with a metal core was patented as the solution.

By the late 1950s the stiletto shoe had become a symbol of young female identity, epitomizing the glamour associated with youth culture and emerging sexuality. The controversy associated with stilettos served only to enhance their appeal.

**Stiletto shoes.** Photo: Shellaine Godbold

For prepubescent girls, a modified high-heeled shoe with a one-inch heel called the kitten became the transitional shoe from childhood flats and asexuality to adult heels and femininity. Once a girl graduated to stilettos, overt sexuality was seen to follow. In films, **fashion photography,** and advertisements showing women removing stilettos symbolized an implied or imminent sexual encounter.

Although the stiletto became an essential piece of footwear, its popularity waxed and waned with the vagaries of fashion. The 1950s generation of stiletto wearers often experienced significant deformation of their toes and balls of the feet. Some women couldn't even put their heels on the ground when bare footed. Medical journals carried articles warning of the dangers of stilettos (in a repeat of the **corset** controversy of the late nineteenth century). This may have deterred (some of) their daughters from adopting the stiletto habit, for the heels of the late 1960s and 1970s tended to be lower and thicker. Fashionable role models preferred footwear more in keeping with the women's liberation movement, which associated stilettos with male oppression. Accompanying this was a "back to nature" movement associated with hippies and early environmentalists, who advocated sensible footwear.

During the 1980s, there were opposing trends regarding stilettos, with career women opting for a modified version of men's suits with sensible conservative footwear, while aggressive female entrepreneurs preferred to flaunt their ambitions with extremely high stilettos. In fashion photography, stilettos continue to be part of the lexicon of sexual libertarianism and transgression and to evoke the figure of the dominatrix. A memorable treatment of stilettos was Vivienne Westwood and Malcolm McLaren's collaboration on black stilettos with parallel rows of studs poking through the back of the shoe for the 1974–76 collection of erotic wear for their boutique, SEX, although perhaps the most famous photograph of ultra-high heels is that of Naomi Campbell's fall in Vivienne Westwood's blue "mock croc" ten-inch platform shoes during the parade of her Anglomania collection of 1993–94.

Of course, different colors convey different qualities—black for power, red for sexuality, and animal-patterned or skin stilettos for lust. The multiple signifiers of stilettos were referenced by artist Allen Jones in his 1972 table sculpture of a female mannequin on all fours dressed in a black latex hooded body suit, black stockings, and knee-length black leather stiletto boots underneath a glass top. The emergence of the fast-growing luxury and erotic lingerie sector accompanied this trend, which sparked controversy about soft-porn connotations, especially once lingerie became popularized as outerwear. This combination of stilettos and suggestive lingerie became the basis of the stage costumes of female performers such as Madonna, Kylie Minogue, the Spice Girls, Grace Jones, and Blondie.

The new female power called girl power was epitomized by Madonna because she "dressed like a sex object, but . . . suggested that the trappings of femininity could be used to make a sexual statement that was powerful rather than passive" (Stoller quoted by Semmelhack 2006: 242, 245). In this take on the stiletto, women could achieve equality and power through the conspicuous consumption of erotic symbols.

Although stilettos remained popular among some groups throughout the late twentieth century, the revival of stilettos as high fashion accompanied the new millennium and growth of shoe couturiers who established stores and franchises globally. Manolo Blahnik, Christian Louboutin, Jimmy Choo, and Dolce & Gabbana become the "It" designers of sexy shoes. Television programs such as *Sex in the City* celebrated extravagant expenditure on stilettos while ridiculing cautious financial planning. The cosmopolitan young female consumers were reveling in short-term hedonistic pleasures afforded by a credit card in the now almost ubiquitous designer boutiques offering a symbol of glamour at a "just affordable" price.

The contradiction between the valorization of high heels as the ultimate fashion statement and their use as an essential prop of prostitution, pornography, and sadomasochistic activities continues to exist without concern.

Jennifer Craik and Sharon Peoples

## CASE STUDY 12: The Magic of Cosmetics

Cosmetics are now taken for granted in contemporary Western culture as a way to present oneself in public or make a social body. But is that all they are? Cosmetics spin in and out of the orbits of sex, love, and culture. Above all, cosmetics establish identity, both social and sexual.

The twentieth-century emphasis on skin, eyes, and mouth in cosmetic practices illustrates the paradoxical resonances of cosmetics. Makeup and seduction are inextricably linked, and facial features are symbols of sexuality. Different cosmetic practices convey different aspects of bodily performance and sexual references, whether it is the blankness of a Kabuki white face; the black-eyed menace of Goths; the overtly sexualized red lips of a Hollywood siren; the stylized, color-coded masquerade of Chinese opera performers; or the exaggerated makeup of a female impersonator.

Cosmetics can be broadly defined as techniques and materials used to enhance a person's appearance according to the cultural norms of the social group to which she or he belongs or with which she or he identifies. These techniques may be temporary or permanent ways of decorating or manipulating the body. Wax (1957) lists a comprehensive range of manipulations: "Bathing, anointing, and colouring the skin; cutting, shaving, plucking, braiding, waving, and setting the hair; deodorising and scenting the body; colouring or marking the lips, hands, nails, eyes, face, or other exposed regions; cleansing, coloring, and filing the teeth; shaping, restraining, and concealing various parts of the body; and so on."

Modern cosmetic practices include embellishing the bodily surface—for example, face makeup, henna (**mehndi**) decoration of the feet and hands, perfume, tattoos—and adding objects to the body (e.g., false eyelashes, body piercings). Cosmetic surgery, from scarification to rhinoplasty, is also a permanent form of bodily augmentation and reinvention.

People are often heard saying, "I must put on my face," and "I feel naked without makeup." The act of putting on cosmetics becomes a habit or routine, almost an unconscious part of getting dressed. The body is like a canvas on which the artist paints a pattern that creates a desired image of the self. Cosmetics are both a mask (to disguise oneself or create a new identity) and a mirror (to reflect a desired identity). We call this "cosmetic behavior."

Although the use of cosmetics is thought of as a modern practice, ethnographic evidence suggests that forms of bodily decoration and manipulation have always been part of human culture, from Cro-Magnon uses of ocher, ancient Egyptian uses of kohl, and the Chinese and Japanese preference for whitening the face to African body painting and Asian tattooing. While Western culture usually makes blended products from artificial ingredients, other cultures use natural ingredients. The myrrh (camphor) and frankincense (conifer) carried by the biblical three wise men are such an example. All kinds of natural ingredients can be used to make cosmetics: floral and vegetable extracts (e.g., patchouli, jasmine, belladonna), animal products (e.g., lanolin, bones, egg whites), minerals, and natural substances (ocher, charcoal, arsenic). Some ingredients—for example, lead—have been used in the pursuit of beauty despite serious physical side effects.

Cosmetic practices are as variable as the cultures in which they are practiced, but within a culture, such practices are regarded as natural. They are internalized and repeated as an essential component of belonging to that culture or subculture. Such historical and cross-cultural uses and meanings of cosmetics have shaped the ways in which modern cosmetics are understood and interpreted today.

If cosmetic practices are relative and context specific, they are linked also to the previous uses that they reject and deliberately differ from as "not statements." Cosmetics are used as means of

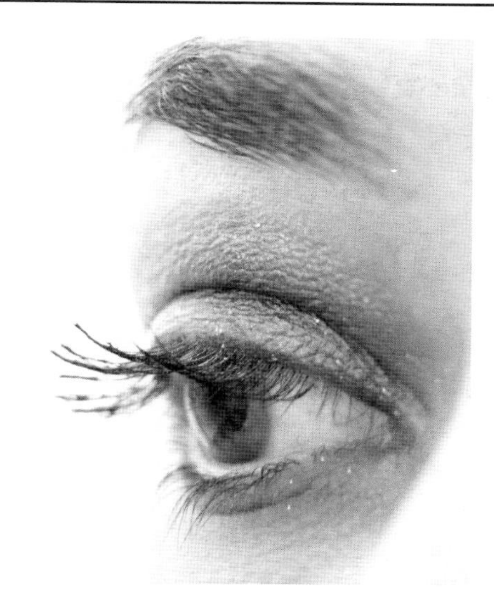

**Eye makeup.** Photo: Esra

identifying with or visually rejecting particular social roles in that they draw on sets of opposites: casualness versus control, exposure versus concealment, plasticity versus fixity. Different ways of scenting the body illustrate the infinite play of cosmetic between these polarities.

Deodorants may be used to conceal natural body odors and control bodily excretions (e.g., perspiration, mucous), while scents may be used to expose the "desirable" body or cover unpleasant smells (e.g., body odor, halitosis, infected flesh). The makers of deodorants often use sports stars to promote their products since the athletic performance of the star can be metonymically linked to both the performance of the product (in stopping perspiration) and the wearer of the product (in enhancing social performance).

Cosmetic manufacturers also segment the market; for example, scents come in different forms—concentrates, aerosols, and eaux de toilette—indicating different strengths of scent and associated cultural connotations, and priced according to their social value. Like deodorants, perfumes use advertisements to project the attributes of the perfume onto the attributes of the intended consumer. By imbuing perfume with the magical power to transform the wearer, consumers purchase the desire to transcend the everyday and assume another perhaps more glamorous, successful, or seductive identity. An effective advertising technique is the use of a popular role model as the face of the brand or product.

At one level, we can think of cosmetics as just another kind of clothing or dress that completes the social body to equip it for the diverse roles it performs. We "wear" our bodies through the ways we decorate, shape, and wrap the body. How we do this is dependent on knowledge of detailed rules of cosmetic and clothing practices, what to use, and how to perform in the made-up body.

Throughout history, references to cosmetics have more often than not been negative; that is, cosmetics have been perceived as a moral problem that poses a threat, incites inappropriate passions, conceals the "real" person, or creates an undesirable persona. Very often, this moral tirade has been an attack on "unruly" women along with the implication of sexual impropriety. Cosmetics, it is argued, cause women to concentrate on the body instead of the spirit, stray from the path of virtue, and deceive people by appearing unnaturally attractive, and they drive the quest for conformity by making all women look the same.

These are the negative connotations of the polarized characteristics of cosmetics: tools for inciting sexual desire and perverting sanctioned social conduct. Indicatively, the word *cosmetic* is also used to mean "false" or "superficial." Accordingly, the use of cosmetics is often denounced as immoral.

Although there is enormous variation in how cosmetics are used and perceived, underlying the discussion of cosmetics in contemporary society is a critical undercurrent that associates cosmetics with undesirable traits: sexual desire, heterosexual norms, sexual transgression, and social disorder—characteristics that usually invoke female sexuality. Terms such as *vamp, painted woman,* and *siren* all describe a sexually provocative woman who displays her sexuality through her body.

Yet these pejorative ideas exist alongside the positive image of cosmetics as the means of perfecting the ideal social self. So, it is the exaggerated use of cosmetics and ideals of beauty (e.g., peroxided hair, lipstick, heavy eye makeup) that are appropriated in non-normative contexts. Parodies of cosmetics lie at the heart of drag shows, vaudeville, cross-dressing, and many subcultures (e.g., hippies, punks, Goths, **new romantics,** Japanese fashions such as ganguro).

There is an intractable clash between good and evil. Ambivalent resonances of cosmetics can be found throughout history in religious tracts, philosophical writings, moral codes, fiction, poetry, and theatrical traditions (from burlesque to Shakespeare). Renaissance dramatists, for example, used face painting and cosmetics to indicate social, political, and sexual corruption, especially sexual sin, unnatural behavior, immoral manners, and the foolishness of disguise. A catalog of makeup routines was used to portray distinct character traits of actors and roles in a way similar to that used in Chinese opera and Japanese Noh theater. This tradition of seeing cosmetics, and especially face color, in moral terms also invoked racial stereotypes. Conventions about desirable and undesirable traits and makeup routines coincide with established racial hierarchies. Common colors of cosmetics (red, black, and white) signified specific attributes as visual shorthand of personality, sexuality, and role. These symbolic markers persisted in the twentieth century and shaped contemporary understandings of cosmetics.

For example, *A Book of Make-Up,* published in 1930 as a manual for stage and film actors, detailed cosmetic techniques to portray male and female characters by different ways of contouring the face, highlighting and shaping the lips, and embellishing the eyes to create particular character types. Instructions to create racial and ethnic types were also given. So the link between cosmetics and character, sensuality, and race/ethnicity was clearly established in cosmetic routines. The American media consistently reports that African American women, as well as those of Asian and Mexican descent, believe that wearing makeup is essential for enhancing their professional status by either concealing or highlighting racial or ethnic features.

The ambivalence toward cosmetics carried through to the twentieth and twenty-first centuries. Whereas preindustrial societies had a normative relationship with cosmetics and body decoration, European societies have had a love-hate relationship with cosmetics that has oscillated from one extreme to another. This ambivalence was bound up with the culture of European courts, which instilled a hierarchy of cosmetic practices among elite and non-elite groups in society. Moral attributes (positive and negative) were associated with cosmetic practices until the nineteenth century. The use of skin care preparations and face powder became widespread and crossed classes; however, the use of visible makeup was confined to theatrical uses and connoted ladies of "ill repute."

By the late nineteenth century, the use of cosmetics was more accepted, and a cottage industry developed. Pale skin was a sign of gentility and status, so products that whitened the skin were especially popular, though discreetly used. There were also successful cosmetic firms offering products for black women, such as Madam C. J. Walker and Annie Turnbo Malone.

This tolerance of subdued cosmetic usage was about to change due to a number of social upheavals: the greater involvement of women in public life, especially in paid work; the development of consumer culture and the increased buying power of women; a fascination with Eastern exoticism; the development of fashion photography and movies; the Hollywood star system and use of star images to promote new cosmetic products and companies; and the development of artificial ingredients to mass-produce cosmetics. No longer were pioneer women mixing potions at home. Women's niche businesses quickly were transformed into major companies complemented by aggressive marketing and retailing. Successful products became brand leaders, and some companies—such as Helena Rubinstein, Elizabeth Arden, and Estée Lauder—became multinationals marketed globally. Sales of hundreds of thousands of dollars in the 1910s multiplied to hundreds of millions in the 1920s.

The advent of Hollywood was particularly important to the manufacture and marketing of cosmetics. Max Factor, an immigrant wig maker and former cosmetics advisor to the Russian court, was an especially important figure, using his knowledge of theatrical makeup to overcome the extremes of light and dark produced by early color film stock. Not only was he a brilliant wig maker, but in 1938 he revolutionized filming by inventing water-soluble pancake that would not cake or crack under studio lights and lip gloss to create a lasting moist look. Later he diversified into other products (lipsticks, eye shadow, mascara, eye pencils, and false eyelashes as well as skin care products) marketed to ordinary women, allowing them to acquire a touch of Hollywood glamour without sacrificing their morals.

This transformation of the production and consumption of cosmetics coincided with major changes in women's lives. The 1920s were particularly important. More women than ever were employed, which meant they had disposable income to make discretionary purchases. The consumer revolution was underway and cosmetics were one of the early products heavily promoted in magazines, film, department stores, and fashion photography. Cosmetics became associated with women's new freedom, independence, individuality, and sense of sexuality.

Throughout the 1930s, the mass marketing of cosmetics reached new heights. Women could choose from 3,000 different face powders and hundreds of rouges and lipsticks. Cosmetics became big business and, with that, became a normal part of everyday life and an essential part of femininity.

The postwar period saw the consolidation of the cosmetics industry with new entrants such as Revlon and increasingly aggressive marketing. Cosmetics were a low-cost, high-profit industry. As little as eight cents covered the cost of ingredients, while marketing accounted for twenty-five cents. Known brands inflated prices, with profit margins up to 900 percent. For department stores, cosmetics were especially profitable, with ground-floor positioning attracting customers and acting as a "traffic generator."

In the search for new consumers, advertising and new products in the 1950s and 1960s were directed toward the emergent youth or teenage market, and products promoted as a means to escape the everyday and traditional female roles and transform oneself into a thoroughly liberated participant in modernity and consumerism. Names of products such as perfumes (see chapter 4) reflected the ambiguous messages and attributes being conveyed by cosmetics: sexuality (Passion, Obsession, Provocative Woman), exoticism (Shalimar, Xanadu), magic (Pure Poison, Hypnôse); rebelliousness (Shocking, Uninhibited), transgression (Tabu, Opium), youthfulness (Charlie, Youth Dew), status (Top Brass, Boss in Motion), science (Chanel No. 5), and romance (True Love, Eternity). It seems that a mix of motives underpins the desire for modern cosmetics and their marketability. As Brain (1979: 137) noted: "Make-up is 'man-proof' and marketed under such names as *Sin* and *Scandal*. However, it is obvious that cosmetics need not express a blatant sexuality to be sold. Youthfulness and social approval are important, especially for older women."

Throughout the 1970s and 1980s, as popular culture came to dominate public debate, new social movements, subcultures, and ethnic groups created new subsectors of consumerism and new ideals of beauty, social mores, and sexual codes. The "natural" look was popularized, and makeup developed to enhance an ostensibly natural beauty. Meanwhile, the black power movement in America in the 1960s led to a "Black Is Beautiful" mantra and growth of cosmetic products specifically for nonwhite markets.

Responding to these trends, new cosmetic market segments catering to men, various ethnic groups, gays, and lesbians emerged in the late millennium. The emergence of gay pride movements and explosion of Mardi Gras celebrations internationally fanned the growth of specialist cosmetics providers and products for non-heterosexual markets. This was ironic, since non-heterosexuals had always been prominent in the cosmetics arena in beauty salons (e.g., Elizabeth Arden), in the theater (e.g., Noël Coward, Jean Cocteau), as fashion photographers (e.g., Cecil Beaton, George Hoyningen-Huene, Horst P. Horst), and as fashion designers (e.g., Christian Dior, Cristóbal Balenciaga, Yves Saint Laurent, Roy Halston, and Rudi Gernreich). Moreover, cosmetics were a key part of the performance of non-heterosexual identities (e.g., drag shows and female impersonators). Making up social identities went hand in hand with reconstructing sexual identities.

The role of cosmetics as a **body technique** for constructing particular desired attributes and traits became more potent than ever. Alongside Hollywood glamour, popular music and street fashion increasingly set the desired role models to emulate. **Anti-establishment** designers such as mod-inspired Mary Quant developed a cosmetics range to complement her clothes and models, because available products did not suit the New Look of Swinging London. Sixties models such as Twiggy, with her boyish bobbed hair, heavy eyeliner and long false eyelashes, cupid lips, and **mini** shifts, epitomized the new waiflike look. It was in stark contrast to both the coiffured, understated elegance of previous generations and the brash, glittering icons of Hollywood.

Popular musicians, models, and television stars had become the new trendsetters, which was partly reflected in the use of celebrities to promote brands. Subcultures and social groups such as hippies, Goths, mods, punks, **glam** rockers, new romantics, grungers, rappers, sports fans, and cheerleaders each created specific looks to match their mood. Cosmetics were a significant tool in the creation of subcultural style.

At the same time, the emphasis on enhancing the face had been shifting from surface cosmetics to skin care products (moisturizers, cleansers, exfoliants) designed to improve the canvas upon which the look was created. Competition between brands and product lines has become ever fiercer, especially with the globalization of the cosmetics industry and the entry of new players into the industry, especially fashion designers diversifying into cosmetic lines. Celebrities also got into the act with their own cosmetic lines and perfumes (e.g., Elizabeth Taylor, David and Victoria Beckham, Britney Spears, and Paris Hilton perfumes). Makeup artists such as Kevin Aucoin have created new cosmetic regimes and in the process become gay icons and role models. All this frenzied activity within the cosmetic industry and new market subsectors creating cut-throat competition between brands and their distributors has become the norm.

The public visibility of popular celebrities reached new heights in the 1990s and 2000s, with saturation promotion of cosmetic products through celebrities accompanied by a vast media industry of cross-promotion of stars, lifestyles, celebrity glamour, and consumer culture. Botox, collagen injections, laser treatments, and similar products called "cosmeceuticals" offer skin rejuvenation without surgery and have proved extremely popular with celebrity devotees and rich clientele.

Cosmetics remain a topic mired in political controversy concerning morality, religious beliefs, feminism, non-normative sexualities, environmentalism, and physical side effects. Behind the look run strong currents of debate and ambivalence surrounding the sensual, sexual, and moral innuendoes behind the act of putting on one's face.

# chapter 4

## fashion, body techniques, and identity

**CHAPTER OUTLINE**



**WHAT DOES THIS CHAPTER COVER?**

This chapter explores the relationship between fashion and identity. The way in which the choice of clothes contributes to the construction of a specific identity is perhaps the main function of fashion. Explanations like modesty, protection, and procreation come as a poor second. But how does this occur? In this chapter, we treat the body as akin to a machine or a technology, in that the ways it is trained, performed, and perceived combine to produce a social body that is regarded as unique—as a person with a specific personality and sense of self. One of the central attributes of a person is gender, and the chapter discusses the construction of femininity and masculinity through fashion and key issues (such as body modification) associated with the performance of a gendered identity. Finally, the chapter looks at the role of uniforms in framing or fashioning the body in socially legible ways that are alluded to in fashion design and everyday dress codes.

The case studies illustrate the arguments and themes of this chapter. They examine the subcultural fashions displayed in Harajuku in Tokyo, the specific training of new female royals to acquire techniques of being royal, how the phenomenon of the metrosexual man has challenged conventional techniques of masculinity, and the significance of the cult of thinness on codes of femininity and fashionable silhouettes.

## i. fashion as a body technique

What does it mean to talk of the body as a technology—or as a technical device? Different cultures think of the norms of their body cultures in quite distinctive ways but are often oblivious to the arbitrariness of these codes. An anthropologist who analyzed cross-cultural forms of body decoration observed that

**early [European] travelers and missionaries, blissfully blind to their own powdered wigs and tight laces, considered all other body techniques signs of barbary and savagery. (Brain 1979: 9)**

Very often, we think of the clothed body as a natural form simply dressed up for a specific occasion. However, the body—although composed of natural parts—is never natural but is always produced by how it is clothed. Think of a newborn baby. Although born naked, a baby is immediately wrapped in clothing or fabric—perhaps having been washed first. Already, the natural body is transformed into a social body by the type of clothes or fabrics and post-natal rituals prescribed by cultural mores. As a baby grows into a toddler, clothing rituals are elaborated. Slowly, a child starts to put on her or his own clothes. Over time, the body learns techniques for how to perform as a trained social body. The body, then, is a technical device that is the outcome of how it has learned to perform. In sum, it is the repository of a constellation of body techniques.

What are body techniques? Using an ethnographic approach following Mauss (1973, 1985) and Bourdieu (1986), this chapter argues that dress and decoration of the body are specialized techniques of display and comportment rather than mere reflections of general and impersonal social forces (Craik 1994). Accordingly, how we dress is a body technique constructed by our clothes, body decoration, language, gestures, and physical comportment (Featherstone 1991; Noyes and Bendix 1998). So body techniques are ways in which the body performs in terms of rules that both construct and constrain its behavior. From the earliest age, our bodies are trained in appropriate ways of behavior in the context in which we live.

This is achieved in a number of ways, including "prestigious imitation"—that is, copying those whom we admire and wish to emulate (e.g., a boy copying how his dad saws wood or digs in the garden, or a girl copying how her mom irons or puts makeup on), and correction or punishment for transgressions (think of how often young children are told: "Don't do that," "Stop it," and "No," and of the more formal modes of correction and punishment used at school). As we grow, we move our bodies in ways learned from training, for example, as when we learn to swim or play a musical instrument. So how we behave is neither natural nor inevitable. Body techniques are the product of specific discourses interacting on different levels of power and knowledge and in different realms, such as social, political, aesthetic, and psychological forms of knowledge. In the same way, we learn how to dress ourselves, what to wear for certain occasions, and how to look after our bodies and groom ourselves from how those around us behave and instruct us.

In short, the body is produced as a social and socialized device and is equipped with technical attributes and mechanisms. Marcel Mauss analyzed this social production of the body through a triple viewpoint, namely the conjunction—or simultaneous fusing—of three modalities of training:

physiological (physical performance), psychological (internalized norms and habits), and sociological (making sense of roles consensually). These training modalities are embedded in wider structural frameworks of power that are manifested in wider contexts such as race, ethnicity, gender, age, and disability. Hence the body is not just technical and social but the embodiment of political arrangements. For example, class position dictates the kinds of trainings, orientations, and performances acquired by an individual. In the same way, techniques are gendered and boys and girls learn specific gestures as well as different clothing regimes.

Thus we can see that there are different ways in which we perform and project our bodies across different places and times; that is to say, body techniques are historically variable (different body ideals proliferate at different historical periods) yet bodies are also culturally specific (that is, framed by our subcultural or broader cultural group—for example, Goth culture, Amish culture, ethnic identities, religious communities—and specifically by the role or roles that we are performing—for example, as a student, policeman, swimmer, father, shopper). In other words, body techniques are highly structured and context dependant. We prepare our bodies for public display and present ourselves in quite deliberate ways. In this sense, our body image forms the basis of our idea of self and identity as an individual, shaped both by our bodily performance and by how others perceive us. Bodies are "worn" through technologies of movement, restraint, precise gesturing, and continual adjustments according to the dynamics of the immediate space occupied by the body.

The performing body refers not only to the body itself but to the space or context in which it performs. Mauss calls this performing aura the **habitus** of the body. Habitus refers to the specialized techniques and internalized knowledge that equip people to negotiate different "departments of existence"—that is, the different spaces they occupy and roles they perform. Like body techniques, habitus is the product of explicit training, imitation, and absorption. Techniques are performed and habituses are occupied as if second nature or unremarkable. That is to say, body techniques are internalized or naturalized to the point where we do not perceive them as learned or arbitrary but simply *the* way to do something specific to the social milieu.

When the body performs a certain role, it brings together specific performances, spatial relationships, specialized knowledge, learned techniques, and the ability to tie these together into a specific performance. These become routine or habitual—just "normal" or taken for granted. Throughout our lives, we adopt specific performances for different roles, occasions, and spaces, sometimes sequentially (from our status in child care, kindergarten, school, college, the workplace, retirement community) or simultaneously (as a college student, part-time employee, son or daughter, competitive athlete, **hip-hop** fan, etc.). While there may be overlap between some roles, other roles may require types of performativity that clash with others.

The combination of roles and performances compose our sense of self or individuality. In contemporary Western culture, the body is the locus or site of individual identity. We take the notion of the individual as a given—as natural and normal—but in fact individuality is a product of our historical moment and our dominant cultural mores. Individuality, then, is a specific contingent social construction unique to our culture and our repository of social performances. Whereas at other times in history and in other cultures, identity has been and is composed by family membership, regional belonging, class position, or gendered performances, in our culture, we struggle to project a unique sense of self. In this we have greater freedom of choice to fashion our identity, and our identity becomes a social entity in itself. Maintaining individuality requires constant maintenance and fashioning. Our culture is flooded with self-help manuals intended to assist us that provide step-by-step guidance to produce a particular individuality that approximates the desired ideal of perfection or a set of attributes that are regarded as normative.

A late 1990s advertising campaign by Nokia offers a good example of the significance of self-help guides in the active construction of a sense of self. The campaign promoted a range of different phones, each of which was illustrated by an ear that represented the type of owner who might aspire to the different models: an unremarkable ear for the everyday user ("I want a simple, basic mobile phone"), a tanned hairy ear for the farmer ("I need a phone that works when I'm miles from the big smoke"), a delicate ear with pearl earrings for the mother ("I need one so that I know the kids are safe"); an ear with multiple rings and a stud ("I'd like a mobile with some really cool features"), a black ear with diamond stud for the successful global career woman of color ("I'd like a phone that I can take overseas"), and a pointy ear for the geek ("I require a phone that is totally logical").

In other words, the phones were matched to particular attributes of personality and lifestyle needs and preferences. The phone stood in for the delineation of particular personality types to the point where a bystander would—ideally—be able to pigeonhole the owner of the phone by her or his choice of phone. Indeed, Nokia's byline was: "Connect yourself with a phone that's been designed for you." This takes the performance of individuality to new heights, where a manufacturer can classify its consumer types in terms of personality traits and fashion a technical device to match. Of course, this is an arbitrary match in the sense that it is culturally contingent and only decipherable by people with knowledge of the depicted personality types and the desired phone features associated with each type.

Just as one can update one's mobile phone by acquiring the latest model, so too can one recreate one's individuality by choosing a different set of attributes as the desired norm. Self-identity is an ongoing project involving techniques of self-fashioning, including diet, cosmetic projection, exercise, spiritual self-help—and the acquisition of a new wardrobe or type of clothing. In the process of self-fashioning, an individual acquires a revised set of body techniques and refines certain attributes by prestigious imitation.

The success of the refashioning project, however, depends on the contingent acquisition of **cultural capital.** This refers to the specific bundle of knowledge that makes sense of the body techniques not only to the individual but also to the observer. That is, one's body techniques must be intelligible to all occupants of a particular habitus. An analogy would be the specialized handshake that Masons use or the high-five gesture of American athletes. Cultural capital refers to how cultural fields are organized, especially the disparate patterning of cultural attributes among a population. This entails a hierarchy of knowledge and attributes that is socially sanctioned so that even in ordinary body habits, there is a differentiation between elites and less culturally equipped groups.

Cultural attributes exhibit a diverse range of levels or skills and a range of knowledges relevant to a specific cultural environment. In other words, cultural capital equips the body to perform the appropriate body techniques in particular roles and contexts. Education and training, as well as imitation of those who are admired, such as family members and role models, are the key sources of cultural capital. As such, there is a positive relationship between cultural capital and the possession of high levels of education and income. Given the right level of cultural capital, the performance of body parts is rendered socially meaningful and culturally intelligible.

Bodies are made up in both senses of the term. They are constructed through the acquisition of body techniques, and known through the ways in which they are made presentable and performed in habituses or living environments. These have also been called "departments of existence," or those specialist spaces that we occupy, such as family, school, workplace, church, and sports groups. Given this, clothes are an extension of the body and its habitus and become another body technique that serves to prepare the body to perform. Techniques of fashioning the body are a visible and primary denotative form of acculturation, which is the way we wear our bodies to present ourselves to our social environment, mapping out our codes of conduct through our clothing behavior. This is also the means by which bodies borrow other techniques to modify established codes of conduct and presentation and create new ones (see Gaugele 2003).

How we clothe the body becomes a barometer of body-habitus relations. As individuals, we use our choice of textiles, clothes, ornamentation, and gesture as extensions of the social body by which we construct and convey our sense of self or persona as our unique identity. Clothes and body decoration thus create distinctiveness. Through different body styles, one wearer is distinguished from another, one group from another. Fashion techniques are also the perfect device for playing on the rules of social interaction through the visual display of calculated transgressions (McCracken 1988).

Clothing is neither simply functional nor symbolic. Codes of dress are technical devices that articulate the relationship between a particular body and its lived milieu, the space occupied by bodies and constituted by bodily performances. Clothes construct the habitus of the self. This enables the achievement of specific bodily performances—including display, presentation, representation, and ritual. In the same way, habituses create codes of recognition and the capacity to accurately read the body so that the meanings intended by the performer are matched by the codes of deciphering.

As well as performing social roles, bodies are fashioned according to one's position in a social group, reflecting one's status in the social hierarchy (how important one is), denoting which subgroups one belongs to or identifies with, displaying one's personality and other attributes of the self and persona, and indicating what statements one wishes to make with one's dress code (e.g., fashionable, traditional, clique-ish, disinterested, "foreign," or ethnic). Sociologists, in particular, analyze fashion and dress in these terms in order to show that we wear our social place on our bodies through the ways we dress and adorn the body.

## ii. fashioning gender: femininity and masculinity

There are a number of key ways of fashioning the self in Western culture. Techniques of refashioning and disciplining the body are central to becoming a gendered self and a consuming self, which are discussed in the next two sections. Acquiring these fundamental techniques of selfhood involves achieving the triple viewpoint referred to previously, namely, the conjunction of physiological, psychological, and sociological techniques. While a person is sexed at birth, the acquisition of a sense of gender is a process that is learned from an early age. Both femininity and masculinity are performances that bodies internalize until they become second nature. Every person in Western culture engages with specific techniques of producing and performing a gendered body and defining her or his relationship with consumer culture. This process begins with pink clothes for girls adorned with the images of female stars (e.g., Britney, Bratz, or Barbie) and blue clothes with the logos of male heroes (e.g., Thomas the Tank Engine, Spiderman, the Hulk) and is reinforced by gender-specific differences in furnishings, toys, DVDs, and gifts—as well as very different interactions (including linguistic utterances) between female and male babies and family and friends. Nicknames and labels, too, reinforce gender stereotypes at an early age—for example, "Princess" or "My best friend."

### Femininity

In terms of fashion and dress, femininity is a much more elaborated and visible domain than masculinity—just compare the floor space devoted to girls' and boys' clothes in any department or fashion store. There is a much greater range of garments—and options within each range—for girls than for boys. Moreover, girls' clothes are modeled on adult clothes and are vestmental signs and symbols that introduce children to adult techniques of femininity at an early age, and public debates about whether a particular look is suitable for children reveal that there is a widespread belief that early introductions to the nuances of adult femininity are inappropriate for young children. Nonetheless, clothes create a specific gendered habitus in that girls clothes are often restricting (e.g., skirts and frills) or prompt a performance (e.g., flounces, bare midriffs, heart logos), while boys clothes tend to be more suitable for roughhousing and physical activity (shirts, pants, and jackets).

The physical coding of children's clothes in terms of gender also conveys psychological messages and symbols of what it means to be a girl or a boy as well as wider sociological conventions about gender that vary between cultures and subcultures. Fashion magazines, fashion advertisements, fashion Web sites, advice columns, music videos, and fashion writings are primarily directly targeted at girls and women, and there is a complex code of femininity inscribed in the symbolic messages and signifiers carried by clothes. But femininity also requires one to learn particular techniques of using the body (moving, facial expressions, ways of speaking, use of language, and interacting with others). Many of the terms associated with femininity— *passive, disciplined, restrained, thoughtful, nurturing, coquettish, seductive*—refer to specific body techniques.

The body work involved in producing an ideal model of femininity involves extensive manipulation and training, including **body modification,** dieting, exercise, and cosmetic enhancement (see case study 16). The extent to which a female will go to achieve her ideal of femininity is positively rewarded as a sign of her commitment to her role model. In some cases, radical denial and self-modification are regarded as a facet of a profession—for example, modeling, airline

**A feminine outfit**

stewarding, and professional sports are sometimes referred to as the anorexic professions due to the high incidence of body imbalances and eating disorders among practitioners. Denial of pleasure or relaxation, extreme body disciplines, and physical and psychological pain are sometimes regarded as normal ways of achieving gendered bodily perfection.

As former **supermodel** Janice Dickinson reflected in her biography, "Beauty is pain—you must agonize for your beauty" (quoted in Gambotto 2004: 18). In this quest, like countless other celebrities, she resorted to cosmetic and surgical procedures, including breast implants, a bunectomy (removal of the ball of the big toe), a blepharoplasty (removal of fat, muscle, and skin from the eyelids), the placement of porcelain veneers (ceramic coating of teeth), a brow lift, and Botox. In the world of modeling, the insouciant sashay down the catwalk disguises the degree of labor that may have been involved in producing a particular look—dieting to extremes, cosmetic surgery, extensive physical workouts, makeup artists, hairdressers, **stylists,** photographers, skilled dressmakers, and so on. Although the images of top models and the garments in designer collections are promoted and marketed to women as the latest must-have fashion and look, in fact, these are contrived forms of artistic manipulation that are unachievable for the ordinary consumer.

Dickinson burst the bubble when she revealed that it is "technically impossible" to "make human flesh behave like an artist's perfectly arranged pixels" (quoted in Gambotto 2004: 18).

As these examples show, the construction of a gendered identity is a deliberate and complex process—irrespective of the fact that one's sex is biologically determined. Gender is a body technique par excellence: *both femininity and masculinity are highly contrived and arbitrary cultural constructs.* The cases of princesses made by marriage (see case study 14) and fashion models exemplify the extremes of techniques of femininity, as they resort to excessive practices of self-denial, masochism, and deprivation, on the one hand, and self-obsession, narcissism, and excess, on the other. Central to this process is the desire to refashion the body and self into a physical form and psychological character decreed by the media and public as well as, respectively, court society (see Elias 1983; Noyes and Bendix 1998: 110–11) and the modeling industry (Quick 1997). Prestigious imitation, technical training (self-help remodeling), and the acquisition of a "stylistic" register are important components of this process. The body is clothed in the desired attributes of femininity—docility, passivity, calculated body performances as spectacle, subservience, and nurturing.

Central to these attributes is the compulsion to discipline the body and mind by denying the self in order to conform to the expectations and dictates of others. Examples of this include dieting, exercise, and learned modes of behavior, gesture, and even one's use of language (see Turner 1991). At the heart of this is a tension between the impulse to be a spectacle and the convention to maintain a decorous and modest demeanor. Despite ostensible revisions of ideal notions of femininity (feminism, girl power, glass ceiling programs to help women reach the top of their professions where invisible barriers impede promotion), traditional notions of femininity persist in Western consumer culture. Even when women—for example, female popular music stars—ostensibly choose to reject dominant conventions of femininity and dress provocatively, they are pressured to conform after they have had children (e.g., Madonna, Victoria Beckham) or readily denigrated if they fall down in conforming to standards of public morality (e.g., Britney Spears, Courtney Love).

But female fashion also has to contend with other aspects of femininity, especially those concerning sexuality and sensuality. Girls' clothes may mimic adult media stars' outfits (revealing flesh, short skirts, leggings, tight shorts—all emblazoned with phrases like "Cheeky Cute Cool," "A List," "Anything boys can do girls can do better," and "Rock Star"), but girls who act *too* provocatively incur sanctions. It's a fine line between celebrating femininity and behaving like a slut. Fashions reflect and deliberately play on this tension and the sexual frisson it implies.

Femininity in fashion is created by body techniques that make the body a spectacle for the enjoyment of others in a process of voyeurism. According to cultural theorists who have adapted psychoanalytic concepts, women become the "object of the gaze," where the spectator takes a normative masculine point of view. Feminine looks are contrived to be looked at by others, so the feminine body is a body under surveillance, which goes some way to explain why women who transgress codes of femininity or codes of female dress are more likely to come under critical scrutiny than men who transgress clothing codes.

Women in the workforce are especially implicated in this bind, with professional and career

**Bikinis.** Photo: Mahesh Shantaram. Creative Commons Attribution 2.0 License

women constantly struggling to look professional (that is, playing down their femininity and playing up their professional attributes by wearing professional clothes such as suits and business shirts, known as power clothes) while at the same time introducing elements that signal their femininity and soften a too masculine look (e.g., scarves, jewelry, bouffant hairstyles, and high heels—or stilettos for the brave; see case study 11). Wearing sexy lingerie underneath corporate clothes (see case study 27) is another popular way for women to retain their sense of femininity while conveying a professional, nongendered occupational image.

### Masculinity

Masculinity, too, is learned, and although it sometimes seems more straightforward, changing codes of masculinity also reveal a complex history. We have already discussed the emergence of the prototype of modern masculinity with the dandy (see case study 5) as well as the emergence of ties as a mark of men's formal dress (see case study 9) and jeans as global everyday dress for men and women (see case study 10). As we have seen, men's clothing in Europe became increasingly austere and pared back beginning in the eighteenth century, arguably in conjunction with the development of modern political, economic, and cultural modes of living. Women's clothes, too, showed some reduction in excess and opulence, but the divergence between the woman as decorated with an elaborated dress code and the man as plain with a restricted dress code increased, especially in Victorian times (Davis 1992: 39). As the modern workforce became male dominated, the workingman's suit became the norm of occupational dress, while fancy women's dress became a sign of leisured and refined status.

While femininity centered on the individual achieving a look as the bearer of a particular image, masculinity became the expression of active roles associated with occupational and social status and the exercise of power. If femininity is characterized by attributes of weakness, passivity, submissiveness, self-control, nurturing, and emotionality, then masculinity invokes the opposite attributes: strength, aggression, dominance, control, and toughness (Craik 1994: 176–78). These attributes have been codified into the basic elements of the modern man's wardrobe—namely, shirt, trousers, and jacket—while individual embellishments of masculine identity can be conveyed in choices in accessories such as tie, socks, sweater, vest, belt, or watch. Twentieth-century men's fashion reflected these restricted codes for the normative male but experimented with deviations in fashion targeted toward male groups and subcultures whose definitions of sexuality, gender, and identity explicitly challenged dominant codes of masculinity, such as gays, cross-dressers, punks, and musicians.

Although the suit has remained the staple of men's fashion, the male wardrobe began to expand in the late twentieth century; however, men in skirts have remained taboo in mainstream fashion (Bolton 2003; see also Chenoune 1993; McDowell 1997). The impact of leisure clothes was one factor, as was the popularization of denim jeans, flower power fashions, stage clothes associated with popular music, and the rapid development of designer fashion and ready-to-wear fashion for the middle market. A softer look for men with more choices presaged the purported emergence of a new type of masculinity, variously called the new man, the SNAG (sensitive new age guy), the new lad, and the **metrosexual** (see case study 15). This man rejected or at least challenged the macho image of men as strong and silent, chauvinistic, authoritative, or ruthless. The new masculinity showed attributes of sensitivity and empathy and was interested in his appearance. In part a reaction to the women's movement and feminism, the new masculinity was also an answer to the prayers of the advertising industry in that it offered up a new type of consumer who could—unlike the traditional man—be seduced by the promises of new products and services. The new man was narcissistic and an active consumer. He was heterosexual but shared attributes with his homosexual peers, who were also becoming a target of marketers as more permissive attitudes toward sexuality made men (and women) less hesitant to reveal their sexual orientations and identities (see image 8).

The overlap of different codes of masculinity, outed forms of sexuality, and reworked codes of femininity were all grist to the mill of the fashion industry, which exploited the bricolage of gendered identities and new market groups. The ambiguity of sexual identities has not only been celebrated in the use of men's clothes in women's fashion and vice versa by cross-dressers and non-heterosexual consumers but has been embraced as a slightly transgressive signifier by mainstream

**Emo boy. Model: Arturo Pozo,** Photo: José Miguel Serrano. Creative Commons Attribution 2.0 License

consumers too. Variously called **androgyny** (neither masculine nor feminine but almost sexless), unisex, metrosexuality, and queer consumerism, this trend has prompted "respectable" brands to market lines such as "His pants for her," sarongs for men, makeup for men, the **G-string** as everyday **underwear,** and erotic lingerie for home shoppers. As male bodies have been transformed into spectacles, objects of the gaze, and subjects of decoration, the codes of sexual desire associated with masculinity have also changed.

Together, these complementary attributes may seem to form the whole of gendered identities, but as notions of gender are destabilized, the emergence of new forms of femininity and masculinity—and a proliferation of other sexual identities—destabilizes one of the central body techniques of Western contemporary culture.

**Board shorts**

## iii. fashioning consumers

Western culture has been built on consumer relations of production and consumption, and the emergence of distinctive personality types and role models in our culture have also embodied this ethos (see McCracken 1988). While individuals strive for uniqueness and difference in the quest to be accepted (i.e., to fit into society), the success of consumer society depends on individual consumers choosing to purchase goods and services to attain the same set of dreams and aspirations. As Bauman (2001: 17) has argued,

**whatever the rationality of consumer society may mean, it does not aim to rest, in stark opposition to the society of producers of the "solid" stage of modernity, on the universalization of rational thought and action, but on a free rein of irrational passions (just like routine rests on catering for the desire for diversion, uniformity on recognition of diversity, and conformity on the agents' liberation).**

Bauman (2001: 17) concludes, "The rationality of consumer society is built on the irrationality of its individualized actors." Modern consumerism has become an integral part of constructing modern identities. Consumerism—identifying with products through the qualities they promote and buying goods in the hope of acquiring the social value ascribed to them—has become the way to create meaning, convey identity, exemplify distinction, and indulge in pleasure. Indeed, consumerism has arguably become the postmodern condition. We design lifestyles by buying the attributes of identity and status by which we can reinforce a desired sense of self or we reinvent the self through new purchases and taste registers. Through our choice of clothes, body decoration, furnishings (bed linen, curtains), and home decoration, we can switch from urban chic to a nostalgic country look to industrial "edginess" to traditional formality by the swipe of a credit card.

We consume images and ideals that we aspire to, and these fuel our consumer behavior—a radical extension of Mauss's observations on human behavior. Shopping has become a primary social activity not only for practical reasons but as a process of acquiring, maintaining, and transforming social identities. Shopping malls and precincts and global brands have become dominant symbolic markers of identity and belonging. Fashion and dress can be seen as the habitus that announces identity. The act of shopping can have a number of motives: the desire to buy a particular identity or status; to differentiate oneself from others through distinctiveness in dress; to overdress or underdress, depending whether one wants to make a statement or blend in; and to select either elite or populist fashion codes that fit one's chosen identity. The topic of fashion and consumer behavior is further explored in chapter 6.

In sum, whether we imagine ourselves as fashionable bodies or mundane ones, body work through the acquisition of body techniques and the refashioning of our sense of self is the key to how we use clothes and body decoration to form our personalities. In this process, we borrow historically and culturally from other times, places, and people. And while we may think of our fashion systems and bodily conventions as normative, there is growing evidence that other cultures, too, purposefully construct bodies and identities. So too do they reinvent and remake identities. While we may think of other cultures as redolent with "exoticism," they are simply different systems of body techniques, dress, and decoration (Craik

**Boxing Day sale.** Photo: Alpha Lau, http://www.flickr.com/photos/avlxyz/2138509455/. Creative Commons Attribution-Share Alike 2.0 Generic

1993). Body work is never done, and clothes will always "maketh the man" or woman.

## iv. uniforms of identity

One of the ironies of fashion is that although fashion is inspired by the desire to be distinctive and to embody now-ness, the practice of fashion creates instantly recognizable signs that can be interpreted by the members of one's clothing milieu. So the pull of fashion demands legibility and thus a degree of uniformity. Even the quest for individuality does not dampen the uniformity impulse. Rather, the fashion slave strives to offset uniqueness with familiarity. Conversely, fashionable looks construct a quasi uniform for the fashion lover. Group photographs of schoolchildren, families, friends, and celebrities and candid shots documenting everyday life reveal the extent of uniformity that overrides distinctiveness and difference.

While the individual in modern culture desires to dress differently, sumptuary laws, or clothing regulation aimed to instill difference between groups by codifying forms of uniformity within groups, have existed throughout history. This regulation was achieved by the prescription and proscription of certain forms of dress. Perhaps, then, it was only to be expected that, at the time when sumptuary laws were abandoned, the idea of the uniform came to the fore. Uniforms are a means to precisely codify a manner of dress according to occupation, status, or role. The word *uniform* is defined as not changing in form or character, unvarying, and conforming to the same standard or rule. As a form of dress, uniform is defined as dress worn by members of the same body (e.g., soldiers, sailors, police officers). A uniform is a standard outfit designed to convey sameness and group membership, the accessories of which (badges, headwear, braid, stripes, etc.) indicate status or specialization.

A uniformed group of people also displays uniform codes of conduct and expresses a uniform demeanor. Just as the body is trained to wear the uniform, so the body techniques of the uniformed person display learned habits and perform certain roles. So uniforms are associated with attributes of unity, authority, status, hierarchy, rules of behavior, and codes of punishment. People in uniform attract attention from bystanders and elicit erotic desire. While some of the history of uniforms involves conforming to the standards that one must achieve to wear a uniform (e.g., joining a scout group, a sports team, a club, or an occupation), other aspects of history have to do with rebelling or subverting the wearing of uniforms—or behaving badly while in a uniform.

In a sense, then, uniforms have two contradictory sets of references: their intended connotations of sameness, order, and authority, and their unintended connotations of difference, disorder, and opposition. This paradox is what makes uniforms so attractive to the language of fashion. Uniforms—or elements denoting uniforms—can symbolize contradictory impulses, emotions, responses, and signals.

The most common uniforms are found among occupations associated with regulating the social order, namely, military forces, the police and law enforcement agencies, religious orders (though their clothing is often referred to as religious "garb"), medical and health workers, security officers, and those in occupations associated with service activities (concerning food, banking, transport, etc.). Uniforms first appeared in modern Europe with the rise of civil society and the recognition of the rights of individuals as citizens. This may see ironic. Yet it seems that the more individualistic a society becomes, the more it depends on signs of sameness, difference, and distinctiveness.

Even in the early twenty-first century, there are more uniforms than ever, with new uniforms for specialized services (e.g., natural therapy practitioners, specialist school uniforms, especially for exclusive private schools, checkout operators, corporate employees, administrators). The reason is that uniforms are an extremely effective and unambiguous sign system that conveys a range of attributes, habits, personality traits, and knowledge. Uniforms are body techniques par excellence. They are acquired by prestigious imitation of those whom we admire or who are in authority. In fact, however, most of the body techniques associated with uniforms entail the acquisition of "not" statements—that is, what to avoid or repress. Uniforms are effective symbols of codified rules of conduct and the internalization of those rules. It is the set of rules and the manner of their enforcement that is more important than the elements of uniforms themselves

**Iraq three soldiers.** Photo by Staff Sgt. Stacy L. Pearsall/U.S. Air Force

in the successful performance of the uniformed body.

The use of uniforms in popular culture has become endemic. Uniforms have been adopted for sports, adapted in the form of quasi uniforms for some occupations (e.g., teachers, hairdressers, arts workers), and reworked for diverse subcultures (e.g., punks, bikers, Goths, revolutionary and resistance groups). Uniforms are also a common device in fashion design, be it haute couture, prêt-à-porter, or ready-to-wear. Fashion artwear is another site of the proliferation of uniforms (see case study 19).

One of the vexatious issues surrounding the use of uniforms is the connotations of sexuality and gender associated with uniforms. Historically, uniforms were associated with idealized attributes of masculinity, particularly the image of the ideal military officer. The phrase "Women love a man in a uniform" sums up the attributes of heterosexual desire wrapped up in the connotations of the uniformed man. Uniformed men, however, have also connoted other forms of sexual desire, as the number of gays and cross-dressers in military forces (especially the navy) has indicated.

Particularly vexatious are the connotations associated with women in uniforms and what kind of sexuality is inscribed by this clothing. The classic elements of uniforms are the button-up shirt, tie, epaulettes, tailored pants or skirt, sensible shoes, and tailored jackets. The misfit between uniforms and femininity is particularly evident in the case of

**U.S. Army Pfc. Rebekah Yokel.** Photo by Master Sgt. Robert W. Valenca/U.S. Air Force

school uniforms for girls. Boys' school uniforms developed out of early military-style uniforms, which emphasized order, discipline, and attention to detail. Classic school uniforms for boys consisted of a button-up shirt, military-style tie, jacket, pleated trousers, belt, and lace-up shoes. These clothes are not so different from adult men's formal business wear.

Girls' school uniforms play a similar role to boys' uniforms in some respects, but also very different and highly problematic roles. While girls' uniforms function as a code of discipline and other attributes of the ideal female pupil, the role of the uniform in relation to acquiring codes of sexuality is radically aberrant. Furthermore, the sexual and sensual connotations associated with uniforms suggest that some deep-seated issues concerning the formation of sexed identities and gendered persona are associated with and inscribed in the nature of uniforms and how they are worn. Indeed, uniforms are an integral prop in subcultures of licentiousness and sexual perversion.

Judith Okely's work (1993) on uniforms in English girls' boarding schools in the 1950s sheds some light on the interpretation of girls and women's uniforms. She speculated on the disjunction between girls' training in schools and female adult attributes of gender. The habits acquired in school were very different from those a girl was expected to possess on graduation. The detailed

**Private school uniform.** Photo by Harold M. Lambert/Hulton Archive/Getty Images. 2006 Getty Images

rules about how uniforms should be worn complemented other training girls received about the highly refined control of their bodies, minds, and language.

Okely traced the contradictions and ambiguities between two kinds of trainings that were offered simultaneously to schoolgirls. In part, much of school training was directed toward the acquisition of a second-rank array of attributes of *masculinity*—discipline, achievement, leadership, conformity. But girls' training was also directed toward the acquisition of attributes of self-control and self-negation. Okely (1993: 112) reflected:

**We did not merely unconsciously imitate movements and gestures, we were consciously made to sit, stand and move in uniform ways. We were drilled and schooled ... by those who had power over us. Our flesh was unscarred, yet our gestures bore their**

**School uniform, Cambodia.** Photo: Lynn Yenkey. Lynn Yenkey

**marks. ... Our minds and understanding of the world were to reflect our custodians. With no private space, we could not even hide in our bodies, which also had to move in unison with their thoughts.**

In the finished product—the "finished" young woman—those latter attributes were intended to prevail, since many of the former became irrelevant on graduation. The term *finishing* was appropriated in the development of finishing schools for young ladies deemed suitable for "good" matrimonial matches and motherhood. The finished young lady would come out as a debutante at a special presentation ball, where she would visibly display her command of feminine attributes (and charms). This contradiction between the rhetoric and the reality was perhaps the reason for adopting a very different approach to enforcement and sanctioning of uniform and other behavioral rules in girls' schools. Instead of relying on corporal punishment, as in boys' schools, girls' schools used psychological and physical forms of enforcement and punishment (including techniques to shape emotion, language, gesture, and deportment). Although ostensibly less brutal, it was a more pervasive strategy that effectively retooled the very ways

**Japanese maids**

of apprehending and communicating with one's surroundings.

Consequently, the nature of girls' training was arguably more effective as a means of training the body as a whole. As Okely (1993: 119) put it, "power may be exercised more completely over girls precisely because it is not visible as physical force." School uniforms and school discipline imbued the body with specific techniques that were building blocks of modes of personal conduct. School girls had to wear their hair short (not reaching below their shirt collars), while their uniforms consisted of an array of garments including tunics (pleated or unpleated—reminiscent of Roman gladiators), thick black or brown stockings, two pairs of large underpants, and knee-length skirts (for modesty), as well as lace-up shoes, striped shirts, blazers, ties, and tie pins.

**Unlike some of the boys' uniforms, ours was discontinuous with the clothes we would wear in adulthood. To us the old school tie had no significance for membership of an "old boy network." We were caught between a male and female image long after puberty, and denied an identity which asserted the dangerous consciousness of sexuality. (Okely 1993: 114)**

However, once the girls left school, they were expected to consciously discard many of the "masculine" attributes acquired at school and acquire a new set of attributes appropriate to adult feminine conduct:

**Immediately we left school, we had to drop all masculine traits, since a very different appearance was required for marriageability. Sexual ripeness, if only expressed in clothes, burst forth. The hated tunics and lace-ups were torn, cut, burnt or flung into the sea. Old girls would return on parade, keen to demonstrate their transformation from androgyny to womanhood. To be wearing the diamond engagement ring was the ultimate achievement. There was no link between our past and our future. In such certainty our confidence was surely broken. (Okely 1993: 114)**

In effect, a radically different triple viewpoint or gendered uniform replaced the girls' school uniform. This contrasts with the experience of boys, who merely swapped one uniform for a similar and related one. But it was not just a question of clothes. Highly prescriptive modes of conduct were conveyed through trainings in correct deportment, gesture, use of language, and tone of voice. These were annexed to the "work" of uniforms and the system of sanctions for transgressions. Even on the athletic field, girls were expected to match sporting aggression with a feminine demeanor. But an athletic body was regarded as unfeminine and inappropriate at any other time.

While contemporary girls' school uniforms are no longer so traditional and masculine, elements of men's clothing linger, and the tension between training a disciplined body and feminine body remains. In its aim of restraining and disciplining the body and mind, it actually incites unrestrained and transgressive conduct that has at its heart a gendered subject that is normatively male and transgressively feminine. And while it could be argued that the English girls' boarding school is an extreme example, there are many parallels with other uniforms and an overwhelming consensus among women about their experiences wearing military-style uniforms during their school days.

The prevalence of uniforms in fashion can be seen in the global incorporation of military uniforms in fashion, and especially the use of camouflage fabric for shoes, trousers, jackets, pajamas, handbags, and hats. Military motifs have been a strong influence in rebellious youth subcultures such as **punk,** skinhead, techno, and hip-hop cultures, and among Rastafarians. Mods in the 1960s favored U.S.-style parkas with German and American emblems. Not only do military uniforms indicate youth group identities, but they have also been appropriated for symbolizing sexual identities, for example, exaggerated heterosexual masculinity or aggressive

**Airline Uniform.** Photo by Alan Band/Keystone/Getty Images. Getty Images

non-normative femininity. As these examples show, uniforms and non-uniforms have been key symbols of signaling identity, one of the key roles of fashion in creating personal and collective identities.

## v. conclusion

This chapter has explored the relationship between fashion and two central forms of identity formation: gender, whether femininity or masculinity

**Camo t-shirt**

(or gendered spaces between), and consumerism as the dominant impulse of contemporary Western culture. The body is trained to take on the attributes, gestures, psychological perspectives, and behavioral codes of particular social identities. Fashion and dress are the outward wrapping or habitus that signifies one's social self.

Although traditionally, fashion has been more intimately entwined with femininity, in recent decades, codes of masculinity have transformed into ways that invite the attention of the fashion industry and marketers to create a strong male consumer market from which have spun off markets for ambiguous gender and sexual identities.

Just as gender and consumerism are entwined in the contemporary person, a radical fashion culture forged in the Harajuku district of Tokyo fuses the spectacle of the performance of exaggerated identities as ultra-consumers yet cultural outsiders (see case study 13). This creation of a subculture based on consumer fashion yet challenging dominant codes of Japanese consumerism and contemporary identities epitomizes the complexity of the nexus between fashion and identity explored in this chapter.

## CHAPTER SUMMARY

- Fashion is more than simply clothes or garments—it involves learned body techniques where a person acquires appropriate modes of behavior by copying esteemed role models so she or he can perform appropriately in the habituses that comprise her or his social milieu.
- There is a dynamic and iterative relationship between the body techniques of the wearer and the interpretations of the viewer and how we understand or read what we see and experience.
- Cultural capital refers to the status occupied by a person due to her or his economic, educational, and social position and is a feature of consumer culture, on which modern fashion systems are based.
- Although the body is sexed as male or female, masculinity and femininity are learned attributes of the gendered self alongside alternative sexual identities.
- Femininity is intimately bound up with fashion, as females contrive to create a certain look that is a spectacle and that becomes the object of the normatively male gaze.
- Masculinity constructs body techniques that communicate power and authority over the body and its habitus as the locus of social status.
- Uniforms have replaced sumptuary laws as a means of regulating the consumption and display of certain social characteristics that can be automatically read by others and that orchestrate behavior and responses.

## CASE STUDY 13: Fashion and Identity in Harajuku

A small district of Tokyo just north of Shibuya, Harajuku is the site of some of the world's most experimental and elaborate youth fashion cultures, where playful interpretations of place and commodities form tactics of resistance, avoidance, escape, and fantasy.

Nowhere have so many niche fashions existed side by side as in the hyper-reality of Harajuku. In their image-saturated world these teens celebrate the superficiality of their posed identities without denying that that is all they are. Hippy, hillbilly, and hip-hop genres, for example, are enacted in a self-reflexive masquerade without regard for appearing natural or authentic. These genres were not grown organically in Tokyo but adapted later with obsessive attention to details of dress, music, dance moves, and other stylistic elements, making evident that subcultural identity is not essential—we constitute ourselves as a techno raver or ragamuffin or glam rocker simply by looking like one. Images are adopted as though in quotation marks, and incongruity is of no concern, as there is no ideological commitment.

In Harajuku they take signs at will out of their original contexts and transform their meanings in a chaotic bricolage where the distinction between reproduction and authenticity is extraneous. The emphasis on incessant change, ambivalence, pluralism, and free-floating signs might be seen to epitomize a postmodern cultural state, but it can just as easily be situated within traditional Japanese culture: identity has been seen as non-essential and performative since long before the advent of the term *postmodern.* Writing in the 1330s, the Buddhist monk Kenko (1967: 73) wrote: "If you run through the streets, saying you are a lunatic, you are in fact a lunatic. If you kill a man, saying you imitate a criminal, you are a criminal yourself. ... A man who studies wisdom, even insincerely, should be called wise."

The best documentation of Harajuku street fashion is *FRUiTS* magazine, which has been published as two books (Aoki 2001, 2005). Founded in 1997 by photographer Shoichi Aoki, it features cover-to-cover full-page photographs of creatively self-styled people on the street. There is very little advertising and the only copy is the individual's name and outfit details, which give each person pictured full credit for her or his creations. *FRUiTS* fashion is less about what one wears than how one wears it, and the wearer supersedes the designer in generating style directions. Fashions often quickly percolate from the minority groups of high-school students up to the imitating privileged classes and global commercial bodies who reproduce them.

In *FRUiTS* we see an emphasis on creative do-it-yourself practice and irreverent but seamless combining of traditional Japanese dress, Western retro fashion from the last half century, avant-garde Japanese couture, futuristic **cyber**-style, and completely new trends with handmade and secondhand fashion and found/cheap mass-produced objects. The magazine represents styles that are too eclectic and diverse to be categorized as a single subculture, but as a whole, *FRUiTS* fashion is best described as "layered," which suggests that their bodies and identities are polyvalent works in progress involving a patchwork of meanings. The hybridity of images demonstrates the Japanese skill at combining novelty and tradition, East and West, the old world and the modern, without compromising an essential identity. In rearranging existing images to give them endless new meanings, their methodically precise processes of self-presentation are not unlike those of the Zen calligrapher. In the words of Rupert Cox (2003: 232), "It is not possible to make a clear distinction between the authenticity of an aesthetic original and the authenticity of its copy, when the culture of the Zen arts is about reproduction and repetition as a valued cultural aesthetic."

**Harajuku.** Photo: Amelia Groom. Amelia Groom

The people in *FRUiTS* magazine are evading the intense panoptic gaze of Japanese culture, evading adulthood, and reveling in their simultaneous invisibility and visibility. The more radical the masquerade, the more attention it earns, but the more they become anonymous behind it: they are as interested in standing out in a city of twenty million as in hiding their biological bodies from identification. Because of the conforming nature of Japanese culture, the intensity of the pleasure in the subversive subculture is heightened—in many other societies, their mischievous eccentricity would be less radical and thus wouldn't have come to exist at the same intensity.

But although subcultural identities are negotiated in opposition to an imagined mainstream, they entail the same self-regulation and omnipresent public scrutiny, imposing an intense pressure to see oneself and be seen in a certain ways. *FRUiTS* and the various other street fashion magazines from Tokyo form a conversation with their readers, rather than a monologue, because they feature images of pedestrians in their own creations who control how they are represented and are granted full agency by the publications. However, their street photographers—who stand with cameras at shopping meccas like Harajuku's Laforet Mall or Omotesando Street—also shape the reality they document. Not only do they distort the representation through selection, exclusion, and repetition, but the very presence of their lens changes behaviors. The possibility of appearing in the publications means the amateur models must forever outdo themselves and each other to be selected for the camera.

In the 1980s the most famed Harajuku *zoku* (tribe) was the rockabillies, and the American 1950s rock-and-roll style is still around today. With faded Levi's, Elvis quiffs, and Peppermint Twists, they wooed on-looking girls in wide poodle skirts and polka-dot cat-eye sunglasses. Quickly growing into a popular tourist attraction, their performances were situated between the pleasure of seeing, the pleasure of being seen, and the pleasure of being unseen. Preceeding the rockabillies was the earliest Harajuku subculture, the *takenoko-zoku* (Baby Bamboo Shoots Tribe, named after the first boutique in Harajuku), which developed in the mid-1970s. They wore garishly colored shiny robes and cheap accessories like plastic whistles, long fake-pearl necklaces, name tags, and kung fu shoes, with stuffed animals stitched to the ensembles. Gathering for hours at Yoyogi Park to perform choreographed dance moves to their boom boxes, they invented a vibrant sphere of inclusion where their costume and performance made them intensely visible but distanced them from the outside world.

The public-private distinction is very important in Japan, and non-public space is marked by, among other gestures, the removal of shoes upon entry. Because the private is so private, the public (including the public self, constituted and read through clothing) is intensely public. According to Richie (1999:

39–40), Tokyo historically had no promenades or public squares, and people would see and be seen only in private spaces. The public spaces that exist today are those constructed by the people of the city—the street culture of Harajuku thus grew from a grassroots process of reclaiming and reusing public space. It became the opposite of the private home: a microcosmic society of communal spectacle where all positioned themselves under intense public surveillance and the separation between performers and spectators was dissolved.

Their creativity and radicalism peaked after 1977 when the main street, Omotesando, was declared *hoko-ten* (a "pedestrian haven")—traffic was banned every Sunday and people would travel from far and wide to parade their latest fantastical creations. In 1998 the *hoko-ten* was abolished by a special decree of the local government, because it was getting too noisy and crowded. The creative aesthetic play no longer exists at the same intensity, but the area remains the best place for young people to see and be seen, to overcome boredom and dissatisfaction in the metropolis of Tokyo, to exchange ideas, and to seek escape through new uses of places and things. Due to the nation's longest economic recession and the inflation of real-estate prices, the majority of young Japanese are choosing to live at home well into their twenties. For many of them, living rent free permits ongoing fashion consumption, and the public street culture offers a respite from the intimate space of the private family home. Their radical fashion is a publicized decorative rejection of what they are expected to aspire to.

Virginia Postrel (2003) gives a good account of how in Western culture we have come to treat appearances as deceptive, frivolous, decadent, or unimportant distractions or distortions of an imagined deeper existence that is beyond mere sensation. This model dates back to Plato, whose theory of the shadows in the cave put deceptive appearances in opposition to the "real" essential truth. But the aesthetic does not have to be seen in this way. The Japanese are good at fashion because they understand how the material and the visual matter to people's internal sense of self and give substance to their outside world. Like the paid models in conventional fashion spreads—like all of us—the "real" people in *FRUiTS* are acting out imagined identities. Their self-decoration is an aggrandizement of their identity: an outward spectacle of how they imagine themselves. If we depart from the idea of a total, obscured truth (the sun outside Plato's cave), we can reexamine self-decoration and find there is no reason why that which is on the surface is less genuine than what is hidden from public scrutiny.

The people in *FRUiTS* should be considered heroic for putting the banal, beautiful, and grotesque side by side. Beyond narcissistic posing, such self-costuming is a public service that exhibits the marvelous in the mundane and shows that artistry can be made anywhere from anything. Through their experimental dressing, they communicate with wider society their disillusionment with it; costume their alienation; and, at times, question the very meaning and function of dress. Presenting themselves outside mass-sanctioned taste, they render everydayness aesthetic; reimagine the type of beauty that is culturally admired, embodying fantasy and optimism; and show that identity is nothing but masquerade.

Amelia Groom

## CASE STUDY 14: Acquiring the Techniques of Royalty

An example of the process of fashioning the self is the transformation of Diana Spencer from minor aristocrat to the Princess of Wales. At the height of her mystique, a book titled *The Princess of Wales Fashion Handbook* (James 1984) illustrated her transformation by charting her changing taste in clothes and designers, hairstyles, makeup, and gestures (waving, smiling, sitting, dancing) (see Craik 1994: 62–64). This was a transformation of the wardrobe of a child-care worker to one suitable for a princess. This was, however, not just about the transformation of Diana but also a manual on how anyone could use her example to refashion herself in her image. The advice concerned the retraining of bodies through the adaptation of Diana's clothes to individual body shapes and redesigned hair and cosmetic routines. The book also adapted royal etiquette to everyday circumstances. In other words, this was a modern instruction manual intended to assist ordinary people in emulating a royal personage. The book assumed that, in contrast to Diana's "new" thin body shape that she worked to achieve after her marriage, readers would have a less perfect body shape—namely, hourglass, pear shaped, short waisted, or top heavy. Diana's iconic clothes were thus adapted to suit the flawed bodies of ordinary commoners.

The tone of this fashion handbook reflected the fluid and dynamic relations between body and habitus as they are inflected through clothing, behavior, demeanor, gesture, and occasion. The style conveyed by our choice of clothes articulates the contours of our habitus—even if it is not a royal one. Diana was portrayed as a role model for everyday lives. A posthumous book, *Diana: Her Life in Fashion* (Howell 1998), also charted the development of her personal style as a way of situating herself in the royal family, and later outside it. British royalty were well known for a stuffy, conservative approach to dress—apart from a few wayward outsiders such as Princess Margaret in her younger days, Princess Alexandra, and Princess Michael of Kent. Diana came from a different generation and had not been versed in the art of aristocratic dress. How Diana dressed became part of her public persona, and she became adept at transmitting "her emotions and feelings through self-presentation, focusing always on the message she wished to communicate" (Howell 1998: 15–16).

A formative influence on Diana's sense of style was the wardrobe of former First Lady Jackie Kennedy, who had revolutionized the culture of the White House and the role of the president's wife and, arguably, had been "the greatest single influence in modern fashion history" (Howell 1998: 166). Diana studied Jackie's clothes, especially her "pastel-suited elegance and ... the simple graphic dignity of her formal evening gowns," and these became "the source of so many Diana outfits," above all, the pillbox hat (Howell 1998: 168). Oleg Cassini had designed the hat to sit on the back of the head so that Jackie's bouffant hairstyle would not be disarranged. Diana quickly recognized this tactic, and she too adopted the fashion, abandoning the hallmark over-the-top hats of other British royals for simple understated headwear.

In her last years, Diana had settled on her sense of style:

> She had come full circle since members of the royal household watched her scanning her press coverage as though searching for clues to her own identity. She did not dress for sympathy any more, but in a uniform of flattering, comfortable dresses that emphasized, without revealing, her figure. In all probability, she didn't even bother to read the dictums of the newspaper fashion police, who now declared that her shoulders were too heavy for low-cut, sleeveless dresses, due to the many hours she had spent in the gym. The famous fashion epigram "less is more" defined her new brand of elegance. (Howell 1998: 182)

**Princess Diana.** Courtesy Ronald Reagan Library

Fittingly, a few months before her death, after her divorce and loss of her royal title, "she symbolically jettisoned her wardrobe of state, selling her weighty embroidered satins, jeweled velvets and sequined laces in seventy-nine lots at Christie's New York" (Howell 1998: 18). Her royal personage was exchanged for a civilian self. Despite her fall from royal favor, Diana's celebrity status as a fashion icon of her time and role model for aspirant commoners remained.

The preoccupation with Diana's public image was repeated in the media with the preparation of Masako Owada, a commoner educated at Oxford and an accomplished and forthright diplomat, to marry the Japanese crown prince, Naruhito, in 1993 and the transformation of Australian-born Mary Donaldson into the wife of Danish crown prince Frederik in 2004. Mary underwent a rigorous self-development training program to equip her for the role, which included "how to relate to people, how to walk into a room, how to socialize, how to perform in front of a camera" (Dennis 2004: 10), how to write "creatively," and how to speak Danish (Smith 2004: 10). She also learned to wear suitably royal clothes (exchanging her casual dress for restrained elegance), to cover her head with suitably royal hats (with pillbox hats and air steward–type caps predominant), and even how to wave in a suitably royal way (with a highly disciplined motion with little movement of the wrist).

In the months after her wedding, the consensus seemed to be that Mary's transformation had been successful: she had acquired the body techniques of a royal personage (Fray 2004: 1, 11; Smith 2004: 10). Indeed, while a senior courtier stressed that what she had been doing since the wedding was "Learning, learning, learning," an ordinary Danish fan exhorted: "She is fabulous. ... You can't teach that kind of naturalness. She's the best thing that has happened here in ages" (quoted by Langley 2004a: 45, 46). The proof of successful acquisition of body techniques is precisely that they are

**Masako.** Photo by TOSHIFUMI KITAMURA/AFP/Getty Images. 2008 AFP

unremarkable (Langley 2007), although recent critics have criticized her for being *too* controlled and wearing the mask of "being royal" too seriously. The quest to become royal thus continues.

The experience of Princess Masako involved a similar transformation but very different outcome. Despite her own reservations about her suitability "for the constraints and obligations of royal life" (Langley 2004c: 67), the wedding was greeted with much enthusiasm in Japan. At the outset, she declared that she would "find a point of harmonious balance between a traditional model of a crown princess and [her] personality," but the 1,200-strong imperial household rebuffed her efforts at reform and succeeded in remaking her in their image of a subservient crown princess:

> Her appearances became less frequent. Her previously stylish wardrobe gave way to the approved court look. She kept her eyes and voice lowered and, most disturbing of all, there was no sign of the baby that everyone was waiting for. (Langley 2004c: 68)

Although Masako had been aware of court protocol, she had not appreciated the extent to which "her entire life as a crown princess would be controlled and regulated to maximize the chances of breeding" (Langley 2004c: 65).

> As the pressure grew on her to produce an heir, so her appetite for independence seemed to dwindle. She gave up skiing and hiking—her favorite recreations—and looked in her rare appearances ever more dejected and resigned to life. (Langley 2004c: 68)

Although she did produce an heir in 2001, an adored girl called Aiko, this posed problems for the line of succession in a regime where only male heirs could assume the monarchy. As pressure for her to produce a useful heir mounted, Princess Masako had a major breakdown. Unusually, Crown Prince Naruhito, on congratulating the Danish engagement, explained that his wife would not be accompanying him because she had become "a virtual prisoner in the palace," not permitted to travel abroad and "physically and mentally exhausted" (Langley 2004: 68)—a distant image from the confident, elaborately dressed and coiffed bride in the twelve-layer, thirty-pound ceremonial robes at her wedding.

The princess was obliged to keep her eyes lowered, speak in a whisper, change her kimono three times a day, walk three steps behind her husband, request fourteen days in advance to travel into Tokyo, and only appear in public when directed. She has no money of her own and is not permitted to have her own telephone. The crown prince concluded: "There were moves which nullified Masako's career and nullified her character based on that career" (Langley 2004c: 65). Her public appearances are still few. In making this claim, Naruhito may have been warning Mary what lay in

**Mary of Denmark** Photo by Chris Jackson/Getty Images. 2006 Getty Images

store for her. Certainly comparisons have been made between the despair of Masako and "the tragedy of Diana," whose fairy-tale marriage unraveled and left her a global superstar without a stage.

Such examples illustrate the point that even in our individualistic culture and obsession with unique identity, the assertion of personality must vie with our habitus. In the case of commoners who marry princes, they are no longer individual personalities but a cog in the machinery of state, subject to the rituals, routines, and expectations of their role—not their sense of self. The courtiers around them precede and succeed them, so training a new incumbent in the codes of court life is of paramount importance for the longevity of the regime. Personality, character, taste, and inclinations must take a backseat to reproducing royal etiquette and protocol. The body, mind, and habitus of novitiate princesses must be retrained—literally refashioned—into those of royal personages recognized by distinctive attributes and roles. They are no longer individuals but occupants of a habitus—mere actors on the stage of royalty.

## CASE STUDY 15: The Metrosexual Man

"Twenty years ago, we sold [men's] clothes and now we sell fashion." (General manager of menswear at David Jones in Melbourne, quoted by Gotting 2003)

The term *metrosexual* was coined in the 1990s to refer to a new form of masculinity that was characterized by softer attitudes and opinions and fondness for shopping and concentrating on enhancing one's appearance. The metrosexual was a new kind of fop or Renaissance man—stylish, socially aware, and narcissistic. There was also an implication that his sexuality was less fixed than that dictated by conventional notions of masculinity. He was not homosexual or effeminate, but his persona contained some traces of both. Another definition of a metrosexual is "a clothes horse wrapped around a dandy fused with a narcissist" (McFedries 2006).

This suggests that the term is a new word for a type of progressive and sensitive man who has been recognized at different points in history. In many ways, the metrosexual is very similar to the Renaissance man of the early modern period, who was sophisticated, intellectual, and cultured. Similar terms include the macaroni, the fop, and the dandy.

In the 1960s, the "new man" made an appearance, reflecting a move away from traditional hard-edged masculinity and a more empathetic attitude toward women, traditional connotations of femininity, and new ideas about being feminine. The women's movement and feminism are purported to have prompted this reevaluation of masculinity. In fashion terms, the new man dressed in unisex casual clothes. In the 1980s he became a SNAG—a "sensitive new age guy." The SNAG is a man who is sensitive, concerned with his appearance and public image, and empathetic, especially to women. He is not as narcissistic and self-obsessed as the metrosexual man.

While there was a vigorous debate about just how sensitive the SNAG really was, the 1980s was a period when men's fashions began to come into their own and deviate from the traditional limited items of dress. Male models also began to proliferate on the runway and in advertisements such as Calvin Klein's advertisements for men's underwear, in which SNAGs began to appear. Fashion magazines for men as well as men's cosmetics, perfumes, and beauty treatments also proliferated. Men's fashion retailers, designer collections of men's clothes, and new products for men appeared on the market through the 1990s to cater for the new male consumer.

In 1994, British journalist Mark Simpson purportedly coined the word *metrosexual* in a newspaper article and the term was quickly adopted to refer to young urban men with a healthy disposable income who were sexually ambiguous and culturally attuned and dressed in flamboyant ultrafashion and reveled in conspicuous consumption and hedonistic lifestyles.

Metrosexual role models—often popular culture celebrities or icons, including actors Hugh Jackman, George Clooney, Robbie Williams, Daniel Craig, and Brad Pitt; sports stars David Beckham, Ian Thorpe, Joe Namath; and businessmen such as Lachlan Murdoch and Richard Branson—were soon identified.

Television programs such as *Queer Eye for the Straight Guy, Will and Grace,* and *Queer as Folk* were quick to characterize the metrosexual. The metrosexual revels in what is known as his feminine side. He is not afraid to cry or show emotions. He loves shopping and pays meticulous attention to color coordination of his clothing and home. He is very body conscious, with a taste for fahsion items that have been traditionally regarded as feminine, such as jewelry, cosmetics, and accessories. He has a different attitude toward the male body than most men and engages in body building and sculpting and dieting and has regular manicures and other forms of body modification that emphasize appearance rather than strength. One wit suggests it is a man who goes to the hairdresser rather than the barber.

Some commentators have suggested that metrosexuals are male impersonators, that is, men who are performing masculinity in a way that makes them attractive to both men and women. While debate persists as to the reality of the metrosexual male and whether this has consequences for gender relations and forms of male sexuality more generally, others argue that the metrosexual has already been eclipsed by the rise of the "übersexual," a man whose sexuality is unambiguously heterosexual but who appreciates a softer, cultured, consumerist persona.

Research suggests that advertising of men's products has shifted to reflect a softer image of masculinity, which is reflected in surveys showing that contemporary 2000s men are more secure in their masculinity and display more sensitivity and commitment to family values and domesticity—a happy home life and good friends—than men at any other time in modernity or postmodernity. What it means to be a male seems to be in flux.

Sharon Peoples and Jennifer Craik.

## CASE STUDY 16: The Cult of Thinness

The title of this case study is taken from a study by Hesse-Biber (2006) in which she argues that the commercial campaigns of the beauty and dieting industry in the 1980s and 1990s imposed unrealistic standards of thinness and beauty on contemporary women in first-world countries. As countries become more cosmopolitan and Westernized, so the cult of thinness grows. In 2008, for example, a media furor was created when leading Indian actresses appeared to sport newly ultrathin bodies at a film premiere, thus abandoning the traditional preference for slightly rounded female stars of Bollywood, India's film industry.

Symptoms of the obsession with weight and beauty include the incidence of dieting (about a quarter of the American population), consumption of diet food and beverages, sales of diet books, membership of weight-loss programs and consumption of products of the fitness industry (health clubs, exercise videos, and exercise clothing and sportswear). Cosmetic surgery (e.g., liposuction, stomach banding, stomach stapling) has also become more widespread in the past decade. While the desire for a svelte physique and toned body has traditionally been a preoccupation of women, men too have increasingly become caught up in it.

There are many ironies in this state of affairs. First, most of these weight-reduction techniques fail, and yet consumers eagerly sign up for more. Second, while some television and media programs, news stories, and advertisements heavily promote weight-loss products and lifestyles, others aggressively promote fast-food outlets, recipes, and food-dependent leisure activities. Third, while role models such as fashion models, actors, musicians, and other celebrities are pressured to become and stay unnaturally thin, this occurs in a media discourse that celebrates their ideal shape, on the one hand, yet castigates as abnormal, unhealthy, and risky this obsession with thinness, on the other. Fourth, the cult of thinness has spawned a myriad of eating disorders (such as anorexia and bulimia) among young women (and increasingly men) and some occupations (such as models, air stewards, dancers, actors, performers, beauty pageant contestants, and gymnasts and other athletes—as well as the wives of rich men) are even being called the anorexic professions. So how did we get to this contradictory state of affairs?

In preindustrial societies, the ideal body shape was often rounded and well endowed because it was associated with health and fertility. However, a trend toward thinner bodies can be detected as modernity took hold of European culture. Partly, this concerned the changing conventions about ideal body shapes that accompanied the emergence of modern fashion systems, but in addition, a succession of moral panics about starving, tight lacing, the condition called consumption, and beauty regimes attests to the underlying concern about body shape and size.

While the Victorian era exalted the S-shaped female body (large bosom, small waist, and large bustle), this silhouette later fell out of favor. Gymnastics for girls and women promoted exercises and ladylike sports that required a more a streamlined figure and muscular physique, and bicycling became a popular pastime for women, who reveled in the freedom it gave them. In the 1920s, the *garçonne* (or boyish) shape for women took hold, at least among the flappers and ultrafashionable avant-garde. This was also the period of the birth of beauty salons that specialized in special regimes using various mechanical contraptions, physical restraint, diets, supplements, chemicals, cosmetics and beauty products, exercises, and treatments such as saunas and mud baths to help women improve their body shape, tone, and attractiveness. The use of these regimes to achieve the desired ideal body shape was the precursor of the cult of thinness, which characterized twentieth-century notions of beauty.

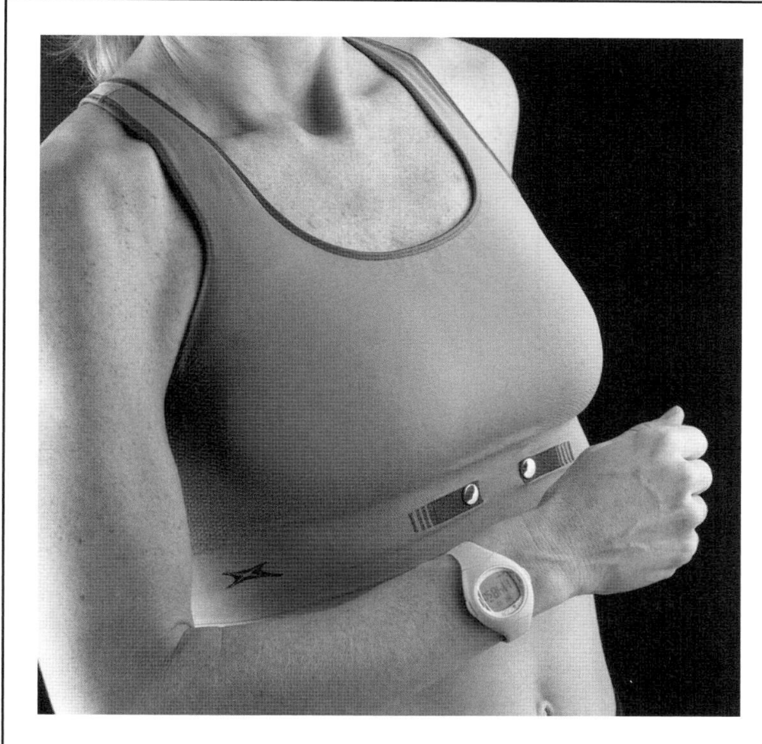

**Exercise top**

It seems to have been a byproduct of two trends: a new focus on youth and youthfulness (which valorized pre-adult bodies and looks) and the development of modern mass-media forms (which enabled the wide distribution of images of fashionable role models and new fads in beauty and exercise). Fashion photography epitomized this promotion of ideals of thinness, reflected in fashion magazines and advertising. The escalation of consumer culture and successful promotion of beauty-related products through advertising became an effective way to attract consumers, who were increasingly desperate to make their bodies conform to the ideal of the fashionable body. Hollywood celebrities, television stars, beauty queens, and fashion models were ever present to remind consumers of the pressure to emulate the ideal. Although erogenous zones shifted over time, that merely nudged the contours of the beauty cult and ideal. One can detect, over the course of the twentieth century, a decrease in the body size of key role models (see Keenan 1977).

Fashions reflected the emphasis on thinness, with designers creating new silhouettes that suited the young lithe mannequin but not the middle-aged matron. The fact that most couturiers were men—and often homosexual—reinforced a seemingly misogynistic attitude toward "normal" female bodies; however, female designers such as Madeleine Vionnet, Coco Chanel, Jeanne Lanvin, Madame Grès, and Elsa Schiaparelli seemed to hold similar views.

The growth of a specific youth culture from the 1950s, and especially the popular music culture of the 1960s and 1970s, produced new role models. The new generation of fashion models, among them England's Twiggy, promoted a childlike figure that has shaped fashion culture ever since and is reflected, for example, in the thinness of Kate Moss. Public debate about models who are too thin has recurred, especially when models have died from the effects of anorexia. Accusations that the media is responsible for increasing incidences of eating disorders by projecting unrealistically thin (and airbrushed) images of ideal bodies and beauty that pressure young women and men into dieting and risky weight-reduction behavior have not been sufficiently addressed. Eating disorder support groups and researchers argue that there is sufficient evidence that the media plays a significant role. The media denies that its influence can be proved.

**Yoga.** Photo by: LocalFitness.com.au

Within the modeling business and fashion industry more generally, dieting is an essential part of securing and maintaining a fashion-related career. There have even been reports of competitions between models to see who can eat the least. As a result, the size of models' bodies has decreased to a point that images of stark rib cages, leg bones, and bosom-less and hipless frames are reproduced on a daily basis as fashionable ideals. In the 2000s, the issue of extreme dieting has received wide public and government denunciation, leading some countries (via modeling agencies, fashion magazines, retailers, and organizers of fashion shows) to impose restrictions on the use of prepubescent models, introduce body mass indexes, impose penalties on those who promote extreme dieting, and outlaw pro-anorexia Web sites. More generally, thinness occurs among an extreme minority in the female population. A 2008 study by the Spanish government, supported by apparel retailer C&A, measured 10,000 women ages twelve to seventy, using a three-dimensional body-scanning system. It found that 56 percent of women had a normal body mass index, 25 percent were slightly overweight, and 12 percent were obese, but only 1.4 percent were thin or very thin (2456.com 2008). Moreover, women's body shapes change with age, with more developing an hourglass or pear-shaped body—shapes a long way from the catwalk waif.

Yet despite such developments, the cult of thinness seems to be here to stay, and increasingly the norm for boys and men as well as women. Public opinion may condemn extreme thinness as ugly and unhealthy, but consumer behavior and celebrity role models suggest that thinness remains the dominant body ideal as the fashion industry shows no sign of promoting a larger body.

Jennifer Craik and Sharon Peoples

# chapter 5

# fashion, aesthetics, and art

**CHAPTER OUTLINE**



**WHAT DOES THIS CHAPTER COVER?**

This chapter explores the issue of whether fashion is art. The field of art history and elite art have both maintained an elitist approach to fashion, at best exhibiting ambivalence as to whether fashion is a true art form or merely a derivative copy. Many fashion designers have been trained in art history and art and/or design practice and draw on previous aesthetic eras and genres in gaining inspiration for their collections. Yet the nature of the fashion industry, with its commercial orientation, media hype, concern with newness, and celebrity obsession, is at odds with the refined world of art, so the ambivalence toward fashion remains deeply seated.

Other aesthetic domains—such as architecture, design, dance, music, and craft—have been more sympathetic to fashion to the extent that closer links and interactions have developed. This chapter charts briefly the debates and contours of the relationship between fashion and aesthetics as well as considering the recent incorporation of fashion in museums, which signals a more receptive attitude toward the aesthetics of fashion.

Case studies explore the politics and aesthetics of fashion photography, the politics of exhibiting the collections of fashion enfant terrible Vivienne Westwood, the challenge of wearable art to fashion, and the aesthetics of the wristwatch as a fashion accessory.

## i. aesthetics and fashion

How does fashion relate to art? Is fashion art on legs? Is fashion a discrete art form with its own aesthetics? Or are art and fashion separate worlds running on divergent logics and different aesthetic codes? These questions are constantly debated by commentators.

In this chapter, we will see that fashion has an ambiguous or ambivalent relationship with the aesthetic realm. Yet the phenomenon of fashion is frequently elided with artistic trends and movements. While much fashion literature proclaims fashion to be the artistic essence of the time or draws parallels between art movements and fashion trends, few commentators have attempted to articulate the nature of the connection—or ask questions like how do the connections work, does art influence fashion or vice versa, or why are some examples of fashion and/or art privileged as exemplifying the relationship rather than others?

My main argument here is that there is little systematic understanding of how fashion fits in the wider aesthetic realm, although there have been discussions about the relationship (Arnold 2001; English 2007; Evans 2003; Hayward Gallery 1999; Mackrell 2005; Troy 2003; Wilson 1985). Sometimes parallels are drawn between fashion and other aesthetic forms; for example, a particular dress is seen as encapsulating a moment in art history or is placed alongside an iconic painting, piece of music, or building, as if they are part of a coordinated aesthetic impulse. Nevertheless, little attention is paid to explaining this coincidence or serendipity—that is to say, how is it that these connections develop within an aesthetic phase or artistic movement, and how is it that subsequent generations read garments, paintings, or buildings as having a taken-for-granted simultaneity?

But first we need to define what is meant by *aesthetics* and its relationship to the more specific term *art.* Dictionary definitions commonly define aesthetics as the philosophy of sensuous perception, theory of taste, criticism of beauty belonging to the appreciation of the beautiful, and relating to principles of good taste. It is a subjective appreciation of beauty—socially constructed and deconstructed.

Raymond Williams (1977: 27–28), in his book *Keywords*, traced the changing meanings and uses of the term *aesthetics.* Although the term is derived from the Greek, Williams notes that it entered English in the early nineteenth century by way of the German usage of the Greek term. At this stage, the emphasis of aesthetics was the importance of "sense perception," that is, the ability to recognize something as having aesthetic value via "apprehension through the senses." It was through the bodily senses that beauty (defined as "phenomenal perfection") could be appreciated. This idea of "subjective sense activity" became the centerpiece of the concepts of art and creativity as an exclusive and restricted individual practice.

By the late nineteenth century, this restriction of aesthetic appreciation to those with refined senses (cultural capital, in today's terms) was under challenge. It was considered snobbish or elitist. Poets and critics such as Samuel Taylor Coleridge (1875–1912) and Matthew Arnold (1822–88) rejected the term *aesthetic,* instead using the terms *taste* and *criticism,* and relegated *aesthetics* and *aesthete* to derogatory uses. Williams (1977: 28) concludes:

**It is clear from this history that aesthetic, with its specialized references to art, to visual appearance, and to a category of what is "fine" or "beautiful," is a key formation in a group of meanings which at once emphasized and isolated subjective sense-activity as the basis of art and beauty as distinct, for example, from *social* or *cultural* interpretations.**

Williams's account of the changing meaning and use of the term helps explain why the realm of aesthetics is imbued with ambivalence and suspicion. For example, the term *art* originally referred to skills, and an artist was one who practiced a particular skill (Williams 1974: 32–34). Indicatively, the terms *artist* and *artisan* were interchangeable until the late sixteenth century. Over the next three centuries, the terms *art* and *artist* gradually became associated with branches of the "fine arts," namely, painting, drawing, engraving, and sculpture, while the term *artisan* increasingly referred to specialist skilled manual or technical workers. By the mid-nineteenth century, *art* was linked to the terms *culture* and *aesthetics,* where a hierarchy of taste and appreciation was implied. The arts occupied a rarefied domain in contrast to (useful) arts (the productions of artisans, craftsmen, and technicians). This antithetical use is especially apparent when the idea of aesthetics is applied to a creative practice that is firmly embedded in everyday habits and consumer culture, namely, the area of fashion.

It is therefore not surprising that other terms employed in explaining fashion have inherited this ambivalence and tension between exclusivity and popularity (as we saw in chapter 1). These different terms refer to particular aspects of the fashion process and distinct moments of an individual's place in the performance of fashion as social practice. There are social and collective meanings of fashion versus individual sanctioned tastes and personal choices from a register of tastes.

Concepts such as aesthetics and beauty are cultural constructs shared by a group and defined within a cultural milieu, while *style* and *taste* refer to nuanced articulations of elements of beauty and aesthetics. These are like building blocks or the pieces of the jigsaw of the aesthetic realm. However, aesthetics is not a matter of personal taste—collective norms and elite or social acceptance hold sway. Hence there is a shared sense of what constitutes style and taste, especially as defined (and practiced) by the cognoscenti of fashion—the fashion setters, fashion police, and **fashion victims.** Terms such as *flair* and *panache* seem to pertain to individual interpretations and manifestations of the act of dressing fashionably.

The difficulty of defining fashion concepts is that, although the link between fashion and aesthetics is central to each term, there is something indefinable that makes a garment, style, or look count as being in fashion by the gatekeepers of the phenomenon. While there is some reference to currently prevailing dominant aesthetic styles (e.g., cubism, ethnic romanticism, postmodernism), only some fashions are singled out as epitomizing a new trend or aesthetic epoch. Periodic stylistic shifts in clothing habits and fashionable behavior as well as individual interpretations of stylistic conventions can be found in *all* cultures, including preindustrial cultures, folk cultures, and transitional cultures. So, the development of European-derived fashion systems can only be comprehensible in relation to the development of particular aesthetic regimes associated with industrialization and the aesthetics of modernity that shaped contemporary European culture.

A mix of formal and informal modes of regulation and authorization of fashion apply in this case. On the formal side, sumptuary laws have been supplanted by organizations' prescriptions of clothing behavior concerning uniforms (e.g., the military, police, schools, hospitals, prisons), codes of morality (e.g., bouncers at nightclubs, public institutions, religions), and ideology (e.g., following revolutions, at national celebrations, among oppositional political groups). Informally, there are also arbiters or trendsetters of fashion and style in subcultures, cults, and friendship groups.

Added to this, the regulation of high fashion has been achieved by gatekeepers or "fashion police" (see Wigley 2003: 35–58), those who count as "polite society" and define the terms of the dominant consensual aesthetic, namely, what qualities constitute good taste, beauty, sensual pleasure, and the like, at any particular moment. These may include the social elite, fashion designers, fashionistas, fashionable celebrities, and avant-garde (or extreme) artists. Instead of being a seamless process, the phenomenon of fashion (the pointy end of continuous change in style) involves challenging the status quo of fashion and introducing some new element to the accepted aesthetic that may deconstruct, reconstruct, un-construct, or remove some component of that aesthetic. But this is only successful if it is legitimated and adopted by influential gatekeepers.

Once legitimated in this way, a new fashion—however absurd—percolates from the fashion arbiters to wider groups and classes. In essence, fashion redresses the void, the space between the body and space (see Quinn 2003a: 63–92). So new innovations in fashion upset the consensus of available choices of beauty and taste yet, if and when accepted, redefine the range of taste and expressive options. It is this process of challenge to the status quo, followed by controversy, rejection or acceptance, and incorporation or obsolescence, that redefines the aesthetic impulse, but this process is the most difficult to conceptualize or explain. Some clues come from the exploration of the relationship between fashion and other aesthetic domains, to which we now turn.

## ii. spatial aesthetics and fashion

One of the few who have attempted to investigate seriously the relationship between fashion and non-art aesthetics is Bradley Quinn, who, as a journalist and author, has explored the links between fashion and other aesthetic forms in his books *Techno Fashion* (2002), *Chinese Style: The Art of Living* (2001), and *Scandinavian Style* (2003). In *The Fashion of Architecture* (2003), for example, Quinn has explored how architecture "is making its presence felt in cutting-edge fashion," with building materials and techniques "creeping onto the catwalk." He begins with the observation that "although the relationship between architecture and fashion was recognized more than a century ago, the connection between them has rarely been explored by historians, designers or practising architects."

At first blush, it may seem strange to link fashion with spatial design, but Quinn shows not only how they have always had close connections (as evident in the sculptural designs of Balenciaga, for instance) but how, now, the two realms are on a collision course. Clothes are becoming "wearable dwellings," while tailoring techniques of "pleating, stapling, cutting and draping" are being incorporated in building design. In fact, in a number of places, fashion and design courses have been moved out of art schools and departments of art history or textiles and relocated to departments and faculties of architecture and design associated with the built environment.

This brings the three-dimensional (volume or architectural) elements of clothing and fashion to the fore. We need to explore the interrelationships between clothes, buildings, and the spaces in which they are animated. Fashion and architecture are increasingly intertwined. Quinn (2003a: 133) argues that

**many exchanges are taking place between art, fashion and architecture. Their fascination for one another seems to spiral around their mutual desire to see life transmuted into art.**

The relationship is intense. While artists like to draw on the themes of "fantasy and desire" that are central to fashion design, architects draw on art, on the one hand, to create new forms that are the physical manifestation of artistic principles, and fashion, on the other, to borrow its interpretations of "imagery, structure and identity" (Quinn 2003a: 133).

These different aesthetic realms are like bees buzzing around the honey pot of the aesthetic zeitgeist of the moment, trying to capture its flavor in diverse artistic forms, each referencing and interconnecting with the other yet maintaining its distinctiveness. Fashion draws on adjacent aesthetic realms such as art and architecture in order to push the boundaries and exaggerate the aesthetic conventions encoded in other artistic forms. By building on the recognized dominant artistic imagery, frameworks, and notions of identity, fashion design translates these concepts into items of clothing and body decoration that encapsulate the contemporary consensus and preoccupations in human "imagination, memory and emotion" (Quinn 2003b: 136).

In translating these into physical forms, fashion works to define the relationship between the body and social space, "between private experience and public content" (Quinn 2003a: 135). But notwithstanding these connections and contiguities, there is still an ambivalent relationship between fashion and other aesthetic forms—not just art and architecture but also photography, cinema, design, music, and new approaches to museum exhibitions—as we explore later in this chapter and case studies.

Quinn's observations (2003a: 136) develop Georg Simmel's metaphorical depiction of "society as a whole" as a garment, relating the "threads of its **weave** and the embroideries of its surface to the manifestations of modern life." The warp and weft, texture and patterning, fold and flow, and shape and structure of garments and textiles spell out the parameters of our cultural lodestones. In the fashioning of these forces in physical forms, positive, negative, and contested impulses are simultaneously encoded—the angst as much as the beauty, now-ness as much as tradition, stability as much as change.

One of the challenges of life is guessing or betting on what aesthetic moments will resonate and become embedded in our cultural history as exemplifying successive artistic moments or trends. Those emanations that don't last become denigrated as mere "fashion" while those that do are exalted as expressing or defining the dominant aesthetic or zeitgeist of the times. The very term *fashion,* then, becomes a pejorative term as much as a description of definitive cultural contours.

Although there were undoubtedly links between art, architecture, and fashion in the development of modernism, architecture later came to despise short-term fashions in design and building. Le Corbusier, for example, sought the "essence" that characterized the "deeper" manifestations of exteriors. "Differences of style, the trivialities (frivolities) of passing fashion, which are only illusions or masquerades, do not concern" him (quoted by Wigley 2003: 38). Describing a "project as 'fashion' is tantamount to excommunication in architectural circles," with iconic examples

**Hussein Chalayan.** Photo by PIERRE VERDY/AFP/Getty Images. 2006 AFP

of cutting-edge architecture "rationalized as aesthetic choices rather than stylistic ones" (Quinn 2003a: 3). To those expressing this view, fashion is merely decoration and ornamentation, superficial renovation of the surface of the body or a building.

A vehement opponent of the link between art and fashion is Richard Martin (1999: 153), who, in his study of fashion and cubism, declares that

**a hundred years ago, the relation between art and fashion was sought in the like sensations of a synaesthetic [the sense impression of a mental image] world. Of late, we have been prone to link art and fashion through the issues of body, gender, and identity that are key to contemporary art and equally crucial to contemporary fashion.**

Despite these similarities, Martin (1999: 153) contends that art and fashion are separate domains that are not "animated by, or heading toward the same aims and criteria," because fashion "is irrevocably commercial" and thus its "system is somewhat different from the system and culture of art." He goes on to argue that art has deeper motives and makes more critical interventions in the desire for social and cultural change, while fashion merely skims the coattails of art and superficially enjoins the battle for change and transformation. Since Martin does not expand on the worthy motives and interventions of art as compared with fashion, this argument merely restates the common argument and prejudice that art has deep meanings while fashion is trivial and ephemeral.

This tense relationship seems to be coming to the fore in postmodernist culture, where leading architects "are employing the principles of fashion design to create membrane structures and mobile buildings" (Quinn 2003a: 4). In the same way, many leading fashion designers are as much influenced by the principles of architecture—both structural and spatial—as they are by art and fashion histories. Reflecting on the work of contemporary cutting-edge designers, Quinn (2003a: 5) argues:

**Garments are wrapped around the body in successive layers of underwear, outer clothing and overcoats that define the outer core of the body. ... Within this system the garments can be seen as more than mere clothing—they form part of a structure that negotiates the relationship between private spaces and public arenas, both defining our identity and place in society.**

As similarities in fashion and architectural practice are identified through layering and structuring to produce distinctive shapes and relationships between the private and the public, fashion and architecture are increasingly sharing a common set of principles (Lee 2005). Both play with mass, volume, line, and flow; both play with deconstructionist principles; both are involved in the development and deployment of new technologies, fibers, and processes; and both are heavily influenced by the backdrop of and debates about urban space and lifestyle.

## iii. fashion as aesthetic zeitgeist

Consequently, histories of aesthetic trends and cultural histories are redolent with iconic examples of art, architecture, and fashion. The mood of a period is often represented by the oeuvre of one particular designer—or even by one garment. For example, the cover of Alice Mackrell's book *Fashion and Art: The Impact of Art on Fashion and Fashion on Art* (2005) reproduces the famous Mondrian dress by Yves Saint Laurent (for which a Mondrian painting was reproduced in fabric). Heralding his subsequent pop art collection, this one dress, part of his 1965–66 collection, came to stand for the Swinging Sixties and cemented Saint Laurent's reputation as a couturier who encapsulated the zeitgeist of the moment—in particular by engaging youth culture rather than the conservative culture of couture and its matron clients (Art Gallery of New South Wales 1987; Buxbaum 2005; see case study 7). Mackrell (2005: 148) describes this dress as "the welding of art and fashion," which

**brought a new elegance and sophistication to *haute couture.* But [it was] also designated by *Harper's Bazaar* in September 1965 as "the dress of tomorrow." Saint Laurent's Mondrian concept of treating these dresses like canvases was a phenomenon, and manufacturers made cheap copies for the mass market.**

Mackrell's analysis involves a retrospective designation of the feel of the time and equation of this with a single garment, although she notes how perceptively Saint Laurent could get a whiff of new cultural moods and how he conceived his prêt-à-porter designs "in terms of machine fabrication" (Mackrell 2005: 148). In other words, although a couturier, he was well attuned to art history, on the one hand, and modern mass production and consumption, on the other. Nonetheless, Mackrell's book is organized around matching artistic movements to designers as if there were a seamless articulation of each aesthetic period in the fashions of the time.

A more nuanced analysis of the relationship between art and fashion is offered by Troy (2003), who analyzes the complex interdependencies between the development of Paris fashion with other aesthetic movements (such as modernism and its expression in theater) and rapid expansion of commercial culture (and its encapsulation in advertising and marketing). She identifies the "fashion conundrum," namely, "the contradiction that characterizes the (supposedly) unique and auratic object when it is subjected to the conditions of mass consumption in an industrialized economy" (Troy 2003: 334). Like art itself, fashion depends on "an audience, a discourse, a profile in the public sphere" for its very success (Troy 2003: 335). For Troy (2003: 336), the ability of the department store to make "exotic" and "unique" fashions available to the "bourgeois mass market" while retaining the tropes of "creative genius" and exclusivity "abruptly leveled the societal playing field." Consumer culture and mass marketing have made aesthetic objects available to ordinary people and made at least populist versions of aesthetic discourse widely available. Consumers can acquire an example of an aesthetic that serves as a talisman of their cultural capital (see box 5.1).

Shoes, too, can be retrospectively designated as expressing an era (see, e.g., Bossan 2004; Mitchell 1997; Pattison and Cawthorne 1997; Pratt and Woolley 1998; Steele 1998): so pumps are identified with the 1900s, bar-strap shoes with the 1910s, decorative Cuban heeled dancing shoes with the 1920s, walking shoes with the 1930s, wedges with the 1940s, stilettos with the 1950s, knee-high boots with the 1960s, platform shoes with the 1970s, **Doc Martens** and athletic shoes with the 1980s, and leisure footwear (boots, athletic shoes, sandals) and a revival of long, pointed stilettos in place of leisure shoes with the 2000s (Pattison and Cawthorne 1997: 134–55). Yet we know that very few people wore these types of footwear during these decades. They were largely confined to the "chic" groups or select self-referential subgroups. Similar lists could be devised for other garments and fashionable accessories, for example, hairstyles, handbags, suits, or headwear.

We also think of Western fashion in terms of chronology—decades representing style eras. So some decades become associated indisputably with fashion figures or defining moments relating to aesthetic movements: the first decade of the 1900s with **Orientalism**; the 1920s with Coco Chanel; the 1930s with Schiaparelli and Hollywood glamour; the 1950s with Christian Dior and Emilio Pucci; the 1960s with Swinging London (Mary Quant, Laura Ashley, Biba) and pop art (Courrèges, Rabanne, YSL); the 1970s with ethnic Yves Saint Laurent, Japanese-born Kenzo Takada, and punk-inspired Westwood; the 1980s with Japanese deconstructionism, radical Gaultier, and erotic Versace; and the 1990s with the global village versus futurism (Buxbaum 2005; Mackrell

### Box 5.1 The Case of Perfume as the Essence of Aesthetics

Fashion is not the only aesthetic form that has been elided retrospectively with the essence of the moment. Fashion accessories or accoutrements also resonate with aesthetic tastes. Perfume is one such example. The distinctive point about perfume is that because it is a scent, it is difficult to encapsulate the essence of a particular perfume in a representational form (see Craik 1994: 164–75; see also chapter 2). Although sachets of scents are now commonly glued into fashion magazines, generally the smell of a perfume cannot be depicted in advertisements and fashion spreads. Instead, advertisers promote perfume by conveying desired attributes of the iconic wearer of the perfume. This may be done through the choice of person who models the perfume (usually a well-known model or actor), narrative imagery conveying emotions or desires associated with the perfume (such as seduction or fantasy), or personal attributes desired by the wearer, which he or she possesses by identifying with a particular scent (adventurous, sexy, glamorous, and dangerous).

As perfume companies compete in this market, some perfumes are more successful than others in capturing the spirit of the time in the way they associate the characteristics of the scent with the feel of the moment (see Aftel 2000; Craik 1994: 164–75; Farkas 1951; Finkelstein 1994; Irvine 1996; Kennett 1975; Pavia 1995–96; Todtri 2002). For example, Coco Chanel's eponymous perfume Chanel No. 5 is often cited as the fragrance of the post–World War I period because of its success in reflecting the personality of the designer herself (as modern and unconventional) as well as the attributes associated with her clothes, that is, satisfying the needs and roles of the "new woman" (see chapter 4).

Perfume has become a highly valuable part of the profitability of designer labels, not so much because it may have an attractive scent, but because it evokes a captivating name, a bottle, a role model, or an idealized image. As designers have recognized the value of fragrance, they have released new lines with increasing frequency, hoping to put the genie of each moment into a bottle.

Perfume by Decade
1920s Arpege (Lanvin)
1930s Joy (Jean Patou) and Shocking (Elsa Schiaparelli)
1940s Miss Dior (Christian Dior), L'Air du Temps (Nina Ricci)
1950s Magie (Lancôme) and Youth Dew (Estée Lauder)
1960s Ô de Lancôme (Lancôme) and Zen (Shiseido)
1970s Rive Gauche and Opium (Yves Saint Laurent), Charlie (Revlon), and Anaïs Anaïs (Cacharel
1980s Samsara (Guerlain)
1990s Eau d'Issey (Issey Miyake), Ysatis (Givenchy), Obsession (Calvin Klein) and Red Door (Elizabeth Arden)
2000s J'adore (Dior), Trésor (Lancôme), Palazzo (Fendi), Elle (Yves Saint Laurent), Ange ou Démon (Givenchy), Gucci by Gucci, and The One (Dolce & Gabbana)

2005). The first decade of the 2000s has become synonymous with global luxury accessories and availability, on the one hand, and with questions of sustainability and "eco" fashion, on the other.

These labels become unquestionable statements and linkages, although, of course, anyone who has experienced any one of these decades may make different iconic designations and have very different memories of the zeitgeist of the time. What is interesting is how and why such taken-for-granted, naturalized aesthetic associations come to be made in the first place.

I would argue that fashion is a complex lexicon of aesthetic trends where aesthetics refers to a complex interplay between or medley of style, beauty, and taste. Links can be made between styles in fashion and styles in other aesthetic realms—art practice, architecture, photography, film, technology, landscape/streetscape. Yet the nature of the link is not explored or even clearly articulated in the fashion world. Rather the connection or correlation is presented as natural and obvious. Aesthetic forms become the material trace or sediment of an era or epoch, the flavor of a specific taste regime. How can we account for this process of encapsulation and retrospective ascription of the aesthetic essence of fashionability?

## iv. artistic fashion and cultural shifts

To construct an aesthetic history of fashion, commentators have related particular moments in aesthetic manifestations to particular designers and particular garments (see, e.g., Buxbaum 2005; De Marly 1980; Mendes and de la Haye 1999; Quinn 2003a). Examples include:

- **Constructivism and the Ballet Russes costume design and its influence on fashion**
- **Orientalism and the work of Paul Poiret, especially the hobble skirt**
- **Body-hugging aesthetics and the clothes of Coco Chanel**
- **Art deco and the fashion illustrations of Èrte**
- **Surrealism and the radical designs of Elsa Schiaparelli**
- **Pop culture aesthetics and op-art clothing and later punk**
- **Postmodernity and the radical asymmetrical structural designs of the Japanese designers such as Kenzo Takada, Issey Miyake, Yohji Yamamoto, and Rei Kawakubo of Comme des Garçons**

Above all, designers have, through their clothes, systematically redefined the contours and volume of the body. Martin (1999) has argued that cubism had a particularly strong influence on the work of early twentieth-century designers such as Poiret, Vionnet, and Chanel (Charles-Roux 1995; de la Haye and Tobin 2001). While this periodization is a useful device, it tends to elide the diversity of fashion looks at any one time or even within a particular designer's collection.

Another designer influenced in part by cubism was the French artist Sonia Delaunay, who in both her art and her clothes dressed the body like a canvas yet saw the body as being mobile and having a dynamic connection with its modernist surroundings (Baron 1995; Craik 1994; Damase 1991). Delaunay explicitly recognized the ways in which the body is clothed as an active process and technical means for constructing and presenting a sense of selfhood or persona. The body performs according to the arrangement of clothing, forms of adornment, and gesture, leading Blaise Cendars, in his poem "The Simultaneous Dress," to reflect on Delaunay's designs: "On her dress she wears a body." Delaunay's revolutionary approach to clothing had two key dimensions. First, she favored simple, practical lines of clothing that followed the shape of the female body rather than producing or modifying it. Second, she used the body as a canvas, draping her clothes around the body and applying bold and colorful geometric patterns that followed bodily vectors. Delaunay's work reflected aesthetic trends (fauvism, cubism, Dada, surrealism, and her term "simultaneity") surrounding the changing role of women in the 1920s as they became more actively involved in the public sphere and dynamically adjusted to rapid changes occurring during the period.

She articulated the influence of painting on fashion and fabric design in a lecture given at the Sorbonne in 1927 (Damase 1991: 69), and although she returned exclusively to painting in 1930, her impact on subsequent fashion design was significant. In a sense, she was translating contemporary aesthetic principles into bodily techniques via her clothes. Artistic impulses were thus captured in fashion and a new fashion aesthetic developed out of her work. In the manner outlined above of eliding a figure with an aesthetic

**Sonia Delanuay.** Photo by Luigi Diaz/Getty Images. 2007 Getty Images

moment, Delaunay was retrospectively designated "the incarnation of her times"—namely, the artistic currents of the 1920s (quoted by Baron 1995: 84).

If Delaunay's experiments in fashion and fabric were revolutionary, they had a much less public dramatic impact than the forays of Elsa Schiaparelli during the next decade. Often retrospectively regarded as synonymous with her 1936 Shocking Pink collection, Schiaparelli was both a brilliant definer of line and form and a revolutionary in her approach to decoration and design. Yet her most common legacy remains her invention of a new kind of pink, neither candy nor magenta. Recognizing that she was on to something, Schiaparelli popularized her new shade by naming her perfume Shocking. After customers requested matching cosmetics, she established a line of Shocking lipstick, rouge, jewelry, and hair accessories, thereby "initiating" designer-manufactured "matching beauty products" (White 1986: 154–58; see also Schiaparelli 2007).

These lines became more profitable than her couture and set in train the practice of designers complementing their clothing collections with designer beauty products and accessories. Women who could not afford couture clothes could still buy an affordable bit of their favorite designer in the form of a scent or eye shadow. The same principle was applied to her Schiap boutique, the first coordinated outlet offering a complete range of clothes and accoutrements for the fashionable aspirant. Schiaparelli was always larger than life, and her designs and catwalk shows adopted racy formats with light shows, music, dancing, stunts, and jokes (White 1986: 164). While she shocked the establishment, the fashionistas and fashion critics loved her exuberance and irreverence. Yves Saint Laurent declared:

**She slapped Paris. She smacked it. She tortured it. She bewitched it. And it madly fell in love with her. (Quoted by White 1986: 11)**

As well as having a distinctive sense of line and cut, Schiaparelli borrowed from a myriad of artistic traditions, cultural referents, and decorative motifs to create exquisite but startling looks often augmented by stunning jewelry, embroidery, sequins, and other decorative devices. These included her Cocteau urn/two-faces dress, her 1937 Dali-inspired Lobster evening dress, her 1938 Harlequin patched coat inspired by the commedia dell'arte, and her 1938 Dali-inspired tear dress, of which White (1986: 134) said: "This extraordinary precursor of punk caused a furor when it appeared." Perhaps her single most famous garment remains her shocking pink wool cape featuring a Medusa head embroidered in gold tweed and sequins.

Although often associated with the interwar 1930s period, when she was regarded as the "undisputed queen of Paris fashion" (White 1986: 172), Schiaparelli survived the war years by relocating to America and attempted to resume her "shocking" career after the war. Although White (1986: 213) claims she prefigured Dior's New Look, Schiaparelli's collections failed to seduce the postwar public and created mounting debts. Her perfume empire was her salvation, but she remained convinced that she was above all a couturier and was always, until her death in 1973, "properly coiffed, made up, dressed in exquisite lingerie, scented in 'Shocking' and surrounded by flowers and photographs of her family and friends" (White 1986: 217).

In some ways, her devotee Yves Saint Laurent (see case study 7) continued her artistic approach by combining exquisitely cut garments with her decorative and irreverent fervor (Art Gallery of New South Wales 1987). He also recognized the need to make his clothes wearable and less shocking than Schiaparelli's designs. Saint Laurent—like Dior—recognized the emergence of a distinctive youth culture and market in the postwar 1950s and 1960s. While continuing to pander to the matronly couture core market, Saint Laurent embellished his collections with historical and artistic references that appealed to a younger generation. These were marketed under his Rive Gauche label. Celebrities, too, loved his garments, and this became an increasingly important means of publicizing his name and oeuvre.

The psychedelic, pop art, and ethnic-inspired motifs in Saint Laurent's collections (from Mondrian, Picasso, Matisse, and Cocteau to inspirations from Africa, Russia, Spain, China, and India) made him the designer of the 1970s, due to his ability to read political and cultural shifts. The popularity and legibility of his collections expanded the outreach of Parisian couture to new consumers, new markets, and new places. But his success simultaneously challenged the elite status of Paris and the couturier as street wear and a younger generation of designers increasingly influenced fashion trends and youth culture, which began to designate the zeitgeist of the times. The traditional haute couture center, Paris, was now in competition with brash new fashion capitals such as New York, London, Milan, and Tokyo (see chapter 2).

## v. from aesthetic innovation to curation

Aesthetic sensibilities again changed in the 1980s and 1990s as Japanese designers appeared in Paris to rewrite the principles of line, space, volume, and bodily form. The Japanese invasion was also a mix of East and West and of old and new. The draping and layered cut of kimonos was combined with new versions of Western garments to create new possibilities and a new fashion aesthetic. The new aesthetic was a combination of Western and Eastern techniques. Jones (1987: 191) argues that it was Vivienne Westwood's 1981 Pirate collection, which

**used deliberately coarse fabric and loose, tied-on, wraparound drapery, [that] prefigure[d] the 1982–83 Japanese coup d'état, which would use the same technique, but with more abstract imagery and without reference to rock, youth culture, or specific quasi-historical parable.**

She observes that Rei Kawakubo

**appropriated torn holes in her 1983 collection, which alluded to concepts in 1977 British punk fashion. Issey Miyake was reported to have attended Westwood showings, and his 1984 line showed great affinity for Westwood's use of Third World sources. (Jones 1987: 191)**

The genius of the Japanese designers was that they fused traditional techniques of dyeing, cutting, weaving, embroidery, shaping, pleating, and sewing with the latest technological advances in fabrics, computer design, and manufacture to create new shapes and seamless garments and produce effects (such as folds, pleats, and crumpling) technically (Mitchell 2005: 9–17). Accordingly, Mitchell (2005: 17) declares that

**the use of technologically advanced fabrics, highly developed skills and ingenuity, and an**

**Comme des Garçons.** Photo by FRANCOIS GUILLOT/AFP/Getty Images. 2006 AFP

**interest in experimentation and innovation are the hallmarks of fashion from Japan.**

The Japanese revolution in Paris fashion signaled the influence of new aesthetics, new techniques, and new approaches to the fashion industry. Between 1970 and 2002, twenty-nine Japanese designers launched collections in Paris, and most relocated to Paris (see box 5.2).

While Kenzo and Hanae Mori were the first to make a mark on Paris, they were soon joined by designers such as Miyake, Yamamoto, and Kawakubo, who also entered the Parisian pantheon of great designers. Since those heady days,

**Box 5.2 Key Japanese Designers in Paris and Year of Their First Paris Collection**

|  |  |
|---|---|
| Kenzo Takada | 1970 |
| Issey Miyake | 1973 |
| Hanae Mori | 1977 |
| Yohji Yamamoto | 1981 |
| Rei Kawakubo of Comme des Garçons | 1981 |
| Junya Watanabe | 1993 |
| Naoki Takizawa (designer for Miyake) | 1994 |
| Miki Mialy | 1996 |
| Yoichi Nagasawa | 1997 |
| Keita Maruyama | 1997 |
| Gomme by Hiroshige Maki | 1997 |
| Yuji Yamada | 1999 |
| Undercover by Jun Takahashi | 2002 |

Source: Kawamura 2004: 105. For specific designers, see Bénaïm 1997; Buxbaum 2005; Callaway 1988; English 2005; Dudjic 1990; Fondation Cartier pour l'Art Contemporain 1999; Fukai 2005; Grand 1998; Mitchell 2005; Miyake Design Studio 1978; Sainderichin 1999.

there has been a steady stream of Japanese designers heading for Paris (Kawamura 2004).

The Japanese approach to aesthetic design generally shaped a revolutionary rethinking of the structure of clothing. It was coined "the aesthetics of poverty" by Harold Koda (quoted by English 2005: 29) and seemed to speak to and for a world experiencing instability, imbalance, and rejection of mainstream aesthetics. Asymmetric clothes that were "torn, ripped and ragged" triggered an antifashion feeling that destabilized the already shaky couture system and hierarchy and instated a youth-driven, anomic, and alienated cultural zeitgeist. Indicative of this was the work of Issey Miyake, arguably the most successful designer of the Japanese design generation. Miyake reconceptualized "the kimono to create a different aesthetic milieu," namely, "the wrapping of the body in cloth":

> **He has created anti-structural, organic clothing which takes on a sculptural quality that suggests a natural freedom, expressed through the simplicity of cut, the abundance of new fabrics, the space between the garment and the body, and its general flexibility. (English 2005: 35)**

The effect of the Japanese designers has been the undoing of assumptions about the inner and outer body, the nature of clothing as "skin," and the tactile quality of how the body is clothed. According to Akiko Fukai (2005: 26–27),

> **in the 1980s, Japanese fashion made an impact with its *wabi sabi*–inspired designs in turn with the minimalist movement. In the 21st century, it is attracting renewed attention with its *manga*-inspired *kawaii* [infantile and childlike] designs. This can be seen as a transitional phase, at a time of uncertainty in which the world is exploring innovative styles and designs as it seeks for a new framework of society.**

Japanese fashion design has also created strong links with other aesthetic forms, notably architecture, theater, sculpture, film, and media. In sum, the Japanese influence on Paris has been profound. Not only have their different approaches to design and construction as well as a distinctively Japanese aesthetic had an impact on fashion design principles. Kawamura argues that the importance of the Japanese designers in threefold: first, they have been included as members of Paris's couture and prêt-à-porter organizations—the inner sanctum of Paris fashion; second, the production of **fragrance** lines confirms the success of these designers; and third, their designs have been shown in exhibitions and collected in museums, thus confirming their status as significant cultural artifacts.

More generally, the Japanese invasion shook up the complacency and inward-looking character of the Paris fashion industry and injected it with a new lease on life and new approaches to design, promotion, and marketing (de la Haye 2001). So, while young Japanese designers have taken advantage of opportunities in Paris to develop their visibility and international profile, it has proved to be

**a mutually beneficial relationship. Each is indispensable to the other. Yet, however successful and famous the Japanese became in Paris, it was still not successful enough to make Tokyo an international fashion city. (Kawamura 2004: 111–12)**

The Japanese designers have been transcending and countering seasonal trends with their distinctive approach to fashion. As de la Haye (2001: 37) concludes,

**critics draw on the terminology of fine art and architecture to describe clothes that can defy standard fashion vocabulary. Defined as conceptual—as mind rather than body clothes—it is often implied that ideas take precedence over function. While some parallels clearly exist, the designers are adamant that they are not artists, they are in the business of selling clothes and do so with impressive commercial success.**

The Japanese contribution to European fashion has been, argues de la Haye, their singular "visions and modernity" in a sea of "pastiche and revival."

Taken together, the designers covered in this chapter exemplify the way in which a name or garment is retrospectively designated as embodying the mood of a particular time. Those chosen here have been significant in challenging the status quo of fashion, redefining body-space relations, redrawing the grammar of the fashion system, and speaking to the cultural mood of the times (Wilcox 2001). Moreover, each has had a popular uptake—as opposed to iconic designers whose work has been profound but in a much more exclusive and limited domain (e.g., Balenciaga, Jean Paul Gaultier, Hussein Chalayan) (Frankel 2001; Steele 2001; Wilcox 2001).

The fashion industry has always been imbued with short-term thinking, infatuation, and chameleon reinvention. Critics would also cite egotism, bitchiness, hypocrisy, and camp following. Its recurring aesthetic tastes inevitably reflect these tensions, where newness is only ever for its own sake and everyday clothing habits continue to only superficially adopt the iconic elements of successive design statements. The zeitgeist of that aesthetic remains elusive, structured by key social, cultural, and political forces but ultimately dependent on its imaginative encapsulation in garments that speak for the time and its people.

Recognition of this has come in the form of fashion exhibitions and fashion collections in museums and art galleries, which began in the 1980s. One of the first was the retrospective of the work of Yves Saint Laurent staged by the Metropolitan Museum of Art in New York in 1983–84. The curator, Richard Martin, acknowledged Saint Laurent's "appropriation of art," which gave his fashions "the same perceptions as art" (quoted by Mackrell 2005: 153). Shortly after, in 1985, the Louvre opened its Musée de la Mode et du Textile and held prêt-à-porter shows in its courtyard. At the launch, minister of culture Jack Lang articulated the connection between fashion and cultural aesthetics:

**There would no doubt be something slightly paradoxical in opening a fashion museum if fashion were just a seasonal trend—a fashion museum is the history of practices and looks. (Quoted by Mackrell 2005: 153–54)**

The challenge for museums and galleries is how to display fashion. Now that clothes are no longer simply regarded as interesting artifacts that represent a period or culture, museums have largely chosen to present fashion as a form of art. Fashion art works are presented with attention to line, shape, color, and movement—as kinesthetic objects. Increasingly, fashion is also placed in its social and cultural context as emblematic of particular currents and trends (the zeitgeist). Where an individual designer is the focus of an exhibition, the curators focus on her or his unique contribution as "creative genius." Initially regarded as not quite appropriate for museums, fashion exhibitions have proved enormously successful and have contributed to the revival of museum culture around the world. The public loves them, sponsors are willing to underwrite them, and curators have developed a new expertise. As Mackrell (2005: 158) has observed,

**whether commenting on themes such as identity, social issues or stereotypes, contemporary artists are utilizing fashion to explore new ideas and issues. As the boundaries continue to be pushed, more ways of engaging the viewer to see new possibilities in the interaction of art and fashion will be developed.**

The overlap between art and fashion has been adopted by many museums and galleries. Designers, too, have increasingly staged events in museums, including Issey Miyake's 1983 "Bodyworks" event, which was one of the first designer-generated exhibitions; Florence's 1996 biennale, Il Tempo e la Moda, which featured a number of fin-de-siècle cutting-edge designers; the Guggenheim Museum Soho's 1997 "Art/Fashion" exhibition; the Metropolitan Museum of Art's 1997–98 Gianni Versace exhibition; the Victoria and Albert Museum's 2004 Vivienne Westwood retrospective; and the Guggenheim Museum's 2000–1 Giorgio Armani exhibition (Mackrell 2005: 154–55). Other exhibitions devoted to other designers are listed in box 5.3.

Many other exhibitions devoted to fashion themes or styles have been staged in museums and galleries across the globe. The significance of fashion exhibitions has been the creation of new audiences and sites of consumption for fashion and widespread awareness of designers and brands. This has spurred both the growth of fashion collections and consumer behavior. Traveling exhibitions have been especially important in this regard. The presentation of fashion and dress in museums and galleries has also assisted the transition of such objects from the periphery to the center of the art world.

While this chapter has traced the aesthetic shifts in twentieth-century fashion into the new millennium, the impact of the **grunge** aesthetic on the cultural habituses in which fashionable bodies

**Box 5.3 Significant Musuem Exhibitions of Major Individual Designers**

| Year | Designer | Exhibition Venue |
|---|---|---|
| 1967 | Mariano Fortuny | Los Angeles County Museum |
| 1974 | Paul Poiret | Musée Jacquemart-André |
| 1978 | Cristobel Balenciaga | Museum of Modern Art |
| 1978 | Missoni | Museum of Modern Art |
| 1980 | Mariano Fortuny | Musée Historique des Tissus, Lyons |
| 1980 | Pierre Cardin | Museum of Modern Art |
| 1980 | Jean Muir | Leeds City Art Gallery |
| 1982 | Charles James | Brooklyn Museum |
| 1983 | Yves Saint Laurent | Museum of Modern Art |
| 1985 | Cristóbal Balenciaga | Musée Historique des Tissus, Lyons |
| 1985 | Pierre Balmain | Musée de la Mode et du Costume (now Musée Gallieria) |
| 1985 | Mariano Fortuny | Kyoto Costume Institute |
| 1985 | Norman Hartnell | Museum of Costume, Bath and Brighton |
| 1985 | Gianni Versace | Victoria and Albert, London |
| 1985 | Salvatore Ferragamo | Palazzo Strozzi, Florence |
| 1986 | Christian Dior | Musée des Arts et de la Mode, Paris |
| 1986 | Paul Poiret | Musée de la Mode et du Costume (now Musée Gallieria) |
| 1986 | Yves Saint Laurent | Musée des Arts et de la Mode, Paris |
| 1991 | Valentino | Accademia Valentino, Bompiani, Milan |
| 1991 | Hubert de Givenchy | Musée de la Mode et du Costume (now Musée Gallieria) |
| 1991 | Pierre Cardin | Victoria and Albert, London |
| 1993 | Rei Kawakubo | Kyoto Costume Institute |
| 1994 | Madame Vionnet | Musée Historique des Tissus, Lyons |
| 1996 | Christian Dior | Museum of Modern Art |
| 1997-8 | Gianni Versace | Museum of Modern Art |
| 2000-1 | Giorgio Armani | Guggenheim, New York |
| 2002-3 | Gianni Versace | Victoria and Albert, London |
| 2003-4 | Ossie Clark | Victoria and Albert, London |
| 2004 | Vivienne Westwood | Victoria and Albert, London |
| 2006 | J.-C. de Castelbajac | Victoria and Albert, London |
| 2008 | Zandra Rhodes | RMIT University, Melbourne |
| 2008 | The House of Viktor and Rolf | The Barbican, London |

are actualized, such as streetscapes, buildings, and landscapes (about which Quinn writes eulogistically), cannot be underestimated. Fashion models have always been controversial in their role as clotheshorses—frames for displaying clothes at their best—but the current preference for fashion models looking blank and expressionless—and sometimes dismembered into body parts or depicted as machine-like robots—may signal a move beyond fashion into a dehumanized world of unconnected aesthetic impulses adrift from the performativity of selfhood.

## vi. conclusion

So, is fashion art? There is no doubt that there has always been a symbiotic relationship between fashion and art, with each drawing on influences and inspirations from the other domain. There have also been close connections and overlaps between the protagonists in the fashion and art worlds, suggesting that the distinction between them and reluctance to accord fashion a place in the art world has been on the part of art institutions rather than practicing creators of fashion and art. Since the late twentieth century, however, the art world has embraced fashion as a legitimate art form with a distinctive aesthetic. In the contemporary global culture, a fashion aesthetic can also be detected in spatial cultures such as architecture and interior design, with the result that fashion now plays a commanding role in orchestrating modern lifestyles and everyday tastes. In sum, then, while some distinctions and reservations may remain, fashion must be acknowledged as a primary artistic form and aesthetic realm with its own theories, language, grammar, and patterns of speech.

The mechanisms that link art and fashion include the copying and reflecting of aesthetic codes; the use of aesthetics as a framing device of fashion codes, aesthetic impulses, and inspirations that shape a fashion trend; aesthetic coordination between fashion and other artistic domains, discursive references, or declarations to aesthetics; and repudiations or refutations of dominant aesthetics through antifashion.

The case studies explore aspects of the relationship between fashion and art, namely, the distinctive aesthetic of fashion photography, the transformation of a counterculture designer to an icon of fashion as art, the blurred boundaries between wearable art and fashion, and a fashion accessory that has served as a barometer of changing aesthetics and a driver of consumer taste.

**CHAPTER SUMMARY**

- Fashion and art share many commonalities and cross-fertilizations—artists and designers draw on and combine artistic and cultural influences that resonate in iconic moments or eras in fashion, architecture, commercial art, performance, and the like.
- Aesthetics has many evolving meanings that have changed over time, from serene beauty with religious or natural connotations to notions of elite style, then mass appeal aesthetics (an aesthetic taste in its own right).
- Fashion is a form of aesthetics or creative practice that links everyday apparel habits with consumer behavior and performance of self.

- The designation of a new look as the prevailing fashion depends on the imprimatur of gatekeepers or arbiters of fashion and promotion to a fashion public.
- Fashion and architecture are increasingly sharing principles and concepts in defining a postmodern spatial aesthetic that defines the body in place.
- The fashion conundrum is the contradiction between the aesthetic ideals of fashion objects and the popularization of these objects as must-have consumer goods by the general public.
- A dominant consensual fashion aesthetic captures the mood or zeitgeist of a time or era.
- The influence of Japanese designers in Paris beginning in the 1970s led to a revision of defining principles of the structure, shape, and technical composition of fashion by the infusion of traditional Japanese aesthetics.
- Fashion exhibitions have, since the 1980s, placed fashion apparel and designers in a curatorial context as significant cultural artifacts and aesthetic objects that create a special language of spectacle, performance, creative genius, and relevance to contemporary culture.

## CASE STUDY 17: Fashion Photography and Heroin Chic

As well as clothing the body, one of the challenges for the fashion system is the representation of fashion primarily in writing or images. Roland Barthes (1984) developed an elaborated grammar of fashion systems that operates both at the level of individual clothing behavior (and the choices made about garments and accessories) and at a systemic level (from the garment and its representation to everyday clothing practices and formal modes of fashion; see chapter 3). Places where fashion representation is seen include fashion magazines, advertisements, the catwalk, shops, films and media, popular music, the workplace, special events, and the street.

Before the invention of photography, however, representational depictions of fashion took the form of portraiture, line drawings, paintings, and written descriptions. Photography changed that (see Craik 1994: 92–114). It became possible to see and circulate more realistic representations of clothing. Fashion photography became a specialist profession and its "creative genius" the subject of historical accounts of the development of fashion photography. Although fashion illustration was still the preferred mode of representation to the end of the 1930s (Packer 1985; Robinson 1986), photographic covers had a growing presence and slowly marginalized the graphic cover (Lloyd 1986: 6).

The use of war photographers during World War II contributed to this trend, especially as a number of the leading war photographers had been fashion photographers and continued this work during the war (e.g., Lee Miller, Cecil Beaton, Erwin Blumenfeld, Norman Parkinson, Toni Frissell). The gritty realism of war photography had an impact on emerging styles of fashion photography as well as reflecting aesthetic moods in genres such as surrealism and Hollywood film. Several themes dominated: mechanical reproduction, likeness and truth, documentary realism, and narrative. Body-clothing-space relations characterized the zeitgeist. These photographs aided and abetted the spread of sportswear, leisure wear, and an obsession with athleticism. Hollywood's creation of stars and their projection through the media supplanted the early photographic use of aristocrats and "well-bred" socialites as the focus of images. Celebrity-driven imagery became the norm. The aesthetics of fashion photography mirrored notions of the aesthetic and good taste, a trend that continued until the 1960s, when the rise of youth culture and popular consumer culture offered new role models (such as fashion models and popular musicians) and new notions of style, sexuality, lifestyle, and gender roles.

The photographs of Helmut Newton may have shocked the establishment, but they have retrospectively been acknowledged as a significant turning point in fashion photography. Gone was any pretence for creating images of glamour. Gone too were the social realism and political nuances of earlier fashion photography. Newton introduced explicit sexuality, erotic desire, and unconventional poses and settings. This linking of fashion photography with pornographic imagery was controversial and unsettling, but this type of imagery became the dominant motif of subsequent fashion photography. Meanwhile, the London three—David Bailey, Terence Donovan, and Brian Duffy—brought a brashness and irreverence from the Swinging London of the 1960s to their photography and the expanding world of modeling. Sexuality, nudity, and suggestiveness oozed from their photographs. Designers and magazine editors tried to turn back the tide, but this only provoked even more outrageous photography. In essence, the new aesthetic focused on the photographer and the model rather than the clothes themselves. The appeal for the viewer was the allure of emulating these swinging lifestyles rather than conforming to rapidly outdated ideas of convention and good taste.

**Kate Moss.** Photo by Rose Hartman//Time Life Pictures/Getty Images. Rose Hartman

While so-called **heroin chic** has been associated with the 1980s (Arnold 2001: 48–55; Quinn 2003a: 187–203), in fact this embryonic aesthetic was well in train by the 1970s (see Craik 1994) and is perhaps most closely associated with the work of Helmut Newton, Guy Bourdin, Deborah Turbeville, and former model Sarah Moon. Their photographs were redolent with sexuality—"homosexuality, transvestitism, and miscegenation, as well as voyeurism, murder and rape" (Hall-Duncan 1979: 196; see also Harrison 1985: 52; Craik 1994: 108–11). These dark and edgy photographs depicted skinny, dazed, unkempt, scruffy models in dysfunctional settings, ordinary urban streets, and hostile landscapes (Evans 2003). The connection between the drug culture of modeling and photography was explicit. In 1997, after the death of New York fashion photographer Davide Sorrenti from a drug overdose at the age of twenty-one, then-president Bill Clinton called on the fashion industry to reject the heroin chic style that glamorized the strung-out look of heroin addicts and encouraged youth experimentation with drugs (National Drug Strategy Network 1997).

Heated debate ensued, but whether fashion photography has abandoned this dark aesthetic is debatable. Ambivalence continues to surround the fame and periodic falls (due to drug use and abuse) of model Kate Moss. One minute, she is the revered face of Calvin Klein or cover girl on *Vanity Fair;* the next she is ensconced in a drug rehabilitation clinic. The mood of the photograph continues to play a greater role than the depiction of the clothing in contemporary fashion photography. Reviews of the Museum of Modern Art's first fashion photography exhibition, "Fashioning Fiction," held in 2004, suggest that the jury is still out on characterizing the mood of 1990s fashion photography. The curators have been accused of reflecting their own "art-world" preference for the "cultural establishment" over the 1990s inspirations of "street fashion, grunge, squatting and the Internet boom" (Halley 2004).

Aletti (2004) argued that the "Fashioning Fiction" show was an attempt to reject "the uneasy, anti-fashion attitude that prevailed for much of the 90s" and had preferred a photographic aesthetic that "turns its back on glamour and embraced ordinary life and all its flaws." For Aletti, the mood of contemporary fashion photography is the "sly rebuke to the reactionary post-heroin-chic happy-face movement" and a new take on "glam and grunge," where

> each image has a strange, offbeat beauty and an oddly melancholy sense of history. These are exactly the sort of pictures that make fashion photography so vital right now.

Clearly, the basis of fashion photography has shifted dramatically. In one account of the history of fashion photography, it has been characterized as a shift from the depiction of clothes as objects of desire to the creation of imagery evoking desired identities and lifestyles:

> Fashion photography has run the gamut of evolution since its birth in the late 1890s, when daguerreotype and "Carte de Viste" was all the rage. Fashion and fashion photography reached a pinnacle of (faux) couture for everyday wear in the days of Coco Chanel, when glamour and

> the *nouveau riche* was something still being explored and discovered. By the 1980s hedonism ran rampant, causing a backlash into the deconstruction to how fashion was represented, with a Dadaist approach to gritty realism that pushed boundaries in reaction to what society saw as beauty, leading to the common opinion that "fashion photography is dead." Grunge to heroin chic broke the mould of how fashion was interpreted, leaving no boundaries or limitations. It's debatable, but the revival of elegance, confidence and beauty will always reflect what we once stereotyped as glamour. You're not always selling the clothes, sometimes it's more about the lifestyle reflected in appearance. (iStock 2005)

It seems unlikely that fashion photography will return to less abstract, mood-driven, and contextual commentaries and that the focus on the clothing will be revived. Instead, fashion photography has propelled a wider revision of what counts as fashion; beauty; aspiration; and, therefore, art. Nowhere is this clearer than in the recent classification of avant-garde fashion designers as artists as their collections become a feted part of museum collections. The dark and edgy image, it would seem, is here to stay.

## CASE STUDY 18: Exhibiting Vivienne Westwood

**Westwood.** Photo by Nathalie Lagneau/ Catwalking/Getty Images. 2008 Catwalking

The dark turn in the fashion aesthetic has transformed the former enfants terribles of antifashion into collectible icons. No one epitomizes this more than Vivienne Westwood, who has been transformed from a rebel to a role model of the new age fashion designer. This shift was illustrated by the major retrospective traveling exhibition curated by the Victoria and Albert Museum in 2004 (Craik and Peoples 2006; McDermott 1999; Wilcox 2004). The self-trained Westwood began her designer career in collaboration with musical entrepreneur Malcolm McLaren and musicians like Johnny Rotten and the Sex Pistols, Adam Ant, Bow Wow Wow, and (in a minor way) Boy George. The start was unrestrained rock and roll, followed by punk and liberal doses of sex and shock. Early collections were titled Too Fast to Live, Too Young to Die (1972), Sex (1974), Seditionaries (1976), Irate (1981), and Savage (1981).

Hers was a rags-to-riches transformation facilitated by her Svengali, Malcolm McLaren, whom she met in 1965, the height of Swinging London. He came from a successful family involved in the East London manufacturing, retailing, and secondhand apparel sector that largely traded goods at the cheaper end of the market and was at art school from 1964 to 1971. However, in his stated aim of "using culture as a way of making trouble," McLaren fashioned himself as a cultural terrorist, eventually becoming a punk guru and entrepreneur. McLaren and Westwood's artistic collaboration lasted from 1970 to 1983, with McLaren being the major shaper of their collections—at least in the early years. On his departure from their partnership in 1983, she—chrysalis like—metamorphosed into a brilliant couturier in her own right—discarding youth street radicals for the better-heeled if quirky haute couture clientele.

As her clothes moved from subcultures to the mainstream, she turned to new muses for inspiration and direction. Collections such as Nostalgia of Mud (1982, more often referred to as "Buffalo"), Punkature (1982), Witches (1983), Mini Crini (1984), and Pagan I (1987) revealed her ability to retrieve historic garments and modes of cut and manufacture and blend them with contemporary underside currents. The low-budget shows designed to subvert and shock were transformed into a glamorous parody. Her work was soon recognized in Paris and later New York, Milan, and Tokyo.

And yet Westwood's story has been presented as an allegory of the transition of British counterculture from the 1970s to the "new" Britishness of a cosmopolitan Euro nation. Westwood has been turned into an icon and labeled "the Queen of Couture" by journalists who credit her with reviving a sense of Englishness. This may be arguable, yet the label serves as recognition of the public revision of her image from a rabble-rouser to a major designer who redefined fashion looks over a forty-year period. In fact, she has continued to focus on high-end and ready-to-wear fashion even since she established her Gold (couture) collection.

By the 1990s, Westwood had become more interested in the detail of cut and silhouette—explicitly borrowing the motifs and tailoring techniques of iconic designers like Dior, Balenciaga, Saint Laurent, and Vionnet. She regarded Chanel as "overrated" and "just a stylist" (*Sydney Morning Herald* 2004; see also Craik and Peoples 2006). Westwood continued her meticulous plundering of historical costuming (corsetry, tailoring, **millinery,** layering, draping, embroidering, and **slashing**). She was regarded no longer as a "cultural troublemaker" but as the muse of the New Britain who had "altered the fabric of the nation" (Januszczak 2004). Accordingly, she was awarded an OBE (which she purportedly received wearing no underwear!) and declared British designer of the year in 1990 and 1991.

Global infatuation followed, with successive exhibitions celebrating her work, culminating in the Victoria and Albert–curated "Vivienne Westwood: 34 Years in Fashion," a traveling exhibition first shown in London in 2004, followed by a world discovery tour to Australia, China, Japan, continental Europe, and the United States. Her empire has restructured to market clothes through worldwide boutiques and department stores by producing different labels for different sections of the market (the Gold Label, the Red Label, etc.) and launching a line of perfumes with names like Boudoir, Libertine, and Anglomania. She recognizes that "having a perfume and license, in general, is a financial necessity" to fund her couture collections (quoted by Fragrance Foundation 2004).

Westwood came of age as a couturier but has built up her credibility and accessibility. Despite the enormous cost of commissioning special fabrics, shoes, beading, and the like, Westwood enjoys $36 million in annual sales in her stores in New York, Paris, Moscow, Hong Kong, and Seoul. She has also moved into department stores with her ready-to-wear Red Label, which is even stocked by Harrods, popularizing her designs among the matrons of Britain, and thereby boosting both recognition and sales (Rosen 2004). She has now also moved into perfume, ceramics (for Coalport), textiles, and furnishings (Hervia 2004). As she has observed,

> when you get to a certain point you must have a fragrance—it puts you at a certain level in the market. I'd done a fragrance before, but in a small way, and now I wanted to wait for the right time to make an important fragrance statement. ... Having a perfume and license, in general, is a financial necessity. A designer must, to reap back the money spent on prototypes and all that sort of thing. (Quoted by Fragrance Foundation 2004)

Clearly, Westwood can no longer be seen as the grandmother of punk and radicalism. Indeed, one commentator concluded that she is "much more suited ... to the role of *grande dame* than punk" (Langley 2004b: 108). With Westwood, we get a sense of how the fashion system constantly redefines its components and parameters, including its aesthetic framework. The phenomenon we are witnessing is the naturalization of the dark and edgy as the linchpin of the new fashion aesthetic and its sedimentation in elite art through its inclusion in museum exhibitions and collections. Like others before her, Westwood epitomizes the balancing act between challenging the status quo and making clothes that are desirable—and affordable—and ensuring that her work will be curated as cultural artifacts.

## CASE STUDY 19: Wearable Art

One should always be a work of art or wear one. (Oscar Wilde)

Wearable art, also called art to wear or artwear, has its origins in experimental clothing from the 1970s, which ostensibly emerged from America as a byproduct of the hippy movement and youth culture. Traces of counterculture and alternative lifestyle connotations remain. Wearable art has a remarkably robust history despite the fact that until recently it was ignored largely by both the cognoscenti of elite art and the mainstream fashion industry (Leventon 2005).

In the 1970s textiles studies emerged in art schools. Traditional skills were reappraised and put into a contemporary context. A name change to "fiber art" ensured that artwear could be incorporated into the art form pantheon rather than remaining a mere craft. Monumental works emerged from international fiber artists such as Magdalena Abakanowicz, who regularly exhibited at the prestigious Biennale Internationale de la Tapisserie in Lausanne, Switzerland, from 1962 to 1979. Techniques that became known as "soft sculpture" evolved, whereby textiles were shaped, carved, and sewn into three-dimensional forms. It was soon realized that the body could be used as a vehicle for expression.

Those unaware of its roots often question the difference between carnivalesque artwear and haute couture designer fashions such as Christian Lacroix's heavily embroidered and beaded garments or

**Wearable art.** Photo: Jennifer Craik

Alexander McQueen's confronting range exploring survivors of psychic, sexual, and political abuse. Wearable art is highly crafted, employing the same skills required by the elite designer. Both are conceptually driven, although elite fashions tend toward ironic postmodern constructions. Would developments such as Vivienne Westwood's critiques of Victorian prudery be seen on the wearable art catwalk? Elite fashions are also self-referential, returning to past periods of fashion for inspiration.

The positioning of wearable art is a key issue. In many ways it can be seen as folk costume within a context of performance. Although wearable art is seen on the catwalk, it is not the catwalks of the fashion cities of Paris, New York, London, or Tokyo. Instead, artwear appears on the catwalks of provincial cities like Wellington, Vancouver, Canberra, and Kamloops in Canada; Berlin; and numerous American cities (Bloomington, Minneapolis; Fort Collins, Colorado; Denton, Texas; and, of course, San Francisco). While both employ theatrical techniques on the catwalk, performance more akin to the ideas of Bahktin is used for exhibiting artwear collections.

The conceptual significance of wearable art is threefold. The language of artwear itself has created arguably a new language of clothes and, with it, new lexicons of visual imagery and verbal representations of the visual, tactile, and sensual. The discursive framework of the elite art world, including its lexicon of curating, exhibition, collection, review, and analysis, has been challenged by the difficulty of acknowledging and incorporating wearable art as a legitimate and recognizable art form. As well, artwear has contributed to the repositioning of fashion academically and institutionally, from the realms of textiles, dressmaking, art history, and couture to those of cultural theory, design, spatial analysis, technological innovation, **smart fibers,** architecture, ecology, and the environment.

The artwear artist, generally the designer as well as the maker, must learn a suitcase of skills: dyeing, felting, knitting, crocheting, machine embroidery, hand stitching, and more. As well the artist needs considerable skills in pattern making and garment construction. Wearable art does not have to be "diluted" to a more realistic product. It is freed from restraints of the quotidian, function, accessibility, and the market. A range is not produced for each season. There is no label that requires an economically viable range to support the top-of-the-range apparel.

Artwear appears not to concern itself with body shape. Thinness of the models—that is, models with celebrity identities—is not part of the system. The prevailing body shape is left to designer labels. The silhouettes of the 1950s "New Look" and 1980s power dressing, with its emphasis on shoulders, do not find currency here. The classic fashion theory of "shifting erogenous zones," with the seasonal focus on the hips, the bust, the legs, or the back, evaporated under the lights of the theatricality.

Major international competitions for artwear have spawned links to the tourist industry. New Zealand's World of Wearable Art, now held in the city of Wellington, attracts large numbers of international tourists to view the extraordinary performances. This is linked to other tourist-drawing attractions. In 1997, a rugby match was scheduled to coincide with the Wearable Art Awards in order to maximize visitor numbers. This helped the city win prestigious tourist awards. In 2008, the Vancouver Museum organized a wearable art award titled Green Is the New Black. The emphasis was on environmental concerns and a tourist program was associated with this.

Over time, artwear has earned its place in the art world and has significantly affected contemporary fashion design and the burgeoning accessories industry. But it remains strongest at the grassroots level, where community-based groups of dyers, felters, knitters, and embroiderers seek inspiration in fiber and fabric in tune with the social, political, and cultural priorities of their localities.

Sharon Peoples and Jennifer Craik

## CASE STUDY 20: Fashion and the Wristwatch

> In our desire to be individuals, the watch continues to be a concise way of expressing our values, interests and aesthetics. (Quan 2008: 31)
>
> A fool … cannot withstand the charms of a toy-shop; snuff-boxes, watches, heads of canes, etc. are his destruction. (Earl of Chesterfield, 1749, quoted by Styles 2008: 50.)

The wristwatch is an apparently basic item of clothing—not quite accessory, jewelry, or garment. It has a very practical function, namely, to tell the time. And yet the wristwatch is a barometer of social change, cultural development, and fashion flows. It is also a highly personal item of dress, as the above quotations suggest. Watches tell us about ourselves and the way we present ourselves in public, making statements about our gender, age, aesthetic preferences, activities, and interests. Watches can also indicate precisely our wealth and aspirations. Watches have become a barometer of aesthetic trends and a driver of shifting consumer tastes: all this in a tiny face on a strap around our wrist.

So what motivates someone to spend $10 on a digital Casio watch at a street market, another to spend $200 on a fake Rolex, and yet another to spend $132,000 on an Omega Constellation Quadrella High Jewellery Snowflake in eighteen-carat white gold with diamonds online? And why does one person have only one watch, which is worn till it breaks, while another has a wardrobe of mix-and-match watches suitable for every occasion?

### *A Brief History of Watches*

The history of the wristwatch is both a technical and practical one, as well as a signifier of fashion and individual identity. A watch is a miniature clock that can be worn on the body, unlike an appliance or a piece of furniture. The invention of clocks and watches stemmed from a major shift in how people lived, from living in tune with natural cycles, phases, and changes—for example, the position of the sun and moon, seasons, the rhythms of day and night, rites of passage, harvests and famines, migration patterns—to living according to artificial divisions of existence. This need to divide up "space" into temporal units coincided with new ways of living that were orchestrated by humans rather than by nature. Clocks and watches were fundamental to that transition (see box 5.4).

It has commonly been argued (for example, by social historian E.P. Thompson) that the development of clocks and watches accompanied the emergence of the Industrial Revolution as a discipline for workers in factory occupations. However, new evidence suggests that clocks and watches were widespread well before the Industrial Revolution. Records of the theft of watches and inventories of pawnbrokers show that watches were a common target for thieves and were commonly pawned by the poor as an easily realizable asset. There was also a healthy secondhand trade in watches. In fact, many more watches were owned by skilled manual workers with relatively high disposable income than by those in manufacturing and mining occupations. Moreover, men tended to leave their watches at home rather than take them to work, except for those in transport industries, for whom keeping time was essential. Instead, watches were worn during leisure time, for example, at the races, in public houses and brothels, and at other social events. The rest of the time, watches were hung up on bedsteads or chimney breasts (making them an easy mark for housebreakers).

This revision of the history of timekeeping suggests that leisure and pleasure and the desire to make timekeeping portable drove the development of watchmaking. But early on, watches were used only in part to keep time. In fact, early watches were unreliable and broke often and it was not until

## Box 5.4 Time Line of Watch History

| Date | Event |
|---|---|
| 1094 | Twelve-meter bronze clock tower using water wheel invented in China created by Su Song |
| C. 1370 | First mechanical clock with driving weights, gear train and escapement in Europe |
| 1480 | First watch using mainspring—miniature of metal clocks—invented in Italy |
| 1500s | Watches adopted in France and Germany; Peter Henlein sometimes credited with first pocket watch |
| 1577 | European clocks brought by Matteo Ricci to China, where the Chinese are intrigued by these magic objects |
| 1600s | Form watches (designed in shape of animals, etc., rather than round) |
| 1680 | Twenty-seven watch workshops opened in the Forbidden City in Beijing during the reign of Emperor Kang Hi |
| 1675 | Balance spring invented by Christiaan Hugyens, giving greater accuracy |
| 1714 | Marine chronometer invented by John Harrison, giving more accurate longitudinal readings at sea and perfected in 1761 |
| 1750 | Rubies used in watch movements, increasing durability and reliability (jewel movement) |
| 1755 | Vacheron established |
| 1775 | Breguet establishes watchmaking shop in Paris |
| 1791 | Forerunner of Girard-Perregaux established |
| 1809 | Luther Goddard, first watchmaker in America, makes firt watch |
| 1833 | Forerunner of Jaeger-LeCoultre established |
| 1837 | Opening of Tiffany |
| 1838 | Stem winding and setting mechanism introduced by Louis Audemars |
| 1847 | Cartier established |
| 1848 | Forerunner of Omega |
| 1853 | Dual-time watch introduced by Tissot |
| 1860 | Heuer established |
| 1868 | First wristwatch introduced by Patek Philippe |
| 1884 | Greenwich, England, established as the zero meridian as basis of twenty-four world time zones, which revolutionized watch making and marketing to global demand |
| 1888 | Lady's wristwatch with diamond and gold bracelet introduced by Cartier |
| 1880s | Growth of popularity of watches |
| 1902 | 93,000 watches sold in Germany |
| 1904 | Famous Santos-Dumont manufactured prototype of modern wristwatch introduced by Cartier |
| 1905 | Rolex established |

| | |
|---|---|
| 1914 | Watch with alarm introduced by Eterna |
| 1918 | Forerunner of Citizen established |
| 1923 | Self-winding watch introduced by John Harwood |
| 1924 | Seiko established |
| 1933 | Children's watch with Mickey Mouse introduced by Ingersoll |
| 1945 | Date and time watch introduced by Rolex |
| 1957 | Battery-powered watch introduced by Hamilton |
| 1962 | Quartz battery movement introduced by ETA |
| 1970 | Electronic digital watch introduced by Pulsar |
| 1972 | LCD (liquid crystal display) introduced by Longines and Seiko |
| 1983 | Swatch established |
| 1985 | Tag-Heuer established |
| 1987 | Analog and digital displays introduced by Tissot |
| 1999 | Built-in global positioning system introduced by Casio |

Source: History of Watches, http://www.paralumun.com/watchhistory.htm; Watch History: Watch Development through the Ages, http://www.which-watches.com/history.html; Answers.com, "Watch," http://www.answers.com/topic/watch

the invention of the balance spring and balance wheel in the second half of the seventh century that watches became reliable keepers of time. Styles (2008) argues that there were two equally important factors in the desire of ordinary people to possess a watch: first, they were a source of prestige, and second, they were realizable assets, the poor man's bank. In addition, it is clear that watches were not just a basic mechanical device but were highly decorative, most commonly made of silver, although more expensive models were made in gold, and cheap watches were made of alloy.

Some watches had china faces, enameled details, diverse decorations, semiprecious stones, and a personal seal (an appendage to a watch guard containing a personalized trinket) featuring all manner of images (such as anchors, angels, ships, portraits, animals, flowers, or the owner's initials). Watches were kept in a pocket, to which they were attached by a silver chain or a decorative ribbon. Consequently early watches were decorative items as much as they were sophisticated pieces of technology. Their compact size, elegant cases in shining silver, reflective watch glasses, and enamel or china dials combined many of the elements of eighteenth-century jewelry (Styles 2008).

Men revealed or extracted their watches with a great flourish, creating a performance in order to emphasize the prestige associated with the ownership of a watch. In fact, a watch became an essential item of dress to convey that a man was a gentleman. It was also a sign of the "masculine command of technology," along with other technical and scientific inventions of the period. So, at this stage, watches were very much a male item of dress and jewelry. Few women could afford to buy or own a watch, and women who did have watches undoubtedly received them as a gift from a benefactor, suitor, or relative.

Although watches are generally represented as a European invention, the first known clock was invented by the Chinese in 1094. This was a huge, intricate water wheel–driven contraption that depicted the path of the sun, moon, and stars and indicated hours and quarter hours with tablets and chimes. Although this early clock-making ability was short lived, the Chinese fascination with clocks was reignited in 1577 when missionary Matteo Ricci brought clocks to China, prompting Emperor Kang Hi to open twenty-seven watch workshops in the Forbidden City in Beijing in 1680. Although the Chinese manufacture of clocks and watches never reached the hoped-for volume, the Chinese became important consumers of European clocks. English, Swiss, and French manufacturers in the eighteenth century created styles that suited Chinese tastes and climatic conditions, using Chinese decorative patterns, musical chimes, precious stones, and pearls for decoration, and exquisitely depicted enamel miniatures (Richemont nd).

The genesis of the modern watch occurred in the second half of the seventeenth century due to John Harrison's invention of the marine chronometer. Subsequent technical developments in watch movements, along with new materials and miniaturization, led to the transformation of pocket watches to wristwatches in the late nineteenth century. Some say it was a nanny who tied a pocket watch to her wrist with a silk ribbon, while others credit Patek Philippe with making the first wristwatch in 1868.

Watches became particularly useful in leisure activities and sports as a means to impose temporal regulations on participants concerning the length of events and the division of rounds and quarters for boxing, horse racing, tennis, and football and other team sports. It became essential for activities where the length of time was crucial, for example, in horse racing, athletics races, and swimming, and later, mechanical races such as cycling and car racing. We can see that watches and sports have had interdependent histories, and consequently watch brands have become synonymous with certain events both as official timekeepers and sponsors. As the returning official timekeeper of the 2008 Beijing Olympic Games, Omega produced a special advertisement featuring the iconic Bird's Nest stadium, the design of which was celebrated as representing "a haven of goodwill and sportsmanship," qualities deemed to extend to Omega watches. Advertising has reflected this in the use of sports-related images and celebrity athlete endorsements. Athletic qualities and achievements have had a strong association with the qualities of watches and influence consumers' buying habits. Instead of buying time, consumers purchase personal attributes and lifestyles associated with their chosen brand or model.

The possibilities for watches worn on the wrist quickly elided with contemporary styles in jewelry. Early watches competed to appeal to the aesthetic tastes of consumers as well as to indicate the technical qualities of the watch mechanism. With this new portability and stylishness, the uptake of watches quickly spread—initially in cities such as London, Paris, Geneva, and Rome, then to regional centers.

Women also began to wear watches, like the elaborate watch bracelets featuring precious stones and extravagant decorations manufactured by Cartier. The **art nouveau** movement also had a significant influence on watch design. Manufacturers experimented with new forms (ovals, rectangles, and squares) as well as new colors and materials and a variety of watchbands.

By the twentieth century, watches were common accessories among the general community, with gradual improvements in watch movements, durability, and power sources. Innovations included waterproofing, capacity depth immersion, anti-magnetism, and the ability to self-wind. The first children's watches, featuring Mickey Mouse, were marketed in 1933; watches displaying the day and date appeared in 1956, battery-driven watches in 1957, quartz battery watches in 1962, and electronic digital watches in 1970. This last development led to a crisis in the watch industry, particularly in countries like Switzerland, which had prided itself on its exquisite craftsmanship and artistry in the manufacture of mechanical watches. In terms of cost, mechanical watches couldn't compete with the cheaper digital variety. It was generally predicted that mechanical watches would become obsolete.

In desperation, the Swatch brand was launched by the Swiss company SMH in 1983. Their ultra-fashionable electronic watch designs were aimed at the youth market and traveling connoisseurs, with the rapid production of short-run new designs. Swatches became must-have accessories and were heavily promoted in the mass media, with consumer outlets in all the main shopping centers and all duty-free airport stores. Swatch was the first company to use celebrity endorsements; capitalized on spectacular popular culture; and was associated with sports events, art, environmental issues, and quality of lifestyle. According to the owner of Swatch, Nicolas Hayek, "Swatch is synonymous with high quality, affordable prices, innovation, joy of life, and just a touch of provocation" (quoted in Childers 1999: 16).

Swatch not only saved the Swiss watchmaking industry but gave it a whole new lease on life. Watches were catapulted into the stratosphere of luxury accessories, and fashion designers and brands entered the watch business, aggressively competing with traditional watchmakers such as Omega, Cartier, Longines, Rolex, Boucheron, Chopard, Tissot, Piranesi, and Bulova. Designers like Pierre Balmain, Calvin Klein, Chanel, Versace, Gucci, and Yves Saint Laurent have become dominant designer brands.

Despite the electronic advances and the inexpensive prices, the consumer demand for traditional mechanical watch movements and hybrid mechanical and electronic watch movements has escalated. Watches can now go to the moon or the bottom of the ocean; they rarely need to be wound manually,

**Swatch store.** Photo: Terence Ong. Creative Commons Attribution 2.5 License

and they provide many more functions than are necessary. Watch manufacturing now occurs at all points of the industrial spectrum from computerized mass production to individually handcrafted and artist-decorated styles for connoisseurs.

In a study of consumer perceptions of the quality and value of watches, Teas and Agarwal (2000) found that brand reputation was the most important factor in consumers' ranking of wristwatches; well-known brands sold in high-ranking retail stores were ranked the highest. The cultural capital invested in the brand name and the retailers' reputation combined to increase the desirability of certain watches over others.

### *Watches, Gender, and Identity*

The history of wristwatches is closely connected with the development of modern masculinity, as the scientific and technical qualities and capacities of the wristwatch are directly mapped onto the qualities of masculinity. These include precision, discipline, and state-of-the-art innovation, as well as scientific knowledge of the technology of watch movements. Men's watches also convey coded signs concerning beauty, craftsmanship, and the design principles underpinning their design. Together, these become analogues of industrialization and modernization as well as mirrors of changing aesthetics and fashions. At the level of gender symbolism, men's watches have a bigger face and wider wristband than women's watches and often feature gadgetry and many knobs and dials with multiple functions. This is ostentation par excellence. Moreover, the overt metallic look of many fashionable men's watches seems to signal traditional occupations and male involvement in machinery, which evokes qualities of hard-edged certainty and the projection of a strong personality.

By contrast, women's watches have been a subset of jewelry and reflect the decorative and stylistic impulses of successive fashion eras, especially through the use of gold and precious metals and precious and semiprecious stones, morphing into bracelets or wearable art as opposed to just being an accessory. These features of watches derive from attributes of femininity such as a sparkling demeanor, frivolity, and lightness. The associated sparseness of technology in the watch face and greater emphasis on the use of fashion materials in the watchband reinforces the feminized appearance. The fact that women's watches are smaller than men's also implies the discreetness of women, with overtones of female accommodation and less importance than men and masculinity. So, for women a watch is a practical convenience and a shorthand stylistic signature, but not as much a declaration of their personality and aspirations as some other items of dress.

Watch advertisements have inevitably been created around images of masculinity and femininity, respectively, promoting qualities of success, avant-garde fashion, sex appeal, luxury, athletic prowess, a beautiful body, artistic sensibility, and leisure interests. Men's watches also promote traditional masculine qualities and values, albeit with a contemporary twist. The watch is one item in which men can invest a sense of fashion and individual aesthetic expression. Although the watch constitutes an apparently unisex item of clothing, in fact it inscribes highly determined signifiers of gender, wealth, aspirations, bodily performance, and the stylistic mores of a particular time. With watches, time never stands still.

Jennifer Craik and Sharon Peoples

# chapter 6

# fashion as a business and cultural industry

**CHAPTER OUTLINE**

I. The structure of the fashion industry

II. Fashion forecasting, marketing and the fashion consumer

III. The changing role of the fashion designer

IV. Luxury brands and global marketing

Case study 21: Celebrity models

Case study 22: Louis Vuitton as luxury accessory

Case study 23: The Gap as global fashion

Case study 24: Secondhand clothing

**WHAT DOES THIS CHAPTER COVER?**

This chapter outlines the main features of the fashion business both as an apparel production industry and a value-adding cultural industry. Like some other industries, such as tourism, fashion is a complex chain of subsectors and interlinking components that combine to produce clothes and accessories, not so much for couture clients as for the broad-based consumer market. After exploring how this industry can be conceptualized, the chapter explores three key aspects: the process of fashion marketing, the process of fashion design, and the trend toward luxury brand retailing within an increasingly global market.

A number of themes are explored, including the role of promotion and advertising; diversifying a label or brand for the global market; licensing and diffusion labels; prêt-à-porter (ready to wear); different retail options, including fast fashion and e-retailing; fashion forecasting; and consumer behaviour—that is, how and why consumers shop for clothes as they do (reception theory).

Case studies investigate the role of fashion models in creating spectacles and attracting media attention to fashion, the rise of Louis Vuitton handbags as an exemplar of a global luxury brand, the success of the Gap as a consumer-focused leisure fashion chain, and the parallel market for secondhand clothes.

## i. the structure of the fashion industry

Neither the glamorous image of the high end of the fashion system nor the ephemeral and derogatory connotations of so-called slaves to fashion reflect the full contours of the fashion business as an industry. Like many industries, it has complicated flows between constituent parts, and many subsectors that feed into the industry. Although interrelated, these components are unequal players in the fashion system in terms of contribution, **sustainability,** power, and prestige. Overall, the industry can be seen as a classic **supply chain** from the production of raw materials to the manufacture of garments to the retailing and consumption of finished products.

In this supply chain, there are four subsystems: a manufacturing system that produces the materials for and products of apparel manufacture; a creative system that designs the products, produces the merchandising and promotion, and underpins consumer tastes; a managerial system that organizes and controls the coordinated stages of sourcing, manufacturing, and distributing apparel; and a communication system that produces product information and advertising of apparel, which highlight salient attributes for consumers.

So, who are the players in this system? Following the chain, we can identify the manufacturers, who are also called vertical producers (Jenkyn Jones 2005). They undertake the production and purchase of materials; the commission or purchase of designs; and the manufacture, distribution, and retailing of apparel. While some manufacturers are large-scale factories, the fashion industry is distinctive in also involving small and artisanal enterprises such as custom tailors, couture specialists, and subcontracted finishers (such as embroiderers, buttonholers, and pleaters).

Equally important are the wholesalers, who commission the manufacturing process, often in small runs to contractors, who, in turn, subcontract the work to outfits (jobbers) that range from medium cut-make-and-trim firms to individual outworkers (who often work from home). Contractors arrange production, packaging, and delivery. Designers tend to produce a range of samples that are tested in the marketplace to determine the best sellers, which are then produced in greater numbers. Because this is a risky process, contractors seek "rolling contracts" with their suppliers to ensure steady work flow. A chosen sample is refined and "sealed" by a docket, which is a contract specifying the production details and run size. Each order is inspected, labeled, and certified

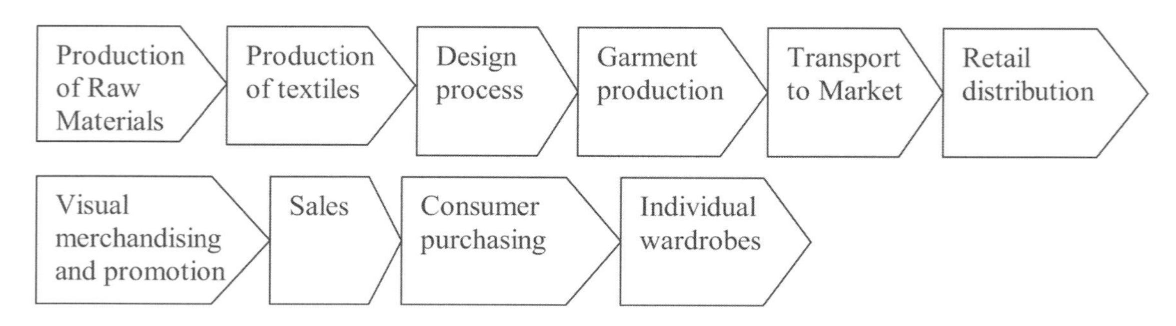


**Source:** Adapted from Hines 2006: 4

with a swing ticket before being kimballed (price tagged) and dispatched to stores.

With an increasingly outsourced supply chain to providers and manufacturers throughout the world, the process of coordinating the fashion industry has become enormously complex as wholesalers and contractors seek cheaper, faster, and more reliable operations to satisfy fashion cycles. Whereas once there were two fashion **seasons**—summer and winter—now there are not only seasonal collections but "fast-fashion" companies, which produce up to twenty collections annually. The complexity of planning and maintaining such schedules is enormous. The use of e-mail and electronic data exchange, computer-aided design, business-to-business e-commerce, automated stocktaking, just-in-time manufacture, and flexible subcontracting enables fast-fashion retailers to order stock for delivery in a week for straightforward designs, and three weeks for complex designs. Box 6.1 shows some other agents in the fashion industry.

Hines (2006) observes that there are some specific features of this industry supply chain, in particular, that it is supply driven. First, it does not include demand factors, which are generated by consumers as end users, but in fact such demand may be whipped up by gatekeepers in the process (designers, fashion writers, trendsetters, cognate cultural products—for example, film or popular music—as well as advertising). Second, the processes in the supply chain operate as discrete cycles within the system, and each cycle has its own time frame (associated with producing synthetics, growing the wool, and harvesting cotton; securing fibers and contracting a textile mill; outsourcing manufacture of apparel; transport time; promotional strategy and retailing cycles; etc.). Third, while the nature of the raw material production involves heavy investment and expensive physical resources, clothing manufacture is generally still labor intensive, relatively small scale, and a mobile industry. As such, it lacks power and must respond to changing circumstances and

**Box 6.1 Roles in Fashion Industry**

|  |  |
|---|---|
| Designer | Designs items of apparel |
| Grader | Determines pattern sizing |
| Merchandiser | Undertakes market research into future style and trends, drawing on fashion forecasts |
| Buyer | Selects and places orders for stock on behalf of the retailer |
| PR department | Marketing and promotion department that organizes promotional material as well as liaising with the public |
| Advertising department | Responsible for developing promotional campaigns and product advertisements |
| Sales person | Employee whose job is to sell fashion merchandise by informing and assisting customers |
| Store manager | Employer with responsibility for overseeing stock levels of merchandise as well as supervising staff and monitoring sales figures and turnover |
| Controller | Manager of the financial organization of the retailer |

pressures rapidly. This pattern of imbalance reproduces historical imbalances in the emergence and development of the contemporary fashion industry.

It is generally recognized that the fashion business as we know it emerged during the Industrial Revolution with the conjunction of several factors: the introduction of raw materials such as wool and cotton from colonial outposts, new processes of mechanical and later mass production, urbanization of the workforce, and birth of a consumer culture. However, Leopold (1992: 102) argues that the distinctiveness of the fashion industry, as opposed to other manufacturing industries, was its "failure to ever fully embrace mass production techniques." This produced an imbalance between the conditions of high-fashion consumption and display and the persistently abysmal conditions of those at the production and manufacture end of the fashion system.

Even today, the manufacture of apparel still relies heavily on craft labor rather than mass production. Alongside the sewing machine, the development of other machines (for buttonholing, button sewing, and blind stitching; over-edgers; pressing machines; etc.) still required skilled labor and the individual handling of garments. One area in which the reliance on hand labor has changed is the development of cutting machines, rotary knifes, and laser cutting, which can cut multiple layers at a time. More recently, laying-up machines, machines that "hand" embroider, and factory "custom" tailoring have increased the automation of sewing and manufacturing processes. Leopold (1992) argues that even where manufacture is divided into special tasks (fellers, basters, snappers, etc.), garments are still being individually handled. In fact, the existence of machine finishing revalues the status of genuine handcrafted manufacture, which often rely on specialist artisans in developing countries to produce exquisite embroidery, beading, and curing that are simply too expensive to be done in the West.

Conditions in developing countries (low pay, poor working conditions, lack of job security, and high markups) have been a constant source of concern. Yet even in the Western world, the industry relies less on factory setups than on outworkers, who work in homes for low pay in largely unregulated conditions. And contrary to expectations, the advent of new synthetic fibers and wonder fabrics has not improved the situation. Arguably, it has exacerbated the imbalances in the supply chain, since synthetics are cheaper and hence unit costs can be reduced, while retail prices have increased because of the prestige value of the new materials.

Thus, the structure of the industry through its internal power relations and cost structure imbalances usually drive the consumer side of the fashion equation far more than the consumers themselves do. From a cynical perspective, fashion consumers may indeed be dupes of the system, albeit nuanced ones. Although demand for mass-produced fashion has grown (for example, mass-produced blue jeans, designer handbags, fashion watches), consumers balance this with individualized apparel that continues to reflect the artisanal and handmade element of fashion items. Designers and fashion retailers must, therefore, constantly make calculations about the balance between the mass-produced (or ready-to-wear) and the individually crafted garment.

The anomalous structure of the fashion industry has continued in the last decades of the twentieth century and early years of the twenty-first century as the economic gap between highly industrialized countries and rapidly developing countries

**Man at sewing machine.** Photo: Steve Evans. Creative Commons Attribution 2.0

has undermined the viability of productive capacity and manufacturing sustainability. With international treaties such as the GATT (General Agreement on Tariffs and Trade) and NAFTA (North American Free Trade Agreement), the production side of the fashion industry has moved offshore to the Caribbean as well as countries like China, Portugal, Vietnam, the Philippines, Mexico, Turkey, and Indonesia. Moreover, global companies move from one place to another at the drop of a hat as economies fluctuate. Increasingly, fashion is designed in one place, manufactured somewhere else, and retailed to "global" Western markets.

On top of this, as tariffs have been abandoned, prices for the mass-produced items of clothing, apparel, and footwear have dropped, creating

**Young girl at loom.** Photo: Zouavman Le Zouave. Creative Commons Attribution Share Alike 3.0

even more pressure on the high-end segment of the fashion industry, which wants to preserve exclusivity and high prices to secure declining margins. Even in countries like China, the majority of the population is clothed in cheap mass-produced everyday apparel while expensive shopping malls housing global designer brands proliferate to capture a growing bourgeois market.

As we have seen, there is a dynamic between supply and demand, or the "push" and "pull" factors of the fashion industry. Products and materials are pushed onto markets to seduce consumers, while a pull system engages in extensive market research of customers to determine tastes, habits, and trends, which are fed into the industry and its product development. The development of new fibers has been especially influential in transforming the industry. Fibers have been developed by major international chemical companies such as **DuPont,** which have invested heavily in the new products and therefore want a good return. The popularization of **rayon,** Dacron, Lycra, neoprene, and smart fibers has largely been the result of heavy marketing and alignment of these new products with the lifestyle and tastes of youth consumers.

Meanwhile, producers of **natural fibers** such as wool, cotton, and silk have faced an uphill battle retaining market share and appealing to consumers. Even schemes such as the Woolmark label and its offspring, Woolblendmark, have not guaranteed the return of faithful consumers. More recently, environmental concerns have also beset the fashion industry with debate about the adverse bio costs of textile production that are non-polluting, eco friendly, and resource efficient. Yet, to date, this has not stemmed questionable methods of dyeing, bleaching, and fertilizing or the use of added chemicals or enormous quantities of water in manufacturing processes.

**Polyamide structure nylon.**

$$\left[ \overset{H}{\underset{|}{N}} - (CH_2)_6 - \overset{H}{\underset{|}{N}} - \overset{O}{\underset{\|}{C}} - (CH_2)_4 - \overset{O}{\underset{\|}{C}} \right]_n$$

**Nylon 66**

$$\left[ \overset{H}{\underset{|}{N}} - (CH_2)_5 - \overset{O}{\underset{\|}{C}} \right]_n$$

**Nylon 6**

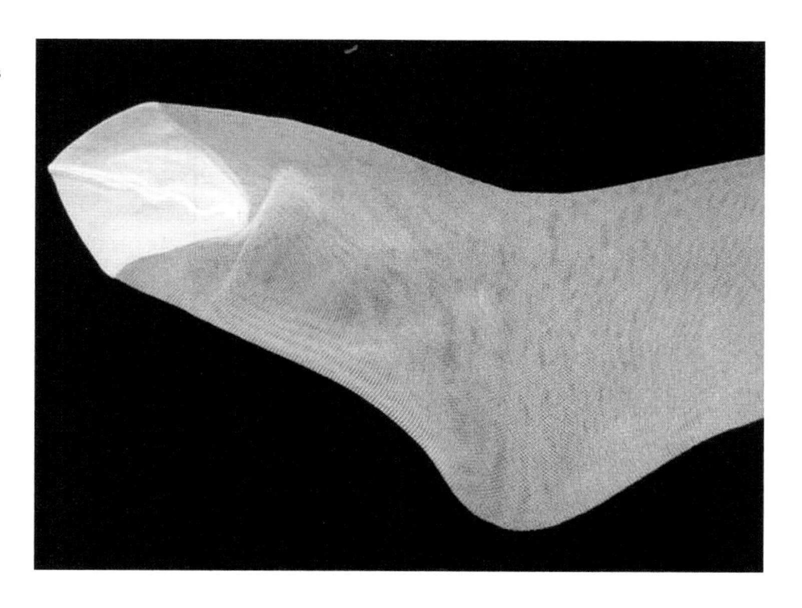

**Detail of white stocking.** Photo: Tranquil Garden. Creative commons attribution 3.0

So far, we have examined fashion as a consumer industry that produces goods for a market. As such, the production end of the system has been treated as normal industry policy by governments keen to encourage the import and processing of raw materials, the transfer of skills, and increased commodity trade, for example, through the encouragement of the construction of docks, mills, chemical facilities, and factories and the subsiding of the expansion of agricultural production of raw materials such as cotton, linen, wool, and silk. England's textile industry was a classic example of this for over two centuries.

Traditionally, governments were also keen to impose regulations on the industry and barrier protection tariffs on the import of finished goods in order to shore up the viability of local fashion industries. Of course, this was not in the interests of consumers, who faced less choice and higher prices. However, such privations were justified as the cost of building and preserving national culture. Governments in industrialized countries have also, usually with pressure from trade unions, instituted a variety of measures designed to regulate work practices and improve working conditions, though often these have barely ameliorated industry practices. So, in this sense, the fashion industry has been of historical interest to governments as a significant part of economic well-being.

However, as we noted in chapter 2, the fashion industry also has some idiosyncratic features that make it distinctive from other industries. The most distinctive aspect of the fashion industry is the fact that it is a cultural industry or phenomenon, that is, an industry that produces and sells intangible values (aesthetic and magical) that ostensibly add quality and status to people's lives (Braham 1997). These days this is called "value adding," where the impulse to purchase goods is not driven by need but by the desire to acquire certain attributes associated with the fashion item or the label it carries. Because of this, it is the promotion, marketing, and retailing of fashion that is crucially important in determining the uptake of a new trend or the sustainability of a designer or brand.

Historically, governments have been much less keen to meddle in the cultural side of the fashion industry. Some exceptions are Italy, New Zealand, Belgium, Spain, Singapore, and Hong Kong, the governments of which have included fashion in their creative industry policies to kick-start local design, manufacture, education, research, and especially the promotion of fashion more generally in their jurisdictions. The perceived benefits of recasting the fashion industry as a cultural industry include fashion's contribution to the creation of a visible national culture; the creation of export opportunities that compensate for the decline of traditional export industries; the generation of spin-off effects that stimulate cognate cultural subsectors such as media, cultural tourism, and design; and the construction of a global profile for a country or state.

## ii. fashion forecasting, marketing, and the fashion consumer

As this chapter has shown, the structure of the fashion industry is a complex one that has undergone a series of changes to become highly diversified and global. It still, however, depends on the existence and corralling of consumer demand driven by trendsetters, celebrities, role models (or fashion slaves), and ordinary shoppers. Every aspect of the fashion industry involves a complex series of strategies and calculations that force designers and brand companies to become agile and flexible in order to move with the times.

Boom can easily turn to bust, and many major labels have either gone to the wall or almost folded on more than one occasion. Reputation, star status, and size are no guarantee of success and the sustainable viability of a fashion business. Part of the problem is the fluid base on which fashion rests. While a particular new style, design, or garment can become feted globally overnight, the history of fashion is also littered with fashion failures where promoted styles have never been accepted by the public. Examples include hobble skirts in the 1920s, flairs and bell-bottoms in the 1960s, **midi**-length dresses in the 1970s, and bubble skirts in the 1980s.

### Fashion Forecasting

The challenge for the fashion industry is to predict future trends due to the long lead time from design to shop floor, which results in substantial investment in fashion forecasting (color forecasting was discussed in chapter 1). The aim of fashion forecasting is to predict trends about eighteen months to two years ahead. It involves predicting mood, behavior, and consumer habits by linking demographic information about consumer segments and statistics on trends in retail sales with guessing how and why people buy fashion and how tastes are changing. Fashion forecasting involves combining information about color and fabrics with socioeconomic and cultural perceptions of the fashion zeitgeist. This requires a combination of intuition, training in design or fashion, and a detailed knowledge of fashion manufacturing and production. Color is of prime importance because of the lead time required for yarn mills to produce yarns of particular colors, which then drives the production of new fabrics and textiles for the upcoming style directions.

Close analysis of trends in the fashion industry, such as new designer collections, catwalk shows, trade shows, and celebrity fashion, are an obvious starting point. In addition, "trend spotters" comb newspapers, business publications, and fashion magazines as well as apprehending trends in popular culture and media (cinema, television, music, advertising, Web sites, CD sleeves, style fliers, and fashion sponsors). More generally fashion forecasters also try to take account of social events, contexts, and major changes, for example, economic upturns and downturns, terrorism, war, the emergence of particular subcultures, and significant social and political debates. In many senses, a fashion forecaster is as much a social forecaster or fortune-teller as a predictor of merchandising trends. The challenge is to turn knowledge about trends into forecasts that can be applied within the industry.

Forecasters draw on many sources for information about changing consumer habits; for example, they may photograph crowds at large festivals, concerts, and sports events to see what they are wearing and how they combine styles and looks. These photographs are categorized and analyzed in order to map out emerging trends and new street fads and identify declining fashions. Trends may trickle down (from the fashion elite), trickle up (from street fashions), or trickle across (from one segment to all market segments). The fashion forecaster attempts to map these flows and deduce the uptake or rejection of new styles and innovations by consumers. Some fashions resonate with the public mood, while others may be avoided and viewed as ridiculous or quirky. Once a trend is identified, it must be mapped onto the target market and their ability to pay.

Trend forecasting has become a major global industry, and the information it generates ranges from publicly available information to niche sector reports to privately commissioned research. Because of the potentially sensitive nature of the information, fashion forecasters charge a premium. Some of the major fashion forecast companies are the New York–based companies Donegar Group, Cotton Inc., and Stylesight; London-based companies Worth Global Style Network (WGSN), FashionInformation.com, and Future Laboratory; and the Paris-based companies Peclers, Trend Union, SachaPacha, PromoStyl, and Au Studio Promostyl. Many fashion forecasters produce online magazines and market research reports. Often fashion trends are slow; a particular look or style gradually morphs into another. An example is Ugg boots (sheepskin flat boots), which may be fashionable one year only to be succeeded by cowboy boots the next year and softer footwear like suede boots in subsequent years.

Fashion forecasting involves consumer research (surveys, interviews, and focus groups with consumers); color forecasting (identifying color trends and new shades that will excite the consumer several years ahead); textile development (creating new fabrics, innovations in the treatment of yarns and textiles, and new fabric patterns and prints); staged industry shows to promote the next fashions (yarn shows, fabric shows, garment design shows, fashion weeks, designer and couture shows); sales forecasting, which estimates production runs, price strategies, and stock levels; and cultural indicators that reflect style and lifestyle shifts and social change. Once these stages have been analyzed, a new season's fashion look is mapped out and promoted through the fashion media before being released to the public. Consumer reaction is the litmus test of this process.

### Fashion Market Segments

There are three main types of fashion wear: women's wear, menswear, and children's wear. Women's wear is by far the largest market segment, accounting for over half of all sales. Accordingly, the majority of designer companies focus their efforts here. The consequence is that there is enormous competition in the women's wear segment, which is exacerbated by quick obsolescence and shorter seasons.

Menswear is a growth sector and now accounts for about a quarter of the market. There are two basic types of menswear: formal suiting or business wear, and leisure and sportswear. Although men's fashions in silhouette and fabric change more slowly than women's, men are more sensitive to quality finishing and details, including brand logos and image.

The smallest market share has been children's fashion, which has subsegments: baby (up to one year of age), toddler (two to four years old), preschoolers (four to six years old), and school age (seven to nine years old, ten- to twelve years old, and young teens). Within this segment, casual and sports clothes predominate, with mini-markets for formal (party) clothes and school uniforms. Traditionally considered to be marginal to fashion trends, children's wear is becoming highly fashion oriented, as preschoolers become knowledgeable about new styles and fashion celebrities.

These clothing segments determine the attributes of groups of customers, but there are also longer-term trends that influence long-range fashion forecasting. For example, in Western countries, a declining birthrate means that populations are aging, and this influences the types of fashion brands and products they will buy. So the fashion industry increasingly caters to the "gray" market, the over-forty-five segment that prefers comfort to cutting-edge style but still wants to look fashionable.

At the same time, however, the lower birthrate means smaller family size and an increased investment in children. This has sparked growing demand for designer clothes and luxury goods for children, with an increasing numbers of labels, including Nike, Tommy Hilfiger, Benetton, and Gap, launching lines for children. At the 2007 Pitti Bimbo trade show for children's clothing in Florence, Italy, designer brands included Burberry, Armani, Alberta Ferretti, Chloé, Missoni, Eva Cavalli, Dior Baby, Gucci Baby, Lavinia Biagiotti's Dolls, and Madonna's English Roses. While analysts claim that the children are driving sales because they already have a sophisticated understanding of fashion, others claim that wealthy parents are creating miniature versions of themselves. The declining size of families has increased the attention given to, and money spent on, children.

Two other market subsegments are teens and college students, both of whom are highly fashion conscious and receptive to promotional campaigns and style gatekeepers, who promote the latest look, although these subsegments have shifting self-images that result in frequent changes in fashion style. In addition to gender and stage-of-life segments, there are also specialist wardrobe segments that cut across the former. These include sportswear, swimwear, lingerie, travel gear, club wear, and loungewear. As fashion-market segments become more differentiated, Jenkyn Jones (2005: 65) has proposed the subsegments shown in box 6.2.

### Consumer Attributes

As well as gender and age, consumer attributes that shape fashion behavior and consumer trends include the following.

Race and Ethnicity—A growing market subsegment is people from distinctive racial or ethnic groups who identify at least partially with the customary or diasporic clothing cultures of their origin, which translates into specific clothing and fashion codes (for example, Muslim expatriates or members of the Indian diaspora; see case studies 29 and 31).

Income and Social Class—Although fashion consumption is broadly related to income (ability to buy), measures of patterns of disposal and income and discretionary expenditure (willingness to buy) are more important indicators of consumer behavior. Social class refers to a combination of income, occupational prestige, and educational levels. These determine how a particular consumer identifies her- or himself in the fashion market. For example, one consumer may only buy designer labels or department store specials, while another consumer may be driven by seasonal fads or preference for a particular color. Fashion is frequently used as a status symbol that indicates actual or aspirational social position and cultural attributes. This is discussed further below.

Place of Residence—Where a consumer lives structures her or his fashion knowledge and clothing consumption. For example, inner-city consumers tend to be more attuned to fast fashion, rural consumers tend to identify with traditional country styles, and residents of college towns effect a more avant-garde or college look. Consumers in beach towns and lively holiday resorts typically wear colorful leisure wear and ostentatious jewelry.

Lifestyle—How consumers live provides a context for clothing behavior that is appropriate to factors such as their occupation (professional versus blue collar), type of community in which they live, exposure to travel, marital status, leisure interests, and sporting pursuits.

Physiognomy—Body shape and size directly determine fashion choices. For example, traditionally tiny Asian bodies are suited to tailored and

### Box 6.2 Market Segments

| EUROPEAN SEGMENTS | U.S. SEGMENTS |
|---|---|
| **Women's Wear** | |
| Haute couture | High end (no couture) |
| Designer | Designer |
| Classic | Missy |
| Middle market | Young designer (fashion forward) |
| High street | Better |
| Budget women's wear | Bridge |
| | Contemporary/trendy |
| | Junior |
| | Moderate |
| | Budget |
| | Private label |
| | Mass market |
| **Menswear** | |
| Bespoke tailoring | Custom tailored |
| Designer | Designer |
| High street | Bridge |
| Sportswear | Furnishings (shirts and ties) |
| Casual | Moderate |
| Budget menswear | Sports and active |
| | Sports |
| | Popular |
| | Supermarket |
| **Children's Wear** | |
| Newborn | Layette |
| Infant | Infant |
| Toddler | Toddler |
| Girls | Girls |
| Boys | Boys |
| Teens | Teens |

structured fashion garments, while many Western countries are experiencing an obesity epidemic that has created a demand for large sizes. African and African American women tend to have prominent bottoms that require a different cut of trousers, panties, skirts, and school uniforms. In Brazil, the bottoms of females are the focus of fashion as the dominant erogenous zone rather than the Eurocentric preference for breasts.

Psychographics (Personality, Values, and Attitudes)—This is the study of fashion attitudes, which anayzes people's susceptibility to fashion trends by distinguishing early and late adopters of new styles. Psychographics entails a combination of measures of psychology, personality, and values. Psychographic measurement in market research is a key element of fashion forecasting (see below).

Stage of Life and Demographic Trends—Where a person is in her or his life cycle relates to rites of passage (e.g., marital status, whether or not one has children) that influence fashion choices. For example, singles and divorcees tend to be more fashion conscious than married couples with young children. Wider social trends such as the baby boom explosion or the aging of a population skew specific patterns of demand.

Religion—As discussed in chapter 8, religion often regulates clothing behavior by formal and informal sanctions as to how adherents should dress, for example, concerning modesty and prescribed social roles (Islamic **veiling,** Amish traditional clothing, Mormons' missionary suits, modest clean-cut shirts and skirts).

### Consumer Motivations

Most intriguing to designers are the factors that persuade a customer to buy or those that deter a customer. Much attention is directed at determining the "motivational drives" that customers exhibit in order to target products to appropriate markets. As outlined above, the study of consumer behavior has become essential to the fashion industry as a way to distinguish between customers on the basis of age and demographic trends; gender balance; location; occupation; and, above all, wealth (Costantino 1998: 22–29). Since the capacity to pay translates into bottom-line profitability, consumer analysts have directed most of their attention to identifying market segments based on occupation, income, and social class—or "purchase behavior," that is, consumer lifestyles. Roughly developed from measures of social or class stratification, consumers are divided into six bands (see box 6.3). These categories are used to target advertisements to different media, place merchandise in different stores, style products in different ways, and seek endorsements that reflect the tastes of a targeted consumer group. A more recent classification system called ACORN uses demographic knowledge of neighborhoods (defined by postal codes or zip codes) to differentiate geodemographic variables that predict purchaser behavior. This is used to target marketing and advertising, select locations for new stores, and strategize mail-order campaigns.

Other techniques use psychographic information about attitudes, values, and beliefs to predict consumer behavior. These techniques are designed to understand consumers' motivations to make purchases and relate this to lifestyle factors that shape consumer behavior. This approach, derived from Abraham Maslow's "pyramid of needs," places fashion at the far end of practical needs (such as basic physiological ones like food and shelter) and views it as bearing attributes such as esteem and status, group membership, and self-actualization. These relate to the desire

**Box 6.3 Socioeconomic Consumer Bands**

A Upper/upper-middle class (managerial or administrative)
B Middle class (middle management, administration, professions)
C1 Lower-middle class (supervisors, clerical, junior managers)
C2 Skilled working class (skilled manual laborers)
D Working class (semiskilled and unskilled manual workers)
E Pensioners, casual workers, unemployed, welfare recipients (Costantino 1998: 29)

An alternative breakdown is:

Upper-upper class
Lower-upper class
Upper-middle class
Lower-middle class
Upper-lower class
Lower-lower class

for recognition and approval from others as well as to discretionary decisions to create a particular self-image. Other analysts have proposed classifications based on personality types, AIOs (activities, interests, opinions), and self-concept types (self-image, ideal self-image, social self-image, ideal social self-image) (Costantino 1998: 31–32). The fashion industry uses many strategies to persuade consumers that certain goods fulfill their social needs by making new products appear relevant to the lifestyles of consumers by appealing to hedonism and novelty, using prominent stimuli and celebrity endorsements, and establishing product or brand bonds with consumers.

This type of market research draws on theories of reception, innovation theory, and self-concept formation to propose models of consumer choice. The fashion industry constantly attempts to manipulate the "push" or supply forces through knowledge gained from market research and fashion forecasting of trends in the "pull" or demand forces in order to keep consumers in suspense and susceptible to every new fad and fashion.

### Types of Retailers

Contemporary fashion consumers have a myriad of ways by which they can buy clothes, depending whether it is a leisure pursuit, serendipitous, or purposeful. As well as understanding consumer types and motivations, fashion retailers need to map this against the specific retail environments, the main types of which are shown in box 6.4.

### Price Points

Determining the price of fashion apparel is a complex and idiosyncratic process since there is no straightforward relationship between the consumer's ability to pay and the cost of goods. Retailers need to calculate the minimum or baseline price that covers costs against the maximum a consumer is prepared to pay (or ceiling price). The profit margin is the difference between these

**Box 6.4 Types of Fashion Retailers**

| | |
|---|---|
| Independents | These are retailers, often sole traders, with fewer than ten outlets who often specialize in certain clothing categories |
| Multiples | Fashion chains such as Benetton, Gap, and French Connection, which have high profile and prime positioning in the market and generate significant turnover. |
| Department stores | Developed in the nineteenth century, department stores offer a range of goods on different floors; they drove the development of fashion consumerism though in recent years have struggled to retain fashion consumers. |
| Concessions | This is space within a store that is rented to a retailer or manufacturer for a fixed percentage of turnover thus minimizing the risk to the store. |
| Franchises | These agreements are made by known brands to franchise the manufacture, distribution, and retailing of fashion apparel exclusively. |
| Factory stores and outlets | These offer excess high-quality stock and seconds to consumers in warehouse facilities at significant discount. |
| Discounters | These buy excess stock from oversupply and failed merchandise, which is offered to budget-conscious consumers. |
| Markets | These are a revival of earlier forms of retailing, where consumers seek bargains and unique fashion merchandise, usually as cash transactions with no guarantee of quality or return. |
| Mail order | Developed in the nineteenth century, mail order is a convenient way for shoppers (especially those in remote communities) to keep up with fashion and purchase from home by making choices from mail-order catalogs. |
| Electronic shopping | This has to some degree replaced mail order as a convenient form of home shopping from fashion Web sites and interactive television. |
| Party plans | Fashion party plans involve an agent selling to groups in private homes in a party atmosphere. |

Source: Adapted from Jenkyn Jones 2005: 65–69.

prices. There are five ways to set prices: cost-plus (basic costs plus a markup), buyer-based (a price determined by how much the target buyer is prepared to pay), psychological pricing (a price point that a buyer will accept as reflecting the attributes of the merchandise, which is then lowered slightly to make it look like a bargain), competition-based (setting a price that undercuts a competitor with a similar product), and dynamic pricing (different prices for different consumers and buying contexts, similar to traditional bargaining).

As well as the strategies for setting prices, there is a time line of changing prices, which relate to or accompany the fashion cycle of the merchandise. The fashion cycle charts the time line from product innovation to stages of promotion and uptake, maximum sales and popularity, declining sales and cheap copies, excess stock, and disappearance. Retailers vary the price point depending on the stage of the fashion cycle. Retailers can be hurt by excess stock, which necessitates markdowns, or alternatively by insufficient stock to meet demand ("stockouts"). Merchandise that fails to sell at any price is often called "slob stock."

### Branding and Consumer Strategies

There are various factors in the development of the brand familiarity, loyalty, and identification that drive fashion consumer behavior. For new products to succeed, the industry must introduce an innovation that is symbolic (an innovation that creates a new social meaning, such as a new style of running shoe) or technological (making some functional change such as introducing smart fibers). Innovations may be continuous (a modification of an existing product, such as a parka or jacket with a foldaway hat), dynamically continuous (a more radical product variation that changes how a garment is worn, such as stiletto-heeled shoes), or discontinuous (something that creates a major change, such as "fast suits" in swimwear). Whether or not an innovation will succeed depends on benefits perceived by the consumer, as well as compatibility with consumer habits, the innovation's suitability for experimentation among consumers, the relatively low complexity of the innovation so that it is easy for the consumer to understand and adopt it, and the visibility of the innovation and consumers' access to it.

Equally contentious is the sustainability of the fashion industry, especially at the couture end. Some argue that despite restructuring, diffusion lines, spin-off products, and the entry of new designers and fashion cities, consumer trends are defying the best-laid plans of the industry gurus. There is evidence that consumers are choosing the lower-priced copies and derivatives available though chain stores and less prestigious designer labels and brands over the exclusive labels (Demasi 2003: 1). It seems not only that the high price tags have deterred fashion followers but that boredom with the lifestyle pitch of the luxury brands can lead to customer disillusion. As fashion forecaster Karen Webster has predicted,

**buying logos for caché is over. People are no longer buying Louis Vuitton because of the LV [logo]. Now what they're buying into is the quality and manufacture of the product. The product has to carry it. (Quoted by Demasi 2003: 1)**

These product and retailing considerations have had a significant impact on the activities of designers.

## iii. the changing role of the fashion designer

The design part of the industry is perhaps the most magical part of all. The manufacturing side is the dark side, with a history of poor employment practices, exploitation, and an enormous gulf between the unit cost of wholesale and retail apparel. The marketing and retailing side is a messy tale of capitalism-unleashed behavioral modifications and short-term horizons that result in boom-and-bust cycles. The representation or transposition of fashion into the media and popular culture is a driven by hyperbole and a self-referential and non-reflective arena of egos, fantasy, and often desperation to remain in vogue. The consumption side of the industry is a murky convergence

**Chanel logo.** Photo: Midorisyu. Creative Commons Attribution 2.0 Generic

of rampant desires, unscrupulous manipulators of psyches, and images overwhelming realities.

The dream of many young people to be a fashion designer or model attests to the lure of the industry and profession. It seems glamorous, creative, fun, global, and a ticket to travel and rub shoulders with the glitterati. The reality is somewhat different, yet the image of the fashion designer remains a potent cultural symbol. Even so, there has been surprisingly little written about the fashion design profession or the place of the designer in the fashion system. In an obvious way, the designer personifies fashion (Kawamura 2005: 57), since a well-designed garment is a precondition for fashion to exist. But even a cursory understanding of the fashion system indicates that it is a long way from an exciting idea for a unique dress or shoe to its uptake as a successful fashion must-have. To bridge the gap, designers must be many things simultaneously.

Design is now recognized as an occupation or profession but emerged organically from the ranks of tailors and dressmakers. In the twentieth century, the usual route was to be apprenticed to a designer or design house and learn the business on the job. Increasingly, couture houses have sought up-and-coming designers to work on collections under the name of the house. Examples include Karl Lagerfeld for Chanel; Alexander McQueen for Givenchy; Stella McCartney for Chloé; John Galliano for Balenciaga, Givenchy, and Dior; Tom Ford for Gucci; Marc Jacobs for Louis Vuitton;

Nicolas Ghesquière for Balenciaga; and Hedi Slimane for YSL and Dior. In these situations, the "appropriated" designer is under dual pressures: first, to be able to produce collections that retain some sense of the iconic look of the house, and second, to be able to develop her or his own signature, which will subsequently be launched under her or his own name. Inevitably, this is a difficult balancing act that often ends in acrimony, disappointment, and sudden departures. However, as the traditional haute couture houses still trade on the name and reputation of the original designer, they are impelled to reproduce the name through new names and lines. For both sides, this can be a make-or-break situation.

This has created challenges for the design industry. Now that designers are bought and sold, they have become dispensable, and their reputations depend on their ability to deliver the right look for the right employer. Designers and labels need to balance flexibility and sensitivity to new fashion trends with tight control of the business through strategies such as controlling the distribution and pricing of merchandise (for example, through franchise agreements or directly owned stores), limiting licensing agreements and monitoring quality, and diversifying their acquisitions and expansion to cross-subsidize underperforming parts of the business but maintaining the integrity of a brand (Andrews 2007).

Since the 1960s, fashion design has become a professional skill taught at technical colleges, art schools, colleges, and universities. Most of the training is directed toward the creative design part of the profession, although it has increasingly been recognized that it is equally important to have a sound sense of the economics of running a designer business (accounting, marketing, small business training, outsourcing, etc.). Nonetheless, a surprising number of designers (both historically and contemporaneously) have had no formal training and have simply fallen into or infiltrated the designer business. Examples of "intuitive" designers include Coco Chanel, Vivienne Westwood, and Rei Kawakubo (who had a graphic design background).

The process of fashion design involves a number of elements: having a conceptual idea of a garment or look and the ability to translate it into a form; choosing the most appropriate fabrics; making samples; building a seasonal collection, typically with a theme; outsourcing manufacture of preorders and likely sales; obtaining exposure and marketing; retailing; evaluating success and financial earnings; and beginning planning for the next season. The designer business is a relentless cycle of anticipating the future yet drawing on resonances of the past. This involves balancing the *now* with the *future* and the *before.* Potential clients may be frightened by trends that are too different from what they wear now but reject anything that looks old fashioned or out of fashion, so a careful balancing act is needed to predict a newness that is exciting but still has some familiarity. There is a tension between newness or uniqueness and themes that are reworked or reinterpreted. And, as we have already noted, some designers take a trickle-down approach by designing elite or avant-garde fashion that appeals to a small coterie and later is taken up by a wider fashion-sensitive group. Other designers raid popular cultural referents from below and translate these into their garments, apparel, and collections.

Interestingly, fashion designers are usually not considered cultural workers by other cultural workers (e.g., artists), industry bureaucrats, or statisticians, even though they are creating cultural products and images, and similar professionals such as costume designers, stylists, and makeup artists are included in this category. Why this should be is not clear, although perhaps designers believe that they are outside or above the realm of cultural workers and are dream weavers of a different order.

This is shown by the ambivalence of fashion designers toward the imitations of star designs and logos (some cheap but some high quality) by the burgeoning fake-fashion or counterfeiting industry. Some designers pursue legal action for breach of copyright and licensing, while others turn a blind eye to it, regarding the fakes as free publicity that generates customer knowledge and brand desirability. The counterfeiting industry is extensive. In June 2007, 500 handbags worth $400,000 were stolen from Gucci's Florence workshop, and a Chinese scheme to counterfeit designer bags and jeans worth $700 million was foiled by U.S. customs officials. Fakes are no longer all poor reproductions shoddily made, but some mimic the quality and craftsmanship, which makes them indistinguishable from the genuine product. The aim is to flood the commercial markets with "elite" brands and labels to force up prices.

To maintain market share, designers and their labels must engage in aggressive marketing and retailing practices that require perhaps a greater range of skills and genius than the design of collections themselves, including:

- **The promotion of new collections through catwalk shows**
- **Promotional fashion weeks**
- **Industry bodies that represent and promote members**
- **Government-sponsored trade shows**
- **Celebrity endorsement in return for the "loan" of collections**
- **Discretionary distribution systems (open, selected, exclusive, or dual)**
- **Franchising (of products to a retailer for a fee)**
- **Licensing (of products and lines)**
- **Mail order (catalogs)**
- **Electronic and online shopping**
- **Directly operated stores**
- **Publicity through fashion spreads and the like (Jackson and Haid 2006: 64)**

The measurement of retail performance can be determined from three different measures:

1. **Financial measures (turnover, margins, returns over costs, cash flow)**
2. **Customer measures (market share, awareness, conversion rate, customer loyalty, etc.)**
3. **Productivity measures (sales to floor space/employee, stock turnover, sell-down rate, turnover rate) (Webb 2006: 119)**

These measures can be refined for the particularities of how different stores operate and perform. Of crucial importance is the success in branding a fashion label as distinctive and embodying "attributes which some may consider intangible but are nevertheless very real to the consumer" (Costantino 1998: 61). Usually, these values are emotional or symbolic, attaching not so much to the product but to the wearer of the product, as enhancements of the person. The challenge for the marketer is to transform a product into a feeling or mood that can be advertised through the product. Once a product has

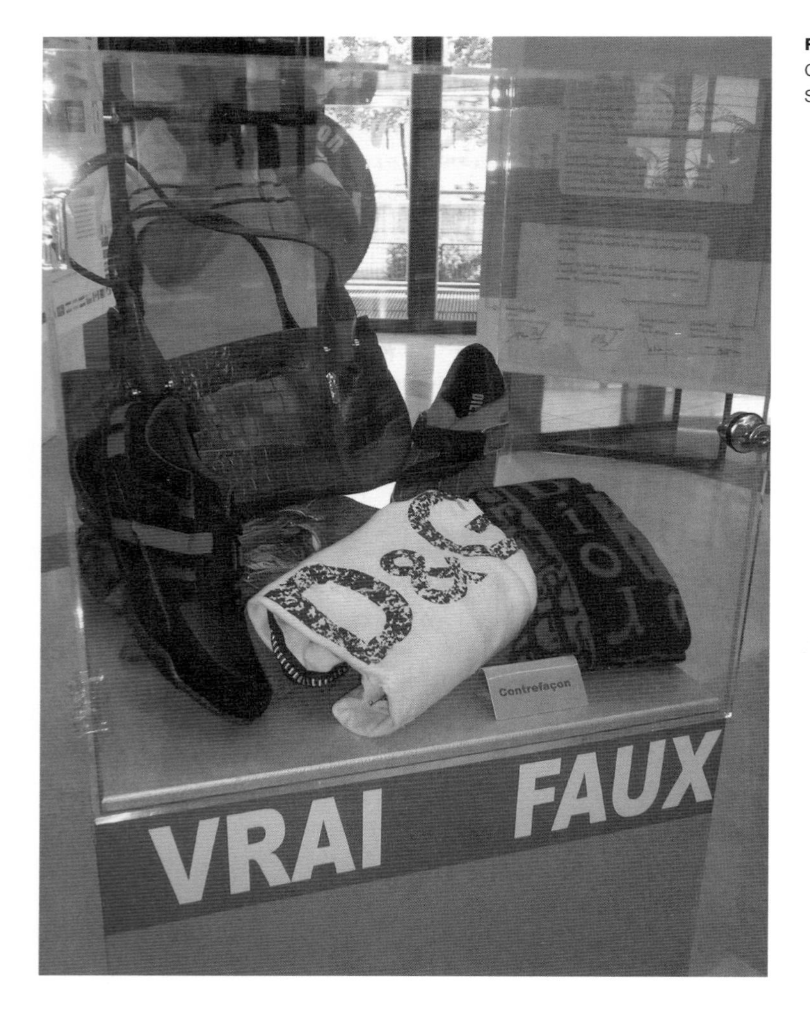


**Fake goods.** Photo: Julien de Koninck. Creative Commons Attribution ShareAlike 2.5 License

achieved value-added status, prices can be increased to reflect its status. Consumers are willing to pay more as a guarantee of the value of the purchase. While some value-added campaigns are short lived, others achieve a permanent brand notoriety and loyalty that persist. Examples include Levi Strauss jeans, Aquascutum fine clothes for English gentry, Hermès accessories, Benetton retail fashion, Swatch watches, Hugo Boss men's clothes, and athletic shoe brands such as **Reebok** and Nike (Costantino 1998: 62–66).

The challenge for designers is to balance the distinctiveness of a product, label, or brand with consumer demand and affordability. Pierre Cardin was the first Paris designer to enter the prêt-à-porter and licensing domains. He established a prêt-à-porter in the French department store Au Printemps in 1959 and the next year signed licensing agreements for men's ties and shirts. In 1958, he signed contracts with the Italian department store La Rinascente and German department stores. Although he was warned that licensing would kill his business, Cardin later claimed it was his salvation. By the 2000s, he had over 800 licensing agreements. While diffusion lines are attractive, and licensing profitable, it is possible to go too down market and diversify into too many products and lines and lose the edge of exclusivity. Cardin was damaged by this in the 1980s, and it took some time to rebuild the brand image. Other designer licensees, including Calvin Klein and Bill Blass, were similarly affected.

Even the global fashion chain stores the Gap (case study 23) and Benetton (case study 28) lost market share as a result of overexposure due to excessive global expansion and deterioration in the quality control of their designs. Some luxury brands (such as Gucci) have also experienced setbacks when certain products or the label has become too popular. When everyone wears apparel featuring a brand logo, the label loses its exclusivity and become ordinary—thus hurting the status of the brand.

## iv. luxury brands and global marketing

The fashion retailing sector changed markedly in the new millennium, building on the impact of changes that had occurred in the second half of the twentieth century. Other designers and brands followed the lead of Pierre Cardin and diversified into prêt-à-porter and licensing during the 1960s. Prêt-à-porter entails the production of special ready-to-wear or off-the-rack collections (rather than custom made) for department stores and boutiques at different price points. These collections are simpler than couture collections and produced according to standard sizes rather than made to measure. As such, they are mass produced and industrially manufactured without the special craft attention given to couture. They are still distinctive of the designer's style and much superior to mainstream fashion company apparel. While many prêt-à-porter collections are sold to retailers, some designers have followed the lead of Yves Saint Laurent, who established his own prêt-à-porter store, Rive Gauche, in Paris in 1965 and London in 1969. Together, these innovations transformed the viability and consumer reach of designer fashion. Almost every well-known elite designer has established prêt-à-porter lines; these include YSL Jeans, Miu Miu, D&G, Marc by Marc Jacobs, Armani Jeans and Armani Exchange, Versace Jeans Couture, See by Chloé, Kors by Michael Kors, and JPG and Gaultier Jeans. Some designers have three or four prêt-à-porter lines priced at different bands.

Major changes in marketing and retailing occurred around the turn of the millennium. The 1970s and 1980s were dominated by designers licensing their agreements with manufacturers and distributors to produce apparel (such as sunglasses, watches, ties, jewelry, perfumes, or cosmetics) in their name. Wearing a label on the outside (as a logo on a T-shirt or handbag) was irresistible to elite and mass markets. Licensing proved to be a lucrative deviation from traditional fashion marketing—generating royalties, global distribution, and label recognition—and created new markets (including tourist markets for known-brand luxury goods as travel souvenirs) (Jackson and Haid 2006: 63; see also Thomas 2007).

By the 1980s, designers and labels were taking a slightly different tack, also experimenting with diffusion lines of products—not only apparel

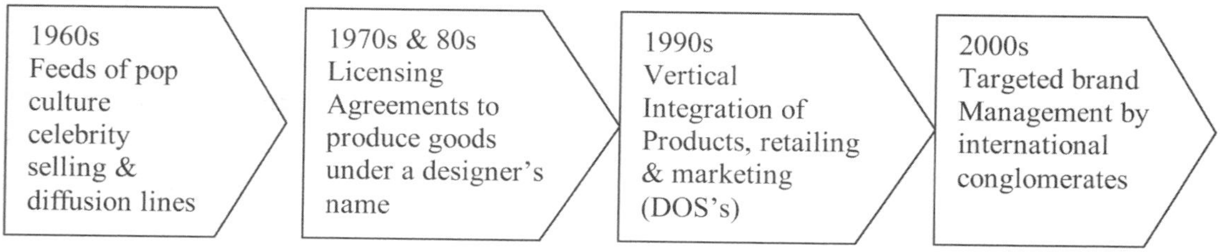

| 1960s Feeds of pop culture celebrity selling & diffusion lines | 1970s & 80s Licensing Agreements to produce goods under a designer's name | 1990s Vertical Integration of Products, retailing & marketing (DOS's) | 2000s Targeted brand Management by international conglomerates |
|---|---|---|---|

**Source:** Adapted from Jackson and Haid 2006: 65

and accessories—that were designed to capture the aesthetic of the designer and bear the designer's name and logo. Merchandise included home ware (crockery, cooking equipment, furnishings), leisure wear (beach paraphernalia, athletic equipment, sports cars, travel gear), and entertainment merchandise (audio equipment, computer accessories). Ironically, while the development of licensing and diffusion lines both popularized elite fashion and increased public awareness of the fashion system and designer stars (that is, arguably democratizing fashion), at the same time, this created a demand for the better brand names and labels and luxury merchandise (and revived elitism and snobbery in fashion).

However, as mentioned above, licensing arrangements can backfire if quality control deteriorates and the brand is overexposed. A number of elite brands suffered a loss of public reputation as a result of dubious licensing agreements, most notably Christian Dior, Gucci, Burberry, YSL, and Pierre Cardin. It took some time for these brands to rebuild their reputations. Meanwhile, new marketing strategies were explored.

In the 1980s, luxury brands began to open directly operated stores (DOSs) in which "control [of] the overall brand identity and customer shopping experience" (Jackson and Haid 2006: 64) could be maintained. As important as the apparel was, the design of the shop was equally important, and creative directors now took center stage, creating the image, mood, and shopping experience of each DOS. This involved blending the qualities of the brand with those of "the selling environment," namely, "advertising, store design, visual display, fashion communication and image activities" (Jackson and Haid 2006: 64). Thus by the 1990s, many brands had created vertical integration into retailing and marketing. While this strategy has proved successful for many brands, it also holds some risks. Umberto Angeloni of the Brioni Group identified three issues (cited by Jackson and Haid 2006: 64):

**Conception**—The standardized model for packaging a brand can become prosaic and too formulaic as the distinctiveness of the brand becomes reduced to a "lifestyle" range of accessories for the mass market.

**Economics**—In contrast to the relatively low capital intensive and flexible cost structure of the traditional designer business, the DOS approach entails financial burdens of high inventories, rental costs, and periodic refurbishing that can crush a company.

**Image**—Rather than enhance a brand image, DOSs can make the brand seem ubiquitous and

**Stella McCartney.** Photo by WILLIAM WEST/AFP/Getty Images. 2007 AFP

its status devalued; this is especially so if stores fail and have to relocate or stock needs to be passed on to outlet stores for cheap disposal.

These problems have led to another retailing strategy. First, goods are divided into "hard" and "soft" categories, with hard goods sold through wholesaling, and soft goods through DOSs. Moreover, a number of brands have been co-opted under the umbrella of large multi-brand conglomerates or franchises that handle some or all of the design, marketing, and distribution of a brand. These conglomerates include LVMH (Louis Vuitton–Moët Hennessy), **PPR** (Pinault-Printemps-Redoute), Compagnie Financière

Richemont, the Prada Group, and the Gucci Group. Bernard Arnault, the power behind LVMH, is credited with reinventing traditional brand cachet by reviving classic products and marketing them globally as a return to old values and quality in the global marketplace. LVMH is the biggest of the conglomerates, representing numerous fashion brands and other lines: wines and spirits (e.g., Moët & Chandon, Krug, Veuve Clicquot, Hennessy), perfumes and cosmetics (Dior, Guerlain, Givenchy), watches and jewelry (Tag Heuer, Zenith, Christian Dior), and selective retailing (DHS, Le Bon Marché) (Jackson and Haid 2006: 67). Box 6.5 shows the fashion brands owned by the major conglomerates.

Sales of luxury goods are now truly global, so there is fierce rivalry between the major conglomerates to poach brands and designers. Although Europe still accounts for 35 percent of sales, other areas are catching up, with the United States capturing 25 percent of sales, Japan 20 percent, and the rest of the world 20 percent. Rapidly growing markets such as China, Hong Kong, Taiwan, Singapore, India, and Russia are already having an impact on these market shares.

One company that famously lost traction through overexposure and poor quality control is Gucci, due to its overreliance on the brand logo and too little attention to the quality or distinctiveness of the products. Box 6.6 shows a brief chronology of the company's fortunes to date.

In the 2007 Milan summer collections, a number of designers toned down or abandoned their distinctive logos, including Donatella Versace ("Logos don't interest people any more"), Dolce & Gabbana ("A logo won't sell on its own any more"), and Fendi (who shredded their logo then braided it into men's bags). According to these designers, consumers are looking for detail, quality, culture, and taste. This shift in the motivations behind consumer behavior is discussed by fashion forecaster Christopher Sanderson:

**We're no longer buying and consuming at any cost—whether that be thousands of dollars for a handbag just because it has a logo on it, or the cost to the child who made a certain product under enforced conditions in a third world country or sweatshop. (Quoted by Demasi 2003: 4)**

Arguably, today's buyers are more astute. They are looking for a combination of value for money, something individual and distinctive, and something personal. Small and independent labels are growing in number and there are signs of a return to customization and tailoring. This has been partly triggered by new possibilities in customizing

**Box 6.5 Brands Owned by Fashion Conglomerates**

| | |
|---|---|
| LVMH | Louis Vuitton, Celine, Kenzo, Givenchy, Christian Dior, Fendi, Emilio Pucci, Marc Jacobs, Donna Karan |
| PPR | Gucci, YSL, Bottega Veneta, Alexander McQueen, Stella McCartney, Balenciaga |
| Richemont | Chloé, Dunhill, Old England, Shanghai Tang |
| Prada | Prada, Miu Miu, Azzedine Alaia, Car Shoe |

manufacture for individual consumers, for example, body scanning techniques that can store a person's body measurements on a smart card, which can be used to order a desired garment to be made to measure. In time, this may compete with ready-to-wear stocks in chain stores and boutiques.

The fashion cycle also means that instant obsolescence builds high levels of excess and waste into the system, a feature only barely addressed by contemporary environmental concerns about the sustainability of raw materials, carbon footprints, use of dangerous chemicals and products, and the environmental impact of the huge amount of discarded items of apparel once the fashion has moved on (Black 2008). A study by the Council of the Textile and Fashion Industries Australia in 2008 estimated that the average Australian woman

**Box 6.6 The Gucci Group**

1904 Guccio Gucci set up a workshop to produce high-quality leather goods in Florence, Italy. He specialized in handcrafted luggage and accessories marketed as luxury goods using equestrian motifs. This became a family business through successive generations.

1925 The duffle bag was launched.

1932 The moccasin shoe with the tongue caught in a gilt bit was popularized.

1938 Gucci coins the slogan 'Quality is remembered long after price is forgotten'

1950s The Gucci double-*G* intertwined trademark was introduced. The firm became highly successful through to the 1970s, selling handbags, belts, and shoes.

1961 The Jackie O bag was launched and the GG logo was printed on canvas bags and luggage.

1970s Company was restructured and sold.

1975 First Gucci perfume was introduced.

1981 First ready-to-wear collection was introduced.

1983 Maurizio Gucci (Guccio's grandson) inherited the company and sparked a bitter family feud.

1993 The investment company Investcorp bought Gucci and in 1994 appointed Tom Ford design director; he turned fortunes around, and the *brand* was relaunched as a highly successful luxury group with Ford as celebrity designer. The brand was famously advertised by *a* G shaved into a model's pubic hair.

1995 Maurizio Gucci was murdered by hit man engaged by ex-wife Patrizia; Domenico de Sole became Gucci CEO.

1999 Gucci was combined with PPR to rebuff a hostile takeover by rival LVMH.

2004 Ford and de Sole resigned and were replaced by three designers: Alessandra Facchinetti for women's wear, John Ray for menswear, and Frida Giannini for accessories.

2006 Ray resigned, and Giannini was appointed overall creative director.

2006 Gucci Baby was launched.

2007 Handbags account for 50 percent, shoes 13 percent, and clothing 12 percent of sales.

Source: Adapted from O'Hara Callan 2002: 118.

**Dolce & Gabbana.** Photo by Chris Moore/Catwalking/Getty Images. 2007 Catwalking

buys fifty-six pieces of clothing (including underwear) each year, while eighteen- through twenty-five-year-olds each buy over one hundred items per year (Australian Broadcasting Corporation News Radio 2008). However, many items are only worn once and charities report receiving twenty-two tons of discarded clothing every day. Despite discounting, secondhand sales, and e-selling, the sheer quantity of "disposable" fashion creates significant environmental issues and ethical trade issues that should drive consumers to reevaluate their consumption habits and drive change in the fashion industry. The scope of disposable fashion is creating social and cultural criticism of the fashion industry as unnecessarily wasteful, exploitative, irresponsible, undemocratic, sexist, and elitist. Despite such polarized feelings, fashion still dominates media and popular culture images. This is the subject of the next chapter.

## v. conclusion

This chapter has introduced elements of the structure of the fashion industry that illustrate the complex system from the production of raw materials through design, manufacture, distribution, and consumption. The fashion industry has undergone major changes since the mid-twentieth century that have revolutionized many aspects of its modus operandi, especially through techniques of prêt-à-porter, licensing, and diffusion and new retailing forms. The field of fashion forecasting and consumer research has become much more sophisticated as the understanding of the marketplace and consumer motivations and habits has become more nuanced, allowing for a greater appreciation of the challenge to balance local and global fashion needs and habits. The unprecedented growth in the demand for luxury fashion and accessories has further challenged prevailing assumptions about the industry and spearheaded aggressive business practices. At the same time, there are new challenges on the horizon, particularly as countries such as China are transformed from sourcing and manufacturing sites as they develop first an effervescent fashion consumer culture (for example, Japan) and then successful fashion design and distribution industries (Reinach 2005). The customary links between rich and poor countries and the West and "the rest" are undergoing significant realignment, which will continue to transform the business of fashion in the future.

**CHAPTER SUMMARY**

- Fashion is an industry, but a complex and diverse one that exhibits a classic supply-and-demand chain.
- The fashion industry is guided by herd-like trends (consumer taste) but constantly reinvents itself as newness and now-ness.
- Despite the prominence of Paris (and Europe more generally) as the fashion capital, its dominance has been challenged by new fashion capitals and shifting patterns of production and consumption globally.
- Fashion forecasting and consumer research indicate expanding segments of the market and complex demographic, psychographical, and lifestyle shifts that shape fashion behavior and patterns of fashion consumption.
- Forms of fashion retailing have expanded, offering consumers a wide range of shopping opportunities.
- The designer has shifted from being seen as an aloof genius to a commodity that is bought and discarded by fashion houses and brands.

- Luxury brands and global marketing characterize the fashion industry of the new millennium.
- New forms of marketing (such as prêt-à-porter and diffusion lines, licensing, vertical and horizontal integration, and international corporate management of brands) have transformed the economics of the fashion industry.

## CASE STUDY 21: Celebrity Models

**Naomi Campbell.** Photo by Bryan Bedder/Getty Images. 2006 Bryan Bedder

We have looked at the rise of the fashion model as a twentieth-century innovation that opened up elite fashion design to wider audiences and gave legitimacy to trickle- or bubble-up fashions from young designers, popular cultural influences, and new sites of fashionability. Despite the early history of modeling, when it was associated with poor morals and improper behavior, modeling gradually gained a positive status as a desirable profession for young women and created role models for generations of teenagers. By the 1960s, models such as Jean Shrimpton, Twiggy, Grace Coddington, Penelope Tree, Iman, and Veruschka had become star celebrities in their own right. They also epitomized thinness, androgyny, indifference, and disdain. The distinction between catwalk models and photographic/advertising models blurred.

These models were—at the time—generally viewed positively. They were joined by a more articulate and confident breed of model, who also commanded huge fees. As Linda Evangelista famously quipped in 1990, "We don't wake up for less than $10,000 a day." The fashion industry realized that models had superseded Hollywood stars as celebrities and household names, and Versace used the same models for the catwalk and advertising under exclusive contracts. These "supermodels" became the faces of leading fashion brands such as Guess? (Claudia Schiffer), Bendon lingerie (Elle Macpherson), Revlon (Cindy Crawford), Lancôme (Isabella Rossellini), Versace (Christy Turlington), and Estée Lauder (Paulina Porizkova). But just as the supermodels seemed to be dominating all aspects of the industry, a new kind of model emerged. These new models were "characterized by more demure personalities" and were "physically smaller and more fragile than their Amazonian predecessors" (Frankel 2007: 48), As Schmid (1999: 92) notes,

> A more feminine notion of beauty returned in the 1970s and 1980s, but the Twiggy type and the ideal of the childlike or sexless woman have experienced a revival since the early 1990s. The ethereal Kate Moss, who has often been compared to Twiggy, introduced this new decade of skinny models or "waifs" that reached a peak in the mid-1990s. Its culmination may be seen in the ultra-thinness of the contemporary fashion model Jodie Kidd … and "Heroin Chic."

This generation of models may have started out as "good girls," but the pressures of the industry led some to acquire a "bad girl" image and, in some cases, led to high-profile counseling, treatment programs, and court cases. Examples include Naomi Campbell (one of the original supermodels), Liz Hurley, and Kate Moss. A bad image became an asset rather than a problem (Rushton 2002). When Moss's turbulent personal life (taking drugs and clubbing with undesirable boyfriends) became tabloid material, the short-term response was ambivalent but ultimately tipped in her favor, escalating her market value and resulting in new contracts (Langley 2005: 62–66; Taher 2006: 16). The diva-like behavior of Naomi Campbell (see box 6.7) has led to legal proceedings and considerable media attention but has not dinted her career (Bearn 2003: 5; Frankel 2007: 45–47). Despite her age (she was born in 1970), Campbell still commands high fees and the top jobs.

Arguably, though, she was eclipsed by Kate Moss (see box 6.8), who has appeared on more magazine covers than any other model and whose image has inspired the Young British Artists to cast her in marble, ice, and bronze. Dubbed the "anorexic Aphrodite of our time," Moss (see image 66) is regarded as "an iconic figure of beauty" for the new millennium (Taher 2006: 16).

Moss came onto the fashion scene via photographs for the *Face* taken by her then-friend, ex-model Corinne Day. In these, she appeared topless on a beach, smiling and squinting at the sun, more as if posing for holiday snapshots than for fashion photos. Although her waifish and childlike appearance

**Box 6.7 Naomi Campbell Bio**

1970 Born in London, England

1985 Discovered by Elite

1993 Fired from Elite, reemployed by Casablancas in 1995

1993 Falls off Vivienne Westwood's platform shoes at London Fashion Show

2000 Legal case for attacking personal assistant

2005 Legal case for hitting employee (ordered to perform community service)

2005 Fired by animal rights group PETA for starring in their anti-fur campaign then wearing fur at Milan fashion show

**Box 6.8 Kate Moss Bio**

1974 Born Katherine Moss in Surrey, England

1988 Discovered by Storm Agency

First job: cover of *The Face;* later *Allure, Harper's Bazaar, Arena, Elle,* and *Vogue*

Appeared in ads for Calvin Klein, Burberry, Cerruti 1881, Dolce & Gabbana, Versace, L'Oreal, Dior, and YSL

1990s Was, with Twiggy and Sarah O'Hare, the face of the Fashion Targets Breast Cancer campaign

2001–7 Face of Chanel

1998 Entered the Priory Clinic in London for "exhaustion"

2000 Ranked the fifth highest-paid model by *BusinessAge*

Linked with photographer Mario Sorrenti, guitarist Antony Langdon, Jesse Wood (son of Rolling Stone Ron Wood), artist Jake Chapman, actor Johnny Depp, musician Pete Doherty

2002 Had a daughter, Lila Grace, with magazine editor Jefferson Hack

2004 Split up with Hack

2005 Photographed taking drugs with Doherty; no charges

2006 Bronze cast of Moss made for a series by Marc Quinn, who calls her the "anorexic Aphrodite of our time"

was similar to Twiggy's, Smedley (2000: 148) argues that whereas images of Twiggy were interpreted as representing the sexual liberation of the 1960s, the images of Moss did not intially have sexual connotations but were read as signaling the ordinariness and poverty of Kate Moss's background. It was only once Moss became tagged as beautiful that these images acquired more complex meanings.

Calvin Klein recognized that the ambivalent connotations attached to images of Moss could work to his advantage. Calvin Klein successfully used models and celebrities to promote his products, especially jeans and perfumes (Obsession, 1985; Eternity, 1989; Escape, 1991; cK one, 1994; cK be, 1997; Contradiction, 1998). In 1980, he became the first designer to "put his name to jeans" (Lehnert 2000: 86), using actor Brooke Shields as a cover girl.

As part of his erotic and provocative advertising series for his personalized jeans and perfumes, he used celebrities (such as Marky Mark in 1982 to launch his underwear for men, which appeared visible above the waistline of his jeans in ads), and he decided to use Moss to promote his new fragrance, Obsession, in 1985. Moss appeared lying down, hair disheveled, with one strap of her top off her shoulder. The imputation of seduction was a theme Klein continued to exploit. The *New York Times* refused to run the advertisements, which they saw as too risqué (Todtri 2002: 34). But the ads cause a sensation and sales went through the roof. Perfume scholar Susan Irvine (1996: 138) recalled:

> When Calvin Klein hired Kate Moss to embody his best-selling fragrance Obsession, there were cries of protest at this "anorexic" and "paedophile" image (feminists scrawled "Feed me!" across billboards showing the ads). But the philosophy of the fragrance had simply changed from the gung-ho writhing bodies of rampant 1980s sexuality to a celebration of youth, tenderness and vulnerability. Moss, by the way, was 19 at the time.

Klein's excessive and explicit imagery was widely copied. According to Lehnert (2000: 117), "His discreet games with androgyny helped to make model Kate Moss famous." Klein used Moss again in 1997 to promote *cK one* again to near hysteria. For Moss, this confirmed her salability and legitimated her lifestyle. In 1998, Kate Moss was used for the Burberry campaign to relaunch the brand for a new generation and younger market in a series of ads shot by celebrity photographer Mario Testino. "The powerful black and white images of Moss in a bikini were key in capturing the attention and imagination of the public" (Jackson and Haid 2006: 80).

In 2007, Moss came back from charges of drug taking and self-imposed rehabilitation to new contracts and public attention. Despite skepticism about her choice of partner, the drug-addicted Babyshambles musician Pete Doherty, they embarked on a joint advertising campaign for Italian designer Roberto Cavalli. Dubbed Brand Moherty, Moss and Doherty were contracted to promote Cavalli's new collection in an advertisement described as "sexy, glamorous, bohemian, dangerous and a little grotty" (*Australian* 2007). Cavalli enunciated the marketing potential like this:

> Kate brings beauty, intensity and personality and a hippie spirit that's perfectly in tune with my collection. Pete is a dreamer and a rebel and not keen on compromises. He's authentic and spontaneous and oozes a new, unexpected brand of sensuality. I think he is perfectly in sync with the spirit of the Cavalli man. (Quoted by *Australian* 2007: 13)

The problem for high-profile models, says fashion photographer Nick Knight, is that

> these people are kids who've been told they're very beautiful and that everyone likes them. … They're told it again and again, and if your whole psyche is built around that you have to be pretty strong to be able to survive. (Quoted by Frankel 2007: 48)

This choice of "bad" celebrities legitimates Moss's decision to trade on improper behavior reminiscent of youth rebellion of the 1960s. Their coupling also parallels other couple brands, such as Brangelina (Hollywood celebrities Brad Pitt and Angelina Jolie) and Brand Beckham (soccer star and pop diva David and Victoria Beckham).

Fashion and celebrity have become intertwined and symbiotic. Today's fashion industry is suffused with celebrity endorsement and deals between stars and the labels that dress them for high-profile public occasions. The late 1970s, the early 1990s, and the early 2000s have been key moments for the cult of the celebrity and celebrity endorsement. According to Frances Bonner,

> Actors like the rise of the visual medium along with substantial decline in newsroom staff pointed to celebrity being a way in which a story could easily and quickly be told visually. It's not so much the power as the volume of celebrity that's changed. There's so many more of them about and it's a standard way in which quite insignificant performers are able to increase product sales. (Quoted by Rushton 2002: 40)

But there are advantages and disadvantages to celebrity endorsement. While attention is brought to a cause or issue, it does not necessarily translate into tangible support or attitude change. And if a celebrity loses cachet or behaves badly, this can cause a downturn in public attention. Nonetheless, celebrity models can earn big money through endorsements. *Forbes* magazine published the incomes of the world's ten leading models in 2007. Brazilian Gisele Bündchen earned $33 million while Kate Moss earned $9 million, and Heidi Klum $8 million. Four models (Adriana Lima, Alessandra Ambrosia, Carolyn Murphy, and Natalia Vodianova) earned over $5 million each, followed by Karolina Kurkova, Daria Werbowy, Gemma Ward, Liya Kebede, Hilary Rhonda, Shalom Harlow, Doutzen Kroes, and Jessica Stam, each of whom earned between $1 and $4 million (Blakely 2007). The fact that most of these models are not household names suggests that the model circuit is much faster paced than it once was, and that models, although earning more than their predecessors, are not getting the same celebrity promotion through endorsements that they used to.

**Agyness Denn.** Photo by Simon James/WireImage. 2008 Simon James

The careers of models today are generally shorter than before because of the competition from up-and-coming aspirants, so models have turned to trying to establish post-modeling businesses. One of the most successful has been Elle Macpherson, who is reputedly worth about $80 million, largely through her lingerie brand through Bendon (McCann 2007: 20). The challenge for a model is to turn her public profile as a desirable image into a brand name that can sell commodities bearing her name before she has reached her use-by date.

## CASE STUDY 22: Louis Vuitton as Luxury Accessory

Show me your wallet and I'll tell you who you are. (Louis Vuitton advertisement, 1921)

There are certain brands in fashion that have become so well known that the brand logo alone is instantly recognized and imbued with the qualities associated with the brand and its products. Coca-Cola's wave bottle and writing, McDonalds' golden arches, Nike's tick, and Lacoste's crocodile are examples. In the world of luxury goods, Louis Vuitton is one of a handful of brands that can claim truly global familiarity. While it is a symbol of up-to-the-minute designer chic and a key member of the luxury group LVMH, Louis Vuitton is also one of the oldest fashion brands, having grown from a manufacturer of luggage (trunks, cases, and bags). According to Jade Hantouche, head of special orders at Louis Vuitton, "Our rule is that if it is not for traveling then it is not a Louis Vuitton product" (quoted by Huckbody 2007). Today it accounts for about one-quarter (over $4 billion) of the LVMH group's annual sales (Thomas 2007).

Established in 1854 by Louis Vuitton (1821–92) in Paris, Louis Vuitton: Malletier à Paris ("Luggage Maker in Paris") manufactured lightweight flat-topped trunks from a poplar wooden fame covered with waterproof canvas whose suitability for travel and convenience for stacking attracted immediate attention. Quality control in the handmade process of manufacture was also to the fore: each item had a serial number and unique keying system, features that have remained. After increased demand following

**Louis Vuitton boutique**

exhibition at the 1867 Paris World Exposition, Vuitton customized his luggage to ward off counterfeiters who were copying this new design, using beige-and-brown stripes in 1876 and introducing the Damier canvas (a chocolate-brown-and-beige checkerboard design) in 1888.

He was succeeded by his son, Georges Vuitton, who expanded the company—especially by entering the American market after exhibiting at the 1893 Chicago World's Fair. The company's fortunes were secured with the design of the distinctive toile monogram on the canvas in 1896. This consisted of entwined LV initials with three motifs—a curved diamond with a four-point star inset, its negative, and a circle with a four-leafed flower inset reflecting the contemporary fashion for Oriental-style graphics. The design was printed in gold on a dark chestnut background. This design has remained the logo of the brand and succeeded in reducing counterfeiting—at least until the 1960s. The company expanded its range of goods and opened new stores worldwide, becoming the largest travel-goods store by the First World War.

Louis Vuitton continued to prosper—despite reportedly being a Nazi collaborator during World War II—by maintaining its traditional lines and complementing them with new products and modifications of design and fabric. By the 1960s, it was an acknowledged fashion **classic** (though considered a bit dowdy) but managed to maintain appeal in youth culture through the introduction of its cylindrical Papillon bag. However, profits were falling, and in the 1970s, the company was restructured to create a vertical integration from production to retailing and turned its fortunes around.

Further changes followed in the 1970s and 1980s, with expansion into Asia, sponsorship of the America's Cup, and introduction of epi leather (soft embossed cowhide products aimed at a lower-cost price point market).

In 1987, Louis Vuitton merged with Moët Hennessy to create the first global luxury group, embarking on another phase of growth with the opening of new stores. In 1990, management of the brand passed acrimoniously from the Vuitton family to Bernard Arnault, who took the luxury group to unprecedented levels of global penetration. Members of the family, however, are still involved in ensuring quality control in the production process. Central to the revamping of Louis Vuitton was the appointment of Marc Jacobs as designer in 1988 to update the appeal of the brand through a three-pronged strategy of promoting its tradition, a new look, and celebrity advertising. LV also launched a clothing line that enabled it to promote its products through high-profile fashion shows. LV had now transformed itself from a classic to a celebrity brand feted by actors, activists, and aesthetes.

A major break with the past came with Jacobs's collaboration with Japanese artist Takashi Murakami, who devised the new monogram multicolore design featuring updated LV symbols interspersed with Murakami's signature symbols (e.g., cherry blossoms and cartoon faces). Eschewing the gold and chestnut, these designs were printed in thirty-three bright (youthful and fresh) colors on a white or black background. They were an overnight sensation, with demand outstripping supply as the must-have or "It" bag of the 2003 season. The new multicolored look was a smash hit with consumers and was quickly copied by competitors. Louis Vuitton, while elated by the unprecedented success of the revamped look, was panicked by the flood of similar bags on the market. In a celebrated case, in 2004, the company took New York handbag company Dooney and Bourke to court for trademark infringement and intellectual property contravention over their DB logo bags on a similar background design. The case centered less on whether the LV logo had been copied, since the letters were different, than on whether a brand had the legal right to "own" a look it had created. Louis Vuitton lost the case, to the relief of the fashion design fraternity.

The popularity of the monogram multicolore design also spawned a new flood of counterfeits, resulting in over twenty legal cases concerning infringement of copyright and intellectual property rights. Although not all these actions were successful, the publicity did the brand no harm, and it remained a leading luxury brand in the new millennium, engaging in publicity campaigns and joint ventures. Louis Vuitton has further developed new lines and products such as pens, accessories, and jewelry. In addition, the company fills special orders for two types of clients: fashionistas who covet the LV logo and Louis Vuitton devotees who value the handmade tradition.

The company has astutely made use of celebrities (including former president of the USSR Mikhail Gorbachev, tennis stars Steffi Graf and Andre Agassi, supermodel Gisele Bündchen, Hollywood starlet Scarlett Johansson, and ageless actor Catherine Deneuve) as the face of LV in carefully targeted campaigns. Aging rocker Keith Richards was signed up to be featured in a 2008 campaign with a custom-made guitar case with the logo on it (though he admitted that he'd "probably never travel with it, because it's just too beautiful"!).

Louis Vuitton was also one of the first luxury brands to move away from uniform design of its stores and commission avant-garde architectural spectacles (Baum 2007). For example, LV used New York–based Peter Marino to redesign its flagship Paris store in 1996, which was followed by makeovers of numerous other stores. Jun Aoki designed the LV Tokyo flagship store as a randomly stacked set of LV trunks and the LV Hong Kong landmark store as a single LV trunk. More recently, Frank Gehry was commissioned to build the Louis Vuitton Foundation for Creation museum in Paris, and Italian artist Fabrizio Plessi to create an art work for the second Hong Kong Vuitton store on Canton Road, for which architect Peter Marino won the 2007 American Institute of Architects' Institute Honor Award for Interior Architecture. Titled "Il lusso e lento" ("Luxury Is Slow"), Plessi's art work features LED lights that screen a river of moving molten gold representing the qualities of LV, namely, "luxury and gold—the golden age" (Plessi quoted by Meagher 2008: 52). To complement this, Plessi also designed eighty-eight (a lucky number to the Chinese) limited-edition black leather handbags featuring a thin LED screen displaying the moving molten gold within the Louis Vuitton logo (and costing almost $50,000).

To ensure its luxury image and market share, Louis Vuitton only sells through its stores (and online, even advising consumers how to spot a fake). Even so, counterfeiting remains an issue. Louis Vuitton has a unique status as one of the most counterfeited brands, with some suggesting that only 1 percent of products bearing the Louis Vuitton logo are genuine, and Louis Vuitton counterfeits accounting for 18 percent of seized accessories in the European Union in 2004. Despite ongoing cases and negative publicity over several issues, Louis Vuitton works hard to maintain its luxury image and marketplace edge for consumers who don't baulk at the price of classicism and fashionable prestige. For those who love the logo but have modest means, a taste of the glamour and glory can always be gotten from the coin purse, diary, pen, or scarf.

## CASE STUDY 23: The Gap as Global Fashion

The Gap (known also as Gap and Gap Inc.) represents a new kind of global apparel chain. It was established in 1969 by Donald and Doris Fisher in San Francisco, California, to focus on the sale of casual clothing and sportswear such as T-shirts, jeans, caps, and sweaters. The distinctiveness of the Gap was its attention to the organization of stock through the arrangement of apparel in logically marked shelving, indicating different sizes. This enabled consumers to select garments of the appropriate size with minimum help from sales assistants. Initially, the Gap focused on stocking Levi's jeans and targeted the large student market of the Bay Area. Success was immediate.

Ostensibly the name of the store came from the phrase "the generation gap," which symbolized youth culture and new forms of consumerism. After its initial success in California, the Gap expanded throughout the United States, with 200 stores by 1976, becoming the largest clothing store chain in North America. The Gap then opened stores in Canada and Europe and, in 1995, Japan. There are now over 3,000 Gap stores worldwide employing about 150,000 people.

Initially, the Gap stocked major brands of casual clothes such as jeans but in 1974 launched its own Gap line of jeans, which quickly became a fashion must-have among actors, musicians, and fashion trendsetters. The Gap capitalized on this by using celebrities in high-profile advertisements. The success of the Gap line gave the company global recognition and catapulted it into a new stage of growth. In 1983 the store acquired Banana Republic, which sported an African safari theme and used khaki and camouflage fabrics in safari-like garments. Sales expanded fivefold in the space of two years.

**Gap store.** Photo by Dimas Ardian / Getty Images. Getty Images 2007

But further expansion was needed to sustain the pace. Gap Kids stores were launched in 1986, followed by the Baby Gap brand in 1990 and Old Navy Clothing Company in 1994. In 1991, the Gap stopped stocking Levi's and thereafter only carried its own brand of clothing. Different segments of the Gap are targeted at different kinds of consumers. While the Gap brand appeals to middle-range consumers, Banana Republic aims at a more up-market customer and Old Navy targets middle-age woman seeking affordable leisure wear for the whole family. In 1997 the Gap initiated online sales, launching the Piperlime online footwear line in 2006.

Advertising was always important for the Gap, which used celebrities in Gap brand ads, while Banana Republic rode the waves of the popularity of the jungle-safari theme in films such as *Raiders of the Lost Ark, Romancing the Stone,* and *Out of Africa.* When this fad passed, Banana Republic was rebranded as an up-market leisure wear label.

While their main market has remained the United States, the United Kingdom, Japan, Canada, and France are their next most successful markets. There are Gap stores throughout Asia and the Middle East. The heyday of the Gap was the 1980s, but in attempting to market its appeal to different types of consumers, the company appeared to lose direction in the 1990s and in the early 2000s underwent major restructuring. Although the Fisher family is still involved in the company, since 2004 there has been a succession of CEOs who have each attempted to reinvigorate the brand and address the decline in sales—parting without ceremony when expectations were not realized. Part of the problem for the Gap has been that new apparel chains—for example, Zara and H&M—have provided stiff competition and offered new marketing techniques.

The Gap has also faced litigation concerning trademark appropriation and has been accused of using sweat shop labor. Although the Gap has introduced a code of ethics covering labor practices and employed inspectors of its offshore factories, child exploitation and workers' rights scandals have persisted. Meanwhile, sales have been gradually declining as consumers turn to new labels and retailers. Despite hiring up-and-coming designers to create new stylistic images and its continuing global presence—for example, in airport shopping precincts and shopping malls—the Gap has failed to retain its preeminence. The Gap has an ambitious expansion plan for the Middle East and Asia for 2008 through 2012. In 2006 their revenue was estimated at almost $16 billion, indicating that although their bubble may have burst as a retail icon, its glow as a global brand remains.

Jennifer Craik and Sharon Peoples

## CASE STUDY 24: Secondhand Clothing

The trade in secondhand clothes has a long history and has existed for almost as long as clothes and garments have been manufactured. Until the eighteenth century, the only clothes that were ready made were secondhand clothes. However, by the late twentieth century, secondhand clothes had become associated with poverty. The modern fashion system has a built-in obsolesce, with the demand for the newest and the best driving the imperative for new clothes. A secondhand system of disposal has always operated to deal with the discards, whether as a perquisite for (gifted to) servants or trading to those dealing in secondhand clothing. Prestigious imitation drives us to want to appear fashionable, but how this is achieved depends on our access to the fashion system.

Today, the terms *antique,* **vintage,** *pre-loved,* and *retro* remove the stigma of secondhand. The secondhand clothing market operates on a number of levels with new hierarchies of consumption (McRobbie 1989). Traders have operated for centuries in marketplaces, as unwanted apparel has been sold in flea markets, by junk dealers, and even to museums. Today in the West, the secondhand clothing trade relies on donations of clothing to charity organizations to help those in need; however, once clothes leave the sorting warehouses, they become solely an economic commodity.

While still in domestic/charitable circulation—that is, intended to clothe people in economic need or to raise revenue for religious organizations—secondhand clothing is sold in thrift, opportunity, and charity stalls and shops. Here, there are other consumers who participate in this market. There are those who choose to buy secondhand clothing for political, environmental, and aesthetic reasons.

Countercultures have raided the wardrobes of discarded clothing to produce specific identities. British Teddy Boys, mods, hippies, punks, new romantics, and those who develop street styles have all worn recycled clothing of previous eras, responding to mass culture in their search for a unique group identity and subcultural authenticity. Part of the fashion cycle is taking from the past. For some, having the original carries prestige. For others, the allure is the antifashion statement that can be made with spurned clothing.

The purchases of this group of consumers are made in accordance with their social identity as well as for aesthetic reasons. They are called collectors and connoisseurs and are characterized by their quest for the thrill of the bargain. Secondhand clothing in this market is now referred to as vintage or even classic clothing. These people have detailed knowledge of the secondhand market and place great economic value on the quality of the textiles; the decoration; the age; or, in the case of designer or haute couture clothing, simply the label.

At the top end are expensive secondhand designer garments. These can also have high social value. This trade usually occurs more formally in fixed shops. Goods are sold on consignment; that is, the owner of the clothing brings the garments to the seller, who only pays the owner once the goods are sold. This can take days or months. These clothes are rarely worn out but are considered out of fashion, even if it may only be by one season.

Since the 1990s, as a backlash to globalization, recycling clothing has been a way of intervening in the ongoing oversupply of new consumer products. The ethical choice of wearing secondhand clothing is seen as a way to reduce environmental impact. So-called thrifters' magazines reflect and celebrate this alternative consumer practice.

Secondhand clothing also has high economic value in the international trade, where garments are baled up and sold to traders from developing countries. This still has the tinge of charity, where the clothing from developing countries is sold to undeveloped countries. The trade has increased enormously since the 1990s, when there was a liberalization of third-world economies as well as the dissipation of barriers between the Eastern Bloc and Western Europe.

Clothing from the first world can represent modernity and progress. Secondhand garments in these new settings can signify social status. Here, the consumer, rather than the producer, plays an active role in creating a fashionable look. The current look, which, in the West, defines what is most suitable to wear, is only sometimes relevant. Secondhand clothing requires greater interpretation and creativity by the individual consumer. Hansen (2005) refers to buying and wearing secondhand clothing in this market as "clothing competence." The reactivation of clothing in other contexts reflects the fact that being in fashion can be achieved in multiple ways.

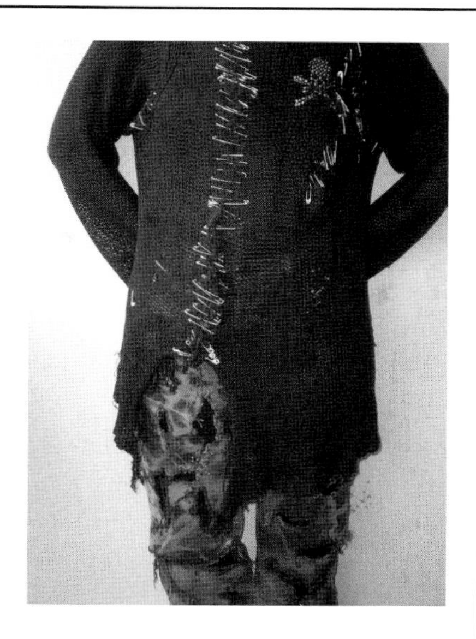

**Slashed clothes.**

However, the secondhand clothing is not a one-way street at the international level. Garments from developing countries still represent the exotic to the West. The trade in Indian saris, where garments are taken apart, cut up, and made into decorative clothing and interior decor (cushions, rugs, wall hangings, lampshades, curtains, etc.), has existed since the 1970s, when the "ethnic look" hit the catwalk.

Similarly, Japanese kimonos, which were seen as highly intimate garments, were baled up and sent to the West. The transformation from intimate apparel to the exotic fashion of the elite has a long history. The fashion for styles from the East was named Orientalism, Japonism, and Chinoiserie by the pre-Raphaelites and impressionists. Today, publications like *FRUiTS,* which illustrates the street fashion of Tokyo, exemplify the two-way traffic of between the East and West.

Sharon Peoples

# chapter 7

## popular culture and fashion

**CHAPTER OUTLINE**

I. Fashion and the rise of popular culture
II. Representing fashion
III. Fashion subcultures and popular music
IV. Fashion journalism, public relations, and stylists
Case study 25: Sports clothing for everyman
Case study 26: Australian bush wear as urban chic
Case study 27: Retailing erotic lingerie
Case study 28: Oliviero Toscani's advertisements for Benetton

**WHAT DOES THIS CHAPTER COVER?**

This chapter addresses the role of the media in projecting fashion and the fashion industry within popular culture. It is no coincidence that the contemporary fashion system developed alongside the development of the mass media and popular cultural forms. The history of fashion is thus intimately bound up with the technologies through which it can be represented, advertised, and visualized.

Specific topics include the intertwined history of fashion and popular culture in Europe and how emerging forms of representation—fashion plates, fashion illustration, fashion magazines, photography, films, and television—created channels that were especially suitable to depict the allure and spectacle of fashion. In the twentieth century, successive genres of popular music also became implicated in the march of fashion in a mutually sycophantic relationship that continues today. As the fashion industry has become conscious of the power of the media in promoting fads and styles, specialist media and fashion professions have developed. These include fashion publicists, fashion editors, and fashion commentators, as well as the increasingly prominent fashion stylists, all of whom are complicit in creating attention-grabbing and seductive images of fashion.

Case studies explore the growth of the sportswear and leisure wear fashion sector as the default clothes for every day as the byproduct of popular cultural projections of this apparel; the transformation of Australian bush clothes from practical clothing for farmers to chic urban fashion not only in Australia but around the world; the emergence of the genre of lingerie (as opposed to underwear), which has increasingly appealed to the general public as normative sensual dress; and the famous series of advertisements photographed by Oliviero Toscani for the Italian fashion chain Benetton, which both transformed the image of the store and promoted awareness of both global social issues and the phenomenon of global fashion.

## i. fashion and the rise of popular culture

Fashion systems of modernity and postmodernity are critically dependent on the media and the marketing of fashion trends to consumers. While the contemporary interdependence is frenetic and sycophantic, how fashion got to this point has a relatively long history. According to Welters (2007: 275), there are two main aspects of this interdependence: first, how the fashion industry uses the media to promote its products to potential consumers, and second, how influential gatekeepers or role models "whose signature styles are … appropriated by the fashion business and repackaged for consumers" are represented in the media and capture the public imagination. We might also add a third element, namely, how the media itself represents fashion independently of the industry. Despite the centrality of the media to fashion systems, there has been surprisingly little critical analysis of the contours of this relationship.

Let's revisit our brief history of modern fashion. Looking one's best or being fashionable has been a long-standing preoccupation of all social elites who could afford it and who had the time to display their finery and be seen. But one had to be seen in person for fashions to catch on before the invention of mechanical (or technological) means of reproduction. There were, of course, sketches, paintings, and illustrations, but the circulation of these was still largely confined to the elite. And, of course, generally the subjects and sitters were the elite, so archival records provide a very biased view of clothing habits and fashions within a society. Cartoons provided a different view: the obverse of fashionable—the extreme, the caricature, the absurd, the vanity, the excess, the indulgence. So the circulation of images of fashion before printing processes can present a highly skewed picture. Nonetheless, there is evidence that fashion did catch on and become widely adopted despite the reliance on word of mouth, if not actual sightings.

For instance, according to fashion historian James Laver, the curious practice of slashing garments to reveal colorful linings was popularized in the fifteenth century. Apparently, when the Swiss beat Charles the Bold, Duke of Burgundy, in 1476, the victors seized the booty of silk and luxury goods, "slashed it to pieces and used it to patch their own ragged clothes" (Laver 1995: 77). Later, slashing was refined as the practice of deliberately cutting slits in the garment (doublet, hose, vests, caps) to expose the most colorful inserts (Denny-Brown 2004). Slashing became an art form that, Laver suggests, was copied initially by German mercenaries and then adopted by the French court. This may be apocryphal, but the fashion for slashing was somehow polarized within the aristocracy and military and then become popular among civilian classes (see image 82).

Inexorably the fashion spread to England, Holland, and other European states among armies, aristocracy, and citizens, until it was "almost universal in the 1500s" (Laver 1995: 78). However, the most extreme forms of slashing were confined to Germany, where complex decorative patterns were achieved by the artful arrangement of slashing:

**For not only the doublet but the breeches were slashed; indeed, quite literally, "cut to ribbons." Nether garments consisted of broad bands of material falling to the knees and sometimes to the ankles. Care was taken that the bands on each leg should form different patterns, and they could even be of different colours. (Laver 1995: 78)**

The popularity of slashing achieved longevity. A self-portrait painted around 1657, a century and a half later, by Dutch artist Frans van Mieris the Elder, depicts him as an officer wearing a black hat decorated with blue satin, feathers, and gold above a velvet doublet with satin lining and slashed sleeves revealing a white shirt. Here we have an artist portraying himself as a person of substance as well as a person with style and a sense of fashion. Slashing also spread to women's clothes, although it was never as popular. Although the slashing craze waned, it still makes periodic appearances in modern fashion and costume, notably in Vivienne Westwood's 1981 Pirate collection.

Portraiture was clearly an important way of depicting the fashions of the day and is often our only source of information about the clothing habits of a period, but we need to remember that portraiture was not a neutral representation of people and their apparel but a highly contrived imaginary portrayal of how the sitter wanted to be seen. European fashion, during the sixteenth and seventeenth centuries, continued to reflect aristocratic styles, and differences could be detected between the fashions of the various courts. But when courtiers intermingled, during wars and through arranged marriages, the fashions of one court were often appropriated and adopted by another.

Examples include the **ruff** and the farthingale, both of which originated in the Spanish court but spread throughout Europe (Laver 1995: 90–93, 97–98), although Elizabethan women modified the ruff with a front opening that exposed the décolletage. Paintings of Elizabeth I invariably depict this fashion adaptation. The farthingale was adopted in England about 1545, and a "wheel farthingale" in France about 1580, while Italy later popularized a whalebone version. Elizabeth I also created the fashion for dying the hair red, which was initially copied by her courtiers, who wished to emulate her and gain patronage, but the fashion for red hair later spread beyond the palace to aristocracy and gentlefolk more generally (Laver 1995: 95).

The popularity of engravings during the seventeenth century means that a much greater archive of changing fashions is available, especially in the form of fashion plates. This means of reproducing and circulating images, along with the political, economic, and social changes that were occurring, meant that fashions began to change more rapidly and spread across Europe more quickly. These fashions persisted into the eighteenth century. Even so, wealthy citizens were so motivated to keep up with the latest modes that fashion dolls were toured through European cities to show off and popularize the latest fashions. Even Marie Antoinette's dressmaker made an annual tour through Europe, showing dolls dressed in the latest Paris modes (Laver 1995: 147). Illustrations and even patterns assisted the uptake of new fashions, while the fashionable elite began to rival the aristocracy as the subject of portraiture (see image 11).

By the 1770s, the development of the fashion plate (reproductions of illustrations of fashions), and early fashion magazines such as the English *Lady's Magazine,* revolutionized the circulation and accessibility of new designs. Initially in black and white, but later hand colored, images of fashion became an important part of the growing etiquette literature and fashion publications in Europe. It was not just the clothes that were featured. Fashion plates usually depicted groups of people dressed fashionably engaging in fashionable pursuits so a whole fashionable lifestyle was being portrayed and promoted in tangible ways for readers to emulate.

By the nineteenth century, fashion and modernity were fused as the symbols of the new social order of modern Europe. The Great Exhibition of 1851, held in London, paid homage to consumer culture, urbanization, and the idea of being fashionable. While the most fashionable looks were only to be found on those with the time and money to see and be seen (epitomized by Charles Baudelaire's observations of well-dressed male flaneurs), the second half of the eighteenth century witnessed major changes in clothing habits as fashionable clothing began to replace customary dress in progressive European cities and increasingly beyond.

One of the factors in the increasing interest in fashion was the advent of department stores such as Bon Marché in Paris in 1952. By the 1870s, department stores like Macy, Wanamaker's, Marshall Field, Bloomingdale's, and Harrods provided both a ready source of the new fashions at affordable prices and a site for conspicuous consumption. They were also regarded as safe places for unaccompanied women, who seemed to revel in the new freedom, social networks, and fashion choices offered by these shopping emporia. While fashion plates were still used extensively, elaborate shop window displays rivaled plate-glass windows in smaller shops as a new mode for disseminating images and settings for fashion and played a vital role in representing fashion to urban consumers. The importance of how fashions were displayed and made attractive to women shoppers spawned a consumer industry of advertisers, shop fitters, window dressers, **mannequins,** and fashion writers. Representing fashion had become a commodity in its own right.

Fashion magazines promoted not only the new apparel but techniques for acquiring a fashionable look (self-help advice—the forerunner of miracle makeovers that are still the staple of women's magazines today) and techniques of looking and consuming. They also included a range of advertising materials—full-page illustrated advertisements, advertorials promoting new products, features, Dear Abby–type columns, and articles on how and where to buy the latest fashions.

## ii. representing fashion

With the development of photography, the possibilities for representing and disseminating fashion suddenly multiplied. Technology allowed for reproduction of images; hence images could be seen in many more places. This led to the advent of fashion magazines with titles such as the *Tatler; Lady's Magazine; Young Englishwoman; Punch;* **La Gazette du Bon Ton**; *Le Journal des Modes; Tailor and Cutter; Ladies' Cabinet of Fashion, Music, and Romance;* and *Ladies' Magazine of Fashion.* Publications like these used the latest techniques in illustrating, coloring, and printing to promote not just the clothes but new ways of living, new moral values, and new habits, "evoking the comforts of an idealized but acquisitive lifestyle with crinolines models inhabiting lush gardens and opulent drawing rooms" (Breward 2003: 120). American magazines had the models "skating, promenading, dancing and shopping ... as aids for bringing the escapist fantasies of the emulative middle-class reader to life (with the help of a maid and a sewing machine)" (Breward 2003: 120). These magazines were forerunners to the new fashion media nexus.

As the titles of the magazines suggest, these were also manuals on acquiring techniques of femininity and civility (see Craik 1994: 44–69). On the one hand, magazines promoted attributes of

**Fashion illustration.** Georges Lepape (1887–1971). Caroline and Erwin Swann Collection of Caricature & Cartoon, Library of Congress

domesticity and the management of everyday life. On the other, they promoted ideal ways of being on display and projecting the female body. There was a tension in the latter between sanctioning forms of conduct that facilitated social engagement and teaching female attributes that credibly reflected one's social position and status. Magazine advice imported a set of moral qualities along with the vestmental ones. A woman could be damned by her choice of clothes and deportment. So, the ways bodies were fashioned in magazines through the choice of clothes, cosmetics, and demeanor simultaneously constructed symbols of identity, social position, and sexuality.

In industrialized societies, women were the visible correlate of the economic and social standing of their menfolk. Their attributes of femininity, then, included techniques of being at leisure or "entertaining," the ultimate signs of social standing. Different magazines were pitched toward different demographics, and sales grew steadily throughout the eighteenth and nineteenth centuries. The demand grew to fever pitch during Victorian times. Between 1870 and 1900, for example, fifty new magazine titles appeared in England and sales soared as women labored to acquire the "right" manners and morals for their social position. The emphasis on domesticity and morality was increasingly balanced with sections devoted to fashion and beauty. The genre was in full bloom. The agenda of the woman's magazine was now set and persisted through the twentieth century. The combination spawned a rash of etiquette manuals and guides, which were also incorporated in magazines. As we have already seen, this was the period when consumerism was taking root, and the advertising industry expanding its seduction of female consumers.

In this context, the impact of photography on the lexicon of the visual and subsequently written language of fashion cannot be underestimated. It extended the symbolic system for representing fashion into "the creative realm of 'the dream'":

**In this sense mass-reproduced fashion imagery can no longer be read as a direct commentary (if it ever really could) on the political economy of style as it is manufactured and worn. (Breward 2003: 122)**

The nineteenth and twentieth centuries became the golden era of the modern fashion journal with the combined forces of fashion editors, major designers (couturiers), fashion illustrators and subsequently photographers, and media magnates (such as Condé Nast and Hearst Publications). See box 7.1 for a list of some early fashion magazines.

Of all the fashion magazines, the most influential and long lasting has been *Vogue* USA (Breward 2003: 122). Arguably, this is because

**Box 7.1 A Sample of Early Fashion Magazines**

| Launch | Title |
|---|---|
| 1798 | *Lady's Monthly Museum* (UK) |
| 1806 | *La Belle Assemblée* (France) |
| 1830 | *Godey's Lady's Book* (U.S.) |
| 1852 | *Englishwoman's Domestic Magazine* (UK) |
| 1861 | *Queen* (UK) |
| 1867 | *Harper's Bazaar* (U.S.) |
| 1873 | *Delineator* (U.S.) |
| 1876 | *McCall's* (U.S.) |
| 1890 | *Woman* (UK) |
| 1892 | *Vogue* (U.S.) |
| 1894 | *Woman's Own* (UK) |
| 1912 | *Gazette du Bon Ton* (France) |
| 1913 | *Vanity Fair* (USA) |
| 1931 | *Apparel Arts* (later *GQ*) (U.S.) |
| 1931 | *Esquire* (U.S.) |
| 1939 | *Glamour* (UK) |
| 1945 | *Elle* (France) |
| 1949 | *Modern Bride* (U.S.) |
| 1953 | *Playboy* (U.S.) |
| 1963 | *Cosmopolitan* (UK) |
| 1965 | *Nova* (UK) |
| 1970 | *Harper's* and *Queen* (UK) |
| 1973 | *W* (U.S.) |
| 1980 | *i-D* (UK) |
| 1980 | *Face* (UK) |
| 1986 | *Arena* (UK) |
| 1991 | *Dazed and Confused* (UK) |
| 1991 | *Visionnaire* (UK) |

it has embraced the new possibilities of fashion photography more fully than other magazines and pushed the connection between fashionable clothes and fashionable lifestyles to an extreme. *Vogue* has also spawned "localized" editions in a range of countries—including the United Kingdom, France, Italy, Brazil, Australia, Germany, Mexico, Spain, Portugal, Korea, Japan, Taiwan, China, Switzerland, Russia, and India.

*Vogue* has long waged a balancing act between representing the pinnacle of haute couture as well as the best of bubble-up new trends in fashion and exposing readers to the social and political contexts shaping fashion. It has featured the most significant fashion photographers of the twentieth century, including Edward Steichen, George Hoyningen-Huene, Horst P. Horst, Norman Parkinson, Cecil Beaton, Irving Penn, Richard Avedon, Lee Miller, David Bailey, Terence Donovan, Antony Armstrong-Jones, Helmut Newton, Sarah Moon, Deborah Turbeville, Herb Ritts, Steven Meisel, Bruce Weber, Corinne Day, Wolfgang Tillmans, and Jürgen Teller. These names are a roll call of the most influential fashion photographers of the century, both controversial and iconic, setting in train a succession of symbolic codes creating visual imagery that has come to stand for the spirit of each generation and fashion phase during the last century.

As discussed in chapters 5 and 6, equally important have been the models they use to construct the fantasies of the fashionable. Initially

***Vogue* magazine.** Photo: Marina Burity. Creative Commons Attribution-Share Alike 2.0 Generic License

using well-known aristocrats and debutantes, *Vogue* later began to use actresses, film stars, mannequins, and models, including Audrey Hepburn, Gloria Guinness, Jean Shrimpton, Suzy Parker, Lauren Hutton, Twiggy, Penelope Tree, Veruschka, Cindy Crawford, Claudia Schiffer, Linda Evangelista, Naomi Campbell, Christy Turlington, Jerry Hall, Nicole Kidman, Brooke Shields, Elle Macpherson, Sarah Murdoch, Kate Moss, Gemma Ward, Lily Donaldson, Raquel Zimmerman, and Coco Rocha.

So although it is easy to trace the changes and continuities in *Vogue,* it is misleading simply to read the magazine as the arbiter of twentieth-century fashion, since its competitors gingered things up and often spearheaded shifts in *Vogue* editorial philosophy in order to update the feel of the magazine and keep abreast of changing times. Of course, *Vogue* was not the only fashion magazine to make an impact, and over time, others have also made their mark. For example, *Harper's Bazaar* and *Marie Claire* have always been more radical and balanced fashion coverage with thoughtful and serious articles examining the cultural context of the moment.

*Cosmopolitan* was even more directly pitched at the contemporary wave of feminism amid the expansion of career, travel, and expressive opportunities for young women that underpinned the so-called sexual revolution of the 1960s and 1970s. Magazines like *Nova, i-D,* the *Face,* and *Elle* have been associated with more youthful fashion and social issues. These have been called style magazines due to their use of new aesthetic conventions and focus on alternative lifestyles and countercultural forms (Breward 2003: 126–29). In the new millennium, style magazines have increasingly confronted the "very premise upon which fashion culture is built" and "the alienation and neuroses that inevitably attend the purchase and display of dress" (Breward 2003: 129).

As we saw in chapter 5, the significance of photography cannot be underestimated. Black-and-white still photography spawned new forms of visual media that also reveled in the imagery of fashion, in particular, film and television. The invention of color film unleashed another set of possibilities for fashion. The links became symbiotic. Hollywood used Parisian couturiers to design the costumes for leading ladies, and later leading ladies became role models for fashion in their own right. The visual language used in filmmaking extended the lexicon of fashion photography because of the moving image and possibility of narratives woven into the representation of clothes (Breward 2003: 131–41). Fashion houses and film studios developed closer relationships and commercial arrangements. For example, film costumes were promoted in fan magazines and fashion journals. Department stores carried modified versions for the mass market. The cosmetics firm Max Factor began as a specialist provider of makeup for cinema.

Breward (2003: 136) identifies the following films as having a major impact on fashion: *Letty Lynton* (1932), *Dinner at Eight* (1933), *Gone with the Wind* (1939), *Roman Holiday* (1953), *Rebel without a Cause* (1955), *And God Created Woman* (1957), *A Bout de Souffle* (1960), *La Dolce Vita* (1960), *Breakfast at Tiffany's* (1961; see image 9), *Bonnie and Clyde* (1967), *Annie Hall* (1977), and *Pulp Fiction* (1994). While other commentators may include different films, this list shows how intimately tied up fashion and film have become. The popular series of James Bond films, for example, not only constitutes a record of changing women's fashions but undoubtedly influenced the fashions and lifestyles of the moment.

And, as Breward notes, it is not just a question of copying the clothes that appear in film, but the ways in which an iconic dress becomes "implicated in a symbolic network of meanings" that creates new role models for (young) people and spearheads the diffusion of new designs into the mass market.

The fact that nine of Breward's list of twelve are Hollywood films testifies to the dominance of the American film industry, and we could argue that there was a symbiotic relationship between the development of a specifically distinctive American fashion sensibility, an American film industry coterie and star system, and (especially after World War II) a palpable American popular culture that was not only different but began to shape popular culture—especially among teenagers—across the globe. Movies aimed at a teenage audience also became vehicles for the promotion of youth and fashion culture.

**Ursula Andress.** Photo by United Artists/Getty Images. 2007 Getty Images

Television has also played a significant role in setting fashion trends. TV shows featuring popular musicians and bands (such as *American Bandstand, Six O'Clock Rock, The Dick Clark Show, The Ed Sullivan Show, Countdown,* and *Ready Steady Go!*), brought more radical stage costumes into everyday fashion, while shows like *Star Trek, Gidget, Lost in Space, Doctor Who, The Avengers, Dynasty, Sex and the City, Miami Vice, Buffy the Vampire Slayer, The X-Files,* and *The Sopranos* have celebrated celebrity fashions and subcultural looks that have been incorporated into mainstream fashion cultures.

Popular culture has been decisive in promoting new cultural forms and challenging the status quo of taken-for-granted conventions and norms. This can be observed across a range of cultural sites—in popular music, in avant-garde art and cultural movements, in subcultures, and in everyday codes of dress and adornment. There are connections between these spheres, and the example of popular music shows how stage clothing has been used to convey radical countercultural messages yet simultaneously has shaped the development of youth fashions more generally (see Craik 2005).

## iii. fashion subcultures and popular music

One of the less recognized cultural forms where fashion trends have been shaped is the world of comic books and cartoons. An exhibition in 2008 titled "Super Heroes: Fashion and Fantasy" at the Museum of Modern Art in New York celebrated the dialectical (mutual or two-way) "influence of fashion on the costumes of superheroes" and "the influential reach of comic-book superheroes on contemporary tastemakers" (de Montebello quoted in Bolton 2008: 7). Costumes like Superman's blue leotard and red cape with an *S*, Wonder Woman's red **bustier** and star-spangled shorts, Catwoman's cat suit, and Spiderman's web have been copied, modified, and parodied in fashion and other popular cultural forms. Fashion alludes to the confronting qualities of a superhero conveyed in the costume but, in transforming it into a fashion garment, modifies the connotations and imprints these onto the fabric of everyday culture. As Bolton (2008: 29) argues,

**fashion designers also magnify the bravado of superhero costumes in an allusive shorthand. When they cite a symbol associated with a superhero, designers extend the conceptual reach of their designs and deploy the graphic body for its most resonant and evocative power.**

He concludes the exhibition catalog by reflecting on revivals of superheroes in films such as *Batman: The Dark Knight Returns* (2008) as drawing on and feeding into the preoccupations of postmodernism:

**Adorned with skulls, hellfire, and other symbols of mortality, they embody both the multifocal eclecticism and semiological complexity that characterize the Postmodern body of both fiction and fashion and the darker terrors of our contemporary world. (Bolton 2008: 143)**

Of all the popular cultural influences on fashion, perhaps popular music epitomizes the convergence between the facets of popular culture on fashion trends and the fashion industry

(Polhemus 1994). Popular music has been a fashion force for most of the twentieth century, typified by successive musical genres including blues, jazz, rock, folk, rap, and disco. Many of the popular music genres have emerged within particular subcultures, so here we track the mutual interconnections between fashions, subcultures, and popular music.

The culture of popular music has been long linked to the adoption of distinctive styles of stage dress. In the 1940s, the **zoot suit,** which was associated with gangsters, was popularized as the look of black music and radical nightclub sounds (Cosgrove 1989; McRobbie 1989; Sims 1999: 19–20). The zoot suit was later adopted as the preferred stage dress for nonblack performers of popular music, while others opted for coordinated business suits. What started as a black musicians' habit quickly became a norm in the mainstream. By contrast, female performers wore glitzy evening gowns.

One of the distinctive aspects of the stage costumes of black musicians was that they were "built," that is, designed and customized for the performer, in contrast to the "pulled" costumes of other popular musicians. Pulled costumes are off the rack, homemade, or purchased from neighborhood stores, whereas built costumes are custom-made outfits designed to create a spectacular and coordinated image. Particularly when worn by black artists in groups or troupes, these costumes guaranteed a visual spectacle heightened by the syncopated performance style. As the twentieth century progressed, built performance costumes tended to become the norm for most popular music genres (Jones 1987: 20).

While black performers experimented with spectacular costuming, most white performers wore sports/leisure wear, even the early rockers. So, although rock had become the dominant form of popular music in 1950s America, musicians were treading a fine line between creating sex appeal and not shocking the largely conservative audience. Along with the preppy shirts and sports jackets, the early rockers sported greased and coiffed hairstyles that were emulated in films and on the street. Both Little Richard and Elvis Presley adopted this look early in their careers. Jones (1987: 187) contends that the idea of specific fashions for rock fans first emerged in 1954, when the link between rock music and counterculture styles was established,

**even though the fad for draped jackets with velvet collars, "brothel creepers" (thick-crepe-soled shoes), and pegged "drain pipe" pants had waned by the time that rock 'n' roll became widely popular.**

By the mid-1950s, Little Richard had developed a new look by wearing glittering suits studded with mirrors with brightly colored shirts, capes, and his hair "piled into a preposterous pompadour or, later, teased into a bouffant" (Jones 1987: 45). This was perhaps the turning point in popular music costuming and complemented his excessive physical exertions in his stage performances—a style that eclipsed Elvis's notorious hip gyrations. Little Richard even performed a striptease at the end of his act, throwing detachable pieces of clothing into the audience, who ripped them into shreds. Although this cost him more than he earned, he later said, "It was worth it because everyone was talking about it and coming to see me do it" (quoted by Jones 1987: 46).

His white counterpart, Elvis, maintained his decorum as the king of rock and roll, although he complemented his costume with his stage mannerisms. In 1959, after his tour of duty in the army, he started dyeing his hair jet black, and this became his trademark, along with a costume style that was regarded as "a caricature of what the middle class deemed backwoods trash, and he gave the image threatening power and a form that was repeated for decades" (Jones 1987: 50). In essence, Elvis succeeded in making white rock stars as virile and sexy as black rhythm-and-blues musicians.

The defining characteristic of the stage costumes of rock musicians became "erotic vitality," which contrasted with the earlier, more conventional look of entertainers (Jones 1987: 185). The ability to convey a vibrant sexuality was the key to the performance of rock and roll. Stage costumes incorporated a number of themes: sexuality (aggressive masculinity, seductive femininity, androgyny), mythology (aliens, outer space, gods and goddesses, myths), technology (lighting effects, sparkles, synthesized effects), and morality (good versus bad, transgression, controversy, destruction). These themes were mixed and matched in unexpected ways and still form the basis of stage costuming.

During the 1960s, Elvis's costumes became more glamorous with touches of lamé, rhinestone lapels, bejeweled belts, and extravagant jewelry that contrasted with his black shirt and trousers. His stage costumes also morphed into film performances in a series of highly popular teen-oriented movies (such as *Jailhouse Rock* in 1957 and *High School Confidential* of 1958). The beach culture films that starred Frankie Avalon and Annette Funicello, such as *Beach Party* in 1963 and *How to Stuff a Wild Bikini* in 1965, also shaped youth fashions. These films can be seen as the forerunner of television music videos.

The challenge for Elvis became maintaining his macho sex-symbol image in his later years, especially after he put on weight, while at the same time competing with new rock stars and new music genres. Other popular musicians of the time included Jerry Lee Lewis, Chuck Berry, Bo Diddley, Pat Boone, Buddy Holly, and Cliff Richard. Each adopted a distinctive mode of stage costume. Female musicians in the late 1950s and early 1960s included Patti Page, Teresa Brewer and LaVerne Baker, Brenda Lee, Connie Francis, the Ronettes, the Shangri-Las, the Chantels, the Supremes, Dusty Springfield, and Martha Reeves and the Vandellas. The women spanned a range of musical genres, but creating a distinctive stage costume was equally essential to their performances.

The different looks offered by different artists were widely copied by their fans and increasingly influenced emerging youth fashions. These overlapped with a range of identity groups that formed the basis of emerging youth subcultures, such as rockers, mods, **surfers**, and beatniks (de la Haye and Dingwall 1997; Lobenthal 1990; Polhemus and Proctor 1984). Music styles like West Coast **psychedelia** and folk music established their own fashion cultures. The common denominator of these subcultures was the emphasis on creating a distinctive look that resonated with each group's beliefs, values, and lifestyle. In other words, "Streetstyle wisely hones in on the most visual aspect of the conscious dissidence of youth—clothes" (Mark Suggitt quoted by de la Haye and Dingwall 1997: np).

During this time, a split developed as some performers wore more and more elaborate and spectacular outfits that were custom made, while other performers crafted images drawn from popular culture or the subcultures with which they identified. The strategic use of costumes became shorthand for the language of radicalism that was associated with the music. Clothes and adornment became an effective means of establishing distinctive identities while also making social comment and attracting media and public interest in this burgeoning phenomenon.

Arguably the epitome of 1960s music culture, the Beatles established new benchmarks for stage costume as much as their distinctive sound. Initially, they wore black leather and jeans (in the style of American rhythm-and-blues artists), but, in an effort to appeal to a broader range of conservative youths (and their popular music gatekeepers), they donned coordinated outfits of collarless jackets (inspired by Cardin), stovepipe trousers, and trademark "mop" haircuts that were purportedly styled by their manager, Brian Epstein (Jones 1987: 189; Sims 1999: 24–25, 171). However, the Beatles also changed their image, regularly moving from the iconic suit to a mod look to hippy fashions and even spectacular versions of historical military uniforms. These experiments coincided with the development of popular music inspirations in designer fashion, and increasingly the world of pop music and youth fashion were inextricably linked.

Other bands followed suit and cultivated a distinctive look for stage performances. For instance, the mod band the Kinks wore hand-crocheted

**The Beatles.** United Press International, Library of Congress

vests with fur edging as their stage costume. This trend inevitably led to a counterreaction. Other popular music bands chose diverse outfits that highlighted differences between band members, with each striving to be distinctive and cultivate a unique look. Often there was fierce rivalry between bands—such as the Beatles and the Rolling Stones—that was reflected in their choice of stage clothes in their determination to stand out as different.

As youths radicalized from the late 1960s and into the 1970s, major changes in dress, gender codes, and lifestyle accompanied the explosion of a popular music–fuelled youth culture. In an ironic gesture, an increasing number of artists adopted formal uniforms as stage dress as a form of social comment (see Chenoune 1993; McDowell 1997; Sims 1999). Jimi Hendrix created controversy in the United States with his disrespectful adoption of a Confederate jacket and other military paraphernalia in the later stages of his career. On the other side of the Atlantic, Pete Townshend of the Who was lambasted for wearing a suit made from a Union Jack flag on stage. Sensing that controversy fuelled their popularity, the band subsequently was photographed under a Union Jack.

Uniforms as stage costume became a fixture of popular music. Public Enemy wore NATO arctic camouflage gear, Duran Duran chose variations of military uniforms, New Order wore Third Reich uniforms, and Adam and the Ants popularized romanticized versions of eighteenth-century costumes. Others chose to parody school uniforms, with the disheveled stage wear of Angus Young of ACDC, Chrissie Hynde of the Pretenders, and Kelly Osbourne. School uniforms were also popular, for example, among Japanese pop groups such as YMO (Yellow Magic Orchestra) (Kinsella 2002: 220).

Retail outlets in the 1960s reflected the obsession with the irreverent use of uniforms, which became a central element of Swinging London's mod look (Fogg 2003: 55–75). This was perhaps best epitomized by the iconic I Was Lord Kitchener's Valet shop on Carnaby Street (the source of avant-garde psychedelic fashions), the front of which was covered in images of Lord Kitchener in military dress (Breward, Gilbert, and Lister 2006; Sims 1999: 63; see also Fogg 2003: 64–65). This niche boutique sold Nazi paraphernalia, Union Jack–adorned garments and accessories, German iron cross pendants, and military surplus wear such as great coats, boots, belts, hats, and jackets. The best-selling item was a recruiting poster of Lord Kitchener exhorting, "Your country needs you," that adorned the bedrooms of countless young people.

Other popular boutiques included Lord John, Mr. Fish, John Stephen, His Clothes, Male W1, Mod Male, Domino Male, and Just Men, while Mary Quant's Bazaar, Barbara Hulinincki's Biba, His & Hers, Gear, Bird Cage, Kleptomania, and Pop catered to a female and "unisex" clientele (Chenoune 1993: 256–59; Fogg 2003: 64–89). Although not all these boutiques were on Carnaby Street, this was the street that became synonymous with Swinging London, gaining a reputation as the epicenter of new trends and styles in pop culture. Celebrities and musicians—and their girlfriends and families—became a significant feature of the high profile of ever-changing London emporia. Above all, these boutiques aimed to subvert conventional ideas about clothes, politics, colors, and sexuality through the use of juxtapositions, unusual combinations, and the unorthodox use of symbols. They aimed for shock value through subversions and parodies of treasured cultural icons.

**The Rolling Stones.** Photo by Steve Wood/Evening Standard/Hulton Archive/Getty Images. 2006 Getty Images

One of the recurring themes of this period was the challenge to traditional gender roles and sexual conventions. Not only was much of the mod and pop look castigated as effeminate or—worse—accused of pandering to homosexual desires, but pop celebrities took to parodying conservative values by wearing unisex clothing and cross-dressing. A now-infamous example is Mick Jagger's costume when he played the July 5, 1969, Hyde Park concert—which had become a memorial to Brian Jones, who had drowned a few days before. Jagger's decision to wear a white semi-**sheer tunic** (which was denounced as a "dress") over trousers instead of a somber "respectful" outfit was seen as a mark of disrespect (Wilson 1985: 165). In fact, the outfit was based on the traditional Greek National Guard uniform. However, by choosing to wear "what was essentially a white moire mini-dress over white trousers," Jagger "gave a performance of unprecedented sexual ambiguity" and established a stage presence that reverberated in his subsequent choices of outfits (Sims 1999: 116).

The controversy over his "dress" became a turning point. It redefined the importance and impact of stage costume as an adjunct to rock music culture. Jagger was quick to capitalize on the payoff of creating shock value and promoting unisex modes of dress. Other musicians such as David Bowie also followed the fashion for men's dresses. The importance of having the right stage clothes to become "a stage person"

**Jimi Hendrix.** Photo by Michael Ochs Archives/Getty Images. 2007 Getty Images

became central to Jagger's image. From then on, the focus was on the Jagger crotch, emphasized by jumpsuits and tight trousers. At the infamous December 1969 Altamont Free Concert in San Francisco, he wore an Uncle Sam hat and a black T-shirt signaling a darker persona. The stabbing death of an audience member by a Hells Angel amid chaotic and violent events (later the subject of the documentary *Gimme Shelter*) overshadowed the musical performances. The oscillation between effeminacy and macho aggression in Jagger's stage image was captured in the 1970 film *Performance,* where he played a reclusive rock star. Ambiguity, shock value, and changing personae became central to the culture of rock music.

The science fiction film *Clockwork Orange* (1971) arguably created a punk look before the term was coined by Vivienne Westwood and Malcolm McLaren in 1972 (Jones 1987: 190). At the same time, performance costumes were incorporating androgyny, on the one hand, and science fiction, on the other. The successive personae of David Bowie, in particular as Ziggy Stardust, epitomized this conflation of looks and inspirations. From the 1970s, the male dominance of the pantheon of popular music was challenged by the increasing number of successful female artists, such as Debbie Harry of Blondie, Annie Lennox, Lori Anderson, Pat Benatar, Cher, Patti Smith, Christine McVie, Grace Jones, Janice Joplin, Cyndi Lauper, Grace Slick, Tina Turner, Cilla Black, and Marianne Faithfull. They too were experimenting with a wide variety of stage looks, both drawing from fashion and influencing new styles.

One of the trademarks was costume changes during a performance and regular reinventions of a trademark look. Madonna—undoubtedly picking up from the Stones, Bowie, and others—adopted a succession of looks (including a serious military phase, a pin-striped suit phase, and a fetish and dominatrix lingerie phase) in her diverse career. She especially conflated "religious and erotic themes" (Garber 1992: 211), expressing ambivalence about her Catholic upbringing and deliberately setting out to shock and subvert public expectations. During her 1990 Blonde Ambition tour, she "evoked Hasidic as well as Catholic images when she and her back-up singers, dressed in long black caftans, waved their hands above their heads as they danced in a 'church' lit with votive candles" (Garber 1992: 211). Her other stage outfit for the tour—Jean Paul Gaultier's conical **bra** and corset—"saved her career" (Sims 1999: 130–131) and later she turned to Dolce & Gabbana to create costumes for her, including costumes for her "Love Kylie" tribute, the Rocco T-shirts celebrating the birth of her son, and "rhinestone cowboy" attire (Cole 2000).

The relationship between stage costumes and youth fashion is complicated by the process of diffusion; that is to say, a stage costume must be able to be adapted for everyday fashion. This means that only elements of a costume rather than the costume as a whole can be appropriated into a street fashion look—for example, a black T-shirt with a swastika, or underwear as outerwear. In other words, "performers' outfits are magnified versions of fashion" (Jones 1987: 196). For example, Jones (1987: 194) argues that while Madonna's "bra straps and bra showing" could be copied, her sexy look for "Material Girl" "was less successful as a style for a rock star because it was impossible for most wanna-be fans to copy."

The adoption of a particular look—or increasingly changing looks—has become part and parcel of the pop-rock scene. Some artists, for example, have adopted distinctive "class" gear, for example, Cyndi Lauper as trailer trash, Bruce Springsteen in denim as a regular New York working class guy, and Jimmy Barnes (Cold Chisel) in the Australian workingman's uniform of singlet and jeans. Michael Jackson also invested heavily in inventing stage personae and "deftly manipulated the stage vocabulary of gender" (Garber 1992: 295), creating a highly marketable commodity and public mask: "His signature white socks, single glove, and sequinned clothing are readily identifiable—and often imitated—marks of his personal style" (Garber 1992: 296). His fall from musical popularity and subsequent legal and ethical troubles perhaps indicate that Jackson was ultimately swallowed by his overly contrived looks.

While some artists were refining marketable images and associations as pop rock became mainstreamed and its radical challenges muted, newer artists began to rebel against the quasi uniform of post-1960s music culture. Glam rock took stage costume to the limit with more and more extreme outfits and identity shifts that were copied across music genres—for example, by Freddie Mercury, Marc Bolan of T. Rex, Gary Glitter, the Bay City Rollers, the New York Dolls, Prince,

**Madonna.** Photo by Kevin Winter/DMI/Time Life Pictures/Getty Images. Time Life Pictures

Kiss, Cher, and Kylie Minogue. Musicals like *The Rocky Horror Show* turned uniforms and costumes into performing arts—theater as well as music. Phenomena like punk, grunge, antifashion, heavy metal, and acid rock generated a new approach to stage wear that aimed to challenge the status quo. Punks typified the new irreverent approach to stage dress. They wore clothes that symbolized the rejection of mainstream values and promoted self-mutilation, asexuality, violence, and bad taste, drawing on props such as slashed clothing, safety pins as fastenings and jewelry, razor blades, chains, latex, and bondage gear—"anything that would annoy adults—nazism, marxism, treason, blasphemy, and sexual perversion" (Mulvagh 2005: 120). Gear like this was sold in boutiques like Sex, the punk shop of Malcolm McLaren and Vivienne Westwood on Kings Road, Chelsea, in the United Kingdom (see chapter 5).

From the 1980s and into the 1990s, new styles emerged in American rap, hip-hop, grunge, acid rock, and techno music. These began as subcultural rallying points of radicalism and resistance but were quickly mainstreamed. Their sartorial

**Kylie Minogue.** Photo: Keven Law, http://www.flickr.com/photos/13914342@N06/ Kevin Law

influences were black street culture and black street wear—typically shiny baggy trousers or track pants, bomber jackets, sunglasses, headwear (cap, scarf, beret, hat), **sneakers,** and heaps of chunky gold jewelry. In Britain, fashion subcultures such as Afrocentrism, cyberpunk, grunge, jungle, old skool, rockabilly, raga, Rasta, ravers, and travelers inflected both music and fashion trends with a huge diversity of looks (de la Haye and Dingwall 1997). Pop rock had moved from appropriating and reworking uniform culture to inventing a new quasi uniform of global urban street wear. At least this was the case for male artists. Female artists have increasingly appeared in versions of fetish lingerie—or "slut" wear—potentially undermining the growing presence of women in popular music by their presentation as objects of desire to be despised rather than admired. If there is a common theme in contemporary music videos, it is shock value and debasement of moral codes. These diverse musical styles and subcultural fashions have inflected popular music into the new millennium.

Repeatedly, the choice of stage outfits by popular musicians and bands has created a distinctive genre of performance costume and influenced youth fashion trends. Many of these have involved forms of cross-dressing, deliberately creating ambiguous sexual references. Often initially controversial, trends among female performers such as cropped hair, men's suits, corsetry, bondage wear, and revealing outfits have subsequently become the inspiration for "high-style looks of the mainstream fashion magazines" and eventually the basis of street fashion (Garber 1992: 136). Popular music fashion and style constantly involve a play between display and spectacle and concealment and understatement, characteristics that have been reproduced in advertising, fashion photography, and the visual components of consumer culture more generally. One analyst has argued that the crossover between music television and the fashion industry is in an "overlap phase" where multiple styles and fashion cycles are layered on top of each other, creating a mélange of possible looks and points of audience identification (Jones 1987: 194). As a consequence, music artists have become increasingly fashion conscious both on and off the stage.

This trend has continued, and as the nexus between popular music and contingent cultures of fashion, film, television, and media expands, it becomes increasingly difficult to separate out the direction of influence. One influential crossover phenomenon has been celebrity events (such as the Academy Awards and MTV Movie Awards), for which celebrities are "loaned" exclusive designer gowns. Designers have recognized the value of the publicity emanating from the coverage of a celebrity flaunting one of their outfits. The choice of designer by an actor, or alternatively the person whom the designer is prepared to have feature his or her gown, becomes the centerpiece of coverage. Moreover, the gowns are rated by media and Internet commentators as to how well (or not) the outfit suited the celebrity and the occasion—and celebrated with hyperbole as successes or pilloried mercilessly as flops. Media reports of such awards ceremonies are framed around these celebrity fashions, often earning more attention than the outcome of the awards themselves. And although these gowns do not directly influence everyday fashion (given the cost and impracticality of these designs), celebrity events have also become a significant force in globalizing brand recognition of celebrity designers, increasing sales of their prêt-à-porter and diffusion lines as well as imperceptibly shaping new styles and fashion trends.

Breward (2003: 141) concludes that the language of fashion and codes of representation have become "impossibly incestuous, confused, and contradictory." How this affects the linguistic, visual, and symbolic lexicons of fashion is yet to be revealed but it may mean that the language and codes of fashion become restratified along new lines of social and cultural fracturing. These might reflect ethnic, political, and locational dynamics along with the conventional signs of class, gender, sexuality, status, and role. So we can see that the entwinement of fashion with media and popular culture has a longer history than is sometimes envisaged. In the new millennium, the possibilities for representation, promotion, interdependence, and coercion of social and cultural politics through fashion and style have become extreme.

## iv. fashion journalism, public relations, and stylists

As mentioned at the start of this chapter, there are three ways in which fashion and the media are connected:

- **Media representations of fashion interdependent of the industry**
- **The use of media by the fashion industry to promote fashion**
- **Fashion take-ups of media representations of role models in new fashions**

Accordingly, the media was implicated in the evolution of the fashion system throughout the twentieth century in diverse forms: fashion illustration, fashion photography, advertising, marketing, fashion forecasting, and modeling. There are also specialist careers within the fashion industry that aim to manipulate the media to promote new trends and market new products, namely, style setters (usually self-appointed arbiters of taste and initiators of new trends or fads, who are adept at sensing a new style and popularizing it, often after first scandalizing the mainstream fashion status quo) and gatekeepers (an official or informal authority who acts as a conduit for permission to perform certain roles or as a veto point for prohibiting certain behavior; in the case of fashion, a concierge or arbiter of changing modes and regulator of fashion behavior).

We also need to distinguish five different kinds of fashion writing:

- **The language of fashion (descriptive and technical ways of writing about clothes, accessories, styles, and particular looks)**
- **Fashion reportage (impressions and images of fashion, as well as opinions, gossip, and scuttlebutt about fashion and fashionable trendsetters)**
- **Promotional writing (explicit or implicit advertising or features promoting fashion)**
- **Critical and analytical writing (evaluations and judgments about fashion offered by specialist fashion arbiters)**
- **Intellectual and scholarly analysis (of the significance, meaning, and contextual understanding of fashion and dress by academics, theorists, and cultural commentators)**

Within the fashion industry, these different forms of fashion discourse are produced respectively by three main types of fashion writers: fashion journalists and editors; public relations people and publicists; and stylists, who coordinate the various parties involved in fashion promotion. One area of fashion journalism where these different discourses and voices converge is fashion advice columns. Here the fashion "expert" offers solutions to readers' clothing dilemmas, almost always in a finger-wagging manner that demolishes the questioner's usual mode of dress and offers an alternative that is frequently elitist, impractical, high maintenance, and faintly ludicrous. Consider this advice from a magazine's "Style Mistress" to a concerned reader:

***Q. I've quit my full-time work to be at home with the kids. Any ideas on how not to fall into the frumpy-mummy trap?***

*I know what you mean—the state of dress of school-gate mums can be alarming. I hear women at my daughter's school say: "I picked these jeans up at so and so. They were really cheap and they're okay for the school run." And I think to myself: "Oh no they're not!" Just because you don't go out to paid work any longer doesn't mean you should lose all sense of style. Admittedly, it does take a little bit of work [mentally mostly] not to become part of the tracksuit brigade. However, I believe it's always important to feel fresh and confident. I always swipe mascara over my eyelashes and dress like I expect to see someone I want to impress. I only ever wear jeans and sneakers, but my jeans are the perfect fit and my white leather sneakers are meticulously clean. I wear well-fitting white T-shirts and a good casual jacket. I look the same every day, but the number of people who comment on what I'm wearing is astounding. Keep your wardrobe really streamlined and wear it with confidence.*

(*Weekend Australian Magazine*, October 2007: 35)

This passage combines the provision of information with the establishment of a hierarchy of fashion looks and a value judgment about how different people choose to dress. Another reader wanted to know how to make stilettos more comfortable, only to be told she should only buy shoes by elite footwear designers such as Manolo Blahnik, Jimmy Choo, and Christian Louboutin because for "their devotees, comfort is key—well, at least on a par with design and cachet" and "this is a case of getting what you pay for, so start saving." This kind of fashion writing exhibits a one-upmanship against the hopelessly unstylish consumer. The message is that to be fashionable, you need to buy designer clothes and eschew the everyday—and, of course, believe the opinions of fashion writers and follow their trend advice.

### Fashion Journalism and Editorial Coverage

The way the media covers fashion is at least a two-edged sword. On the simplest level, the media gives coverage about fashion—for example, by reporting a new season's collection; profiling a designer, brand, or fashion store; or reporting on a passing or new trend. But the media can also shape fashion and influence responses to fashion through its role as an agenda setter—for example, by profiling a new brand so often or so conspicuously that it becomes a household name even if a reader has never bought a product. This role is especially important when the media smells a controversy whose flames it can fan through headlines and relentless coverage. The collapse of a brand-name business, drug taking by the "face" of a brand, and upheavals in personal relationships are familiar themes of fashion exposés—rumors on rumors.

The media can use fashion to frame a news story or make a story newsworthy by emphasizing the fashion angle, for example, when celebrities find themselves in court and choose their court appearance outfits to portray themselves as demure and responsible (though still stylish). A number of high-profile models who have fronted court have chosen to wear Chanel outfits since Chanel is seen to be a symbol of traditional and respectable haute couture (see chapter 2). Examples include Naomi Campbell (on assault charges) and Jerry Hall (on a drug charge). Reportage of the case often begins with what the defendant wore to court. Women's sports are also frequently covered in the mainstream media *only* because of the catchy or idiosyncratic outfits worn by high-profile athletes (for example, coverage of tennis or golf).

So **fashion journalism** is a complex, multipronged activity. Fashion journalists may be attached to a newspaper or a fashion journal, although some commentators argue that there is a big difference between them in terms of what they do. Polan (2006: 166) argues that fashion journalists for newspapers and general-interest women's magazines are constrained to produce coverage that is "utilitarian, didactic, analytical, occasionally critical, practical, value-driven." She suggests this is because fashion is accorded a low priority in newsrooms as a serious pursuit and is largely included because of its titillating and controversial nature. As a result of the latter, there is generally a huge amount of fashion coverage in newspapers even though the coverage is anodyne. Newspaper editors are also sensitive to the power of advertisers and thus shy away from pointing out the pros and cons of rival brands or products. Because of this, fashion journalism does not exhibit the critical edge expected of an arts critic (Kawamura 2005: 81). Often it degenerates into advertorials and commercial endorsements in the guise of exclusive features or fashion show reportage.

By contrast, Polan (2006: 166) argues that fashion editors of fashion journals and magazines do a range of activities: style photographs; cover news stories; interview and profile designers, retailers, collectors, and archivists; comment on lifestyle trends; and advise readers on new looks (often through "miracle makeovers"). So although fashion editors collaborate with industry players, they have two key weapons—silence and space—so they are more able to take an independent line in covering fashion. At least this is the theory.

All fashion journalists are subject to persuasive inducements and promotional tactics such as sample bags, presents, invitations to shows, access to fashion celebrities (designers, elite clients, etc.), and invitations to parties and launches. Fashion firms, especially cosmetic ones, use powerful strategies to have their brand featured on covers and specials. Makeover features use crude techniques to exaggerate the "before" look and polish up the "after" look. These techniques have expanded with the spread of fashion journalism to radio, television, and the Internet. The first Paris fashion show to be broadcast on television was in 1962, when Christian Dior and Pierre Balmain broke ranks with the Chambre and gave CBS global broadcast rights (Polan 2006: 163). This was the start of a rash of razzamatazz fashion shows and the entrance into the arena of new young designers who reveled in experimenting with new approaches and new media opportunities.

Fashion journalism changed as the fashion industry became truly global and fast paced. Fashion editors have hectic nonstop schedules covering fashion shows and fashion weeks in fashion cities around the world. Coverage has emphasized higher-profile designers, star models, celebrity guests, and more and more extravagance. Arguably the quality of fashion writing has declined, now suffused in hyperbole and the mirage of celebrity. Fashion became a world unto itself even as it expanded to global distribution and new markets. The business of fashion has become more and more hard nosed, with expensive arrangements and complex organizational decisions.

During the 1980s, the range of fashion media outlets expanded to include new fashion lifestyle publications such as the *Face* and *i-D.* Long-running magazines—especially those targeting a male readership, such as *GQ, Esquire,* and *FHM*—revamped their style and fashion content to reflect contemporary lifestyles and the new male fashion consumer (Polan 2006: 167). These publications were infused with the spirit of "new journalism," where fact, fantasy, and opinion were intermingled, and fashion journalism became much less descriptive and informative, becoming instead a patchwork of breathless celebration of designer genius and elite consumer extravagance.

Some fashion editors such as Suzy Menkes, Colin McDowell, Diana Vreeland, Anna Piaggi (see image 2), and Anna Wintour became treated as fashion royalty. Alongside this, however, critical insider accounts began to appear that looked behind the gloss and glitter and revealed the entrails and downsides of the fashion industry, including Nicholas Coleridge's *The Fashion Conspiracy* (1989) and later Teri Agins's *The End of Fashion* (1999) and Naomi Klein's *No Logo* (2000) (Polan 2006: 168–69).

Polan (2006: 169–70) concludes that there are a number of credibility challenges faced by contemporary fashion journalism:

- **The cult of the celebrity, which overdetermines every aspect of the craft of fashion coverage**
- **The preponderance of mindless personal opinion that masquerades as journalism**
- **The huge power of the public relations industry, which increasingly masterminds the puppetry of fashion**
- **The Internet, which has become a major new medium for all forms of fashion reportage, both good and bad**

This is not to say that the art of quality fashion journalism has entirely disappeared; rather, "there must be a bedrock of good, fact-based journalism, not a froth of self-regarding nonsensical nonsense" (Polan 2006: 170).

### The Growing Public Relations Industry for Fashion

The space between the fashion industry and the media-consuming public has been filled by a gigantic publicity machine filled with public relations exponents, publicists, and stylists.

**Public relations is defined as the practice (sometimes described as the art and social science) of analyzing trends, predicting their consequences, counseling organization leaders and implementing planned programs of action which will serve both the organization's and the public's interests. (Costantino 1998: 84)**

Just as the dimensions and global reach of the fashion industry have proliferated, so too has the appetite of fashion journalists for "news" about fashion. Often news amounts to no more than gossip, catty asides, gloating, commiserating, and speculation, but it has nonetheless fueled the publicity machine. Publicity has always been around, but it has become a sophisticated practice, though maybe not a transparent one. How the industry communicates to the media has become vital, and this involves not just advertising but ways to annex contextual information surrounding advertising campaigns and convey this to the media and public. Moreover, an astute public relations strategy can be much cheaper and arguably more effective than an advertising blitz.

In the fashion business, public relations is often regarded as one of the most glamorous occupations. It is also high profile, and some fashion publicists have become as famous as their clients. Company public relations staff disseminate information about their products and brands to the media and other organizations by cultivating relationships with media representatives and lubricating these links through various means. Publicists stage various media events (such as press conferences, press receptions, staged debates, and "facility visits") as well as issuing press releases and photographs of new products.

Often the media are plied with "exclusive" press releases, product samples, kits, **look books** (an abbreviated catalog for each season's apparel), catalogs, and visuals—as well as gifts, free lunches, and receptions. Publicists are also responsible for organizing media invitations to fashion shows, guest appearances, trunk shows, celebrity opportunities, and charity events. The other main task of fashion publicists is commissioning and strategizing advertising as the creative force that draws on market research to set the theme and look of a particular campaign. Occasionally, such ploys are exposed as a form of payola (paid inducements), but generally these practices are accepted as a necessary part of doing business.

Fashion journalists spend much of their time at fashion shows and presentations of collections, from which they craft "hot" stories for the media by focusing on distinctive trends, controversies, and lessons for the fashion public. In addition, fashion journalists contribute to regular columns and features on fashion trends to maintain the salience of fashion news. New media forms such as fashion Web sites and fashion television shows have expanded the scope of fashion journalism.

### Stylists

> *The stylist is the person who frames the setting, mood, clothes, hair styling, makeup, photographs, and the overall look of every image of a collection, agreement, or brand. The stylist pays attention to the detail of the presentation of a product to enhance its desirability and attention-getting qualities. Fashion shoots and advertising campaigns are increasingly being produced by professional stylists, who coordinate every aspect of the campaign. They may work freelance or be attached to an agency or fashion label. Their aim is to choreograph the presentation of a garment, collection, or brand to enhance or target its appeal. To do so, they are engaged in all aspects of the project, from the briefing of the theme through setting the budget, organization of the fashion shoot, choice of clothes and accessories, selection of models and photographer, and the commissioning of a hair stylist, makeup artist, and the selection and setting up of the fashion shoot location. After the shoot, the stylist works on the proof images to prepare them for publication in the print media or for broadcast and video release.*

As well as this, stylists are responsible for producing a range of other fashion materials including look books, advertising campaigns that epitomize the theme or mood of the season or brand, catalogs, advertorials that can be given to media outlets to promote a product for free, and still-life photo shoots (or shopping pages) or posters for placing products in print media. There are two main kinds of fashion stylists: those who work with an editor or a photographer on a regular basis, and those who work with designers to help visualize the overarching concept of fashion shows and collections. Stylists are also increasingly involved in producing fashion shows and trunk shows and styling celebrities in the apparel of a brand.

Stylists also select celebrity endorsement and promotion. So now the involvement of celebrities in all aspects of publicity and media exposure has become extreme as a range of celebrities—actors, artists, sports stars, models, creative leaders, and popular singers—have become "the icons of the twenty-first century" (Haid, Jackson, and Shaw 2006: 179). Whereas celebrity endorsement was traditionally confined to the heading names of haute couture, it has now become almost de rigueur in promoting all brands and new product lines. Many celebrities and brands have contractual arrangements for the star to exclusively wear the label. While some celebrities buy the garments, most borrow samples or are given products as "gifts." The publicity gained from a celebrity wearing a particular brand is regarded as exceeding the value of an advertising campaign because "celebrities belong to the elite of opinion formers and have a considerable following" (Haid et al. 2006: 180). Each time a photograph of a celebrity is reprinted, free publicity for the designer is ensured.

By collaborating with and manipulating the media through these means, the fashion industry seeks to persuade those who spearhead new fashion trends of their novelty value, choice of mode, and marketability. They hope to win the favor of fashionable personalities, celebrities, editorial gatekeepers, and elite patrons. Examples of high-profile stylists include Isabella Blow (see image 1), L'Wren Scott, Amanda Grieve, and Katy England. When this is achieved, a collection, label, or brand is virtually guaranteed sales and a media profile that keeps the name circulating in the wider fashion orbit. In this process the role of journalists, publicists, and stylists has become crucial to success.

## v. conclusion

This chapter has discussed the dialectical relationship between fashion and popular culture, particularly through the role of the media as the medium of visualizing fashion trends and looks as well as the means for promoting and selling new fashions. As new media forms have been invented, the fashion industry has been adept at exploiting opportunities to annex its representational possibilities.

At the same time, media forms have been part and parcel of developments in popular culture, which has seen the democratization of fashion, opening it up to more and more groups in society and across the globe. Post–World War II developments saw the fracturing of class divisions and the emergence of taste cultures and subcultures based on shared values and lifestyles. These, too, became intimately bound up with fashion cultures as they proliferated into distinctive dress codes. Popular music was a central feature of twentieth-century fashion trends as sexuality and spectacle converged in the images projected by the stage costumes of performers.

In addition to media representation of fashion, the fashion industry actively recruits the media to promote and project changing styles through different kinds of style setters and gatekeepers. At the new millennium, fashion and popular culture cannot be separated but together create a potent force of identity management and the unconscious of the consumer. In this process, media no longer reflect trends in the street but is complicit in fanning new styles and mediating public reaction and the general acceptance and conversion of stylistic elements into everyday fashions.

The first case study in this chapter investigates the decisive place of sportswear in contemporary fashion both as a specific type of clothing and as the basis of everyday dress codes and how this has shaped fashion trends. As a specific example, another case study traces how the practical dress of rural Australians (bush wear) has been repackaged for urban consumers as high fashion and how the Internet has been used to create a global market. The third case study looks at the marketing of erotic lingerie to the general public in ways that overcame traditional connotations of sexy underwear as naughty. Finally, the controversial, attention-grabbing advertisements created for Benetton by Oliviero Toscani are analyzed in terms of the development of global merchandising as the forerunner of fast fashion.

## CHAPTER SUMMARY

- The media translates fashion impulses by disseminating new trends and focusing on elements that can be appropriated and reworked into mainstream fashions.
- The relationship between the media and the fashion industry has three components: the fashion industry uses the media to promote its products, influential gatekeepers sift through media trends and selectively reinforce the popularity of some styles over others, and the media represents fashion as a complex compromise between the vision of the fashion producers and the aesthetic sensibilities and shifting tastes of its diverse publics.
- The spread of modern fashion was dependent on the development of mechanical and technological means of production of imagery, including etching, printing, photography, the moving image, and electronic circulation.
- The promotion of new fashions equally involved the promotion of new fashionable lifestyles.
- The advent of department stores was a key to the democratization of fashion in that it introduced innovative strategies of display, access, and consumer habits.
- Fashion magazines such as *Vogue* and lifestyle magazines such as *i-D* have also been a specialist form of media that has promoted fashion and projected new trends to wide audiences, creating new consumer groups.
- Since the 1950s, youth popular cultures and subcultures have become a major force shaping fashion trends.
- Within popular music, the stage costumes of performers have both borrowed from fashion and costume traditions and shaped new styles and street fashions.
- Shifting notions of gender and sexuality, especially concerning transgression, androgyny, counterculture, and antifashion, have been inflected in fashion trends and media reportage of fashion.
- Style setters and gatekeepers are key elements of fashion journalism and the fashion media.
- Public relations and fashion stylists have become increasingly important in their roles as the intermediaries who shape how fashion innovations and change are manipulated and massaged into media images and representations.
- There is a symbiotic but also mutually destructive and exploitative relationship among fashion creators, fashion icons (such as models and celebrities), and fashion disseminators (fashion media)—for example, high-profile models are created by media hype then destroyed when they fail to live up to their image.

## CASE STUDY 25: Sports Clothing for Everyman

**Basketball game.** Photo by Photographer's Mate 2nd Class Damon J. Moritz/U.S. Navy

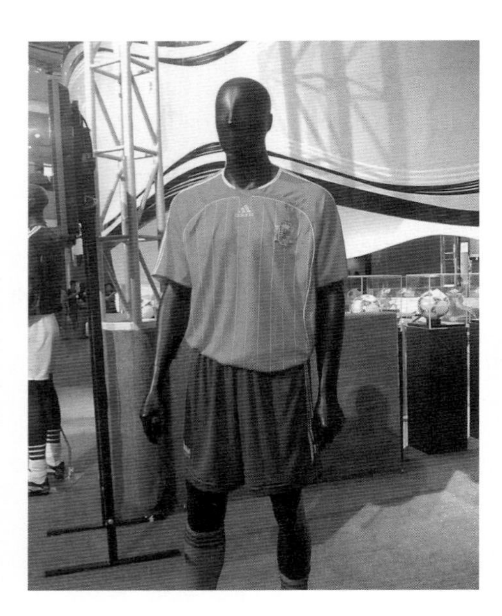

**Football jersey.** Photo: Chong Fat

Over time, but especially during the last century, clothes have become looser, more informal, and more suited to leisure and recreational activities, leading to the observation that "All-purpose clothing [has] transcended role demarcation" (Joseph 1986: 178). Sportswear has been the obvious beneficiary of this trend. As well as using sports uniforms for other activities, designers are increasingly designing and producing sports-influenced casual clothing (e.g., T-shirts, leggings, athletic shoes, Lycra swimwear and exercise wear, sports jackets, facsimile sports jerseys, football stripes, and baseball caps). These garments and their details focus on the utilitarian and the egalitarian, with the "emphasis as much on the structural quality and everyday practicality as on the visual surface of the garment" (Danielsen 1999).

Designer cargo pants, military-style trousers, jumpsuits, hooded jackets, fleecy vests, and zippered tops proliferate in recent collections. These borrow heavily from winter wear and mountaineering apparel with brand and style names like Himalayan and Patagonia. Sportswear has become the mainstay of many designers and the last resort in hard times. There is an increasing incidence of specialized wear for leisure activities for those who may not actually be into sports—for fishing, horse riding, golf, tennis, martial arts, yoga, and the like. The quasi uniform is derived from the appropriate sports uniform and outfits, then commercialized into specialist activity wear and popularized as leisure and recreation fashion.

The theme of this chapter has been the play between the maintenance of tradition and the impact of innovation—factors that have simultaneously characterized the development of the modern fashion industry and the manufacture of outfits specifically for sports. From the earliest appearance of sports outfits, fashion has been either never far behind in incorporating elements of the athletic look into mainstream fashion or influencing the design and/or acceptability of new athletic looks. As the cult of the body has asserted itself cyclically, the credibility of sportswear has been enhanced. This has created opportunities for manufacturers of sportswear to increase sales to non-athletic consumers and develop everyday sports-look lines. Competitive teams often change their stripes each season and have different home and away colors. This increases sales among supporters, who want the latest team look—and sometimes a star player's number. Clubs and sporting-goods stores satisfy this demand while creating new ways to enhance it further. Sports stores have proliferated in airports, offering accessible stock to new markets. Chain and department stores are quick to manufacture facsimile versions for the cheaper end of the market.

**Serena Williams.** Photo by Getty Images for Nike. 2004 Getty Images

Of course, this becomes a double-edged sword, for while a core of sports-conscious consumers may prove reliable, the fashion-conscious consumer is not. One of the notable success stories of athletic clothing being mainstreamed is that of athletic shoes, variously called sneakers, trainers, and tennis shoes (Gill 2006; O'Mahony and Braddock 2002: 105, 169–74; Quinn 2002: 197–99). While soft shoes or slippers for sports were systematized in the invention of tennis shoes, it was relatively recently that manufacturers reworked the design of athletic shoes to maximize flexibility, support, and sport-specific requirements by rethinking support and cushioning. What they did not count on was the translation of the athletic shoe into youth culture as the generic shoe of young people. It has become the tip of new trends, necessitating constantly updated models and features—with fashion and style as much in mind as practicality for sports. Manufacturers of athletic shoes, for example, produce and retailers stock only limited numbers of high-end street designs to make purchases more exclusive. Sneaker stores only get a limited number, usually in the low hundreds, of each style, which sell out quickly. Rather than ordering more, the store waits for the next release and pent-up consumer demand among sneaker aficionados. Collectors acquire special-edition shoes as an investment—never to be worn! Indeed, collecting athletic shoes has become a popular hobby, with enthusiasts owning up to 500 pairs and specialist Web sites and magazines serving collectors (Lunn 2003).

According to Alderson (2002: 29), an estimated 430 million pairs of athletic shoes are sold annually, accounting for a quarter of the footwear market. Yet only a fifth of these are worn for sports; the rest are lifestyle purchases. In America, the athletic footwear industry has been valued in excess of $16 billion a year (Lunn 2003). Perhaps not surprisingly, couture designers have joined the fray, producing "status sneakers" for the fashionista and bowling shoes (a cross between a "nanna" shoe and an athletic shoe) for the chic urban worker. Not only must sportswear manufacturers produce garments that enhance performance and are durable, but they are equally concerned with producing goods that are viewed as stylish: cool vies with function in the sportswear war and, all too often, cool has won out.

Sometimes, though, cool fashions become the focus of moral panics. The sneaker brand Heelys was introduced in 2000. Modified gym shoes, they have wheel sockets in each heel that pop out when the weight shifts and can be used to roll instead of walk. Indicatively, one brand is called Street Gliders. In 2007, the "heeling" craze created a medical emergency in the seventy countries in which they are sold. For example, the United States Consumer Product Safety Commission received reports of one death and sixty-four roller-shoe injuries in the last four months of 2006 (Tanner 2007: 3). In Singapore in 2006, thirty-seven children were hospitalized, while one hospital in Dublin treated sixty-seven children during the ten-week summer holiday of 2006. Despite the injuries—and controversy, including bans in schools and shopping centers—Heelys has sold more than 10 million pairs since 2000 and reported a first-quarter income of $8.5 million in 2007 alone (Tanner 2007: 3).

While many sports have sacrificed sporting performance and tradition for fashionability, some sports have resisted new approaches to sports clothes design—for example, tennis, baseball, and football. So some sports embrace new developments, while others lag behind. Thus we find that cycling, skiing, scuba diving, swimming, and luge have adopted one-piece outfits as standard wear while other sports resist. One recent case concerned the decision of the Cameroon soccer team to wear a one-piece **microfiber** bodysuit in the African Cup of Nations in Tunisia in 2004. As a result, they were docked vital championship points on the grounds that the governing body, FIFA, had rules insisting on a two-piece outfit. The Cameroon's defense was that they had merely joined the two pieces together. Despite this setback, it can be predicted that the sport of soccer will, in time, permit one-piece bodysuits in new climatically suitable and ergonomically appropriate fabrics.

According to Quinn (2002: 199), we are seeing a new dialogue between sports technicians and fashion designers that

> forever disrupt[s] the historical narrative of fashion, making it less apparent where the boundaries between fashion and sport now lie. From sportswear, fashion has learnt to protect and equip the body, while from fashion, sportswear has learned to decorate the body and tailor clothing to follow its shape. ... The combined sense of utility, functionality, performance and transformability inherent in sportswear is moving fashion forward.

But is this as radical as some commentators suggest? Quinn (2002: 200) concludes that the sports-techno revolution in fashion is overdue—a belated recognition of the centrality of characteristics of "functionality, performance and transformability" in clothing. In a sense, this is a revival of fundamental principles of clothing design developed among early societies, such as the waterproof, weatherproof clothes of the Inuit (parkas and sealskin boots) and Scandinavians (two-thumbed mittens knitted from human hair to repel water and provide a wet and dry thumb for fishermen) (O'Mahony and Braddock 2002: 92, 94, 111–12). The wheel of fashion may have turned full circle, with the sports obsession redrafting our ideas about clothing, dress, and bodily performance in general.

## CASE STUDY 26: Australian Bush Wear as Urban Chic

**Bush wear.** Photo: Jennifer Craik

Let's now turn to the example of Australian style, namely the legacy of "bush wear" in contemporary fashion. Bush wear evolved informally as the Australian outback was settled and settlers had to make do with uncertain supplies of clothes and fabric, harsh climatic and working conditions, and limited opportunities for dressing up in their finery. Clothes had to be practical and hard wearing. Over time, a distinctive colonialist mode of dress evolved, one that was intimately connected with the remoteness and mateship of outback life.

Similar fashions evolved in other settler societies such as South Africa, Canada, and New Zealand and in pre-independence India. In all cases, the clothes became synonymous with the qualities of hardship, practicality, and egalitarianism that characterized the pioneer settler in the bush—living with and overcoming adversity. Many commentators have noted that the bush is a foreign land to most Australians—Australia is one of the most urbanized countries in the world, with its population concentrated in coastal nodes. Yet the bush continues to occupy a central place in the national imagination and constructions of national identity and character.

The Akubra hat (a felted, broad-brimmed hat) and moleskins (brushed drill cotton trousers) form an indelible part of this vision in the eyes of not only Australians but also outsiders. American cultural analyst Alison Lurie, in her book *The Language of Clothes* (1992), identified the distinctive dress of Australians and Canadians as a legacy of regional and rural British dress that took on a peculiarly "colonial" set of adaptations. For Lurie (1992: 105), Australians provided a spectacle through their informal bush clothes: "khaki shirts and jackets, clumsy sheepskin vests, high leather boots and the famous bush hat."

Lurie's description of outback gear translates the vernacular into internationally recognized national costume and establishes a connection between the clothes and national character located in the outback: a masculine, outdoors, and outback folk community. Central, too, is the notion of a lifestyle that is casual and informal. These elements have characterized the distinctiveness of Australian style and fashion. The combination of the two influences (the bush and informality) has given freshness and vitality to what is in reality a language of mundane garments and combinations. In other words, a distinctively Australian sense of style has evolved from dominant cultural influences, climatic pressures, and lifestyles (see Symons 1983).

In this process, the role of outback clothes is symptomatic. The kind of outfits described by Lurie emerged in rural Australia as early settlers came to abandon the more formal wear favored by Europeans and develop specific kinds of clothing suitable for a tough, rough life in the outback—suitable for everyday working life yet smart enough to wear to town. These clothes seem to have had a range of sources: elements of some military clothing (khaki shirts and shorts, hard-wearing boots, adaptations of the **slouch hat**), while other elements may have been borrowed from American settlers, especially those involved in gold digging and westward settlement (e.g., moleskins). Other elements were devised or adapted in Australia.

Margaret Maynard (1994a) suggests that the concept of Australian bush clothes was itself a myth that stemmed from the widespread mythology of the outback, the bush, and egalitarianism that came to characterize ideas about Australia in the mid- to late nineteenth century. The centrality of outback life on farms and goldfields in accounts and representations of colonial Australia invoked a polarization of bush versus city and men versus women. The life of the bush and dress associated with it were resolutely masculine (as in Lurie's depiction) and this informed emerging concepts of national identity and character. By the 1890s, the bushman was "the one powerful and unique national type," kitted out in "a broad-brimmed felt hat, riding boots and moleskin trousers" (Maynard 1994a: 176).

Yet these were the clothes of the bosses—the squatters and property owners. Workers wore very different outfits—flannel shirts and trousers, jackets, and the like. That is to say, there were quite evident class differences between the bosses and the workers, yet these differences were elided in the elevation of outback wear as *the* clothing of the iconic Australian. Within this genre, it was the cream of outback gear—the most expensive and exclusive—that became synonymous with national identity. Cheaper brands were undoubtedly more common and more popular but did not achieve iconic status. Bush wear was also quintessentially masculine, the exclusive province of "blokes."

According to Maynard (1994a: 179), women in outback Australia "were completely excluded from the folklore of the typical Australian and his dress," and accounts of their clothing and interest in fashion largely derive from letters and diaries from the period. While the everyday demands of outback life necessitated hard-wearing clothing, many women retained best clothes for special occasions and photographic opportunities (see Maynard 1994b).

Yet there is some evidence in recent studies of a strong interest in clothes and fashion among outback women, with clear codes and rules about who could wear what and when. Much of this has been gleaned from photographic records. But insofar as representations of bush women and their dress occurred, they depict such women as "surrogate" men—as "unaffected, fearless and frank" or as having "acquired a kind of second-rate masculinity" (Maynard 1994a: 176; see also Elliott 1997).

The situation changed somewhat during the 1920s and 1930s, when *The Squatter's Daughter* and aviatrix role models enabled the construction of female bush figures, concepts that were also dependent on the influence of modernity in shaping new ideas of Australian nationality and culture. Even so, the outback has remained the primary province of men and rugged masculinity.

Of all the garments that became identified as bush wear, the Akubra hat perhaps epitomizes the look. These hats, made from rabbit fur in a mechanized felt-making process, date from the 1870s (Eager 1998). The label Akubra was coined in 1918 and has become synonymous with the hats themselves. Initially, the hats were popular with workingmen, especially those working outdoors. The securing of contracts to manufacture military slouch hats in both world wars gave the company its strength. In the 1950s Akubra won the lucrative contract to produce Stetsons, thus guaranteeing international recognition.

Not only has the name Akubra become the colloquial term for "hat" in Australia, but the Akubra has become an icon of Australianness and a favorite gift for visiting dignitaries—and souvenir for tourists.

Playing on other Australian myths, the Akubra is promoted as having been worn by "the famous and the infamous" around the world, from bush rangers to athletic stars to celebrities. In recent years, Akubra has expanded its range to meet the tastes of different groups of consumers. The best-selling styles, however, have retained names resonant of the Aussie outback tradition: Cattleman, Territory, Snowy River, Stockman, Plainsman, Bronco, Pastoralist, the Arena, Coober Pedy, and Coolabah.

Despite the growing diversification of the market for Akubras within Australia, the Akubra has also become synonymous with a concern for the rural sector and, more recently, regional Australia. Thus it is that politicians venturing out into rural electorates shed their suits and don an Akubra because, as Maynard (2001: 182) notes, "Akubra-wearing politicians send messages about their commitment to rural values by the signage of their headwear." The Akubra hat has become the most visible icon of the outback and the epitome of outback gear.

The total range of bush wear products—boots, moleskins (shirts, jeans, and skirts), oilskins, leather goods, camping gear, and riding gear—has come to epitomize "a strong image of the bush that tourists identify as being uniquely Australian" (Collins 1997). In recent years, bush wear companies have embarked on aggressive marketing campaigns on a global scale, with retailing and advertising accompanied by snazzy Web sites and sophisticated distribution techniques. This is indicative of not only the success of these companies and products but their integration into something that is recognized as distinctively Australian and that appeals to locals and visitors alike.

The appeal of bush wear has also migrated from the bush to the city and from work clothes to fashion clothes. Increasingly, the sales pitch is increasingly toward the urban yuppie and international consumer to buy garments that exude nostalgia for a dreamtime. Items such as traditional oilskin coats (or Driza-bones) as well as new ranges of casual clothes for men, women, young people, and children are indicative of the reorientation of outback gear to new consumer markets.

Yet recent collections have also tried to balance contemporary lifestyles and urban living with traditional images of bush wear and outback life like mustering and horse riding. As the marketing reveals, the continuation of traditional approaches to manufacturing, design, and production—preferably within a family- or at least Australian-owned company—is part of this appeal of bush wear to an essential sense of Australianness and a sense of national identification and belonging. It is a form of simulacrum that draws on an imaginary and nostalgic idea of the Australian outback, but increasingly the bush comes to the city—and other global spaces. This example underscores the importance of modes of representation to popularize—even globalize—fashion and dress trends. Without the popularization of the image and brand recognition of bush wear in popular culture, it might have remained just clothes for "bushies" in the outback.

## CASE STUDY 27: Retailing Erotic Lingerie

Lingerie window display

Brevity is the soul of lingerie. (Dorothy Parker)

From the 1960s, lingerie became the target of erotic retailing, which aimed to promote products and images that were sexually arousing but not pornographic. This phenomenon seemed to be associated with a combination of factors: new approaches to sexuality and sexual identity, the phenomenon of feminism, the growing role of women and girls in public life, subcultures such as punk, and the revolution in sports and activity clothes (Bressler, Newman, and Proctor 2003; Fontanel 1992). Forms of erotic retailing included the opening of sex shops, mail-order and later electronic retailing, and the production of new types of sex products—underwear, sex toys, and fetish items.

The new stores contrasted with the traditional sex shops located in seedy backstreets selling pornographic (and often illegal) merchandise to men in trench coats. The perception of sex stores changed as the number of new-style stores increased as government began to legalize pornography. Scandinavia and Western Europe—where there were already so-called marital aid shops, which sold sex technologies, erotic and exotic lingerie, contraceptives, films, and literature—led the charge.

In the United Kingdom, the first entrepreneur to dabble in sexy or erotic lingerie was Janet Reger, who started her business in 1958, though it really took off in the late 1970s. Lingerie party queen Ann Summers opened her first store in 1970, and Victoria's Secret also began in the early 1970s, primarily as a mail-order company. Agent Provocateur was set up by Vivienne Westwood's son Joseph Corré in 1994. In the United States, Good Vibration set up in the 1990s. In 2001, Sam Roddick—daughter of the Body Shop's Anita Roddick—opened Coco de Mer in London. Most of these enterprises combined shops with mail-order and catalog retailing.

Tupperware-style parties were the mainstay of Ann Summers, who encouraged working-class women to get an introduction to the world of erotica through alcohol-fuelled parties in friends' homes, where trying on erotic merchandise occurred amid ribald joking and comments about their partners. As public and media acceptance of erotica grew, retailing moved from behind closed doors and shop fronts to entertainment venues where men performed and stripped for all-women audiences, thus redressing the historic existence of female reviews targeting male consumers, which persists in the form of lap-dancing clubs and pole dancing.

**Agent Provocateur shop**

The rapid expansion of erotic lingerie retailing indicates how much moral standards were changing and created a distinction—albeit controversial—between shops selling hard-core pornographic material and those selling sex toys and soft porn with adult-only provisos. Central to the marketing strategies of the new-generation retailers was the need to make the products as well as the mode of selling attractive to women—or at least not threatening to women. So instead of blacked-out shop fronts in seedy backstreets, this new generation of erotic stores was located in mainstream shopping precincts and emphasized attractive and eye-catching displays of their products.

Increasingly, the new generation of erotic retailing involves online retailing offering a range of products including sex toys, accessories, books and magazines, DVDs, clothing, and advisory services. The design of erotic lingerie has changed in concert with this trend (Storr 2003). This reflects the ambivalent and ambiguous connotations of erotic lingerie. As recent commentators have noted,

> there is a double meaning of underwear; it covers up and acts as sexual signal or substitute of the body or (for fetishists) becomes the sexual object itself. (Kent and Brown 2006: 204)

There is now a much greater range of fabrics, ornamentation, finishings, and color in erotic lingerie to make it attractive to both women wearing the lingerie and the observers, who are nominally male. The use of silk and embroidery is designed both to make the garments more seductive and to satisfy the narcissistic and autoerotic desires of the wearers, embodying what one erotic chain calls "Naughty but Nice."

Women were becoming more articulate about matters to do with eroticism and sex and increasingly becoming the initiators rather than passive recipients of sexual desire. Subcultures such as punk contributed to this by promoting extreme sexuality in sadomasochistic clothing and performances. They combine images of prostitution and **fetishism** and promote extreme sexual rebellion as an antidote to conventional morality. In mainstream culture, the advent of body-conscious athletic and exercise regimes, in conjunction with the whole new approach to sports and leisure wear, placed a previously untapped emphasis on showing off the body and its clothed and unclothed silhouette.

The dance wear designs of the 1980s created a demand for body-clinging lingerie, epitomized by the popularity of the G-string in the 1990s and the increasing use of black underwear. Until then, black underwear had largely been associated with infusing "its wearers with the erotic charge of racialised and therefore transgressive sexuality" (Fields 2006: 611). By then, erotic lingerie and erotic garments had explicitly inflected designer fashion with fabrics appearing regularly on the catwalks, such as leather, rubber, and **PVC.** Before long, lingerie and underwear had become outerwear.

Nonetheless, women have maintained clear distinctions between lingerie that is "respectable" and lingerie that is "about sex" (regarded as sleazy or "harlot" clothes). Debate persists as to whether lingerie is important because of what it *does* or because of what it *means,* but perhaps it is a combination of the two (Amy-Chinn, Jantzen, and Østergaard 2006). Women under the age of forty-five are more likely to buy and wear erotic lingerie, and lifestyle/stage of life is also related to consumer habits. There are also cultural differences in the attitudes of women toward lingerie, which determine their consumer behavior. Above all it seems that women want to be seen as "being sexy the 'right' way" (Amy-Chinn et al. 2006: 388).

As recent fashions in erotic lingerie suggest, the play between the clothed and the unclothed persists as the primary driver of lingerie habits, as the following quotation makes clear.

> The rather radical shift from **thongs** to boy-shorts is probably best understood according to "laws of fashion." ... Whereas g-strings have a sensual effect by unveiling the body, boy-shorts can be erotic precisely because they veil the body, and leave things up to the (imagined) spectator's imagination. An explicit period is followed by a more discreet one; thongs may become not respectable—an outdated token. (Amy-Chinn et al. 2006: 399)

Erotic lingerie has come a long way from the licentious titillation of whalebone corsets and fishnet stockings, but it seems that some form of cover over the naked body in intimate encounters remains the impulse for sensuality and sexuality.

Jennifer Craik and Sharon Peoples

## CASE STUDY 28: Oliviero Toscani's Advertisements for Benetton

The fashion house of Benetton was established in 1965 in Treviso, Italy, by the Benetton siblings: Luciano, Giuliana, Gilberto, and Carlo. They were manufacturers of high-quality colorful yet affordable knitwear aimed at the prêt-à-porter market. It was a successful company but constrained by its orientation to a primarily domestic client base. Its transformation into a globally recognized brand was largely due to the phenomenal success of the advertising campaigns of Oliviero Toscani between 1983 and 2000. Currently there are 7,000 shops in 120 countries. Since 2000 they have opened a number of superstores in Moscow; Paris; Cardiff, Wales; Kyoto and Osaka, Japan; St. Moritz, Switzerland; and Hong Kong.

Capitalizing on the advertising profile, Benetton also established a then-unique system of computer-coordinated and high-tech production called Robot Store Logistics. This system organizes the entire manufacturing and distribution of the entire process from cutting and dyeing of raw materials to manufacture, quality control, distribution, and stocktaking. This system means that they have almost no warehousing, thus reducing the cost of storage and excess production of less successful lines. In 2000, they set up Fabrica, a center of research and development of strategies for improving fabric quality and design techniques. Part of their success has been due to this innovative approach to all aspects of apparel production and retailing. This model has since been adopted by other companies such as Zara and H&M.

With revenue in 2008 of $2,8005 million, half the sales are from sportswear and accessories under the brands Benetton, Benetton 012, Sisley, Killer Loop, Playlife, Zerotondo, and Tutti i Colori del Mondo (United Colors of Benetton). The remainder of sales comes from the licenses for accessories, underwear, beachwear, cosmetics, and bed linen. They have also acquired brands such as Nordica and Prince Rollerblade.

The turning point for their success was the development of the United Colors of Benetton brand, with its controversial advertising campaign (Falk 1997; Salvemini 2002). From 1966 to 1983, advertising campaigns were traditional, although in the mid-1970s, they used celebrities such as Mick Jagger, Andy Warhol, and Frank Zappa to appeal to the youth market and attempt to build an international profile.

Toscani was already a controversial figure in advertising. Born in Milan in 1942, he was captivated by his father's occupation as a photojournalist for the newspaper *Corriere della Sera.* As a teenager, he began to take photographs for the newspaper. Toscani then studied art in Zurich but increasingly began to mix and manipulate his artistic images with those of the mass media. Gradually his unique approach to photography emerged from this mix. He first gained attention around 1972 for his advertisements for Jesus Jeans, in which he depicted the back of a girl in very tight denim Jesus shorts with the slogan "Who loves me follows me." This attracted an outcry from the Vatican, and the poster was censored and withdrawn from public display.

In 1983 Toscani was given the task of taking the Benetton brand out of Italy, positioning and promoting it to an international audience. While still emphasizing the themes of youth, happiness, and color, Toscani abandoned scenic locations and celebrity models for abstracted representation of adults and children of all races wearing colorful clothing. This appealed to multiple global markets. In subsequent campaigns, Toscani emphasized ethnicity and incorporated folk references to highlight the global village through juxtaposition. This conveyed messages of racial tolerance and international harmony rather than simply advertising Benetton's clothes. These eye-catching advertisements inevitably created controversy and made Benetton a household brand worldwide.

Some of Toscani's campaigns featured, for example, photographs of prepubescent children portrayed as Adam and Eve in blue denim, children with animal face masks, parodies of famous paintings, black and white toddlers sitting on potties against a field of warm gray, and an array of multicolored condoms. Another advertisement showing a black mother breastfeeding a white baby evoked the American memory of black wet nurses succoring white babies and escalated the public debate about whether Benetton's advertisements were pushing the accepted boundaries of advertising.

Toscani's advertising campaigns became increasingly and overtly political, with each successive campaign reigniting public censure. Images of a multiracial family, a bloody newborn baby still attached to the umbilical cord, and a young priest and nun kissing appeared between 1989 and 1991.

Beginning in 1992 Toscani increasingly became obsessed with extreme realism and incorporated news photographs of major disasters in his advertisements, including terrorist bombings, electric chairs, a deathbed scene of a man with AIDS and his family, refugees clambering desperately up the side of an already overcrowded boat, and the bloodied body of a Mafia victim, as well as the alienation of an albino African.

His work then moved on to reflect environmental concerns, showing images of oil tanker spillage on wildlife and pigs foraging in a garbage dump. In 1995 he photographed a naked hermaphrodite. In 1996 he focused on racial tolerance, with three hearts bearing the words *red*, *black,* and *yellow*. In 1996–97, images of the world food crisis appeared. Then Toscani produced a series around nudity, including an array of penises, women's genitals, and men tattooed as HIV positive, a theme he returned to in subsequent campaigns. As well as issues around homosexuality, Toscani also tackled disability. His final controversial series in 2000 featured portraits of American criminals on death row.

Taking this wide range of themes and addressing major public debates, Toscani and Benetton attracted controversy as well as publicity. A moral panic emerged about the appropriateness of these confronting and politicized images and themes. As a result of pressure exerted in the United States, Benetton agreed to withdraw some advertisements, much to Toscani's anger. It was not only the death row series but also the interviews with the condemned men, which accompanied the ads, that brought the misunderstanding and disagreements between the photographer and Benetton to a head. This led to dissolution of their long-standing partnership.

Toscani has remained one of the foremost influential contemporary commercial photographers, still in demand for his fashion shoots and avant-garde approach to consumer culture. Subsequent Benetton advertising campaigns returned to more traditional forms of promotion of the Benetton brand, but they have failed to recapture the attention that Toscani attracted.

Jennifer Craik and Sharon Peoples

# chapter 8

## the politics of fashion

**CHAPTER OUTLINE**

I. What are the politics of fashion?
II. Endogenous and exogenous factors
III. Fashion and colonialism
IV. Fashion and postcolonialism
V. Conclusion: global fashion futures?
Case study 29: The politics of veiling
Case study 30: Renegotiating Chinese fashion
Case study 31: Indian fashion: from diasporas to designers
Case study 32: Burberry's brand of Britishness

**WHAT DOES THIS CHAPTER COVER?**

The final chapter offers some insights into the politics of fashion. Sometimes fashion seems a long way from the arena (or bear pit) of politics, and yet fashion provokes fierce debates within politics—for example, concerning labor practices, the exploitation of non-industrialized countries, excessive production of waste, conspicuous consumption, elitism, and oppression. So while fashion may seem to be just about clothing habits, in fact politics is deeply implicated within its underpinnings, ideologies, and practices.

In this chapter, we begin by exploring the different types of politics that are involved in fashion, namely, relations with authoritative politics, anti-establishment politics, identity politics, and industry politics. The chapter then investigates the link between fashion developments and colonialism before looking at more recent trends in fashion in the postcolonial era. Finally, the conclusion to the chapter and the book speculates on the future of fashion in a global culture.

Case studies examine several issues that illustrate the themes of the chapter. First, the reinvention of the custom of veiling among Muslim women is explored, followed in the second case study by an examination of the reinvention of Chinese identity in fashion. The third case study looks at two different yet connected expressions of contemporary Indiana identity in fashion, namely, the transitional fashions of the Indian diaspora and the emergence of a contemporary high-fashion culture in India. The final case study locates the appropriation of a sense of British identity within the operations of the successful apparel brand Burberry.

## i. what are the politics of fashion?

*Fashion is not something that exists in dresses only. Fashion is in the sky, fashion has to do with ideas, the way we live, what is happening. (Coco Chanel)*

*Fashion is born by small facts, trends, or even politics, never by trying to make little pleats and furbelows*, by trinkets, by clothes easy to copy, or by the shortening or lengthening of a skirt. (Elsa Schiaparelli)*

* **Furbelow** *C18. 1. A flounce; the pleated border of a petticoat or gown. Now often in* **pl.** *as a contemptuous term for showy ornaments or trimming. (The Shorter Oxford English Dictionary)*

Fashion has been analyzed from various perspectives: as a symbolic system, an aesthetic form, a global industry, a media phenomenon, an individual indulgence or sign of group membership, and a technique of creating and re-creating a sense of self and persona. The statements above, made by two of the most significant fashion designers of the twentieth century, place the determinants of fashion in wider cultural and political contexts than simply the cut of a garment or clever choice of embellishment. Yet popular perceptions of fashion generally cast it as ephemeral, trivial, and idiosyncratic. In a much-cited quip, British designer Bruce Oldfield defined fashion as "more usually a gentle progression of revisited ideas." As a result, fashion has largely remained on the periphery of analysis as an important force shaping societies and cultures. Moreover, many students of fashion are not interested in the study of politics or do not think of fashion as a political phenomenon. More often than not, they are motivated by a desire to make clothes that make an impact and, hopefully, set a new style or trend.

However, this chapter argues that clothing and its regulation have been a powerful means of establishing power relations, reaffirming hierarchical structures, articulating gendered habits, and asserting ethnic and cultural distinctiveness. Very often, overt political action and ideology have been at the heart of clothing conventions. As we have seen in the preceding chapters, there are many instances where fashion and clothing are a lot more than froth and bubble. Fashion and dress—throughout history—not only have been controversial but have been implicated in different kinds of politics. Examples include the politics of employment conditions, exploitation of third-world resources and labor, legislative regulation of clothing, the use of clothing in political movements and actions, and even the codes of dress adopted by high-profile politicians (especially women). Contemporary debates about the veiling of Muslim women, the production of sneakers in offshore factories, the weight and age of fashion models, and the appropriation of indigenous motifs in Western fashion are all examples of the **cultural politics** of fashion.

Daniel Roche's (1996) masterful analysis of the role of clothing in the maintenance and transformation of political rule and the rise of civil society in France's ancien régime demonstrates the combination of overt and subtle ways in which fashion and dress can become political mechanisms, tools, and weapons. Wendy Parkins's (2002) anthology shows how centrally fashion and dress have been implicated in political participation and protest, in both forging inclusive political regimes and forming people's political identities as citizens.

She includes studies of the role of clothing in revolutionary France, imperial Russia, the suffragette movement, the Italian fascist Blackshirts, the Spanish Falange, Australian indigenous politics, and contemporary Chinese citizenship, as well as the role of the scouting movement in empire building. But studies like these are rare.

So we have an odd situation where the phenomenon of fashion can be shown to be highly political and politicized, creating controversies and public debate that sometimes leads to severe repercussions—and yet most followers of fashion do not usually think of fashion as being political! This seems to have occurred because fashion tends to be appropriated as costume or style, while other aspects of its symbolic systems and referents are neglected. Hence, the neglect of or inattention to the cultural politics of fashion may not be unique or idiosyncratic. Many other aspects of fashion are also eschewed in contemporary scholarship (e.g., in sociology, anthropology, discourse analysis, and semiotics). Possibly this is because serious fashion studies has only been with us for a relatively short time. As Sophie Woodward (2002: 346) argued in a review of Berg's *Dress, Body, Culture* series,

**the analytic focus upon dress would seem to lend itself to an approach wherein the materiality of the clothing is central to the understanding of facets such as culture, identity and gender. Yet, with a few notable exceptions, the clothing—ostensibly the subject matter of the series—remains a ghostly presence, coming to appear immaterial by the very lack of engagement with the physicality of clothing itself.**

Here she is pointing to the lack of analytical attention to clothing as items of materiality—despite the fact that such appreciations are the "ghostly presence" behind our readings and understandings of them. It is also apparent that the political meanings and uses of fashion and clothing are largely underemphasized—even when fashion writers accept that there are political messages in clothing. However, these reflections are usually more an aside or footnote rather than a substantive departure point in their commentary.

Hence, we could take this critique further and argue that not only is the materiality of fashion and dress largely absent from discussion and analysis but so too are the circumstances in which certain modes of dress are proscribed, prescribed, contested, and fetishized, that is to say, the ways in which dress is understood and circulates as political force within the broader polity. I have begun this process in a modest way in relation to the politics of uniforms (Craik 2005)—but this chapter aims to identify a more systematic representation of the cultural politics of dress in its widest forms.

## ii. endogenous and exogenous factors

So, the cultural politics of fashion are very broad and involve multiple competing domains. The term *cultural politics* can be defined as the play between endogenous forces within the fashion system and exogenous forces from the outside that converge to shape the production, circulation, and consumption of cultural products, ideas, and phenomena.

Some of these factors are external, such as regulatory mechanisms, and some are internal to the fashion industry, for example, rules for membership of elite designer groups and craft professions and stylistic consensus about trends.

Sometimes, external and internal political forces converge. For example, many fashion designers are inspired by political sentiments, especially young street designers. Kathryn Hamnett's T-shirts emblazoned with political slogans in the 1980s are an oft-cited case. The widespread use of the image of Che Guevara and the Chinese red star on fashion apparel are other examples. The popularity of wearing the Palestinian *kuffiya* (head scarf) without any reference to its political symbolism typifies this appropriation. While some political forces may be overt and explicit (e.g., etiquette manuals, sanctions), others are covert and implicit (e.g., peer pressure to conform to a stylistic convention, consensus among key trendsetters). Here, four types of fashion politics are proposed: authoritative politics, anti-establishment politics, identity politics, and industry politics.

**Chinese red star cap.** Photo: S. Tormod. Creative Commons Attribution-Share Alike 2.0 Generic License

### Authoritative (Or Top-Down) Politics

The authoritative cultural politics of fashion entails overt political uses of fashion as political statements. In some cases, the clothes or particular garments acquire politicized connotations or become unambiguous political statements. These politics are imposed by an institution (religion, army, school, employer), regime (legislature, corporate culture, police, or security force), or regulatory mechanism (legal provisions, protocols, international covenant, penal codes). Examples include sumptuary laws; religious prescriptions or proscriptions, such as veiling for women or bans on immodest dress; cultural conventions such as business suits for male professionals and politicians; and power dressing for female executives and "femocrats" (female bureaucrats).

The best-known example of clothing regulation is sumptuary laws (see chapter 1), which have been enacted by many regimes—China, the Ottoman Empire, courtly societies, Western Europe—and even attempted in the United States. Such regulations are justified as modulating "gender, communal, political, and social relations within and among ... administrative, military, and subject classes" (Quataert 1997: 404). Similar overt forms of clothing regulation were implemented (with varying degrees of success and resistance) in colonial contexts by administrators, political regimes, and missionaries (e.g., Reid 1988; Schulte Nordholt 1997a, 1997b). In the twentieth century, an example of the imposition of clothing codes on citizens occurred during the leadership of Mustafa Kamal Atatürk (known as the father of Turkey) during the 1930s. Atatürk was keen to adopt Western and modern practices in preference to Islamic ways and customs. As part of this strategy, he banned men from wearing the form of headwear traditionally worn by men, the **fez,** and opposed the veiling of women. More generally, he discouraged the wearing of customary dress.

Another similar example was driven by the opposite desire, namely the desire to reject Western clothes and customs and impose "revolutionary" ones. This involved banning the traditional robes of courtiers, the Western-style clothing of the educated middle class, and the traditional cheongsam (also called also called **qipao**) worn by many Chinese women. Instead, loyal comrades were exhorted to wear loose blue jackets and pants typical of the peasants. This outfit became notorious as the Mao suit during the Cultural Revolution of the 1960s (see case study 30).

These examples illustrate how clothing codes have been employed as a force in civilizing societies or creating a civil society, for example, as associated with colonial and postcolonial politics (Parkins 2002). The role of clothing prescriptions and proscriptions by colonial administrations is discussed later.

### Anti-Establishment (Or Bottom-Up) Politics

This type of fashion politics bubbles up from an ideology, subculture, or political movement among groups seeking political or cultural change. Examples include T-shirts with political slogans, the adoption of military or camouflage gear by revolutionary groups and "freedom fighters," distinctive subcultural dress codes, and the adoption of distinctive garments or symbols by alternative political groups. Sometimes these political types overlap; for example, a clothing statement may start out as anti-establishment but be taken up as a symbol of a political movement or expression of identity politics.

#### *Ideological Anti-Establishment Politics*

Here, a group opposes a dominant ideology, but within the parameters of the political system.

**Atatürk**

Examples include conservation or green movements where activists use existing political channels as well as community mobilization and media attention to expose issues and advocate new political approaches.

The punk movement began in the 1970s as an anti-establishment movement, confronting, shocking, and rebelling against the ideology of democratic liberalism epitomized by Western democracies, initially in Britain. Punks advocated anarchy and the celebration of fascism. Stylistically, this took the form of radical clothing, for example, pastiches and reconstructions of other styles emblazoned with slogans that offended mainstream values and conventional fashion. These were accessorized by symbols such as crucifixes, swastikas, iron crosses, and depictions of controversial political leaders (such as Hitler, Marx, Stalin, and Mussolini).

Punks were recognizable by their extreme-colored radical hair designs (such as Mohawks and spiky styles) and heavy-duty, thick-soled Doc Martens boots. Leather, chains, body **piercing,** tattoos, badges, and chunky jewelry completed the look. The punk movement was galvanized by punk music and anti-establishment sentiments among disaffected parts of youth culture. The best-known exponents were bands like the Sex Pistols, the Ramones, Siouxsie and the Banshees, and the Clash as well as the musical and fashion exploits of Malcolm McLaren and Vivienne Westwood.

**Mao suit worn by Deng Xiaoping.** Photo: NASA

Punk also became implicated in racist political movements even though advocates of punk have subsequently denied accusations of racist intentions. In interviews with the curators of the "Surfers Soulies Skinheads and Skaters" exhibit for the Victoria and Albert, skinheads "were adamant that they should not be portrayed as fascist and racist thugs" (de la Haye and Dingwall 1997: np). The political party the British National Front, whose members dressed as skinheads, opposed immigration policies and was accused of racism. Their views were purportedly echoed by rock star Eric Clapton at a concert in 1976. The conjunction of these expressions of racism drew fierce opposition from the mainstream media, which galvanized public opinion, culminating in Rock against Racism campaigns and concerts. By the 1980s, what had begun as an anti-establishment ideological movement had become much more of a subcultural phenomenon influencing the fad for antifashion, a neo-punk music scene, and popularization of punk fashion as mainstream.

### *Subcultural Anti-Establishment Politics*

Many subcultures have begun as informal movements against establishment ideologies. The hippy movement of the late 1960s epitomizes a subculture that galvanized a number of anti-establishment causes into a visible subculture that adopted a distinctive form of dress that became a fashion. The term *hippy* came from the word *hep* (meaning "to be with it"), which was used during the jitterbug craze of 1930s America. The word evolved into *hip* and *hipster* and was incorporated into the bebop and beatnik subcultures of the 1950s. Beatnik style influenced the youth dropouts of the 1960s, who coalesced as the first hippies in San Francisco's Haight-Ashbury neighborhood and New York's East Village in 1966. Hippies rejected "straight" society, namely, mainstream American values of authoritarian politics, institutions, and commercialization of culture. Public hysteria about this new subculture was captured by an issue of the influential magazine *Time,* which devoted its July 7, 1967, issue to explaining "The Hippie: The Philosophy of a Subculture" to a bewildered and frightened American public.

The hippy mantra was cooperation (love, peace, and goodwill—"flower power") instead of competition (war, profit, aggression). Their slogan was "Turn on, tune in, drop out." Hippies set out a plan to establish alternative communities based on equality among all members and relying on self-sufficiency and consensus. Drugs like marijuana and LSD were a mind-expanding part of everyday hippy life. But other stylistic forces were also part of the hippy subculture: the vibrant alternative popular music of musicians like the Beatles, Jefferson Airplane, Big Brother and the Holding Company, Cream, Bob Dylan, and Jimi Hendrix; alternative architecture and design, such as the invention of revolutionary geodesic buildings, which became synonymous with hippydom; the anti–Vietnam War movement, which was boosted by the spread of the hippy movement among young people; anti-racist campaigns; organic farming; alternative education; and alternative religion and spiritualism. In addition, in America, young people in huge numbers began to travel what became known as the Hashish Trail from London to Southeast Asia

The subculture gained further attention due to the actions of high-profile celebrities like Timothy Leary (who advocated drug taking), Jack Kerouac (who wrote the beat generation bible *On the Road,* in 1957), Hunter S. Thompson (and his demolition of the 1968 presidential election in *Fear and Loathing in Las Vegas*), Andy Warhol (who scandalized the art world with his pop art and outrageous lifestyle), Ravi Shankar (who mentored George Harrison and spawned a Western craze for Eastern music and religion), and Abbie Hoffman (who began the Yippies). The late 1960s was a turbulent time with countless major disruptive political events, including the messy withdrawal from Vietnam and its aftermath, race riots and the assassinations of Martin Luther King and Bobby Kennedy, the establishment of proto-terrorist movements like the Black Panthers and the Weathermen, a perceived drug crisis in the Western world, and the death of the

**Hippy.** Photo: Alexander Konovalenko. Copyright 2005 Alexander Konovalenko Creative Commons Attribution-Share Alike 3.0 Unported License

Cuban revolutionary Che Guevara in Bolivia (by American-trained troops).

Yet many memories of the hippy era are of guys in paisley shirts and bell-bottom trousers and girls in lace tops and tie-dyed skirts; of colored eye glasses, hippy beads, long hair, velvet pants, Indian shirts, unisex gear, and patchwork shoulder bags. The image of the August 1968 Woodstock Festival as a peaceful gathering of a half-million people to hear music "that changed the world" is perhaps the most potent image of a subculture that is remembered as being benign and stylish. Although the fortunes of the hippy movement arguably died at the Altamont Free Concert later in 1968, hippy subculture remains a model of anti-establishment cultural politics.

In 2000 the Kent State University Museum celebrated hippy fashion in an exhibition called

"Revolutionizing Fashion: The Politics of Style"—ironic, given the 1970 shootings of Kent State students opposing the American invasion of Cambodia. Hippy fashion borrowed from folk cultures to produce clothes with bright colors and flamboyant styles juxtaposed with mundane garments like jeans and T-shirts to proclaim their non-conformism and anti-establishment beliefs. As with other subcultures, although the subcultural craze waned in the early 1970s, the uptake of hippy-inspired fashion and style in mainstream street wear and designer collections continued, perhaps epitomized by Yves Saint Laurent's succession of "ethnic" collections.

### *Political Movement Politics*

In this case, groups forge political collective identities through fashion—including statements of resistance to **colonialism** and movements for nationalism (e.g., the Indonesian cap or *peci*), independence (e.g., Ghandi's adoption of the **dhoti** in the Indian independence movement), and resistance (e.g., the black berets and military-like clothing of the IRA or Black Panthers), and the adoption of the black-and-white checked head scarf in the Palestinian campaign for a homeland, which later became an alternative fashion item. This type of cultural politics is discussed later in this chapter.

### Identity Politics

The cultural politics of identity in fashion emanates from particular feminist, queer, ethnic, and religious subgroups. The slogan "The personal is political" was a common catchphrase in the 1970s expressing the belief that one should articulate one's ideology though one's behavior and appearance. Examples include the veiling (and reveiling) of Muslim women (discussed later), cross-dressing, reinvention of "ethnic" costume, and power dressing for female executives.

Symbols of less radical or "conformist" uses may include the conscious adoption of business suits by the Japanese and Korean socialist parties in the 1970s to signify they were able to be responsible, run businesses, and engage with the West. Although Western dress codes have become normative, some politicians have simultaneously revived customary and traditional ethnic costume, which is interspersed with Western dress. This is especially noticeable among female Korean politicians, who have a wardrobe of Western and "exotic" garments, which are worn on different occasions (Goldstein-Gidoni 1999; Ruhlen 2003; Skov 2003; Soh 1992; Suga 1995). Libya's Colonel Muammar al-Gaddafi and Zimbabwe's President Robert Mugabe also mixed Western suits with customary garments.

The adoption of national dress, or the outlawing of other forms of dress, has been a common feature of colonized societies as part of the "civilizing" process of subjecting indigenous people to colonial administration and political regimes. While these may be effective at the time, there has often been overt or passive resistance and frequently the reinvention—or reimposition of—traditional or customary dress codes under postcolonial regimes. For example, in Zimbabwe, some British vestmental trappings remained, even amid the investiture of President Mugabe, although he also advocated customary national dress to show anti-British sentiment.

In the diasporic communities of the West, many groups have reinvented forms of customary dress to display their ethnic distinctiveness, including the hairstyles of the Hmong in the United States (Lynch 1995), head wraps of Jamaican-origin

**South Korean female politician with former U.S. Secretary of State, Condoleezza Rice.** Photo: Michael Gross/State Department

black British women (Tulloch 1998), and South Asian clothing identities in Britain (Dwyer 1999; Puwar 2002).

In Scotland, kilts—which themselves have multiple resonances—were once suppressed, then incorporated in military regiments (similar to Gurka uniforms in the British army). Subsequently, kilts became a symbol first of the folk heritage of "Scottishness" and later of the assertion of Scottish independence. Kilts have also been incorporated partially in the outfits of bagpipers in Hong Kong and troupes of acrobatic kung fu drummers as the symbol of the British colonial legacy in the period following unification with China.

A potent form of the cultural politics of identity concerns gender and sexuality. Symbols of gender are an intrinsic part of the language of clothes and conventionally signs of normative femininity and masculinity and the traditional sex roles associated with gender. However, the history of fashion is also littered with examples of fashion creating alternative messages and subversive symbols of gender and sexuality. Issues include the articulation of concepts of femininity, the impact of feminism on dress, the projection of masculinity, and the subgenres of gay and queer fashion and, more generally, of transgressive and "mobile" identities. Examples of the gender politics of fashion include

**Nelson Mandela.** Photo by Michelly Rall/WireImage. 2008 Michelly Rall

the choice of lounge suits among 1970s feminists (Entwistle 1997), gay clone dressing, dominatrix fashion, men in skirts and dresses (Bolton 2003), and coveralls for lesbians. Detailed studies include Paulicelli's (2002) study of the role of dress codes and gender and the politics of pre-fascist and fascist Italy.

## Industry Politics

Industry politics relates to the politics surrounding issues of production, distribution, and consumption of fashion. Instances of the cultural politics of the fashion industry include government subsidies, tariffs, assistance schemes and industry incentives, employment conditions (sweatshops and indentured factories), third-world exploitation for first-world luxury markets, distribution cartels, counterfeiting, contra-deals, celebrity endorsement, and advertorials.

Historically, there has been a tension between the need for large-scale factories for mass-produced fashion products (e.g., athletic shoes) and small-scale (artisan-based) companies for high-end, high-quality fashion products. Increasingly, large-scale production has moved offshore to a succession of cites and countries that can provide cheap labor and raw materials. This has inevitably aroused human rights concerns about employment conditions, quality control, ethical issues, and environmental concerns that some organizations, ethical designers and brands, and retailers have attempted to address. Despite the attention

**Kilts, Hong Kong.** Photo: Jennifer Craik

to offshore production issues, the situation is not much better in advanced societies engaged in fashion manufacture where patterns of immigration have been reflected in employment and manufacture (often small-scale family-based piecework—always exploitative). For example, Rabine and Kaiser (2006: 246–47) have exposed the "'disconnect' between dream machine representations for consumers and the grim realities facing immigrant garment workers" in Los Angeles. Although there have been sustained efforts to redress the worst features of the imbalance between the glamour of high fashion and the exploitation of production, contracts are often negotiated elsewhere before effective action can be taken.

Perhaps more so than conventional industries, the nature of the processes of design, production, distribution, marketing, and consumption of the fashion industry is highly complex and contentious. Because of this and its transnational interconnections, the fashion industry has been resistant to global reform or regularization. Many of these issues have been already examined in other chapters.

**Fairtrade Certified Cotton TShirt**

## iii. fashion and colonialism

As the examples above show, the cultural politics of fashion is a very broad topic. This chapter has explored some of the different ways in which clothing and dress codes have been employed in political circumstances. In most cases, these case studies cross the boundaries of different forms of politics. To summarize the argument, fashion has been used as a civilizing force in many societies, and therefore dress habits and behavioral codes are inherently sites of contestation. Consequently, dress has been the subject of forms of regulation throughout cultures and history both in preindustrial and industrial contexts. Obviously, in the minds of these government leaders, changing people's outward appearance, whether by force of law or social pressures, was a means of changing people's values.

The uses to which clothing can be put range from overt declarations of ideology or allegiance to disguises of oppositional or subversive political movements. This has worked in two ways. Some leaders and regimes have unquestioningly accepted Westernization as the path to modernization. Others have rejected Western ways and sought to impose indigenous or alternative cultural codes. These political struggles have entailed the use of clothing edicts (formal and informal) in an effort to persuade people to join a particular course of action and ideological outlook. The history of fashion over the past two to three centuries has been intimately bound up with the political and economic shifts under colonization and **postcolonialism**—and the cultural politics of fashion entailed therein. Although primarily focused on political revolution or resistance, many of these figures remained highly conscious of looking fashionable and wearing their revolutionary garb or symbols in a stylish manner.

There is a growing literature charting the role of dress codes and uniforms in explicit and covert campaigns to "civilize" the population in colonial and postcolonial contexts. Very often, colonists imposed dress codes that combined aspects of the uniforms of officials (military or administrative) with elements of local dress. Sometimes, indigenous rulers chose to wear European uniforms. For example, in the 1860s, Cambodia's King Norodom I was photographed in a French field marshal's uniform. Ten years later, he wore a French general's cap and jacket with a *sampot* (Edwards 2001). Still later, administrators adopted the colonial suit as their uniform. In some cases, locals used the adoption of Westernized dress codes in order to gain the approval of the colonists. At the same time, dress codes were a means of social control used by colonists over the colonized. Dress codes were also resorted to as a means of expressing nationalist and indigenous claims (Bean 1989; Callaway 1997; Edwards 2001; Schulte Nordholt 1997a, 1997b).

Cohn (1989: 304) has traced the role of clothing in Britain's colonization of India, arguing that the dispute about the Sikh turban was emblematic of clothing skirmishes in colonial India that eventually led to "the creation of a uniform of rebellion by the Indians in the twentieth century." At first, the British chose to dress distinctively in order to emphasize their difference from the locals, but soon, the exchange of clothing and fabric was recognized as a means to negotiate power:

**Clothes are not just body coverings and adornments, nor can they be understood only as metaphors of power and authority, nor as symbols; in many cases, clothes literally *are* authority. ... Authority is literally part of the body of those who possess it. It can be transferred from person to person through acts of incorporation, which not only create followers or subordinates, but a body of companions of the ruler who have shared some of his substance. (Cohn 1989: 312–13; see also Schulte Nordholt 1997a: 9)**

In establishing their colonial power, British rulers modified English modes of ceremonial dress to bestow on "deserving" Indians, while they borrowed some aspects of Indian dress for modified forms of ruling dress. But when Indian princes visited Queen Victoria at Windsor, they "were required ... to appear in their 'traditional' Indian royal dress rather than Western clothes" (Cohn 1989: 321). This two-way exchange of sartorial signs also occurred in the military, with British troops adopting some "Indian" affectations (e.g., cummerbunds and puggarees—linen covers wrapped around their wicker helmets or cloth caps and hats) and even turbans and scimitars (Cohn 1989: 324), while Indian troops were dressed in plain British military uniforms or as British fantasies of how exotic people should look.

Not surprisingly, when the push for Indian independence came, part of the struggle was a sartorial one with distinctive dress. This involved adopting a khaddar uniform of a white cotton dhoti, sari, kurta, and a small white cap (Cohn 1989: 343). Due to

**The landing of Columbus.** Library of Congress, Prints and Photographs Division, Washington, D.C

this distinctive dress, activists could be easily identified, and eventually, Gandhi made this outfit the "uniform of the Indian National Congress" (Cohn 1989: 344). Through manipulation of the meaning of cloth and clothing, Bean (1989: 373) suggests, the khaddar "had become, in Nehru's words, 'the livery of freedom.'"

In these processes, codes of civil dress and "uniform fever" were an essential tool in the transformation of far-flung outposts. Some genres, such as the safari suit and the sarong, have become permanent legacies of this era (Frederick 1997; Sekimoto 1997; van Dijk 1997). While men were more likely to be subject to explicit codes or uniforms, dress codes were also applied informally, though often ruthlessly, to girls and women (Callaway 1997; Locher-Scholten 1997; Taylor 1997). The imposition of school uniforms among girls proved an effective technique for instilling Western attitudes—especially the gendered identities and codes of conduct that were being instilled by the colonial administrators.

These instances illustrate that fashion has been a highly charged political tool in successive

**Gandhi statue**

**Prince Charles in safari suit.** Photo: Tim Graham/Getty Images

scenarios that have accompanied encounters between Western and Eastern forms of civility, especially in situations of colonial occupation and transformation and subsequent moves toward regaining independence and a sense of national identity. The impetus behind these examples of politicization has been a mixture of efforts to homogenize different cultures and impose visible and effective distinctions and hierarchies. Because of the materiality, tactility, and visibility of clothing, dress codes have proved to be an extremely flexible and ruthless way of achieving political, economic, administrative, and "civilizing" objectives.

While dress codes have been part and parcel of revolutionary, resistance, and self-determination movements, many of the key figures in these movements also recognized the politics of fashionable dress. Schulte Nordholt (1997a: 19) cites the obsession of Indonesia's President Sukarno with shirts: "When Hatta, Sjahrir, and Sukarno were imprisoned by the Dutch during the Revolution, they were allowed to ask for a limited number of things. Hatta wanted books, Sjahrir Dutch newspapers, and Sukarno a new Arrow shirt." As mentioned above, Nelson Mandela also carefully crafted an accessible political image through his choice of the long-sleeved Madiba shirt made from patterned cotton or silk and similar to Indonesian batik shirts. Garbed in this spectacular way, Mandela embodied the qualities given off by the shirt:

**It seems a relaxed, leisurely garment, a popular style with which the people can have sympathy. This constellation of meanings has suited the widely admired leader extremely well, and sits with the warm hearted, elder statesman image he has calculated in his later years. (Maynard 2004: 56–57)**

His statue in London, unveiled in 2007, depicts him in this costume. As this example illustrates, fashion can generate and reflect changing power balances between regions, countries, groups, and religions.

## iv. fashion and postcolonialism

One of the stylistic consequences of postcolonialism has been the invigoration of ethnic dress and ethnicity as fashion inspiration. In the fashion industry, designers are always looking for new inspirations and ideas. Inevitably, ethnic fashions, costumes, decorative motifs, ornaments, garments, and fabrics have figured strongly in designer collections, for example, in a number of Yves Saint Laurent's collections. This has popularized Western ideas of Japanese-ness, Chinese-ness, Orientalism, Gypsy-ness, and the like. These ethnic referents signify otherness and exoticism, and it is this richly connotative symbolism that has colored the persistence of ethnic dress as costume and fashion in transforming developing cultures. Examples abound in places such as Indonesia (Jones 2003; Molnar 1998; Niessen 2003b), China (Li 1998; Skov 2003), Vietnam (Jonsson and Taylor 2003), and Korea (Ruhlen 2003).

There are tensions between wearing Western clothes to appear modern and avoiding the negative moral messages often attached to such clothing, as well as debates about the messages conveyed by wearing customary dress or modified versions of customary dress. In the field of fashion, designers also struggle to reconcile the temptation to make ethnic and local references in their work by drawing on ethnic themes with the desire to compete in the global fashion market with designs that have a global resonance but still retain a touch of localism. In short, there is tension between global zeitgeist and its propulsion of local cultures to differentiate themselves through distinctive fashion statements and local variants

Even in Western fashion capitals and other cosmopolitan sites, the issue of ethnicity lurks beneath the surface as diasporic communities come to terms with blending in or standing out, sparking modern adaptive fashions such as the **shalwar kameez,** which has been popularized among Asian communities in the United Kingdom and ethnic-inspired high-fashion-with-modesty collections and providers such as Bombay Connection, EAST, and Damanis (Bhachu 2003; Dwyer 2006). As

**Cheongsam.** Robbie Sproule. 

these examples show, transnational flows between fashion capitals, aspirant fashion centers, and the rest of the world are palpable and virulent. As the length of fashion cycles decreases and fashion centers interpret trends in highly localized ways, the pace of fashion is constantly speeding up.

## v. conclusion: global fashion futures?

This chapter has located the study of fashion concepts within the wider politics in which the industry is located. By exploring the different dimensions of fashion as a political phenomenon and how the diverse ways of wearing clothes and being fashionable become politicized, we have attempted to hint at an underexplored agenda for fashion studies. As fashion becomes an increasingly globalized phenomenon with new patterns of fashion flows (from designer to sourcing of materials to sites of production, distribution, and consumption), new issues and challenges have been raised that will continue to transform the field of fashion.

Whether—as analysts—we are prepared to ask difficult questions and investigate contentious issues remains to be seen, but with the rapid growth of fashions studies as an academic field, there are many possibilities for new research into the political contours of fashion. Although traditionally, the fashion industry has been reluctant to be involved in cooperative research and sponsor empirical and critical research—beyond market research—while hiding behind the mantra of commercial in confidence—the time has come for a more engaged relationship between the industry, designers, and intellectuals. The generous involvement of Giorgio Armani and Condé Nast in staging the "Super Heroes" exhibition at the Museum of Modern Art in New York hints at a new dawn.

Some major issues and challenges face the future fashion industry and fashion culture. These include:

- **The impact of fast fashion on the sustainability of the industry in terms of resources, employment conditions, and accelerated fashion flows**
- **The extent to which eco (environmental) and ethical concerns among consumers will influence the reshaping of the fashion industry**
- **The degree to which social and political uncertainties will impose a negativity and obsession with destruction and disaster on fashion culture**
- **The ways in which new gender roles and alternative forms of sexuality might create different assumptions underpinning fashion design and practice**
- **The impact of the dissolution of "mediascapes" and public spaces and sites into a virtual reality of fashion representation and promotion**
- **The implications of new forms of clothing regulation, especially in Islamic culture**
- **The challenge of reconciling the pressure to achieve idealized body images with the increasing obesity epidemic within advanced societies**
- **The need to marshal new approaches to managing and sustaining the natural and manufactured (artificial) resources required in fashion production**
- **The significance of new patterns of fashion flows between traditional sites of fashion action and emerging centers of fashion designs, manufacture, distribution, consumption, and innovation**

These are the questions that face analysts of fashion.

Our fashions and dress do indeed wear our bodies. Perhaps, then, it is not surprising that the march of globalization and transnationalism has spurred a new phase of politicizing fashion and dress with the objective of both identifying with the global village and asserting distinctiveness and difference. As noted above, politicians—especially women—have been quick to recognize that their choice of attire is a critical factor in their public image. As Maynard (2004: 58) has suggested, "If the courtroom is a dramatic stage, how much more significant then is the global, political stage." Fashion has become a key political force that can make and—more importantly—break political careers and fortunes. Clothes do, indeed, maketh the man—or woman—but only when strategically calculated and cunningly contrived.

**Armani.** Photo by Dave Benett/Getty Images. 2003 Dave Benett

## CHAPTER SUMMARY

- The cultural politics of fashion refers to external and internal forces that converge to shape the structure and symbolic codes of fashion systems.
- There are four types of cultural politics of fashion: authoritative, anti-establishment, identity, and industry.
- Colonial powers used a mixture of formal and informal proscriptions and prescriptions concerning clothing and fashion as a visible index to, and tool of, policies designed to impose European economic, social, and cultural values on colonized people with the aim of creating their sense of a modern civility.

- Societies under colonial regimes used clothing and fashion systems and symbols to variously embrace, resist, modify, and/or reject colonist ways—for example, in struggles for nationalism, independence, and the assertion of cultural identity.
- Postcolonialism has witnessed the strategic use of clothing and fashion to assert cultural, ethnic and diasporic identities as well as renegotiate transnational exchanges in the global village.

## CASE STUDY 29: The Politics of Veiling

This case study explores a clothing practice that exemplifies the complexities and convergence of the cultural politics of fashion. Head coverings are a common feature of global dress codes from earliest times. While there are practical reasons for this, Georgia Scott's survey entitled *Headwraps* (2003) suggests that the meanings and uses of head wraps are diverse and complex. Rarely is the purpose of a head covering as simple as it might seem. Let's take three examples: Arafat's head scarf, Atatürk's ban on the fez, and the reveiling of Muslim women.

Former leader of the Palestinian movement Yasser Arafat became synonymous with his choice of head covering, a black-and-white checked scarf or *kuffiya*, which he wore with either military uniform, customary robes, or Western dress (Maynard 2004: 56; Scott 2003: 98). He wore the *kuffiya* for explicitly political reasons, namely, as a symbol of the Palestinian struggle for a homeland and independence. But it was also a sign of his Arab heritage, a meaning that was merged in the way in which he wore his *kuffiya*:

> The shape of his signature black and white kuffiya [was] carefully fashioned to represent a map of Palestine—and its meaning has thus been the subject of controversy. The kuffiya [became] his trademark. (Scott 2003: 98)

So this head covering is interpreted as a sign of political activism and a threat to the balance of power in the Middle East. By contrast, the ban imposed on the fez by Turkey's Atatürk in 1925 has been read as a symbol of the Westernization and modernization of Turkey (Scott 2003: 86). In fact, this episode was just a footnote to a protracted history of clothing (or sumptuary) laws in the Ottoman Empire designed "to control and reshape state and society":

> The 1829 law specified the clothing and headgear to be worn by the varying ranks of civil and religious officials. It sought to replace ancient community and occupational signs of differentiation by dress with a homogenizing status marker—the fez—that placed the state at the centre of Ottoman life as the sole remaining arbiter of identity. (Quataert 1997: 403)

As well as standing as a sign of political authority and indicating status and rank, the laws "sought to demolish not only the elite but also the popular sources of opposition to the consolidation of [Mahmud II's] personal power" (Quataert 1997: 403). This included many ethnic minority migrants, who were effectively exiled. One of the most visible forms of regulation was on the head wear one could wear, which since the fourteenth century had been subject to regulations on color and type (turban, fez, etc.). While their primary function was to "maintain discipline" and "state control … over functionaries and subjects," the clothing laws were also "instruments of negotiation, used by both the state and its elites as well as by the various (occupational and religious) communal groups" (Quataert 1997: 406–7). In sum, "clothing laws delineated, maintained, and reinforced gender, religious, and social distinction" (Quataert 1997: 407). Yet the adoption of a uniform fez for Ottoman bureaucrats effectively broke down vestmental distinctions between Muslims and non-Muslims and reinforced the "laissez-faire economic policies of" Sultan Mahmud II (Quataert 1997: 414). The design of fezzes proliferated throughout the nineteenth century, in some respects as a counterpoint to the abandonment of clothing laws elsewhere.

> The Ottoman state in 1829 sought to dominate Ottoman society by creating a uniform, state-centered dress code. In so doing the government turned clothing laws on their head. For perhaps

> the first time, a state sought to use clothing laws to promote homogeneity, uniformity in dress instead of distinctiveness. In at least this respect, the 1829 law stands out as unique in the annals of European, American, and Ottoman clothing laws. (Quataert 1997: 419–20)

However, this attempt to impose modesty and uniformity in dress foundered as non-Muslim influences came to dominate public space, fashionable styles, and cultural role models:

> The state was mired between legitimacies. Long-standing religious distinctions were embroiled in emerging class differentiations that clashed with immature notions of a common subjecthood/citizenry. The Ottoman Empire had no face. (Quataert 1997: 421)

In this context, Atatürk's ban on the fez is not an aberration but a continuity of long-standing clothing laws (see Norton 1997; Fandy 1998 on clothing regulation in Egypt). Nor were such laws restricted to male dress. Female dress, too, came to the attention of the state. A thick black veil replaced the traditional flimsy white yashmak in the late nineteenth century, and this became the norm for almost all Turkish women (Norton 1997: 155). But the allure of Western fashion also took hold. Atatürk's reforms aimed to modernize the economy and Westernize the culture. Although most of his efforts were directed toward male attire, he also outlawed "the tyranny" of the veil for women and ordered Turkish women to keep their faces uncovered. Despite initial reservations, these laws were adopted, particularly in urban areas, and remained in place after Atatürk's death. Until the 1960 military coup, men and women in public life wore almost exclusively Western clothing.

During the 1960s and 1970s, however, the reversion to an Islamic state led to the reimposition of Islamic dress codes. Gradually, forms of cover-up dress appeared in the form of head scarves, turbans, and the black *çarşaf,* a shapeless full-body gown (Norton 1997: 168). Despite attempts to ban women wearing Islamic dress from universities, there has been a citizen-led imposition of modest dress codes for women amid heated public debate about its interpretation as symbolizing "religiously inspired political dissent" (Breu and Marchese 2000: 25; see Baker 1997 for the similar debate in Iran).

> At stake … are more than political and religious ideologies. The subtler concerns of human sexuality, freedom of expression, and Islamic *and* secular feminism are at the core of the debate. To focus on the headscarf as *the* issue of modern Turkish society and life misses the depth and breadth of the appearance or absence of the headscarf not only in Turkish society but in the broader context of the Middle East. (Breu and Marchese 2000: 26)

To understand the head scarf, Breu and Marchese distinguish four groups who "use the headscarf as an expression of social identity": the traditionalists (who wear customary dress); the Islamic middle class (urban Turks who wear modest but fashionable dress); the fundamentalists (a growing group who wear the *çarşaf* or chador and identify with calls for the institution of an Islamic state); and the secularists/modernists, or Kemalists, who wear "mass-produced fashion-inspired dress, many of Western design, and … do not cover their heads with scarves" (Breu and Marchese 2000: 27–34).

What we can see, then, is the transformation of the political connotations of head coverings for men and women, which chart changing political, economic, diplomatic, and cultural formations. In the current climate, the imposed or voluntary adoption of a form of head covering or modest body dress has become "a potent political symbol" for Islamic identification and affiliation rather than a reference to the political state itself: "a conglomerate of abstract meanings related to Muslim identity and female modesty, which are juxtaposed against the sociopolitical situation of" modern Islamic states (Breu and Marchese 2000: 35).

**Mannequin wearing hijab.** Photo: Jonathan McIntosh. Creative Commons Attribution 2.0 License

Veiling has become almost an epidemic in Muslim-dominated and aspirational societies. Chatty (1997) has charted the revival of the veil in the Middle East, especially many states in the Middle East, be it the hijab, niqab, or burka. Meanings have varied, ranging from social status and economic privilege, purity and virginity, and the Islamic resurgence and reinvented assertions of ethnic identity to feminist consciousness and Westernization and colonization and postcolonialism (see Abu-Lughod 1990; Yamani 1997). Even in Western secular societies, veiling has become a preoccupation in some ethnic communities (see Dwyer 1999; MacMaster and Lewis 1998; Puwar 2002).

This trend has been controversial, with the practice of veiling being denounced as being a conflation of political, sexual, religious, and cultural meanings and motives. This fad is called "hyperveiling" by MacMaster and Lewis (1998: 132) in their account of changing interpretations of veiling from colonial to postcolonial times:

> Representations of the veil over the last two hundred years [have] been that they have invariably been ideological fabrications. But the major shift in form has been away from unveiling as a metaphor for colonial domination, towards a radical hyperveiling as a marker of political and cultural danger.

This example shows that the issue of head covering is neither a new nor a postmodern concern. Head scarves, veils, burkas, and fezzes have been political fixtures whose meanings may vary

**Veiled woman**

but whose political potency remains a tool of change, challenge, and resistance. In the West, there has been belated recognition of the size of the Muslim market by manufacturers and retailers of clothing, head wraps, soft drinks, electronic goods, financial services, and food, perhaps a reflection of the fact that there are now over 15 million Muslims in the European Union, a figure that is expected to double by 2015 (Carter 2005). The veil has become—once again—a statement of the political ambitions of Islam for Muslim leaders and is now worn as a political statement of Islamic culture and identity in Muslim countries and diasporic communities.

## CASE STUDY 30: Renegotiating Chinese Fashion

This case study examines successive cultural politics of fashion in the increasingly important fashion center of China. Like the Middle East, China has a long history of sophisticated culture and society, until the twentieth century based on imperial dynasties. China also has an extensive history of active interest in aesthetic pursuits and silk, featured in many of these as fabrics or as the thread of embroidery. For the elite, at least, this meant that men and women were clothed in exquisite robes heavily embroidered with silk and gold thread. The "rapacious appetite" of the elite for signs of conspicuous consumption "fuelled advances in technique and creativity in style" (Rutherford and Menzies 2004: 9). These aesthetic possibilities were shaped and monitored by clothing laws.

> Highly elaborate and rigid dress regulations specified in minute detail the colour, cut and symbols that could be worn by the emperor, different ranks of officials and nobles for a variety of occasions and ceremonies. ... The codes varied but persisted throughout imperial times, although they were often flouted. (Rutherford and Menzies 2004: 9–10)

The result was splendid robes for all occasions, from padded cold-weather protection to exquisite gowns and cloaks for ceremonial occasions. This tradition persisted for centuries, but everything changed under European occupation and attention. While the silks were valued in Europe as artifacts and as the aesthetic inspiration for European decorative art and fashion design, the demise of imperial China coincided with the rise of Western influences in China and the denouncement of distinctive Chinese forms of dress. While customary dress could still be found in rural areas and remote provinces, urban dress became imbued—albeit ambivalently—with the modernizing influences of European fashion. Like other cultures subjected to colonial incursions, China was ambivalent about balancing traditional cultural habits with so-called modernizing influences from Europe. This directly stemmed from political upheavals and ideologies, especially with respect to modernism, nationalism, and global connections (Finnane 1999, 2007; Roberts 1997; Steele and Major 1999).

The gradual infiltration of European-style uniforms into the ranks of the leadership (political, military, and administrative) quickly influenced styles of civilian Chinese dress (Finnane 1999). These high collars, close-fitting jackets, gold buttons, gold braid, frogging, and epaulettes were a legacy of military uniforms. Sun Yat-sens's influence was especially significant in "changing from western suit to Chinese robe and back again," and he even came "up with a style of his own—the Sun Yat-sen suit" (Finnane 1999: 130). This outfit was modeled on military dress and was but one of a succession of influences of military culture on Chinese dress. Another was the cheongsam, which was popularized in the 1930s and 1940s, serving as a de facto national dress for women until it was "displaced by the dress of the women's revolutionary army" (Finnane 1999: 131). Finnane (1999: 131) concludes that:

> The green and blue army and naval suits sported by Mao Zedong's teenage fans during the year of Cultural Revolution were thus not a quixotic or aberrant fashion, but rather a logical product of a process of dress reform which had its origins in new uniforms for the soldiers in the service of the Manchu dynasty.

Chen's (2001) study of women's dress from the 1940s through to the Cultural Revolution in China argues that there were two interlinking forces. First, clothing habits were much more complex and varied than officially sanctioned models of dress seem to suggest. Far from looking "shapeless" and "sexless," Chinese women experimented with all kinds of modifications and uses of color to personalize their clothing. Second, the Communist Party quickly realized the importance of dress as a technique to produce particular kinds of citizens and preferred codes of femininity. In this process, women mixed traditional elements of dress (such as patterned blouses) with newly sanctioned ones, such as the cheongsam, belted Mao jacket, and soft cloth cap.

The Mao suit was an interestingly ambiguous outfit. On the one hand, it promoted uniformity and an image of the new nationalism of the Cultural Revolution. But it also functioned to make distinctions within the party, between the party and ordinary citizens, and between some ordinary citizens and others. Accordingly,

> during the Maoist period, sartorial discourse increasingly placed value on the uniformity of militaristic fashion and promoted this form of clothing and concomitant behavior as that to which all citizens should work. This increased presence of militaristic uniformity did not destroy other clothing conventions; but it did necessitate that alternatives to the uniform be measured against the uniform. (Chen 2001: 156)

This resulted in fine distinctions being made between "the various manifestations of the Mao suit as well as between the Mao suit and clothing made from coloured fabric" (Chen 2001: 157). Despite the importance of dress reform to the implementation of the Maoist doctrine, the elaboration of dress habits and subtle resistance to officially sanctioned modes of dress illustrated the complexities and multiple responses to the regime.

A little later, the opening up of China and ambivalent fascination with an exotic yet austere culture led to an on-again, off-again love affair with the Mao suit—and derivations in fashion design. The Mao suit had been designed as a uniform of nationality—a garment to be worn by all classes—but its appropriation was as a marker of difference (Steele and Major 1999). In Western fashion, it represented a deliberate though insincere allusion to the drab reality of the Cultural Revolution.

**Woman's patriotic suit.** Collection: Powerhouse Museum Sydney/Photo: Sue Stafford. Powerhouse Museum

The Mao suit even made it to the cover of *Vogue*. In October 1979, *Vogue* UK went to China and featured a model in the Mao suit in front of a silk tapestry. An even more startling cover on Australian *Vogue* in March 1981 showed a model in a Mao suit, a cap with a red star badge, sunglasses, and a red scarf. These images guaranteed that the Mao suit gained a new life as high fashion (Lloyd 1986: 198, 204). The red star became a ubiquitous fashion accessory, while jackets adapted from the severe lines of the Mao jacket, high collars, caps, and military insignia created something of a controversy. While some derivations intended to make a sympathetic political statement, fashion aficionados preferred an irreverent appropriation purely as style. It was a very different fashion statement from the long-standing derivations from the elegant cheongsam, *qianlian mei* ("pretty face" jacket typically worn by peasants), and *xiao'ao* (wedding jacket) (Clark and Wong 1997; Szeto 1997; Ye 1997).

Since the end of the Cultural Revolution in 1976, and especially since the opening up of trade with the world, China has—at least in urban areas—resumed its love affair with Western high fashion and modernization (Kunz 1996; Mead 2007). This has taken several forms: China has become a major manufacturer of apparel for the West, Western fashion has shaped Chinese fashion and dress codes, wealthy Chinese have become serious elite designer fashion shoppers, and Chinese-identifying designers have developed a distinctive fashion aesthetic. Apparel has been an important factor in China's economic transformation: "a high fashion discourse modeled on elite fashion in capitalist consumer culture has come to dominate … the nature of China's modernization" (Li 1998: 74). At the same time,

> modernization became the major driving force behind the development of new fashion systems in China. In fact, the Chinese term *shizhuang* (fashion) has always signified the modern, as it is clearly contrasted to *fushi* (costume), which refers to clothing styles in Imperial China and of ethnic minorities. It is *shizhuang* (fashion), not *fushi* (costume), that links China to the outside world. If *fushi* always points to tradition and past, *shizhuang* is closely associated with internationalization and modernization. (Li 1998: 75)

**Fashion show at Attica, Shanghai.** Photo: Daniel Lehnberg, http://lehnberg.net Daniel Lehnberg

One of the visible signs of this is the popularity of fashion shows and fashion fairs in Chinese cities and towns beginning in the 1980s as well as the proliferation of high-end fashion malls in most Chinese urban areas, Taiwan, and Hong Kong. The uptake of Western fashions in everyday dress was slow at first and mostly promoted through the media; however, fashionable young people adopted Western celebrity styles and subcultural looks, which by the 1990s had taken root in Chinese dress consciousness. Like other fashion-center aspirants, China has struggled to reconcile "global" fashion trends with the assertion of a distinctive local fashion aesthetic, oscillating between designers and brands that explicitly draw on "chinesey" aesthetics (reworked allusions to Orientalism and the exotic) (Skov 2003: 223), responses and reactions to the still authoritarian role of the Chinese state, and innovative efforts to embrace a borderless aesthetic of "global" fashion design (Mingxin and Lijun 2008).

This play is especially noticeable in Hong Kong, which, since annexation to the mainland in 1997, has struggled to reconcile its long heritage as an independent colony that looked to the West and its both ancient and contemporary reintegration with traditional Chinese heritage (Skov 2003; Wong 2006). Fashion influences draw on well-known stereotypes such as images of

**Asian-inspired haute couture, Christian Dior.** Photo: Tony Barson/WireImage, WireImage

Chinese women and women of Chinese heritage as Suzy Wong and China dolls, although the dominance of global luxury designer names and brands is overwhelming and Western models are generally used to display the latest fashion collections. Nonetheless, customary elements of Chinese dress persist in everyday dress and in the more remote areas of mainland and offshore China—and have been reinvented in Chinese couture.

As Chinese people still struggle for a truly democratic political system, fashion and dress are one way of expressing resistance and a desire for other cultural identifications. The state endorses a fashion-led policy of economic development, and establishing Chinese cities like Shanghai and Hong Kong as global fashion cities is part of numerous urban policies (Gilbert 2006: 3). Commentators believe that "Shanghai will surely be able to establish its own image as a city of fashion and culture" (Zhang quoted by Gilbert 2006: 3), while Hong Kong achieves a truly "transnational" fashion status.

## CASE STUDY 31: Indian Fashion: From Diasporas to Designers

The case of India (and, to an extent, Pakistan and Bangladesh) provides a convenient snapshot of many aspects of the contemporary fashion industry and changing patterns of fashion flows between fashion capitals and new hubs, on the one hand, and producers, on the other (Bhachu 2003; Bhandari 2005). These characteristics include:

- The reinvention of traditional Indian fashion amid growing Western fashion habits in India
- The reworking of traditional Indian fashion for diasporic Indian women
- The position of India as a major exporter of fabrics and garments to Western fashion hubs
- The use of Indian subcontractors for production of fashion, especially skilled workers for embroidery, beading, and the like
- The ability of Indian manufacturers to meet the time lines demanded for fast fashion
- The emergence of Indian fashion designers as local and international figures

**Shalwar kameez.** Photo: Tim Thomas. Collection: Amanda Russell

The dress of India is probably best known for the **sari** (the wrapped garment for women worn over a short tight blouse, the **choli**) and the dhoti (men's loin cloth, most often associated with Mahatma Ghandi) (Bean 1989), although there is a rich and varied range of clothing types across the different regions of India (Bhatia 2003; Biswas 2003; Fabri 1961; Lynton and Singh 1995). The sheer variety of styles, fabrics, colors, and finishings (for example embroidery, beadwork) is truly astonishing, and there can be no doubt that a fine appreciation of the minutiae of clothes and how to wear them has underpinned the changing fashions of Indian cultural history.

In the West, however, the image of the sari is generally of a customary garment or costume denoting tradition and national/ethnic identity, with little realization of the range of styles and possibilities—as well as meanings of the sari. The sari has two connotations: on the one hand, as a timeless and elegant costume, and on the other, as the sign of migrants from the subcontinent who have not yet adapted to "Western" ways. Yet there are many other images that could be added to this.

But the focus here is on the challenge to the sari from new forms of Indian dress, in particular the *shalwar kameez* (also known as *salwar kameez*), made up of a *shalwar* (loose-fitting trousers secured at the waist with a drawstring and narrowed at the ankles, or alternatively *churidar,* tight leggings) and *kameez* (a tunic worn on top, which may be long or short, loose-fitting or body hugging, with long sleeves or sleeveless, also called a *kurti*). In fact, this form of dress has roots back to AD 750, when it arrived with conquering Muslim moguls from Central Asia. Over time many regional and ethnic variations occurred.

After partition and the formation of the Indian state in 1947, the sari was deemed national costume in India, while the *shalwar kameez* was adopted in Pakistan. While still common in everyday life in the subcontinent, the *kameez* was revived with the emergence of second-generation Indian immigrants in Britain (and elsewhere), who were articulate and aspired to embrace their cultural heritage with modern Western lifestyles. The *shalwar kameez* proved to be a garment that served the purpose. A similar revival occurred in the subcontinent itself with the new generation of young emancipated urban women.

**Benazir Bhutto.** Photo: SRA Gerald B. Johnson/United States Department of Defense

Initially, in Britain, specialist stores targeting the migrant market were the source of imported clothes, but gradually local production began and United Kingdom–raised diasporic designers began to experiment with modifications to the classic garments (Bhachu 2003; Jones and Leshkowich 2003; Khan 1992).

Now, the *shalwar kameez* appears in countless variants from everyday wear to exclusive designer couture in a transnational industry that spans the globe (Dwyer 2006). Indeed, the *shalwar kameez* has arguably displaced the sari as the sign of Indian identity (Kaur 2003). Online stores have contributed to its wide availability in a myriad of styles that combine comfort and elegance and can be worn modestly (with a **dupatta,** or shawl covering the head) or to highlight the body (in designer versions). Western role models such as the late Diana, Princess of Wales, and Jemima Goldsmith Khan made global headline news wearing the suits and enhanced their appeal to non-Asian women. This boosted their popularity worldwide and helped transform the image of the suit as traditional and backwards to contemporary and glamorous.

The late Benazir Bhutto, former prime minister of Pakistan, wore stylish Western clothes when she first returned from Oxford to Pakistan but was soon pressured to adopt local clothing codes, wearing the *shalwar kameez* with a shawl draped over her shoulders and partially covering her hair. This indicated the shifting symbolism of the suit from the assertion of ethnic identity within contemporary diasporic Asian fashion to its redefinition as part of the politicization of Islam as a cultural, as well as religious, force. This politicization of Islam has resulted in many Muslim women across the world adopting forms of veiling (see case study 29).

In addition to contemporary diasporic Asian clothing, India has also seen a massive expansion of its fashion industry. This has taken several forms. First, India is second only to China as the biggest exporter of textiles and low price point apparel. Second, within India, high-end designers have developed innovation fusion fashion for India's growing urban middle class. And third, India's highly skilled but poorly paid artisans who specialize in fine finishings are subcontracted by Western fast-fashion designers, who demand tight scheduling (up to three weeks for intricate detailing but a few days for relatively straightforward manufacturing).

India then can be seen as a microcosm of the transnational components and flows of contemporary fashion and the contradictions and tensions between the various subsectors of the industry.

Jennifer Craik and Sharon Peoples

## CASE STUDY 32: Burberry's Brand of Britishness

Recently we were discussing tartans with a friend and mentioned the Burberry tartan, commenting how dull it is. "Oh," she said, "but it's *so* classic." That got us thinking—how does a fabric, logo, or brand acquire status as a "classic"?

Burberry is known as a quintessential symbol of British style and British culture, with its distinctive tartan seen worldwide and frequently copied. How did this come about? Burberry began as a traditional English company, established by Thomas Burberry in 1856. Working with a cotton mill, Burberry created a prototype raincoat-overcoat made from a cotton fabric called **gabardine,** which was waterproofed first during the spinning of the fiber and then again after being woven into a fabric. The style derived from the weave and style of an agricultural smock. After 1891, Burberry began to specialize in active and leisure wear and sports. In 1902 gabardine was registered as a trademark, and in 1909 the name Burberry was registered as trademark for the company.

The turning point in Burberry's fortunes came when he was commissioned to produce a trench coat for the British military that was suitable for the horrific conditions of trench warfare. This became the model of subsequent military coats. After World War I, the trench coat was marketed to civilians. Beginning in 1920, Burberry targeted an upper-middle-class clientele that aspired to emulate the aristocracy. It became the accepted uniform of the country squire, perfectly suited for hunting, shooting, and fishing.

**Burberry, Kok Leng.** Photo: Maurice Yeo. Creative Commons Attribution 2.0

In 1924, the Haymarket check, a tartan of beige with black-and-red stripes, was introduced. This fabric has become synonymous with the Burberry brand as an enduring global fashion. Adopted by Hollywood actors such as Humphrey Bogart and Peter Sellers, the coats were popularized to new markets. By the 1960s, Burberry was synonymous with conservative and traditional brutish antifashion and rejected by Swinging London, although its main domestic clientele remained loyal.

From 1967, the check was used not just as a lining fabric but as the fabric for numerous items such as scarves, umbrellas, luggage, handbags, watches, sunglasses, and fragrance lines. Despite many imitations of this iconic tartan, Burberry has remained a British byword in fashion and achieved worldwide preeminence in the outerwear and accessories market. With its tartan pattern, Burberry is still an instantly recognizable logo of luxury and imprimatur of good taste. Vivienne Westwood is just one designer who has played on traditional tartans such as Burberry to create collections that focus on tailoring and British style.

In 1980s Burberry's fortunes turned a corner, with the popularity of their apparel growing among a new generation of young European and Asian Anglophiles. Burberry became a symbol of global cosmopolitanism. Up to 75 percent of Burberry's sales are outside Britain, but the company still trades on the different versions or essence of British style in far-flung fashion capitals. But its success became a problem, and fashionistas began to tire of the brand, resulting in declining sales. To address this, at the end of 1990s, a designer was employed to create new looks and invigorate the market. This led to new connotations of the brand to appeal to highly mobile cosmopolitan careerists and fashion followers.

The company has also attracted controversy. In 2006, Burberry was attacked by animal-rights organization PETA over the company's use of fur. Further criticism followed when Burberry decided to relocate its production from Wales to mainland China in 2007. Despite a major celebrity-led campaign to "Keep Burberry British," the company relocated. However, the campaign succeeded in keeping the British symbolism of Burberry and arguably contributed to revived fortunes in the new millennium. They are now marketed under the name Burberry Prosum in most fashion cities.

Jennifer Craik and Sharon Peoples

# glossary

**Accessories** – Items of apparel that enhance or complete an outfit, including head wear, shoes, handbags, jewelry, body piercings, hairstyles, neckwear, umbrellas and parasols, gloves, belts, cosmetics, and perfume.

**Adidas** – German sportswear and accessories brand established in 1920 by Adolph and Rudolph Dassler. The name was a contraction of "Adi" and "Das." The brand name was registered in 1948, and the three-stripe logo adopted in 1949. Adidas has become one of the dominant global sportswear companies and is frequently adopted as the major licensed brand for major sporting events such as the Olympic Games.

**Advertising** – Diverse forms of communication about products and ideas, most commonly associated with mass media and consumer society. Advertising messages may convey information as well as qualities associated with products. Symbols and techniques associated with the product enhance an individual's sense of identity. See *Benetton.*

**Aesthetics** – Artistic trends and movement, regimes of good taste and appreciation, a critical appreciation of artistic values and conventions, contemporary notions of beauty, apprehension through the senses.

**Aglet** – Cladding wrapped around the end of a ribbon (cf. shoelaces) used to tie sleeves to bodice or doublet.

**Androgyny** – The combination of references to masculine and feminine gender to convey through dress and behavior overtly effeminate and masculine traits, which are blurred. Terms such as "butch" and "queen" are used to denote androgyny.

**Anti-establishment** – Movements, styles, or trends that explicitly oppose or challenge established cultural norms and conventions, oppositional politics or political movements, or change-oriented or revolutionary philosophies or identities.

**Antifashion** – An outfit or style that is outside the fashion system—perhaps one that is customary, traditional, or unchanging. The dress of groups such as Sloane Rangers, European royalty, Hassidic Jews, and traditional Muslims can be described as antifashion.

**Art deco** – An artistic style that began in the 1910s with Paul Iribe's style of illustrating the fashion designs of Paul Poiret. The name was coined for the 1925 Exposition Internationale des Arts Décoratifs et Industriels Modernes in Paris, which heralded the modernist movement. Art deco was an eclectic fusion of the styles of different cultures and periods, marked by purity of line borrowed from neoclassicism and Orientalism.

**Art nouveau** – A European decorative art form in the 1880s and 1890s, expressed particularly in architecture, interior decoration, furniture design, posters, glasswork, jewelry, and fabric design, characterized by distinctive graceful curved lines ending in curlicues (dashing curls or twists), frequently framed with flowers and leaf motifs. Art nouveau fashion reflected this free-flowing style with soft, flowing fabrics and designs and the use of scarves over layered and draped garments. Art nouveau overlapped with art deco and is associated with the posters of Henri Toulouse-Lautrec and the glasswork of René Lalique. It was revived in the Liberty fabrics in the 1960s.

**Atelier** – A specialist studio or workshop associated with fashion that provided finishings such as beadwork, embroidery, and decorative stitching for the haute couture industry.

**Avant-garde** – The vanguard of a new stylistic movement or fashion usually associated with artistic trends that challenge established conventions.

**Ballets Russes** – The ballet company founded in 1909 by Serge Diaghilev, who revolutionized the foundations of modern dance. Its emphasis on the spectacular had a major influence on art, music, and decor. The color, exuberance, and originality of the costumes had a profound influence on trends in fashion.

**Bandana** – Cotton kerchief tied around the forehead, neck, or mouth as protection against the sun and sweat. It is associated with revolutionaries, pirates, gangs, and cowboys. The word "bandana" derives from the Hindi word meaning "to tie."

**Bandeau** – A narrow piece of fabric worn around the chest as an alternative to a bra.

**Bauhaus** – The Weimar school of art and design that was active from 1920 to 1933 and was founded by Georg Muche. It initially housed textile, craft, furniture, and furnishings workshops. The Bauhaus focused on the concept of "total architecture." It was the incubator for the genre of interior design. Key educators were Walter Gropius, Johannes Itten, Annie Albers, and Mies van der Rohe.

**Bell-bottoms** – Trousers with extremely wide cuffs, originally worn by sailors because they were suitable for rolling up the leg for deck work and for removing quickly over shoes. They were revived as a fashion item in the 1960 and 1970s and became associated with the hippy era and radicalism.

**Belle Epoque** – Style of dress at the end of the nineteenth century that emphasized the hourglass figure. Dresses were made in pale lustrous silks with swags and sashes billowing behind. Charles Worth was a key designer of the Belle Epoque.

**Benetton** – An Italian prêt-à-porter fashion house begun in 1965 by siblings Luciano, Guiliana, Gilberto, and Carlo Benetton. The idea was to manufacture well-designed but affordable knitwear. Later the company diversified into sportswear and accessories, particularly trading on the global success of the United Colors of Benetton campaign. Benetton became notorious for innovative and provocative advertising campaigns created by Oliviero Toscani from 1983 till 2000. See case study 28.

**Bertin, Rose** – The most famous French *marchande de mode* of the eighteenth century. She dressed the elite French aristocracy and the rising bourgeoisie. Her most famous client was Marie Antoinette, wife of Louis XVI. Bertin's success came from her ability to flatter her clients by building on their preferred costume, adding new and unexpected elements.

**Bias** – A line drawn or cut at a forty-five degree angle. In fashion, cutting fabric on the bias became popular in the interwar years. This technique emphasized the fall of the fabric, which seemed to hang, producing a more curvaceous silhouette. It was first used for clothes designed by Madame Vionnet circa 1918 and is still popular in contemporary fashion collections.

**Biba** – An avant-garde London boutique founded by Barbara Hulanicki in 1964. She designed a new style for young people that was modeled by thin models like Twiggy. Her styles of maxi and mini skirts used new and artificial fabrics such as PVC. The shop closed in 1975, but it is still an important influence on fashion.

**Bikini** – A controversial two-piece bathing costume based on folded newspaper triangles daringly cut away. Strings were used to tie the pieces together. The designer Louis Réard, a mechanical engineer, named it after the U.S. nuclear tests at Bikini Atoll in the Pacific Ocean in the 1946. It was adopted as the official swimming costume for Miss World contests in 1951 but was withdrawn the following year. Despite cultural sensitivities, the bikini became popular in the 1950s and early 1960s and has remained a mainstay of swimwear since.

**Black** – A dominant and enduring fashion color. Its meaning has changed over time, and its use often sends contradictory messages. Its connotations range from death, power, and danger to sexual allure and the avant-garde. These multiple signifiers account for its continued attraction as shorthand for mystery and magic. The little black dress, the versatile mainstay of the fashionable woman's wardrobe, is attributed to Coco Chanel. See case study 6.

**Body modification** – Different ways of reshaping the body, including the use of piercings, tattooing, scarification, binding, stretching, insertions, dieting, bondage, and plastic surgery, that have been common in all cultures since ancient times. It is often a marker for group identity, for example, among sailors, Chinese women with bound feet, irezumi (a form of tattooing) among the yakuza in Japan, sado masochists, and Goths. It became mainstream after the development of the subculture of punks in the 1970s. In contemporary culture, body modification has spiritual, ornamental, and sexual meanings and is also a fashionable form of self-expression. The artist Orlan is exemplary in celebrating continuous body modifications.

**Body technique** – Ways of behavior, gesture, and presentation usually learned through imitation of the actions of those a person seeks to emulate. See chapter 3.

**Bohemian** – Unconventional and individual dress arising in the late nineteenth century and common among artists, writers, dissidents, and rebellious characters who rejected dominant cultural values. Their behavior connoted transgression, excess, sexual extremism, and eccentricity. Bohemian clothing is often colorful and typified by flowing garments that emulate popular conceptions of Gypsies and connotes a contrived, unstructured approach to dress.

**Boutique** – A small specialist and designer fashion and accessories retail outlet that became popular beginning in the 1960s. The word derives from the French word for "small studio" or "workshop."

**Le Bon Marché** – The Parisian department store, founded in 1852, offering floors of diverse merchandise including fashion, cosmetics, and home wares that used new and innovative techniques of display and marketing to entice new consumers and make fashion more accessible to the growing middle classes.

**Bra** – A garment designed as an undergarment to cup and support the breasts, usually with shoulder straps, and fastening with hook and eyes at the back; also called a brassiere.

**Brand** – Identifying symbol of a particular product designed to differentiate it from its competitors. Consumers often identify with a particular brand as reflecting their aspirations and lifestyle. The success of certain brands in dominating the fashion industry has given them significant market share in the consumption of apparel.

**Breeches** – Knee-length pants worn by men, usually fitted and fastened just below the knee. They were generally worn by members of the middle and upper classes during the late sixteenth through the early nineteenth centuries.

**Bricoleur** – The improvisation and assemblage of items reconstituted in fashion garments to create a new and individual appearance and style; from the French *bricol,* meaning "trifle."

**Burka** – A loose black or light blue robe covering the entire female body, often covering the eyes, designed for modesty in public. Imposed by fundamentalist Muslim regimes such as the Taliban in Afghanistan and the Iranian government. Other forms are the chador, yashmak, and hijab.

**Burkini** – A modified form of swimwear designed to ensure modesty for female Muslims. It consists of a tunic over leggings with long sleeves with a hood. Originating in Australia, burkinis are now marketed globally.

**Bustier** – A long-line brassiere.

**Buyer** – A purchasing agent for a chain or department store who attempts to anticipate trends and consumer demand.

**Camisole** – A short sleeveless undergarment like a vest with thin straps.

**Camlet** – Fabric from camel or fur angora wool.

**Capitalism** – A private production system based on private property, the use of waged labor, and profit created by entrepreneurialism that is inherently inequitable.

**Capri pants** – Three-quarter pants first designed by Emilio Pucci in 1949 on the island of Capri in Italy. They were popularized by Hollywood actresses such Audrey Hepburn. Variations are pedal pushers and clam diggers.

**Cargo pants** – Three-quarter-length pants popularized in the 1990s, originally made in lightweight khaki-colored cotton, featuring external pockets with accordion folds in the side and flaps that are secured by buttons, press-studs, or Velcro. Cargo pants are derived from the styling of military trousers.

**Celebrity** – A high-profile person (now often in the sports or entertainment industries) who attracts excessive media visibility and whose private life becomes more important than his or her professional life and achievements; a larger-than-life public figure.

**Chemisette** – A piece of lightweight fabric that covers or fills in a low bodice or décolletage

**Chemise** – Simple dress-like undergarment with sleeves, much like a petticoat, worn by women. Made from fine cotton, linen, or silk.

**Cheongsam** – A tight-fitting embroidered silk A-line sheath with a high collar that opens at the front via a diagonal slit to the underarm and is fastened with satin knot buttons and loop (cf. a toggle); also called *qipao.* It may be sleeveless or have cap sleeves or full-length sleeves with a curved edge at the wrist. The cheongsam was a hybrid outfit designed by modern urban Chinese women in the 1920s. Known as the "banner gown," the cheongsam was regarded as very daring because it revealed the shape of a woman's body. It is popular both as customary dress and as a silhouette and influence in contemporary fashion although it was banned during the Chinese Cultural Revolution.

**Chic** – A word of French origin to indicate elegance, taste, and style that probably developed during the Belle Epoque.

**Choli** – A short, tight-fitting tailored blouse worn under a sari.

**Class** – Hierarchies denoting divisions of economic and social status.

**Classic** – A style that lasts for an indefinite period of time and is immune to fads and fashions.

**Clothing** – Garments collectively; raiment; clothes; apparel, covering.

**Colonialism** – A relationship indicating domination and hegemony, often associated with the political rule of European countries in the New World and after military conquests; often used interchangeably with imperialism; related to decolonization and postcolonialism.

**Color wheel** – A system using the color spectrum and classifying colors as primary, secondary, and tertiary hues that is used in fashion to determine compatible and contrasting color combinations.

**Commodity** – Objects and services produced for use or sale; usually involved the processing of raw materials into things that are given a use value and exchange value. Commodification involves the modification of an object to enhance mass production, distribution, and promotion.

**Communism** – An economic system in which there is collective ownership of production (by the state) and abolition of private ownership for the benefit of the people (aka the proletariat). In fashion, communism is associated with the fashions in Bolshevik Russia, the Mao suit in China, and black jackets and trousers worn by workers in communist countries in Asia.

**Conspicuous consumption** – A phrase coined by Theodor Veblen in 1899 to describe the tendency to mark social status through the competitive display of possessions.

**Constructivism** – A Soviet abstract art movement that grew out of cubism and futurism in the early twentieth century as part of Bolshevik cultural censorship. It referred to art forms that were minimalist, geometric, spatial, architectonic, and experimental.

**Consumer culture** – A culture permeated by consumerism in which people take their identity from the value of the goods they purchase as much as from social values.

**Consumption** – The market relationship between a producer and consumer; the act of purchasing commodities and the consequences of these financial connections. The act of consumption is the defining characteristic of consumer culture.

**Cornet** – Lowest-ranking commissioned cavalry officer, who carried the standard.

**Corset** – Garment developed in the nineteenth century that was used to restrict and reshape the torso, particularly the waist and hips; traditionally made from whalebone inserted in the fabric. Corsets were originally fastened with lacing, which led to moral panic over tight lacing. First worn over a chemise, the corset became an undergarment, but by the late twentieth century, it had become a fashionable outer garment. A corselette is a tubular corset incorporating bra, girdle, and suspenders.

**Couture** – Clothing that is individually created, usually by commission, involving the highest-quality artisanal handcrafting; commonly associated with Parisian fashion.

**Cowl** – Hood or long hooded cloak

**Cravat** – A scarf worn by men around the neck with a slip knot and long ends hanging down the front of the shirt; a forerunner of the tie. Originating in the seventeenth century, cravats were worn by Croatian mercenaries in France and were subsequently popularized in Britain. They are now worn as formal attire with the ends tucked into the shirt or jacket.

**Crinoline** – Stiff petticoat structure modified into a hooped underskirt in the 1840s. It reached a maximum length of two meters in the 1860s.

**Cubism** – Artistic movement associated with Pablo Picasso and Georges Braque, who rejected representational likeness for the fragmentation of subjects into components that were then reassembled in new arrangements on canvas; the breaking down of form and space into geometrical shapes, enabling multiple perspectives and viewpoints. Cubism appealed to cognitive readings rather than visual recognition. There were two phases of cubism: analytic (1907–12) and synthetic (1913–20s). Robert Delaunay and Marcel Duchamp were among the artists influenced by cubism.

**Culture** – Ways of living, traditions, and habits particular to a social group that are transmitted from one generation to another; development or improvement by education or training; a particular stage or state of civilization; the act of cultivating or tending. Cultural industry refers to an industry based on transforming art forms into commodities.

**Cultural capital** – A form of social value that enables a person to achieve higher status through the acquisition of skills, knowledge, and qualifications that give him or her an advantage in performing social roles. Family background and educational achievements are central to the acquisition of cultural capital, which equips a person to achieve other forms of value, including economic advantage.

**Cultural politics** – The play between endogenous forces within the fashion system and exogenous forces from the outside that converge to shape the production, circulation, and consumption of cultural products, ideas, and phenomena.

**Customary** – Common; habitual; traditional; the quality of persisting over time.

**Cyber** – Subculture mixture of Goth and rave using anime symbolism and recognizable body modifications and color contrasts of black, red, and white.

**Dada** – Movement established in Zurich in 1916 by expatriate artists who challenged political ideologies and established conventions of art, philosophy, and morality through outrageous and excessive performances and art works.

**Damask** – Fabric of reverse Jacquard (raised-weave) pattern.

**Dandy** – A male who pays fastidious attention to his appearance and the details of dress. This emerged in the late eighteenth and early nineteenth centuries and was commonly associated with the aristocracy. The best-known dandy was Beau Brummell.

**Deconstruction** – The genre of clothing whereby clothes are deliberately taken apart and reassembled in a partially finished state, or whereby parts of garments are reassigned; typified by features such as turning pieces of clothing inside out, fraying, ripping, and using fastenings in an unusual and decorative manner.

**Denim** – A durable cotton fabric identified by its diagonal twill, traditionally dyed from indigo. The word "denim" is a contraction of the French *serge de Nîmes,* the fabric named after its town of origin. Denim was popularized on the Californian goldfields by Levi Strauss, who systematized the production of tough working trousers made from denim and strengthened with rivets. These soon became known as jeans.

**Designer** – The key person associated with the design and production of fashion apparel who gives the creative signature of distinction— both an occupation and the personification of fashion. Designers have become the apex of the fashion system since Charles Worth and Paul Poiret in the early twentieth century.

**Dhoti** – A long cotton loincloth, traditionally woven from khaddar, that is wrapped between the legs and worn by Hindu men.

**Diagliev theater** – See Ballets Russes.

**Diffusion** – Lines of apparel, accessories, and other merchandise created by a fashion designer and bearing their name (or a derivative thereof) as a mass-produced affordable alternative to couture or custom fashion.

**Disco** – A 1970s fashion style associated with popular dance. Disco dance dress included leotards, stretch jeans, and leggings often made from Spandex (stretch fiber) in fluorescent colors and extravagantly decorated.

**Draping** – System of cutting garments that relies on the fall of the fabric on the body, which determines the line and seaming.

**Drawers** – Type of loose underwear with open or closed crotch, drawn together at the waist.

**Dress** – Clothing, apparel, or garb as well as ornaments or adornment of the body. Dress also refers to everyday or functional modes of dress. Sometimes dress is used to denote a specific stable genre of clothing that is not subject to rapid change or fashion (e.g., religious dress).

**Drill** – Weave of coarse twill fabric from the eighteenth century that is used for heavy utilitarian clothing.

**Doc Martens** – An ankle-length, round-toe boot that was originally handmade for orthopedic wear with thick soles stitched to the upper, with laces. Doc Martens were popularized in the 1970s by punks and skinheads. Since the 1980s, they have become mainstream casual wear.

**Dupatta** – The long scarf often worn with the shalwar kameez to cover the head or across one or both shoulders.

**DuPont** – Multinational chemical company established in 1802 that is especially known for the development of synthetic and smart fibers for the apparel industry (including rayon, nylon, Dacron, Orlon, Tactel, and microfiber).

**Edwardian** – Period of King Edward (1890s–1910) but denotes the fin de siècle in Britain and the Gibson Girl period in America as well as the period of the (unsuccessful) dress reform campaign promoting less structured menswear. Women's dress was typified by a high collar, an ample bosom, a tight waist, and full hips. Bustles were worn to enhance the back of the skirt and the *S*-shape silhouette.

**Enlightenment** – Seventeenth-century period when new ideas of rational thinking and aesthetics were combined.

**Elizabethan** – The English Renaissance period during the reign of Elizabeth I (1558–1603), which was characterized by extravagant fabrics, jewels, and the shaping of garments through padding and frames.

**Eroticism** – Aesthetic focus on sexual desire through the manipulation of the spectacle of dress and display of the unclothed body; from the Greek word *eros*, the name of the god of love. Fashion associated with eroticism includes lingerie and fetish wear.

**Ethnographic** – Scientific classification of ethnic and racial groups in terms of distinctive cultural practices and social mores. Ethnographic dress is generally regarded as customary or traditional.

**Existentialism** – A school of philosophy that investigates the meaning of existence.

**Fabric** – Any material made from weaving, knitting, crocheting, or bonding of yarns and threads to create a textile that is a fabric or cloth from which garments are made.

**Fads** – Short-term styles that are fashionable for a moment but quickly discarded.

**Fashion** – A prevailing custom or style of dress, etiquette, or procedures and internalized sense of the modish style of the time; appearances, styles of behavior, and social status; a clothing system denoting occupation, gender, ethnicity, and status; clothing habits that are subject to changes of style in a short space of time.

**Fashionability** – Conforming to fashion; visible markers of identity, status, and gender.

**Fashion cycle** – The regular reappearance and regeneration of distinctive periodic styles that serve as inspirations for new fashions and trends.

**Fashion illustrations** – Art work depicting fashions and the construction of garments that developed as a specialized art form before photography and digital methods. Its appearance coincides with the development of fashion magazines in the eighteenth century.

**Fashion journalism** – Specialized form of journalism that reports on current trends and forecasting fashion news with a focus on newness and now-ness. Much fashion journalism is descriptive, though some is hyperbolic (advertorial) and some cruelly dismissive. Although there is only a small tradition of intellectually critical fashion journalism, hagiographic or damning reports can make or break a designer or fashion house.

**Fashion magazines** – Specialist magazine reporting on latest trends, cultures, tastemakers, and technologies. Fashion magazines rely heavily on advertising and “contra” deals (convenient exchanges or arrangements) between editors and agents and representatives of the fashion industry.

**Fashion photography** – A special form of photography that focuses on not only clothing but moods and qualities associated with fashion looks.

**Fashion system** – The organized system of designing, manufacturing, promoting, distributing, and selling apparel. The term is also used to refer to the factors that shape public taste in apparel that drives consumer fashion behavior.

**Fashion victims** – Consumers who devour the latest fashion trends with no regard for cost, the appropriateness of the attire, or the sustainability of the environment; also called fashion slaves.

**Femininity** – Ideal attributes of a woman; expressing womanly characteristics; often defined as self-disciplined, demure, self-aware, passive, nurturing, and supportive of others.

**Fetishism** – The obsession with objects or things that are imbued with magical qualities and powers, especially concerning sexuality and sensuality; apparel that connotes erotic attraction, such as stilettos, corsets, or rubber wear.

**Fez** – A red felt hat with black tassel originating in Morocco and often associated with traditional male Islamic dress.

**Flapper** – A young woman in the Roaring Twenties who showed disdain for conventional dress and behavior. Flappers wore loose-fitting sleeveless shift dresses with a dropped waistline, which allowed for greater movement, for example, when dancing. The style was associated with hedonistic lifestyles associated with jazz and the Charleston dance craze.

**Fragrance** – Perfumes produced from natural and synthetic oils and compounds to produce scents that complement fashion moods. Fragrance has become a major line for couturiers, fashion houses, and brands.

**Gabardine** – A woven dress fabric made from cotton or silk with wool lining; patented by Thomas Burberry in 1904.

**Gap** – American brand label begun in 1969 in San Francisco. It internationalized its selling point of the open display of well-organized and well-stocked shelves of apparel arranged by size for selection by consumers. Launched its Gap line of jeans, which took it to international prominence. Subsidiaries include Banana Republic, Gap Kids, Baby Gap, and Old Navy Clothing Co.

**Garçonne** – The figure of the garçonne came to be associated with a young woman with short boyish-styled hair, a thin (almost androgynous) body, and little makeup. The garçonne typically wore a man's shirt, tie, and jacket with either skirt or trousers. It connoted transgression of gender and was commonly associated with the fashions of Coco Chanel.

**Garment** – A textile fashioned into clothing.

**Gatekeepers** – Official or informal authorities who act as a conduit for permission to perform certain roles or as a veto point for prohibiting certain behavior; arbiters of changing modes and regulators of fashion behavior.

***Gazette du Bon Ton*** – A leading French magazine founded in 1912 to promote trends in fashion and lifestyle and beauty aids.

**Geometric** – Designs based on abstract or nonrepresentational motif or simple shapes such as circles, squares, triangles, and rectangles producing an angular look; also includes a range of designs incorporating stripes, polka dots, and checks as well as lozenges and polygons. Geometric designs have been a staple feature of textiles and clothing perhaps due to their suitability for weaving techniques.

**Girdle** – A lightweight corset extending from waist to upper thigh, usually elasticized or rubberized. "Step-ins" are a super lightweight type of girdle constructed of stretch fabrics.

**Glam** – The 1970s music-related subculture of glam rock, whose bands wore androgynous, glamorous, and showy outfits, such as one-piece jumpsuits and platform shoes made from extravagant fabrics such as satin and metallic materials.

**Globalization** – The phenomenon of the twentieth and twenty-first centuries that relates to social and economic relations and interdependence that span many counties and economies. The term specifically refers to the spread of the economic system of capitalism.

**Goths** – A subculture that emerged in the early 1980s and embraced distinctive forms of music, aesthetics, and fashion shaped by an obsession with nihilism, alienation, darkness, death, and mysticism. Goth fashion in a mixture of styles influenced by death rock, punk, androgynous, medieval, Renaissance, and Victorian aesthetics, usually black in color and complemented by thick black makeup and hair over artificially pale skin.

**Grosgrain** – Silk woven with crosswise ribs or stripes.

**Grunge** – Style that evolved from street cultures originally from Seattle and is linked to the philosophy of deconstruction to make political and anti-consumerist statements. It was epitomized by the band Nirvana. See *deconstructionist.*

**G-string** – A narrow piece of cloth that passes between the buttocks to cover the genitals and is attached to a band at the hips; also called a thong.

**Habitus** – A set of dispositions that form the attributes (practices and perceptions) of a person in terms of his or her relationship with other people and the contexts inhabited by the person. Habitus also refers to a person's deportment and the manner and style in which a person performs as a social being, sometimes called the practical "departments of existence" occupied by a person.

**Haute couture** – From the French words *haute*, meaning high, and *couture*, meaning sewing; high-quality fashion design produced by a designer or couturier, usually for a specific client. Haute couture is custom made and fitted on a client. Garments are handmade and finished by skilled artisans. Haute couture is associated with the Paris fashion industry and the peak designer body, La Chambre Syndicale de la Couture.

**Heroin chic** – A term coined in the 1980s to refer to the fashion for models to appear to look disheveled, pale, anorexic, and apparently under the influence of drugs or other substances.

**Hip-hop** – Hip-hop music and fashion originated among African American youths in the late 1970s, originally as a fringe subculture but gaining mainstream attention in the 1980s as sportswear companies like Nike and Adidas used hip-hop entertainers to promote hip-hop-inspired fashion ranges. The distinctiveness of the subculture was baggy, colorful clothes such as tracksuits, jackets, boots, or sneakers and oversized gold jewelry. Shaped by black identity politics and misogyny, hip-hop musicians, rappers, and break dancers have remained controversial in mainstream popular music culture. Nonetheless, fashion designers have incorporated hip-hop influences, including Calvin Klein, Tommy Hilfiger, and DKNY. Contemporary hip-hop fashion consists of baggy pants, ostentatious jewelry or chains, large T-shirt, boots or sneakers, and a bandana or do-rag.

**Hippies** – Participants in a youth culture movement associated with the late 1960s that started in the United States (notably in the Haight-Ashbury neighborhood of San Francisco) and spread internationally in the early 1970s. Hippies rejected mainstream values and embraced counterculture values of peace and love (many being pacifists and the peace symbol becoming the symbol of hippies), collective living in communes, advocated free love, "unisex" dress, and sexual equality) and promoted health food and organic farming. It coincided with social and political crises (including the Vietnam War) that polarized societies. Hippies embraced Eastern cultures, music, philosophies and customary dress that became distinctive fashions. These included muslin or cheesecloth blouses and shirts; long hair; headbands and beads; jeans and velvet bell-bottom pants for men and women; sheepskin coats; sandals and bare feet; tie-dyed clothes; full, peasant-like, and layered skirts for women; and floral and paisley fabrics. Hippies became synonymous with psychedelic (mind-expanding) drugs, music (epitomized by the 1969 Woodstock Festival), and pop art.

**Hosiery** – Tight-fighting knitted garment covering the foot and leg made from stretch fabrics such as silk, nylon, Lycra, mesh, or microfiber. Also called stockings and tights, hosiery was originally worn with garters and suspender belts but newer technologies allowed for the creation of a one-piece garment with elasticized waist.

**Houndstooth** – Duo-tone weaving pattern. Houndstooth fabric is generally used for outwear jackets, suits, and accessories.

**House of Worth** – The first couture house, named after Charles Frederick Worth, who dominated nineteenth-century Paris fashion.

**Identity** – A person's projection of a sense of self and distinctiveness; an appearance of recognizable continuity and coherence that is visible in the attributes of character, personality, experience, social position, and lifestyle.

**Indigo** – A blue-violet dye made from a deciduous shrub grown in many countries.

**Industrial Revolution** – A technological, social, and economic revolution in the eighteenth century that changed labor configurations by way of the development of mass production in factories. It was accompanied by urbanization and the rise of a wealthy middle class. The textile and wool industries were among the first to be transformed by the Industrial Revolution, particularly in the north of England. Subsequently this new form of industrial relations occurred in other Western European countries.

**Jeans** – Sturdy work trousers made from the fabric known now as denim but originally called jean or jeane, reflecting its origins in Genoa, Italy. Jeans were worn by sailors from the Middle Ages. During the 1850s, denim trousers were adopted by Californian miners and marketed as jeans by Levi Strauss, whose company became the premier jeans brand. Since the 1950s, jeans have been a staple fashion item initially for young people but now for all ages. Designs have proliferated and diversified from grunge to designer jeans, though the use of denim is intrinsic to the distinctive form of casual wear. See denim.

**Jersey** – Knitted fabric deriving from the Channel Island of Jersey in the late nineteenth century that is soft and stretchable and manufactured using cotton, wool, silk, or artificial threads. Coco Chanel famously used jersey (then an underwear fabric) to make outwear cardigans, jackets skirts, and trousers that initially shocked public sensibilities but later became fashion classics.

**Kilt** – A traditional Scottish garment made from plaid cloth, partially pleated, wrapped around the lower torso, and fastened at the side with buckled straps. Complemented by a sporran or pouch, a kilt is reputedly worn without underpants. Kilts have also become an evergreen fashion inspiration.

**Kimono** – Traditional Japanese T-shaped robe, with wide hanging sleeves and a stand-up collar, wrapped over the left side and tied with a wide belt, or obi, at the back.

**Kitsch** – Overly sentimental, previously disdained mass-produced items that are typically garish and ironic.

**Kirtles** – Tunic-like dresses worn over a dress and under an outer gown.

**Knitwear** – Garments made from knitted textiles from variety of yarns. Knitwear may be manufactured through domestic or industrial processes. It was popularized as healthy clothing in the late nineteenth century, especially after its use in sportswear.

**Leather wear** – Garments produced from animal hides and skins or synthetics that have become associated with erotic dress, fetishism, and sexual practices.

**Leisure wear** – Casual dress for everyday living that adopted unstructured lines suited to physical activity, including sportswear, jeans, T-shirts, sweat shirts, track pants, and athletic shoes.

**Licensing** – Commercial arrangements for producing and selling brand goods under the name of a designer or fashion label (e.g., Pierre Cardin or D&G sunglasses, suitcases, or watches) by which the designer receives an upfront payment and percentage of sales.

**Livery** – Uniform worn by domestic or military servants or employees.

**Logo** – Distinctive graphic devised as a shorthand symbol of a brand, product or service such as the Nike tick, the Adidas three stripes, or the Chanel double Cs.

**Look book** – A publication produced by designers to illustrate a few key pieces, evoking themes and moods that epitomize or illustrate the upcoming seasonal silhouette and styles. Look books are circulated to fashion editors and stylists.

**LVMH** – A leading French-based multinational group associated with luxury products (Louis Vuitton-Moët-Hennessy). It is a grouping of luxury brands whose products include fashion, wines and champagnes, perfumes, and cosmetics. The president is Bernard Arnault.

**Lycra** – Elasticized artificial knitted fabric initially manufactured by Du Pont in 1958, but not widely used until the 1970s. The special qualities of Lycra include abrasion resistance and a high "stretch and recovery" quotient that is especially suitable for active sportswear and underwear.

**Mandarin suits** – A Chinese style of suit with a distinctive high collar and central opening fastened by satin knot buttons and toggles.

**Mannequins** – Life-sized fashion display dolls first used in department stores windows in the 1880s; popularized in the 1930s when new technologies enabled the manufacture of realistic facial features. Mannequins are now made from fiberglass and plastic.

**Mao suits** – Distinctive Chinese dress introduced by Mao Zedong in 1950 to mark the foundation of the Republic of China. It consisted of green or blue high-collared jacket with buttoned pockets and baggy trousers for both men and women. Initially, the Mao suit denoted membership of the Communist Party but later was universal wear in mainland China.

***Marchandes des modes*** – French term for sellers of fashion usually in salons or studios; the forerunner of couture houses.

**Marketing** – The science of selling consumer goods to create market share, reinforce brand image, and create new consumer demands through the use of techniques such as advertising and consumer market research.

**Marks and Spencer** – An English department store established in 1884 famous for guaranteed quality and value for money merchandise that targeted midlevel consumers. Marks and Spencer developed its own labels by buying apparel directly from manufacturers. M&S became a British institution, introducing product research (e.g., for new fabrics) and diversifying into many other consumer products and services.

**Masculinity** – Attributes deemed to be appropriate for a person of the male gender. Masculine attributes include virility, vigor, and power. The term is also used to refer to socially sanctioned qualities such as superiority or strength.

**Mauveine** – A reddish-purple aniline dye developed in the nineteenth century as the first synthetic organic dye used to produce red textiles.

***Mehndi*** – A form of temporary body decoration using henna, which is applied to the hands to create intricate and very fine designs. It has a long history of use in the Middle East, Asia, and North Africa and was traditionally associated with dancers and brides. The custom was revived in the 1980s by diasporic Asian communities especially as wedding ritual but also gained popularity outside Asian communities after it was adopted by celebrities such a Madonna, Brittany Spears, and Hollywood actors. Although traditionally used to decorate the hands of brides, it is now used to decorate arms, stomachs and other body surfaces.

**Metrosexual** – A term popularized in the 1990s to refer to urban heterosexual males who have high disposable income and are obsessed with their appearance and lifestyle, interests usually associated with homosexual men. The term implies diverse or ambiguous sexual identities and orientations and replaced the late 1970s "the new man" and is sometimes used interchangeably with the term "übersexual."

**Microfiber** – A new kind of synthetic made of polyester or viscose that was first used for knitwear but is now common in rain gear, parkas and sportswear due to its lightweight and soft texture, water resistance, and quick drying properties.

**Millinery** – The craft of designing and manufacturing hats and head wear.

**Minimalist** – An aesthetic philosophy of paring down to the minimum to clean and simple principles and lines. Minimalism eschews elaborate decoration and embellishment in art, architecture, interior design and fashion. Popular in the 1990s, minimalist fashion featured monochromes (black, gray, white, khaki) and avoided accessorizing clothing and looks.

**Midi** – A calf-length skirt. Despite concerted publicity campaigns (e.g., in the 1967 film *Bonnie and Clyde*), the midi, an attempt to counter the mini in the 1960s, never captured the fashion mood.

**Mini** – A very short skirt (up to the thighs) popularized in the 1960s youth pop fashions.

**Mod** – A 1960s British youth subculture that emerged among the newly enfranchised working class and embraced a distinctive mode of dress based on Edwardian suits, clothes emblazoned with union jacks, and helmet haircuts. Mods followed rhythm and blues, soul, and ska music of black American and Jamaican artists as well as the British bands the Small Faces, the Yardbirds, and the Who. Mods rode motor cycles and clashed with rockers (who wore black leather, rode motor bikes and favored rock and roll). Depicted in the

1979 film *Quadrophenia,* mod fashion became the vanguard of Swinging London's style and fashion.

**Model** – Live mannequins who show apparel at fashion shows and appear in fashion advertisements and magazines. First initiated in 1853 by Marie Worth, wife of Charles Worth, to promote his fashions, modeling took off in the twentieth century and became a glamorous career for young girls.

**Modernity** – The late eighteenth-century characterization of European societies as progressive and civilizing, based on continuous growth and change in science, technology, industry, secular government, bureaucracy, social mobility, urbanization, and new aesthetic conventions.

**Monochrome** – The use of a single color.

**Natural fibers** – Fibers derived from natural materials such as linen, cotton, silk, jute, and wool.

**New romantics** – A London youth movement that emerged in early 1980s and opposed punk by reinventing historical themes in fashion such as the use of lace, velvet cloaks, loose billowing shirts, pantaloons and scarves. This was typified by Vivienne Westwood's Pirate collection of 1981–82, which presented a neo-dandy look. New romantic bands and singers included Spandeau Ballet, Duran Duran, Depeche Mode, Boy George, and Steve Strange.

**Nike** – An American brand of sports footwear and trainers that was established in the 1960s and later endorsed by basketball player Michael Jordan in a series of famous advertising campaigns. Nike's special feature was to insert pockets of air into the sole and heel to give trademark of Nike Air using its universally recognized tick logo.

**Nudity** – The state of full or partial undress. Nudity is socially defined and varies according to conventions relating to the concealment and revelation of bare skin.

**Nylon** – A strong artificial fiber first manufactured by Du Pont in 1930s and used for women's stockings from the 1940s. It is characterized by its elasticity, sheerness, and luster.

**Orientalism** – A European term referring to the character, quality or style associated with the philosophies, expressions and fashions of Eastern nations. Orientalism became the aesthetic fashion for motifs redolent of the ancient and exotic (unknown and fabulous) as well as the cultural symbolism of the East (from Turkey to Japan). Orientalism drew on longstanding elaborate decorative traditions that influenced the choice of fabrics (e.g., silks), fabric design (e.g., exotic motifs) and the cut of garments (e.g., kimono influences, cheong-sam, draping). Ideologically, Orientalism came to be conflated with colonialism and polarized with European or Western modes of thought and traditions as the unknowable, mysterious, threatening, and exotic.

**Partlet** – Chemissette or fill-in for low décolletage.

**Peacock Revolution** – A 1960s movement in men's fashion, associated with Swinging London in the 1960s. It is typified by bold colors and prints replacing normative dull men's clothing. It overlapped with the unisex fashions of the time.

**Peek-a-boo** – A garment that involves sections cut out to reveal skin and/or underwear.

**Performativity** – The ways in which a person acts out a social role or assumes the attributes of an identity.

**Piercing** – A form of body modification that features in traditional dress but more recently as part of subcultures, sadomasochism, and bondage. Piercing has increasingly become a form of fashionable self-expression. It involves the insertion of a piece of jewelry into the skin such as the ear, nostril, tongue, belly button and eyebrows, other parts of the face.

**Plaid** – A patterned woolen cloth featuring horizontal and vertical interwoven stripes to form squares of graduating shapes, patterns, and colors; also called tartan.

**Pop art** – An artistic movement that emerged in the 1950s and shaped 1960s art fashion, borrowing from Dadaism to challenge and satirize established art forms and the mainstream art world while celebrating everyday life and ordinary, culture especially through the mass media and consumer objects. Art works were highly stylized, colorful, and easily mass produced. Exponents of pop art include Andy Warhol and Roy Lichtenstein.

**Polychrome** – The simultaneous use of many colors.

**Postcolonialism** – The term refers to cultures after colonialism but still influenced by the legacies of European occupation. In cultural theory, postcolonialism invokes the tensions and unresolved issues concerning the "between" status of former colonies whose elites may continue to identify with European values yet wish to promote the resurgence of "local" politics, identities, and cultures.

**Postmodernism** – The period from the late 1960s when the certainties of the Enlightenment period were challenges by new cultural, social, and political changes that accompanied the transformation of capitalism from extractive and manufacturing economies to service-based, globally networked and consumption-based ones. These changes heralded time-space compression, a cornucopia of choice, and new ideologies and perspectives that challenged established norms and conventions. Postmodernism influenced intellectual debate by replacing accepted theorization with meta-narratives and competing frameworks of understanding.

**PPR (Pinault-Printemps-Redoute)** – A luxury French brand foundered in 1963 by François Pinault and is now one of the largest global distributors of luxury products including Yves St Laurent, Balenciaga, Gucci, Stella McCartney, and Alexander McQueen.

**Prêt-à-porter** – The French term for ready-to-wear. In contradistinction to haute couture, it refers to clothes that carry a designer label that has been specifically produced for a modified and less exclusive collection that is mass produced in quantities for off-the-rack purchase.

**Psychedelia** – A term that originated in the 1960s to denote irregularly, brightly colored, and luminescent patterning in art, filmmaking, fabric, and lighting that attempted to replicate the effects of hallucinogenic drugs during the hippy era.

**Psychology of fashion** – Explanations for fashion in terms of individual motivations and needs. It is often associated with the writings of J. C. Flügel and René König.

**Punk** – A mid-1970s subculture that emerged among British working-class youths who had few life chances and felt alienated from mainstream culture and other youth subcultures. Punks poured their disaffection into clothing and lifestyles that confronted mainstream society and challenged dominant shibboleths with anti-social sentiments, fascist politics, misogynist attitudes, and anti-consumerist behavior. Punks wore crudely made unconventional clothing (often ripped and reconstituted) that was made from unconventional materials as well as liking bondage wear, stark makeup, Mohawks and garish-dyed hair, body piercings and tattoos, outrageous jewelry and Doc Martens. Iron crosses, Nazi swastikas, and sexually explicit and politically irreverent slogans, motifs, and symbols adorned their apparel and shocked mainstream society. Punk music, visual art, and fashion followed suit though subsequently elements were incorporated into other styles.

**Purple** – Formerly a luxurious dye extracted from thousands of gastropod mollusks to produce richly colored fabrics. The color purple became a status marker that was associated with nobility and high-ranking officials in ancient societies. Now it is artificially manufactured and has generally lost such connotations although purple is still used for certain royal and high status ceremonial garb.

**PVC** – Polyvinyl chloride, a synthetic fabric that was invented around 1930s and 1940s from the waste material of industrial processes. It was popularized in fashion in the 1960s.

***Qipao*** – (see Cheongsam)

**Rayon** – An artificial fiber made from viscose that was invented in early twentieth-century France as an alternative to silk, and used extensively in fabrics and knitwear. It was marketed for its silk-like qualities as a continuous thread and for its cotton-like toughness.

**Rap** – A 1980s youth protest movement initiated in rundown American urban areas that opposed mainstream consumer culture. Rap culture includes music (rap or hip-hop), art (graffiti), and fashion (oversized pants, sportswear, bomber jackets, and baseball caps).

**Rastas** – The Rastafarian youth movement developed in Jamaica in the 1970s and was linked to reggae music and black self-determination orchestrated around the celebration of the mysterious death in 1975 of the last Ethiopian emperor, Haile Selassie, who became a symbol of African independence and opposition to colonialism. Rasta clothing includes camouflage uniforms, jeans and woollen caps in the colors of Ethiopian flag (red, green, and gold), and dreadlocks.

**Ravers** – An antifashion statement that originated in the summer of 1987 and rejected mainstream values and embraced hedonism most visible at drug-fueled, often illegal, marathon dance parties. These were held typically in industrial warehouses or open-air venues accompanied by acid house, Afro, and funk music.

**Red** – One of the first colors used to dye fabric and apparel by the use of the madder root, kermes, and cochineal dyes. Red became important symbolically because of its similarity to the color of blood.

**Reebok** – An English athletic shoe manufacturer established in 1895, but repositioned in 1958. The company took its name from the African gazelle, the rebook. In 1979, a new direction was taken in aerobic shoes expressly designed for dance and exercise. In 1988, the Pump shoe, which automatically pumped up shoes to mould to the shape of the foot, was introduced.

**Resort wear** – A casual style of dress dating from the 1920s and 1930s that was suitable for the beach; sports such as tennis, cycling, and swimming; and other holiday and outdoor leisure activities. Resort ear is also referred to as leisure wear.

**Retailing** – The diverse forms of selling and buying, including targeted marketing and advertising, mail order, boutique, home shopping, Internet shopping, e-commerce, and lifestyle shopping. It is geared directly at the consumer, as opposed to wholesaling, which sells to an intermediary between manufacturer and consumer.

**Ruff** – A detachable and elaborate starched frill collar that was invented in Italy in the sixteenth century and spread to Elizabethan England.

**Sable** – The (usually black) fur of the African antelope.

**Safari suit** – The slang name for a two-piece men's suit of short-sleeved shirts and shorts or trousers usually made in light khaki or white fabric such as cotton or gabardine. They were adapted from the military styling of colonial administrators' uniforms, that is, with cargo pockets, epaulettes, and military-type tailoring. Typically, safari suits were worn with long white socks and lace-up shoes (leading Australian Aboriginals to call administrators "the white socks"). Safari suits were advocated as rational wear for men during the late nineteenth century and spasmodically during the twentieth century as practical wear for men in subtropical and tropical climates.

**Sailor suit** – Traditionally, a middy blouse with a large v-shaped collar at the front and low flap at the back, bell-bottom trousers, dark-colored necktie, wide-brimmed hat, and lanyard. Blue and white with dark colored contrasts were the predominant colors used for sailor suits. Stripes, arrows, anchor, sea creature or ship motifs (often embroidered), buttons, braid, and even lace embellished these uniforms. They were popularized in the mid-nineteenth century after the four-year-old Prince of Wales, Albert Edward (later King Edward VII), was painted wearing one. Thereafter, sailor suits became perennial popular wear for children.

**Sarcenet** – A fine soft silk fabric for linings.

**Sari** – A length of material that is often very brightly colored and with intricate embroidered or beaded designs that is worn by Indian (and to a lesser extent, Bangladeshi and Pakistani) women. It is draped around the body to form a skirt or trousers while the remaining long end may be slung over the shoulders or draped over the head. There are numerous draping styles and lengths dependent on regional differences. It is worn over a short tight blouse called a *choli.*

**Seasons** – A fashion term used to describe the biannual spring/summer and autumn/winter collections produced by many designers months in advance.

**Semiology of fashion** – The meaning of the formal properties and signs of garment decorations.

**Sexuality** – The cultural connotations relating to matters pertaining to sex and gender, involving biological, psychological, and sociological dimensions. Developed in the early nineteenth century to denote the quality of being sexual, sexuality refers both to normative heterosexual behavior and to other sexual leanings and so-called perversions. The term has attracted controversy concerning whether sexuality is natural or socially constructed in different cultural and historical contexts.

***Shalwar kameez*** – A two-piece outfit consisting of a long tunic top worn over loose pants. It is worn by the diaspora of Indian subcontinent women to bridge the divide between traditional dress (e.g., the sari) and Western fashions. The *kameez* is also called a *kurta,* and *churidar,* or tapered pants, are sometimes worn instead of the *shalwar.*

**Sheer** – A fine, semitransparent, or flimsy fabric that is used to produce lingerie, blouses, tights and leggings.

**Silhouette** – The outline or contour that a garment creates when worn on the body. It varies subject to changing conventions of ideal body shapes, such as the S-shape or androgynous look.

**Silk** – A natural fiber spun from the cocoon of the silkworm to produce a yarn that is then woven into luxurious fabrics.

**Slashing** – The practice of deliberately slashing or pleating the fabric to reveal the linings (often rich colorful satin or velvet). Popularized in mid-fifteenth-century Italy, the practice spread throughout Europe as a mark of distinction and stylishness. Slashing has become part of the grammar of modern fashion design.

**Sloane Ranger** – Term coined in 1979 by *Harper's* and *Queen* magazines to describe its target readers, who lived around Sloane Square in London. Female Sloanes were characterized as wearing Laura Ashley blouses, pleated skirts, flat shoes, and strings of pearls, while male Sloanes wore tweed jackets, Shetland Pullovers and green Wellington boots. They were aristocratic and aspirant upper middle-class young people who opposed or were dismissive of other youth subcultures.

**Slouch hat** – A World War I military hat made of felt (often from tufted rabbit fur) with a soft brim turned up on one side.

**Smart fibers** – New generation artificial fibers manufactured to assist the performance of the body and enhance comfort. Smart fibers can incorporate chemical, atmospheric, and electronically controlled elements to the fibers that can heat, deodorize, moisturize, and add vitamins to the body of the wearer. They have become popular for use in extreme sportswear as well as military uniforms and high fashion.

**Sneakers** – Another name for athletic shoes.

**Sportswear** – Clothes designed for sporting activities, such as swimwear, T-shirts, shorts, athletic shoes, hiking apparel, and equestrian wear.

**Style** – A combination of silhouette, construction, fabric, and details that make the performance of an outfit distinctive of an aesthetic form or individual.

**Style setters** – Usually self-appointed arbiters of taste and initiators of new trends or fads who are adept at sensing a new style and popularize it often after first scandalizing the mainstream fashion status quo.

**Stylist** – The person who frames the setting, mood, clothes, hair styling, makeup, photographs, and the overall look of every image of a collection, agreement or brand. The stylist pays attention to the detail of the presentation of a product to enhance its desirability and attention-getting qualities.

**Subculture** – A distinctive network of behavior, beliefs, and attitudes existing within a wider culture; a subgroup who share certain behavior, beliefs, values, and ways of living and dressing that unite the members of the group and distinguish the group from mainstream culture.

**Suit** – A set of clothes cut from the same fabric, generally consisting of a tailored jacket and long pants or skirt and sometimes a waistcoat. Suits may be worn with a tie and business shirt or blouse.

**Sumptuary laws** – Legislation that was enacted in Europe between the fourteenth and sixteenth centuries to control what conspicuous consumption by prescribing what different groups of people could own and wear. Prohibitions on luxury goods (such as gold and silver, velvet, silk, fur, and jewels) supplemented laws about proscribed clothes and accessories. Similar clothing regulations have been inscribed in many other cultures, including ancient China, Japan, and the Middle East.

**Supermodel** – A term popularized in the 1980s to refer to celebrity models who dominated popular culture by moving from the catwalk to become the face of global brands such as cosmetics and accessories.

**Supply chain** – All the processes and actors involved in transforming a raw material into a consumer product, that is, through the process of production, distribution, and consumption. In the apparel industry, the supply chain specifically refers to the conversion of natural fibers and chemical-based products into fabrics and other materials; the production of apparel; and distribution to wholesalers, retail suppliers, and middlemen for marketing to consumers. Key issues for the supply chain are coordination, cost, quality, reliability, and timing.

**Surfers** – A youth movement that emerged out of 1960s California beach culture associated with surfboard riders. Typified by baggy pants and short, sweat shirts, T-shirts, and sandals or thongs, surf culture later became a mainstream youth culture that spawned a distinctive style of leisure wear.

**Surrealism** – Art movement established by André Breton in 1924, best known through the work of Salvador Dali, who resolved contradictions between dream and reality by establishing a super-reality that drew on the subconscious to project fantasy and create impossible images. Surrealism influenced fashion beginning in the late 1920s, particularly in the work of Elsa Schiaparelli.

**Sustainability** – An ideology typified by late twentieth century, reflecting environmental concerns of excessive production and consumption on the destruction of natural resources upon which postmodern lifestyles depend.

**Swimming costume** – A single garment encasing the body from the neck to the leg, designed to facilitate the sport of swimming by streamlining the body. See *bikini.*

**Swinging London** – London from the mid-1960s to the early 1970s, during which time it was the centerpiece of youth culture and youth fashion. In contrast to established adult-oriented fashions sold in department stores, young art school graduates began to design clothes that appealed to devotees of popular music such as rock and roll, blues, and mod bands. Shocking older generations, young people embraced relatively cheap, counterculture, political, unisex clothing that complemented emerging youth lifestyles and purchasing power. Fascination with Eastern and ethnic cultures and beliefs also heavily influenced hippy and youth fashions and lifestyles. Swinging London became synonymous with Carnaby Street and Kings Road boutiques (such as Biba and I Was Lord Kitchener's Valet) and designers such as Mary Quant, Ossie Clark, Malcolm McLaren, and Vivienne Westwood.

**Symbols** – Accessories and the rules of combining items of apparel, to which consumers attach shared meanings and interpretations.

**Tailoring** – The system of customized (individually fitted) production of apparel where the measurement of individual customers guides the construction of unique garments.

**Tartan** – See *plaid.*

**Taste** – The abstract capacity to make cultural discriminations and choice. Good taste is defined by the knowledge of high cultural aesthetic values, while bad taste refers to the failure to recognize the conventions of beauty and quality.

**Tattooing** – A system of dyeing the skins with indelible dyes that is associated with traditional body modification to denote status and rank but increasingly has become a mainstream form of permanent body decoration.

**Taxonomy** – The classification or laws of describing and differentiating objects or phenomena of a similar kind.

**Teddy** – Combination of camisole and underwear.

**Thongs** – A narrow piece of cloth that passes between the buttocks to cover the genitals and is attached to a band around the hips; also a type of footwear that has a bifurcated strap that is attached to the sole and passes between the big toe and second toe (or makes a loop around the big toe) and is attached to the inner and outer mid-sole that slips easily on and off the foot.

**Tie** – A narrow piece of cloth tied in a knot at the neck that was first worn at the court of Charles II in fifteenth-century England.

**Toile** – A test garment of a new pattern or design made of muslin or cotton.

**Trend** – The direction in which a fashion or style is heading.

**Trickle-down theory** – Georg Simmel's theory that the elites set the fashions that are copied by the lower classes or masses thereby producing a cycle of creation and innovation followed by imitation and modification. As a fashion ceases to be distinctive because of its dissemination to wider groups, the elite adopt new fashions to remain different. The cycle of fashion speeds up during periods of rapid social change as the elite seek to maintain their aloof status.

**Trickle-up theory** – The theory that reverses the trickle-down thesis and argues that more often, especially in recent decades, fashion impulses come from everyday, subcultural, or street influences and are adopted by an influential set of fashion aspirants. Once new fads and fashions are popularized, they are appropriated by the mainstream fashion industry. While the street style embodies a badge of identity and difference, the designer version is oriented around stylishness and nowness.

**Tudor** – An English period between 1485 and 1603, named after the Tudor royal house.

**Tunic** – A tubular dress worn over a chemise and under an outer gown

**Underwear** – Garments designed to worn directly on the body under outerwear; also called intimate apparel and lingerie.

**Uniform** – Identical clothes and accoutrements. Uniforms were first associated with identical clothing manufactured for military forces to distinguish one side from another and to create a sense of collective identity and bonding.

**Utilitarian** – Practical, functional, and protective. For example, the word "utilitarian" might be used to describe clothes for manual work, gardening, and military garb for active duties (as opposed to mess or parade uniforms).

**Veiling** – The (typically) Islamic custom of covering part or all of a woman's face and other body parts with scarves or gowns to preserve modesty in public. The custom of veiling was revived in the 2000s with the resurgence of Islamic religion, law, and culture in diasporic Muslim communities. It is sometimes imposed by law but also adopted voluntarily as part of Muslim identity.

**Victorian** – An English period associated with Queen Victoria, who ruled from 1837 to 1901, during which there was great conservatism in fashion and strict moral codes.

**Vintage** – Secondhand clothing marketed as recycled fashion.

***Vogue*** – One of the most important and long-lasting associated fashion magazines, published by Condé Naste, *Vogue* was founded in 1892 in America and has subsequently published editions in many other countries.

**Weave** – A system of manufacturing cloth by interlinking yarns with warp (length-wise thread) and weft (horizontal thread) on a loom.

**White** – The color associated with purity, virginity, youth, and (in some cultures) death. In contrast to black, white is a commonly used to reflect the absence of color.

**Witches breeches** – A type of pantaloon with an elasticized waist extending to the mid-thigh. Witches breeches were made of a nylon knit fabric and were popular in the 1970s.

**Woad** – The plant from the Brassica family that is used to obtain blue dye.

**Wool** – A natural fiber from the woolen coat of sheep, goats, yaks, and alpacas. The wool is shorn from the animal and spun into woolen yarn, which is carded and knitted by hand or machine to manufacture woolen cloth or directly as garments.

**Yarn** – Any long continuous fiber used in the production of textiles and knitwear.

**Yoke** – A shaped piece of fabric at the top of a garment from which the clothing falls. It can be a decorative feature.

**Zara** – A Spanish brand and chain of fast fashion created in 1963. It is now a global firm offering menswear, women's wear, and children's clothes. It is distinguished by a "just-in-time" system where frequent runs of small numbers of garments are produced to constantly updating the range and introduce new styles.

**Zeitgeist** – The thought or feeling peculiar to a generation, period, or era.

**Zoot suit** – An outfit worn in the 1930s by African Americans who had a connection to Harlem and black dandies who patronized the jazz clubs. The suits consisted of wide and long double-breasted jackets worn with wide-legged baggy trousers and ostentatious wide ties. The zoot suit was recycled as a fashion statement in the 1980s.

# fashion milestones

## Prehistory

1310 Shoes first made for the right and left feet
1500s Slashing popularized throughout Europe
1600s Fashions set by courts and aristocracy
1661–1715 Court of Louis XIV

## 1700s

1733 The Flying Shuttle (invented by John Kay) increases the output of handloom weavers and marks the revolution of the English textile industry
1768 James Hargreaves's (1732–92) spinning jenny, which enabled spanning multiple threads at the same time
1769 Richard Arkwright's (1768–1845) water frame, which used water-run rollers to produce yarn of specified thickness and strength
James Watt's (1736–1819) steam engine, which improved means of transportation and augured a new era of tolls and machines
1778 Beau Brummell born (d. 1840)
1779 Samuel Crompton's (1753–1827) spinning mule, which combined the spinning jenny and the water frame to mechanically produce strong, soft, and fine yarn
1780s Industrial Revolution
1770s Publication of the first fashion plates and magazines (*Lady's Magazine, La Galerie des Modes*)
1789 French Revolution (subsequent changes to post-revolutionary fashion)

## 1800–50

1804 Jacquard loom for machine knitting
1810s English men's dress influenced by Beau Brummell
1821 Louis Vuitton born (d. 1892)
1822 Tight-lacing fashion changes the shape of women's fashions
1825 Charles Worth born (d. 1895)
1846 The sewing machine patented (500,000 sold in 1871)
1851 Emily Bloomer's unsuccessful campaign to introduce bloomers for women

## 1851–99

1852 Home dressmaking popularized by marketing of patterns and instructions

Source: Adapted from Christopher Breward. 2003. "Timeline." In *Fashion.* 256–60. Oxford: Oxford University Press and other sources.

Le Bon Marché department store opens in Paris

1854 Louis Vuitton opens shop in Paris

1858 Charles Worth (regarded as the founder of haute couture) establishes his own dressmaking business in Paris, signaling new approach to fashion and dress

1868 The Chambre Syndicale de la Confection et de la Couture pour Dames et Fillettes formed in Paris to stop the copying of designs

1870 Helena Rubinstein born (d. 1965)

1871 Mariano Fortuny born (d. 1949)

1873 Levi Strauss patents the metal rivets on jeans

1875 Liberty shop opens in London

1877 American fashion editor Edna Woolman Chase born (d. 1957)

1879 Paul Poiret born (d. 1944)

1880 Jean Patou born (d. 1936)

1883 Coco Chanel born (d. 1971)

1880s The rational dress movement
Fashion, including bloomers for female cyclists, influenced by sports clothes

1885 Marshall Field's store opens in Chicago

1890 Elsa Schiaparelli born (d. 1973)

1892 Vogue (USA) launched

1895 Cristóbal Balenciaga born (d. 1972)

## 1900s

1903 Paul Poiret opens haute couture salon

1904 Max Factor born (d. 1996)
Cecil Beaton born (d. 1980)

1905 Christian Dior born (d. 1957)
Claire McCardell born (d. 1958)

1907 Art nouveau influence on fashion

1908 Estée Lauder born (d. 2004)

1909 Selfridges store opens in London

## 1910s

1910 Coco Chanel opens her first boutique
Influence of Orientalism in fashion
Paul Poiret's hobble skirt
The Chambre Syndicale de la Couture Parisienne holds shows of Paris fashion overseas

1914 Pierre Balmain born (d. 1962)
Emilio Pucci born (d. 1992)

1914–18 The First World War

1916 *Vogue* (UK) launched

1917 Irving Penn born

1919 Jean Patou opens salon in Paris

## 1920s

1920 *Vogue* (Paris) launched
Chanel launches jersey knit clothing range
Sonia Delaunay (1885–1979) promotes futurist designs

1921 Chanel markets Chanel No. 5 perfume
Guccio Gucci (1881–1953) opens leather accessories shop in Florence, Italy

1922 Bill Blass born (d. 2002)
Pierre Cardin born

1923 Madeleine Vionnet (1876–1975) introduces the **bias**-cut skirt
Elsa Schiaparelli introduces knitwear line
Anne Klein born
André Courrèges born

1924 Rayon launched

1926 Chanel introduces the little black dress

1927 Hubert de Givenchy born (retired 1995)

| | |
|---|---|
| | Geoffrey Beene born (d. 2004) |
| 1928 | Levi's becomes a trademark |
| | Elsa Schiaparelli opens studio in Paris |
| 1929 | Elsa Schiaparelli launches first collection |

## 1930s

| | |
|---|---|
| 1936 | Yves Saint Laurent born (d. 2008) |
| 1931 | Lastex invented |
| 1932 | Roy Halston born (d.1990) |
| | Valentino born (sells business 1998) |
| 1933 | René Lacoste establishes Lacoste brand and Le Crocodile logo (the first logo reproduced on a garment) |
| 1937 | Cristóbal Balenciaga opens boutique in Paris |
| | Schiaparelli launches Shocking perfume and Shocking Pink range |
| | Nylon launched by DuPont |
| 1938 | Claire McCardell launches Monastic dress range, influencing New York fashion |
| | Elsa Schiaparelli launches Shocking perfume |
| | Karl Lagerfeld born |
| 1939 | Ralph Lauren born |
| 1939 | Coco Chanel closes her salon |
| 1939–45 | The Second World War |

## 1940s

| | |
|---|---|
| 1940 | Nylon stockings marketed |
| 1941 | Britain's utility scheme introduced to ration fabric and clothing |
| 1945 | Chambre de la Couture holds traveling fashion exhibitions to highlight Paris fashion |
| | Norma Kamali born |
| 1946 | Louis Réard is credited with inventing the two-piece swimsuit, the **bikini** |
| | Christian Dior sets up own boutique |
| 1947 | Dior launches the New Look, purportedly revolutionizing postwar fashion |
| 1948 | Donna Karan born |
| | Christian Dior signs the first fashion licensing agreements (or fur, stockings, and perfumes) |

## 1950s

| | |
|---|---|
| 1950 | *Vogue* (Italy) launched |
| 1951 | Haute couture in Italy launched |
| | *A Streetcar Named Desire* (film version of musical), which fans the development of youth culture and street style, opens |
| | Dacron marketed |
| 1952 | House of Worth closes |
| 1953 | Coco Chanel reopens her salon |
| 1954 | *The Wild One,* starring Marlon Brando, has a major influence on popular culture |
| | Elsa Schiaparelli closes business |
| | Balenciaga creates semi-fit clothes |
| 1955 | *Rebel without a Cause*, starring James Dean, popularizes blue jeans and youth rebelliousness |
| 1954 | Chanel reopens her Paris boutique while Schiaparelli closes |
| | Laura Ashley (1925–85) establishes boutique in the United Kingdom |
| 1955 | Mary Quant (b. 1934) opens Bazaar on Kings Road in London |
| | Velcro invented |
| 1957 | Yves Saint Laurent becomes head designer at Dior (after the sudden death of Christian Dior) |

| | |
|---|---|
| | Chanel launches her signature black quilted handbag |
| 1958 | Balenciaga launches his pillbox hat, popularized by Jackie Kennedy |
| 1959 | Lycra invented by DuPont |

## 1960s

| | |
|---|---|
| 1960 | Marc Bohan (b. 1926) appointed chief designer at Dior |
| | Barbie doll launched by Mattel |
| 1962 | Yves Saint Laurent's first collection |
| | Council of Fashion Designers of America formed |
| 1963 | Mary Quant (b. 1934) launches the mini (copied by Cardin 1965/66, Courrèges 1965) |
| | Diana Vreeland becomes editor of *Vogue* (USA) |
| 1965 | *Nova* magazine launched |
| | Zara fashion chain established |
| 1964 | Rudi Gernreich (b. 1922) launches the topless monokini |
| | Biba boutique opens in London on Kings Road |
| 1965 | Benetton group established |
| 1966 | The term "Swinging London" popularized typified by youth cultures (mods, rockers, beatniks, hippies) |
| | The film *Blow Up* gains cult following |
| | Yves Saint Laurent launches Le Smoking collection (the women's tuxedo and suit), promotes the midi, opens his ready-to-wear Rive Gauche boutique, and launches his Rive Gauche perfume |
| | Op art popularized in fashion and design (e.g., in Yves Saint Laurent's Pop Art collection, 1966/67) |
| | Twiggy becomes first supermodel epitomizing pop fashion |
| 1967 | The Beatles' *Sergeant Pepper* album sets new exotic fashion in youth clothing |
| | Peggy Moffitt models Rudi Gernreich's topless bathing suit (the monokini) |
| 1968 | Ralph Lauren (b. 1939) launches Polo range |
| | Balenciaga retires |
| | Calvin Klein (b. 1942) founds Calvin Klein Ltd. |
| 1969 | Barbara Hulanicki opens Biba on Kensington Road in London |
| | Levi Strauss markets bell-bottom jeans |
| | The Gap founded |

## 1970s

| | |
|---|---|
| 1970 | Takada Kenzo (b. 1939) opens Jungle Jap boutique in Paris |
| 1971 | Malcolm McLaren (b. 1946) and Vivienne Westwood (b. 1941) open Let It Rock in London (later known by other names—e.g., Sex in 1974, Seditionaries in 1976) |
| | Yves Saint Laurent launches his perfume Pour Homme with advertisements showing him photographed in the nude, creating controversy |
| 1972 | Nike shoes start production |
| 1973 | Rei Kawakubo (b. 1942) opens Comme des Garçons |
| | Issey Miyake (b. 1938) holds first Paris collection |
| 1974 | Zandra Rhodes (b. 1940) founds own label |
| 1975 | Yves Saint Laurent launches the pantsuit for women |

John Molloy publishes *Dress for Success,* launching power dressing (the padded, broad-shouldered power suit), initially aimed at men but attracting media and public interest in how career women should dress

Giorgio Armani (b. 1934) founds Armani label

1976 Calvin Klein launches jeans label

Kenzo Takada launches own label

Yves Saint Laurent launches Russian and Peasant collections, igniting an "ethnic" phase in fashion

1977 Farah Fawcett popularizes sneakers in a fashion shoot

*Saturday Night Fever* popularizes disco clothing and fabrics as fashion

Yves Saint Laurent launches his perfume Opium, again appearing in the advertisement

1978 Derek Jarman's *Jubilee* becomes a cult film for the emerging punk movement

Jean Paul Gaultier (b. 1952) launches label

Gianni Versace (b. 1946) launches label

Velcro marketed

1979 John Molloy publishes *Women's Dress for Success*, a guide for career women

1979 Claude Montana (b. 1949) establishes couture house

## 1980s

1980 *i-D* magazine launched

1981 Vivienne Westwood launches first solo collection, Pirate

Olivia Newton-John popularizes disco and aerobics with the song "Let's Get Physical"

The *Face* magazine launched

1981 Yohji Yamamoto (b. 1943) has first collection in Paris

1982 The United Colors of Benetton fashion chain launches controversial advertisements that establish the iconic status of brand

Westwood launches Buffalo Girls collection in Paris to acclaim

Issey Miyake launches Bodyworks collection, challenging perceptions of line and cut in Paris fashion

Domenico Dolce (b. 1958) and Stefano Gabbana (b. 1962) open Dolce & Gabbana

1983 Jean Paul Gaultier promotes underwear as outerwear

Karl Lagerfeld appointed chief designer at Chanel

1984 Donna Karan (b. 1948) establishes DKNY label, offering casual knits

Tommy Hilfiger establishes the Tommy Hilfiger Corporation

Nike signs Michael Jordan for five-year celebrity endorsement

Yves Saint Laurent retrospective exhibition at the MOMA, New York

1985 Miuccia Prada (b. 1949) launches first ready-to-wear collection

Jean Paul Gaultier creates skirts for men

Vivienne Westwood designs the minicrini

Donna Karan launches first collection

Dior bought by Bernard Arnault

1986 Levi Strauss markets Dockers (casual trousers for baby boomers who had outgrown their jeans)

Marc Jacobs (b. 1963) establishes own label

1987 Luxury fashion group LVMH created by Bernard Arnault
1988 Christian Lacroix (b. 1951) opens own couture house
1988 Lacroix establishes his first ready-to-wear line
1989 Armani launches Emporio Armani (designer global superstore)
Gianfranco Ferré (1944–2002) appointed head of women's wear, couture, and fur at Christian Dior, becoming the first non-French designer to head a Paris house

## 1990s

1990 Jean Paul Gaultier designs costumes for Madonna's Blonde Ambition tour, including the famous conical bra and corset as outerwear
1990 Tom Ford (b. 1961) appointed at Gucci
1991 Gianni Versace launches his Bondage collection
*Dazed and Confused* magazine launched
1992 Deconstructionist fashion (e.g., Hussein Chalayan)
1993 Marc Jacobs launches Grunge collection
1995 John Galliano (b. 1960) appointed at Givenchy
1994 Alexander McQueen (b. 1969) establishes his own label
Hussain Chalayan (b. 1970) introduces ready-to-wear line
1995 Maurizio Gucci (b. 1948) is murdered and Paolo Gucci (b. 1931) dies, initiating a period of instability for the company
1996 John Galliano (b. 1960) appointed to Dior
1997 Gianni Versace is murdered, label assumed by sister Donatella (b. 1955)
1997 Stella McCartney (b. 1971) appointed chief designer at Chloé
Martin Margiela (b. 1957) appointed to Hermès
Alexander McQueen succeeds John Galliano at Givenchy and is crowned the "daring new designer"
Nicolas Ghesquière (b. 1972) appointed to design for Balenciaga
Marc Jacobs appointed creative director at Louis Vuitton
1999 Gucci purchases Yves Saint Laurent and enters an arrangement with PPR

## 2000s

2000 Net-a-Porter (among other luxury fashion e-retailers) launched to become the most successful fashion "e-tailer" to date
Alexander McQueen appointed to Gucci
2001 Stella McCartney (b. 1971) establishes own label in conjunction with Gucci
Prada sold to LVMH
2002 Christian Lacroix appointed creative director at Emilio Pucci (resigns 2005)
Armani exhibition at the Guggenheim Museum, New York
2001 Stella McCartney establishes own label in conjunction with Gucci
2002 Yves Saint Laurent retires
Exhibition of Gianni and Donatella Versace's couture at the Victoria and Albert, London

2004 Tom Ford leaves Gucci and establishes own label

2006 Burberry moves its production offshore from Wales to China, creating public opposition

2007 Gianfranco Ferré dies

A voluntary BMI (body mass index) adopted by some fashion shows to set a minimum weight and size for fashion models after the deaths of several models due to anorexia

Karl Lagerfeld signs agreement with Coty to produce own fragrance line; also establishes own accessories line

Tom Ford boutique opens in New York

2008 Yves Saint Laurent dies and is acclaimed as the style muse of the late twentieth century

Louis Vuitton reinterprets its 120-year-old black-and-gray check range accessories as Damier Graphite

Karl Lagerfeld establishes ready-to-wear Lifestyle collection

# questions for essays and class discussion

## introduction: why study fashion?

0.1 What qualities make an outfit or particular look fashionable rather than mere everyday dress?

0.2 Compare two subcultures and identify the adoption of a distinctive mode of dress as part of their subcultural practices.

0.3 What are the strengths and weaknesses of analyses of fashion from (a) anthropological, (b) economic, (c) sociological, and (d) dress history approaches?

## chapter 1. the fashion impulse

1.1 What elements of contemporary Western fashion make it similar to and different from other fashion systems (of other cultures or other times)?

1.2 How do the trickle-down and bubble-up theories of fashion explain the appearance and adoption of successive fashions and fads?

1.3 What is the importance of color in fashion, and why are some colors fashion perennials, and others mere fads? Illustrate your answer with examples.

1.4 Why were sumptuary laws important in regulating civil conduct? Why did they fail?

1.5 How has the sailor suit been incorporated in recent examples of designer fashion, and how have these nautical references created distinctive meanings and symbols in these fashions?

## chapter 2. the eurocentric fashion system

2.1 How do you account for the preeminence of Paris as the fashion capital of the twentieth century?

2.2 Is haute couture an irrelevant anachronism in the new millennium and global fashion cultures?

2.3 Use examples to explain the ways in which two other fashion cities have contributed to trends in global fashion.

2.4 To what extent is the legacy of Beau Brummell still relevant for contemporary men's fashion?

2.5 Is it possible for fashion systems to exist outside consumer culture?

## chapter 3. fashion cycles, symbols, and flows

3.1 Undertake a semiotic or symbolic analysis of the messages conveyed by the little black dress or a particular brand of perfume and the different ways or contexts in which it can be worn.

3.2 Use the terms *denotation* and *connotation* to contrast how the symbolism of two items of clothing has changed as a consequence of changing dress habits and/or marketing.

3.3 Is body modification (e.g., cosmetic surgery, tattooing, piecing) just a body technique used to achieve a sense of self or does it radically undermine self-identity and the control of one's body?

3.4 New fashion merely recycles the old. Discuss.

3.5 What are the advantages and disadvantages of using an interdisciplinary framework in fashion studies? Illustrate how you would develop an analytic framework to explore the meaning and significance of either a uniform or a nightclub fashion.

## chapter 4. fashion, body techniques, and identity

4.1 Analyze and interpret the body techniques that professionals in two occupations (e.g., an artist and a zoo keeper) need to acquire, the role of clothes and deportment in their jobs, and the messages they convey to observers.

4.2 How does a body technique approach lend itself to understanding cross-cultural differences or alternative sexualities in conventions of dress? Provide some examples and analyze how body techniques create specific social bodies and performances.

4.3 What body techniques and modes of dress and deportment are recommended for job interviews? Can you analyze why particular advice (dos and don'ts) is given so dogmatically?

4.4 To what extent do the imperatives of fashion drive the cult of thinness?

4.5 Have new models of masculinity created a new language of male dress and new codes of masculinity and sexuality?

## chapter 5. fashion, aesthetics, and art

5.1 Does art determine fashion or do fashions determine art?

5.2 How does fashion differ from taste, style, and flair?

5.3 What do you think is the zeitgeist of fashion in the 2000s?

5.4 Does contemporary fashion photography provide positive or negative role models for people seeking a fashion look?

5.5 Evaluate the significance of the designs and influence of Vivienne Westwood. Does she represent an innovative turn in couture or simply an eye for controversy, parody, and pastiche?

## chapter 6. fashion as a business and cultural industry

6.1. Do copyists and counterfeiters benefit or undermine the dynamics of the fashion industry?

6.2 In what ways is fashion a cultural industry rather than just a manufacturing part of consumer culture?
6.3 To what extent has the development of prêt-à-porter and luxury brand fashion transformed the global fashion industry and consumer habits?
6.4 Why are fashion houses and brands so susceptible to boom-and-bust cycles?
6.5 Critics argue that the fashion industry is inherently exploitative in terms of manufacturing, production, and promotion. What measures can you identify that would address these issues?

## chapter 7. popular culture and fashion

7.1 What has been the legacy of the modeling industry in terms of ideal body techniques of femininity (and masculinity) and associated techniques of body management (e.g., dieting, exercise, eating disorders)?
7.2 What roles have fashion magazines and fashion shows (e.g., on television, the Internet) played in hastening cycles of fashion?
7.3 Investigate the influence of Parisian fashion on Hollywood, and Hollywood costumes and stars on Parisian fashion.
7.4 Use two or three examples to explain to what degree—and how—pop culture celebrities have influenced fashion trends.
7.5 In what ways have recent trends in popular culture transformed either sportswear or lingerie?

## chapter 8. the politics of fashion

8.1 Why is fashion commonly regarded as trivial and ephemeral when it is in fact highly politically charged and implicated in a range of political issues?
8.2 Has globalization depoliticized fashion or exacerbated its politics?
8.3 Why is the regulation of clothes so effective as both a civilizing technique and a technique of resistance?
8.4 Why has the recent trend toward veiling among Muslim women been so controversial in secular societies and among diasporic Islamic communities?
8.5 Take the example of a modernizing society (such as China, India, or Africa) to discuss what role fashion has played in kick-starting modernization and constructing a modern identity.

# annotated guide for further reading

## introduction: why study fashion?

The following references are useful for all chapters in the book as key writings on understanding fashion concepts.


Breward, Christopher. 2003. *Fashion.* Oxford: Oxford University Press.

An excellent overview and analysis of the modern fashion industry.

Carter, Michael. 2003. *Fashion Classics: From Carlyle to Barthes.* Oxford and New York: Berg.

Excerpts from influential fashion writers.

Craik, Jennifer. 1994. *The Face of Fashion: Cultural Studies in Fashion.* New York: Routledge.

An interdisciplinary perspective on fashion as a cultural form and industry.

Laver, James. 1995. *Costume and Fashion.* Rev. ed. London: Thames and Hudson.

A social history of the emergence of European fashion.

O'Hara Callan, Georgina. 2002. *Thames and Hudson Dictionary of Fashion and Fashion Designers.* London: Thames and Hudson.

An authoritative reference volume with short dictionary entries on many key aspects, figures, and details of fashion.


## chapter 1. the fashion impulse


Breward, Christopher. 1998. "Cultures, Identities, Histories: Fashioning a Cultural Approach to Dress." *Fashion Theory,* 2(4): 301–13.

Excellent overview of major recent theoretical approaches to understanding fashion.

Davis, Fred. 1992. *Fashion, Culture and Identity.* Chicago: Chicago University Press.

Contemporary sociological analysis of fashion and dress as a communicative system.

Hunt, Alan 1996. *Governance of the Consuming Passions: A History of Sumptuary Laws.* New York: St. Martin's Press.

Stimulating history of the cultural significance of sumptuary laws.

Kawamura, Yuniya. 2005. *Fashion-ology: An Introduction to Fashion Studies.* Oxford and New York: Berg.

Engaging introduction to the art of "fashion-ology" covering most aspects of the industry.

Welters, Linda and Lillethun, Abby, eds. 2007. *The Fashion Reader.* Oxford and New York: Berg.

A comprehensive reader of significant writings on all aspects of the fashion industry.


## chapter 2. the eurocentric fashion system


Breward, Christopher, and David Gilbert, eds. 2006. *Fashion's World Cities.* Oxford and New York: Berg.

Collection of chapters on emerging new fashion capitals and transnational fashion.

Buxbaum, Gerda, ed. 2005. *Icons of Fashion: The 20th Century.* New York: Prestel Verlag.

Accessible snapshots of key fashion moments of the twentieth century.

de Marly, Diana. 1980. *The History of Haute Couture, 1850–1950.* New York: Holmes and Meier.

Excellent history of the development of high fashion.

English, Bonnie. 2007. *A Cultural History of Fashion in the 20th Century.* Oxford and New York: Berg.

An overview of twentieth-century fashion from an art history perspective.

Mendes, Valerie, and Amy de la Haye. 1999. *20th Century Fashion.* London: Thames and Hudson.

Invaluable resource charting key moments in fashion history.

Steele, Valerie. 1988. *Paris Fashion: A Cultural History.* Oxford: Oxford University Press.

Brilliant analysis of the phenomenon of Paris as a fashion center.

Steele, Valerie. 2003. *Fashion, Italian Style.* New Haven, CT: Yale University Press.

Authoritative history of the emergence of the Italian fashion industry.

Welters, Linda, and Patricia Cunningham, eds. 2005. *Twentieth-Century American Fashion.* Oxford and New York: Berg.

Diverse collection of chapters on the development of the American fashion industry.

## chapter 3. fashion cycles, symbols, and flows

Barnard, Malcolm. 1996. *Fashion as Communication.* New York: Routledge.

Excellent analysis of fashion as a communicative practice.

Breward, Christopher. 2003. *Fashion.* Oxford: Oxford University Press.

Outstanding introduction to major themes in fashion studies.

Calefato, Patrizia. 2004. *The Clothed Body.* Oxford and New York: Berg.

A semiotic approach to analyzing the relationship between fashion and the body.

Craik, Jennifer. 1994. "Cosmetic Attributes: Techniques of Make-up and Perfume." In *The Face of Fashion: Cultural Studies in Fashion.* New York: Routledge. 153–75.

Analysis of the cultural meaning of cosmetics and perfume.

Hollander, Anne. 1980. *Seeing through Clothes.* New York: Avon Books.

A classic history of the development of European fashion through the interpretation of visual representations of fashion.

## chapter 4. fashion, body techniques, and identity

Bolton, Andrew. 2003. *Men in Skirts.* London: V&A Publications.

Lively study of men who wear dresses and skirts.

Chenoune, Farid. 1993. *A History of Men's Fashion.* Paris: Flammarion.

A comprehensive analysis of men's fashion from a French perspective.

Craik, Jennifer. 1994. *The Face of Fashion: Cultural Studies in Fashion.* New York: Routledge. Chapters 1 and 3.

Analysis of fashion as body techniques and the acquisition of techniques of femininity.

Mauss, Marcel. 1973. "Techniques of the Body." *Economy and Society,* 2(1): 70–87.

The classic text on body techniques.

McCracken, Grant. 1990. *Culture and Consumption: New Approaches to the Symbolic Character of Consumption, Goods and Activities.* Bloomington: Indiana University Press.

Masterful study of the emergence of consumer culture.

McDowell, Colin. 1997. *The Man of Fashion: Peacock Males and Perfect Gentlemen.* London: Thames and Hudson.

Excellent and well-illustrated reference on men's fashion history.

## chapter 5. fashion, aesthetics, and art

Brydon, Anne and Niessen, Sandra. eds. 1998. *Consuming Fashion. Adorning the Transnational Body.* Oxford and New York: Berg.

Anthology of writings on global fashion identities.

Buxbaum, Gerda, ed. 2005. *Icons of Fashion: The 20th Century.* New York: Prestel Verlag.

Accessible snapshots of key fashion moments of the twentieth century.

Kawamura, Yuniya. 2005. *Fashion-ology: An Introduction to Fashion Studies.* Oxford and New York: Berg.

Explores the factors behind fashion design and the figure of the designer.

Mackrell, Alice. 2005. *Fashion and Art.* London: Batsford.

Analysis of the relationship between aesthetic movements and fashion design.

Quinn, Bradley. 2003. *The Fashion of Architecture.* Oxford and New York: Berg.

Explores the convergence between avant-garde fashion and postmodern architectural design.

Wilson, Elizabeth. 1985. *Adorned in Dreams: Fashion and Modernity.* London: Virago.

Classic study of the intertwining of the development of the modern fashion system and the articulation of modernity in European culture.

## chapter 6. fashion as a business and cultural industry

Costantino, Maria. 1998. *Fashion Marketing and PR.* London: Batsford.

Accessible introduction to the dynamics of the fashion industry as a business.

Gill, Alison. 2006. "Limousines for the Feet." In *Shoes: A History From Sandals to Sneakers,* ed. Giorgio Riello and Peter McNeil 372–85. Oxford and New York: Berg.

A cultural history of contemporary athletic shoes.

Jackson, Tim, and David Shaw, eds. 2006. *The Fashion Handbook.* New York: Routledge.

Detailed analysis of the anatomy of the fashion industry.

Jenkyns Jones, Sue. 2005. *Fashion Design.* London: Lawrence King.

Excellent textbook on the structure of the fashion industry concerning design and industry occupations.

Leopold, Ellen. 1992. "The Manufacture of the Fashion System." In *Chic Thrills: A Fashion Reader,* ed. Juliet Ash and Elizabeth Wilson 101–17. London: Pandora Press:

Exploration of the often invisible manufacturing side of fashion.

O'Mahony, Marie, and Sarah Braddock. 2002. *Sportstech: Revolutionary Fabrics, Fashion and Design.* London: Thames and Hudson.

Coffee-table book study of new fabrics and their move from sportswear to fashion.

Quinn, Bradley. 2002. *Techno Fashion.* Oxford and New York: Berg.

Analysis of high-tech fashion design and use of fabrics.

## chapter 7. popular culture and fashion

Breward, Christopher. 2003. *Fashion.* Oxford: Oxford University Press.

Traces the representation of fashion in the popular media.

Coleridge, Nicholas. 1989. *The Fashion Conspiracy.* London: Mandarin.

Still relevant exposé of the less visible dynamics of the fashion industry.

Garber, Marjorie. 1992. *Vested Interests: Cross-Dressing and Cultural Anxiety.* New York: Routledge.

Acclaimed study of cross-dressing in straight and alternative sexual subcultures.

Jackson, Tim, and David Shaw, eds. 2006. *The Fashion Handbook.* New York: Routledge.

Includes chapters analyzing the structure of fashion promotion and marketing.

Klein, Naomi. 2000. *No Logo*. London: Flamingo.

Polemic against third world labor exploitation in fashion manufacturing by global brands.

Laver, James. 1995. *Costume and Fashion*. Rev. ed. London: Thames and Hudson.

A social history of the representation of fashion from portraiture to fashion photography to popular media.

Sims, Joshua. 1999. *Rock/Fashion.* London: Octopus.

Coffee-table look at the nexus between rock music and fashion trends.

Welters, Linda, and Abby Lillethun, eds. 2007. *The Fashion Reader.* Oxford and New York: Berg.

Includes sections on the representation of fashion in the media.

## chapter 8. the politics of fashion

Breu, Marlene, and Ronald Marchese. 2000. "Social Commentary and Political Action: The Headscarf as Popular Culture and Symbol of Political Confrontation in Modern Turkey." *Journal of Popular Culture,* 33(4): 25–38.

Fascinating analysis of the diverse forms and meanings of veiling.

Breward, Christopher, and David Gilbert, eds. 2006. *Fashion's World Cities.* Oxford and New York: Berg.

Anthology of writings on new fashion cities and the transnational movement of fashion.

Lindisfarne-Tapper, Nancy, and Bruce Ingham, eds. 1997. *Languages of Dress in the Middle East.* Richmond, Surrey, UK: Curzon Press.

Classic anthology of the politics of modes of dress (particularly veiling) in the Middle East.

Maynard, Margaret. 2004. *Dress and Globalisation.* Manchester, UK: Manchester University Press.

Groundbreaking study of the emergence of global forms of dress and fashion.

Niessen, Sandra, Ann Marie Leshkowich, and Carla Jones, eds. 2003. *Re-orienting Fashion: The Globalization of Asian Dress.* Oxford and New York: Berg.

The first comprehensive look at the development of distinctively Asian approaches to fashion and dress.

Parkins, Wendy, ed. 2002. *Fashioning the Body Politic: Dress, Gender, Citizenship.* Oxford and New York: Berg.

The first anthology of writings about the politics of dress addressing a range of issues and contexts.

Steele, Valerie, and John Major, eds. 1999. *China Chic: East Meets West.* New Haven, CT: Yale University Press.

Compelling anthology of analyses of Western influences on styles of Chinese fashion.

# bibliography


Abu-Lughod, Lila. 1990. "The Romance of Resistance: Tracing Transforming of Power Through Bedouin Women." *American Ethnologist* 17 (1): 41–55.

Adams, Marie Jeanne. 1973. "Structural Aspects of a Village Art." *American Anthropologist* 75 (February): 265–79.

Aftel, Mandy. 2000. *Essence and Alchemy: A Natural History of Perfume.* New York: North Point Press.

Agins, Teri. 1999. *The End of Fashion.* London: William Morrow.

Alderson, Maggie. 2002. "Status Sneakers." *Sydney Morning Herald* (April 18–20): 29.

Aletti, Vince. 2004. "Story Time." *Village Voice* (April 16). Available at: http://www.villagevoice.com/art/0415,aletti2,52611,13.html

Ambrose, Gavin, and Harris, Paul. 2007. *The Visual Dictionary of Fashion Design.* Lausanne, Switzerland: Ava.

Amy-Chinn, Dee, Christian Jantzen, and Per Østergaard. 2006. "Doing and Meaning: Towards and Integrated Approach to the Study of Women's Relationship to Underwear." *Journal of Consumer Culture* 6 (3): 379–401.

Andrews, John. 2007. "Business Sense: It Takes a Lot More Than Individual Flair to Stay at the Top." In *The Fashion Reader,* ed. L. Welters and A. Lillethun 357–60. Oxford: Berg.

Aoki, S. 2001. *Fruits.* London: Phaidon Press.

Aoki, S. 2005. *Fresh Fruits.* London: Phaidon Press.

Arnold, Rebecca. 2001. *Fashion, Desire and Anxiety: Image and Morality in the 20th Century.* London: I. B. Tauris.

Arnould, Eric, and Richard Wilk. 1984. "Why Do the Nativess Wear Adidas?" *Advances in Consumer Research* 11: 748–52.

Art Gallery of New South Wales. 1987. *Yves Saint Laurent Retrospective.* Sydney, Australia: Art Gallery of New South Wales.

*Australian*. 2007. "After Brangelina Comes Kate and Pete Inc." June 25: 13.

Australian Broadcasting Corporation News Radio. 2008. Interview between Jo Kellock, Executive Director of the Textile and Fashion Industry Association, and Jennifer Byrne. July 22.

Baker, Patricia. 1997. "Politics of Dress: The Dress Reform Laws of 1920–1930s Iran." In *Languages of Dress in the Middle East,* ed. N. Lindisfarne-Tapper and B. Ingham 178–92. Richmond, Surrey, UK: Curzon Press.

Baron, Stanley. 1995. *Sonia Delaunay: The Life of an Artist.* London: Thames and Hudson.

Barthes, Roland. 1984. *The Fashion System.* New York: Hill and Wang.

Barthes, Roland. 2006. *The Language of Fashion.* Trans. Andy Stafford, ed. A. Stafford and M. Carter. Sydney, Australia: Power.

Bartlett, Djurdja. 2004. Review of *Fashion under the Occupation,* by Dominique Veillon. *Fashion Theory* 8 (1): 117–22.

Baum, Caroline. 2007. "Retail revamp." *Qantas*, August, pp. 105–8.

Bauman, Zygmunt. 2001. "Consuming Life." *Journal of Consumer Culture* 1 (1): 9–29.

Bayley, Stephen. 1991. "Fashion: Being and Dressing." In *Taste: The Secret Meaning of Things* 142–72. New York: Pantheon Books.

Bean, Susan. 1989. "Ghandi and *Khadi,* the Fabric of Indian Independence." In *Cloth and the Human Experience,* ed. A. Weiner and J. Schneider 356–82. Washington, DC: Smithsonian Institution Press.

Bearn, Emily. 2003. "Lost Claws." *Sydney Morning Herald Weekend* (August 9–10): 5.

Belfanti, Carlo, and Fabio Giusberti. 2000. "Clothing and Social Inequality in Early Modern Europe: Introductory Remarks." *Continuity and Change* 15 (3): 359–65.

Bénaïm, Laurence. 1997. *Issey Miyake.* London: Thames and Hudson.

Benedict, Ruth. 1931. "Dress." *Encyclopedia of the Social Sciences,* Vol. 5. New York: Macmillan. 235–37.

Bhachu, Parminder. 2003. "Designing Diasporic Markets: Asian Fashion Entrepreneurs in London." In *Re-Orienting Fashion: The Globalization of Asian Dress,* ed. S. Niessen, A. M. Leshkowich, and C. Jones 139–84. Oxford: Berg.

Bhandari, Vandana. 2005. "Fashion in India." In *The Fashion Reader,* ed. L. Welters and A. Lillethun 387–91. Oxford: Berg.

Bhatia, Nandi. 2003. "Fashioning Women in Colonial India." *Fashion Theory* 7 (3/4): 327–44.

Biswas, A. 2003. *Indian Costumes.* New Delhi: Ministry of Information and Broadcasting, Government of India.

Black, Sandy. 2008. *Eco-Chic: The Fashion Paradox.* London: Black Dog.

Blakeley, Kiri. 2007. "The World's Top Earning Models." *Forbes* (July 16). Available at: http://www.msnbc.msn.com/id/19791212/

Blumer, Herbert. 1968. "Fashion." *Encyclopaedia of Social Sciences,* ed. David Sills and Robert Merton 341–45. New York: Macmillan.

Bogatyrev, Peter. 1971. *The Functions of Folk Costume in Moravian Slovakia.* The Hague: Mouton.

Bolton, Andrew. 2003. *Men in Skirts.* London: V&A Publishing.

Bolton, Andrew. 2008. *Super Heroes: Fashion and Fantasy.* New York: Metropolitan Museum of Art.

Bossan, Mari-Josèphe. 2004. *The Art of the Shoe.* Paris: Parkstone International.

Bourdieu, Pierre. 1980. "Haute couture et haute culture." In *Questions de Sociologie.* Paris: Les Editions de Minuit. 196–200.

Bourdieu, Pierre. 1986. "The Biographical Illusion." *Actes de la Recherche en Sciences Sociales.* Paris: Les Editions de Minuit. 196–206.

Braham, Peter. 1997. "Fashion: Unpacking a Cultural Production." In *Production of Culture/Cultures of Production*, ed. P. du Gay 119–65. London: Sage.

Brain, Robert. 1979. *The Decorated Body.* London: Hutchinson.

Brenninkmeyer, Ingrid. 1963. *The Sociology of Fashion.* Paris: Librarie du Recueil Sirey.

Bressler, Karen, Karoline Newman, and Gillian Proctor. 2000. *A Century of Lingerie.* Royston, Hertfordshire, UK: Eagle Editions.

Breu, Marlene, and Ronald Marchese. 2000. "Social Commentary and Political Action: The Headscarf as Popular Culture and Symbol of Political Confrontation in Modern Turkey." *Journal of Popular Culture* 33 (4): 25–38.

Breward, Christopher. 1998. "Cultures, Identities, Histories: Fashioning a Cultural Approach to Dress." *Fashion Theory* 2 (4): 301–13.

Breward, Christopher. 2003. *Fashion.* Oxford: Oxford University Press.

Breward, Christopher. 2004. *Fashioning London: Clothing and the Modern Metropolis.* Oxford: Berg.

Breward, Christopher, and David Gilbert, eds. 2006. *Fashion's World Cities.* Oxford: Berg.

Breward, Christopher, Becky Conekin, and Caroline Cox, eds. 2002. *The Englishness of English Dress.* Oxford: Berg.

Breward, Christopher, Davis Gilbert, and Jenny Lister, eds. 2006. *Swinging Sixties.* London: V&A Publications.

Buxbaum, Gerda, ed. 2005. *Icons of Fashion: The 20th Century.* Munich: Prestel Verlag.

Callaway, Helen. 1997. "Dressing for Dinner in the Bush: Rituals of Self-Definition and British Imperial

Authority." In *Dress and Gender: Making and Meaning,* ed. R. Barnes and J. Eicher 232–47. Oxford: Berg.

Callaway, Nicholas. 1988. *Issey Miyake: Photographs by Irving Penn.* New York: New York Graphic Society.

Cammann, Schuyler. 1952. *China's Dragon Robes*. New York: Ronald Press.

Cannon, Aubrey. 1998. "The Cultural and Historical Contexts of Fashion." In *Consuming Fashion: Adorning the Transnational Body,* ed. A. Bryden and S. Niessen 23–38. Oxford: Berg.

Cardon, Dominique. 2004. "Fashion in Colors and Natural Dyes: History under Tension." In *Fashion in Colors.* Akiko Fukai. New York: Assouline. 229–32.

Carter, Meg. 2005. "EU Brands Pilgrims on Path to Muslim Market." *The Australian* (August 12): 23.

Carter, Michael. 2003. *Fashion Classics: From Carlyle to Barthes.* Oxford: Berg.

Cassin-Scott, Jack. 1997. *The Illustrated Encyclopaedia of Costume and Fashion: From 1066 to the Present.* London: Studio Vista.

Charles-Roux, Edmonde. 1995. *Chanel.* London: Harvill Press.

Chatty, Dawn. 1997. "The Burqua Face Cover: An Aspect of Dress in Southeastern Arabia." In *Languages of Dress in the Middle East,* ed. N. Lindisfarne-Tapper and B. Ingham 127–48. Richmond, Surrey, UK: Curzon Press.

Chen, Tina Mai. 2001. "Dressing for the Party: Clothing, Citizenship, and Gender-Formation." *Fashion Theory* 5 (2): 143–71.

Chenoune, Farid. 1993. *A History of Men's Fashion.* Paris: Flammarion.

Childers, Caroline. 1999. *Designers of Time.* New York: BW Publishing Associates.

Clark, Hazel, and Agnes Wong. 1997. "Who Still Wears the Cheungsam?" In *Evolution and Revolution: Chinese Dress, 1700s–1990s,* ed. C. Roberts 65–74. Sydney, Australia: Powerhouse.

Clarke, Alison, and Daniel Miller. 2002. "Fashion and Anxiety." *Fashion Theory* 6 (2): 191–214.

Cohn, Bernard. 1989. "Cloth, Clothes, and Colonialism: India in the Nineteenth Century." In *Cloth and the Human Experience,* ed. A. Weiner and J. Schneider 304–55. Washington, DC: Smithsonian Institution Press.

Cole, Shaun. 2000. " 'Macho Man': Clones and the Development of a Masculine Stereotype." *Fashion Theory* 4 (2): 125–40.

Coleridge, Nicholas. 1989. *The Fashion Conspiracy.* London: Mandarin.

Collins, Carolyn. 1997. "The Long Reach of R.M. Williams." *Australian* (October 4–5).

Color Me Beautiful. 2008. "Hello Spring!" Available at: http://www.colormebeautiful.com/seasons/spring/index.html

Colour Affects. 2007. "Colour in Fashion." Available at: http://www.colour-affects.co.uk/fashion.html

Comaroff, Jean. 2003. "The Empire's Old Clothes." In *The Consumption Reader,* ed. D. Clarke, M. Doel, and K. Housiaux 100–6. London: Routledge.

Cosgrove, Stuart. 1989. "The Zoot Suit and Style Warfare." In *Zoot Suits and Second Hand Dresses,* ed. A. McRobbie 3–22. London: Macmillan.

Cosic, Miriam. 2001. "Paris Unmatched." *Australian* (March 17–18): 20–23.

Costantino, Maria. 1998. *Fashion Marketing and PR.* London: B. T. Batsford.

Cox, R. 2003. *The Zen Arts: An Anthropological Study of the Culture of Aesthetic Form in Japan.* London: Royal Asiatic Society Books, Routledge Curzon.

Craik, Jennifer. 1993. "Exotic Impulses in Fashion." *Southern Review* 26 (3): 397–418.

Craik, Jennifer. 1994. *The Face of Fashion: Cultural Studies in Fashion.* London: Routledge.

Craik, Jennifer. 2005. *Uniforms Exposed: From Conformity to Transgression.* Oxford: Berg.

Craik, Jennifer, and Sharon Peoples. 2006. "Review of Vivienne Westwood: 34 Years in Fashion." *Fashion Theory* 10 (3): 387–99.

Crawford, Joanna. 2004. "Clothing Distribution and Social Relations c. 1350–1500." In *Clothing Culture, 1350–1650,* ed. C. Richardson 153–64. Aldershot, UK: Ashgate.

Crawley, A. E. 1912. "Dress." In *Encyclopedia of Religion and Ethics.* Vol. 5. New York: Charles Scribner's Sons. 40–72.

Cunnington, Phillis, and C. W. Cunnington. 1951. *The History of Underclothes.* London: Michael Joseph.

Dalby, Lisa. 1993. *Kimono: Fashioning Culture.* New Haven, CT: Yale University Press.

Damase, Jacques. 1991. *Sonia Delaunay: Fashion and Fabrics.* New York: Harry N. Abrams.

Danielsen, Shane. 1999. "Sporty but Nice." *Australian* (February 1): 15.

Davis, Fred. 1992. *Fashion, Culture and Identity.* Chicago: Chicago University Press.

De la Haye, Amy, ed. 1997. *The Cutting Edge: 50 Years of British Fashion.* London: V&A Publications.

De la Haye, Amy 2001. "'A Dress Is No Longer a Little, Flat Closed Thing': Issey Miyake, Rei Kawakubo and Junya Watanabe." In *Radical Fashion,* ed. C. Wilcox 28–37. London: V&A Publications.

De la Haye, Amy 2002. "Gilded Brocade Gowns and Impeccable Tailored Tweeds: Vistor Stiebel (1907–76) a Quintessentially English Designer." In *The Englishness of English Dress,* ed. C. Breward, B. Conekin, and C. Cox 147–57. Oxford: Berg.

De la Haye, Amy, and Cathie Dingwall. 1997. *Surfers Soulies Skinheads and Skaters: Subcultural Style: From the Forties to the Nineties.* London: V&A Publications.

De la Haye, Amy, and Shelley Tobin. 2001. *Chanel. The Couturière at Work.* London: Victoria and Albert Museum.

De Marly, Diana. 1980. *The History of Haute Couture, 1850–1950.* New York: Holmes and Meier.

Demasi, Laura. 2003. "Fashion's Latest Trend: Clothes." *Sydney Morning Herald Weekend* (November 1–2): sec. 6, 1, 4.

Dennis, Anthony. 2004. "So, This Princess Walks into a Bar..." *Sydney Morning Herald* (May 15–16): 1, 10.

Denny-Brown, Andrea. 2004. "Rips and Slits: The Torn Garment and the Medieval Self." In *Clothing Culture, 1350–1650,* ed. C. Richardson 223–37. Aldershot, UK: Ashgate.

Di Trocchio, Paola. 2008. "Black Magic." In *Black in Fashion: From Mourning to Night,* ed. National Gallery of Victoria 57–68. Melbourne, Australia: National Gallery of Victoria.

Drake, Alicia. 2007. *Before the Fall: Fashion, Genius and Glorious Excess in Paris.* New York: Little, Brown.

Drewal, Henry, and Margaret Drewal. 1990. *Gẹlẹdẹ: Art and Female Power Among the Yoruba.* Bloomington: Indiana University Press.

Dudjic, Deyan. 1990. *Rei Kawakubo and Comme des Garçons.* New York: Rizzoli International.

Dwyer, Claire. 1999. "Veiled Meanings: Young Muslim Women and the Negotiation of Differences." *Gender, Place and Culture* 6 (1): 5–26.

Dwyer, Claire. 2006. "Fabrications of India: Transnational Fashion Networks." In *Fashion's World Cities,* ed. C. Breward and D. Gilbert 217–34. Oxford: Berg.

Eager, Alan. 1998. "Akubra: An Aussie Icon." *Outback: The Heart of Australia* 1: 58–62.

Ebin, Victoria. 1979. *The Body Decorated.* London: Thames and Hudson.

Eco, Umberto. 2007. "Lumbar Thought." In *Fashion Theory: A Reader,* ed. M. Barnard 315–17. London: Routledge.

Edwards, Bronwen. 2006. "Shaping the Fashion City: Master Plans and Pipe Dreams in the Post-war West End of London." In *Fashion's World Cities,* ed. C. Breward and D. Gilbert 159–73. Oxford: Berg.

Edwards, Penny. 2001. "Restyling Colonial Cambodia (1860–1954): French Dressing, Indigenous Custom and National Costume." *Fashion Theory* 5 (4): 389–416.

Ehrman, Edwina. 2002. "The Spirit of English Style: Hardy Amies, Royal Dressmaker and International Businessman." In *The Englishness of English Dress,* ed. C. Breward, B. Conekin, and C. Cox 133–45. Oxford: Berg.

Ekland, Brit. 1984. *Sensual Beauty and How to Achieve It.* London: Sidgwick and Jackson.

Elias, Norbert. 1983. *The Court Society.* Oxford: Basil Blackwell.

Elliott, Jane. 1997. "The Politics of Antipodean Dress." *Journal of Australian Studies* 52: 20–33.

English, Bonnie. 2005. "Fashion as Art: Postmodernist Japanese Fashion." In *The Cutting Edge: Fashion from Japan,* ed. L. Mitchell 29–41. Sydney, Australia: Powerhouse.

English, Bonnie. 2007. *A Cultural History of Fashion in the 20th Century.* Oxford: Berg.

Entwistle, Joanne. 1997. "'Power Dressing' and the Construction of the Career Woman." In *Buy This Book: Studies in Advertising and Consumption,* ed. M. Nava, A. Blake, I. MacRury, and B. Richards 311–23. London: Routledge.

Evans, Caroline. 2003. *Fashion at the Edge: Spectacle, Modernity and Deathliness.* New Haven, CT: Yale University Press.

Fabri, Charles. 1961. *A History of Indian Dress.* Calcutta: Orient Longmans.

Falk, Pasi. 1997. "The Benetton-Toscani Effect: Testing the Limits of Conventional Advertising." In *Buy This Book: Studies in Advertising and Consumption,* ed. M. Nava, A. Blake, I. MacRury, and B. Richards 64–83. London: Routledge.

Fandy, Mamoun. 1998. "Political Science Without Clothes: The Politics of Dress or Contesting the Spatiality of the State in Egypt." *Arab Studies Quarterly* 20 (2): 87–105.

Farkas, Alexander. 1951. *Perfume Thru the Ages: A Brief History of the Civilizing Influence of Fragrance.* New York: Psychological Publishing.

Featherstone, Mike. 1991. "The Body in Consumer Culture." In *The Body: Social Process and Cultural Theory,* ed. M. Featherstone, M. Hepworth, and B. Turner 170–96. London: Sage.

Fields, Jill. 2006. "From Black Venus to Blonde Venus: The Meaning of Black Lingerie." *Women's History Review* 1 (4): 611–23.

Fine, Ben, and Ellen Leopold. 1993. *The World of Consumption.* London: Routledge.

Finkelstein, Joanne. 1994. *Slaves of Chic: An A–Z of Consumer Fashion.* Port Melbourne, Victoria, Australia: Minerva.

Finnane, Antonia. 1999. "What Should Chinese Women Wear? A National Problem." In *Dress, Sex and Text in Chinese Culture,* ed. A. Finnane and A. McLaren 3–36. Clayton, Victoria, Australia: Monash Asia Institute, Monash University.

Finnane, Antonia. 2007. *Changing Clothes in China: Fashion, History, Nation.* Sydney, Australia: University of New South Wales Press.

Fogg, Marnie. 2003. *Boutique. A '60s Cultural Phenomenon.* London: Michael Beazley.

Foley, Caroline. 1893. "Fashion." *Economic Journal* 3 (11): 458–74.

Fondation Cartier pour l'Art Contemporain. 1999. *Issey Miyake: Making Things.* New York: Scalo.

Fontanel, Béatrice. 1992. *Support and Seduction: The History of Corsets and Bras.* New York: Harry N. Abrams.

Fragrance Foundation. 2004. "Vivienne Westwood Interview." Available at: http://www.fragrance.org/Ftforum_vivienne.html

Frankel, Susannah. 2001. "Radical Traditionalists. Azzadine Alaïa and Jean Paul Gaultier." In *Radical Fashion,* ed. C. Wilcox 18–27. London: V&A Publications.

Frankel, Susannah. 2007. "Deconstructing Naomi." *Weekend Australian Magazine* (March 31–April 1): 46–8.

Fray, Peter. 2004. "Homegrown Royal New Jewel in the Crown." *Sydney Morning Herald* (May 15–16): 1, 11.

Frederick, William. 1997. "The Appearance of Revolution. Cloth, Uniform, and the Permuda Style in East

Java, 1945–1949." In *Outward Appearances: Dressing State and Society in Indonesia,* ed. H. Schulte Nordholt 199–248. Leiden: KITLV Press.

Fukai, Akiko. 2004. *Fashion in Colors.* New York: Assouline.

Fukai, Akiko. 2005. "A New Design Aesthetic." In *The Cutting Edge: Fashion from Japan,* ed. L. Mitchell 19–27. Sydney: Powerhouse.

Gambotto, Antonella. 2004. "A Model Train Wreck." *Australian* (August 20): 18.

Gaines, Jane, and Jane Herzog, eds. 1990. *Fabrications: Costume and the Female Body.* London: Routledge.

Garber, Marjorie. 1992. *Vested Interests: Cross-Dressing and Cultural Anxiety.* London: Routledge.

Garrett, Valery. 2007. *Chinese Dress: From the Qing Dynasty to the Present.* Vermont and Singapore: Tuttle.

Gaugele, Elke. 2003. "Unter dem Kleid sitzt immer Fleisch—Plastische Korper und formende Blicke der Kleiderreformbewegung um 1900." In *Femme fashion 1780–2004. Der Modellierung des Weiblichen in der Mode,* ed. Patricia Brattig 59–81. Stuttgart: Arnoldsche Art.

Gilbert, David. 2000. "Urban Outfitting: The City and the Spaces of Fashion Culture." In *Fashion Cultures: Theories, Explorations and Analysis,* ed. S. Bruzzi and P. Church Gibson 7–24. London: Routledge.

Gilbert, David. 2006. "From Paris to Shanghai: The Changing Geographies of Fashion's World Cities." In *Fashion's World Cities,* ed. C. Breward and D. Gilbert 3–32. Oxford: Berg.

Gill, Alison. 2006. "Limousines for the Feet." In *Shoes: A History from Sandals to Sneakers,* ed. G. Riello and P. McNeil 372–85. Oxford: Berg.

Goldstein-Gidoni, Ofra. 1999. "Kimono and the Construction of Gendered and Cultural Identities." *Ethnology* 38 (4): 351–371.

Gotting, Peter. 2003. "Rise of the Metrosexual." *The Age* (March 11). Available at: http://www.theage.com.au/articles/2003/03/10/1047144914842.html

Grand, France. 1998. *Comme des Garçons.* London: Thames and Hudson.

Gröning, Karl. 2001. *Decorated Skin: A World Survey of Body Art.* London: Thames and Hudson.

Grove-White, Annie. 2001. "No Rules, Only Choices? Repositioning the Self within the Fashion System in Relation to Expertise and Meaning: A Case Study of Colour and Image Consultancy." *Journal of Material Culture* 6 (2): 193–211.

Guenther, Irene. 2004. *Nazi Chic: Fashioning Women in the Third Reich.* Oxford: Berg.

Haid, Carmen, Tim Jackson, and David Shaw. 2006. "Fashion PR and Styling." In *The Fashion Handbook,* ed. T. Jackson and D. Shaw 172–87. London: Routledge.

Hall, Marian. 2002. *California Fashion: From the Old West to New Hollywood*. New York: Harry N. Abrams.

Hall-Duncan, Nancy. 1979. *The History of Fashion Photography.* New York: Alpine Book.

Halley, Peter. 2004. "Fashion Victims." *ArtForum.* Available at: http://www.findarticles.com/p/articles/mi_m0268/is_9_42/ai_n6081702/print

Hansen, Karen Tranberg. 2005. "Crafting Appearances: The Second Hand Clothing Trade and Dress Practices in Zambia." In *Old Clothes, New Looks: Second Hand Fashion,* ed. A. Palmer and H. Clark 103 –18. Oxford: Berg.

Harrison, Martin. 1985. Introduction. In *Shots of Style,* ed. D. Bailey 13–55. London: Victoria and Albert Museum.

Hayward Gallery. 1999. *Addressing the Century: 100 Years of Art and Fashion.* London: Hayward Gallery.

Heller, Sarah-Grace. 2004. "Anxiety, Hierarchy, and Appearance in Thirteenth-Century Sumptuary Laws and the Roman de la Rose." *French Historical Studies* 27 (2): 311–48.

Hervia. 2004. "Menswear Collection SS2005—a Letter from Vivienne." Available at: http://www.hervia.com/news/news.asp

Hesse-Biber, Sharlene. 2006. *The Cult of Thinness.* Oxford: Oxford University Press.

Hibbert. Adam. 2004. *Fashion.* London: Franklin Watts.

Hines, Tony. 2006. "The Nature of the Clothing and Textiles Industries: Structure, Context and Processes." In *The Fashion Handbook,* ed. T. Jackson and D. Shaw 3–19. London: Routledge.

Hollander, Anne. 1978. *Seeing Through Clothes.* New York: Avon.

Hongxing, Zhang, and Lauren Parker, eds. 2008. *China Design Now.* London: V&A Publications.

Howell, Georgina. 1998. *Diana: Her Life in Fashion.* Ringwood, Victoria, Australia: Viking Penguin Books.

Huckbody, Jamie. 2007. "Trunk Show." *Harpers Bazaar,* November. Available at: http://www.harpersbazaar.com.au/Fame/2007-11-13_Fame_Interviews_Trunk+show.htm

Hume, Marion. 1997. "Tailoring." In *The Cutting Edge: 50 Years of British Fashion,* ed. A. de la Haye 36–61. London: V&A Publications.

Hunt, Alan. 1996. *Governance of the Consuming Passions: A History of Sumptuary Laws.* New York: St. Martin's Press.

International Trade Centre. 2001. "Don't Be Off-Colour." *International Trade Forum* Available at: http://www.tradeforum.org/news/printpage.php/aid/418/Don't_Be_Off-colour.html

Irvine, Susan. 1996. *Perfume: The Creation and Allure of Classic Fragrance.* London: Aurum.

iStock. 2005. "Dernier Cri: A Peep to Fashion Photography." Available at: http://www.istockphoto.com/article_view_print.php?ID=26

Jackson, Tim. 2006. "Fashion Design." In *The Fashion Handbook,* ed. T. Jackson and D. Shaw 29–56. London: Routledge.

Jackson, Tim, and Carmen Haid. 2006. "Global Luxury Brands." In *The Fashion Handbook,* ed. T. Jackson and D. Shaw 57–82. London: Routledge.

James, S. 1984. *The Princess of Wales Fashion Handbook.* London: Orbis.

Januszczak, Waldemar. 2004. "Art: Vivienne Westwood." May 18. Available at: http://travel.timesonline.co.uk/printFriendly/0..2004_12629-1-66081-12629.00.html

Januszczak, Waldemar. 2007. "Bright Stars in the Gloom." *Australian* (August 6): 8.

Jenkyn Jones, Sue. 2005. *Fashion Design.* London: Lawrence King.

Johnson, Kim, Susan Torntore, and Joanne Eicher, eds. 2003. *Fashion Foundations: Early Writings on Fashion and Dress.* Oxford: Berg.

Jones, Carla. 2003. "Dress for *Sukses:* Fashioning Femininity and Nationality in Urban Indonesia." In *Re-Orienting Fashion: The Globalization of Asian Dress,* ed. S. Niessen, A. M. Leshkowich, and C. Jones 185–214. Oxford: Berg.

Jones, Carla, and Ann Marie Leshkowich. 2003. "Introduction: The Globalization of Asian Dress: Re-Orienting Fashion or Re-Orienting Asia?" In *Re-Orienting Fashion: The Globalization of Asian Dress,* ed. S. Niessen, A. M. Leshkowich, and C. Jones 1–48. Oxford: Berg.

Jones, Mablen. 1987. *Getting It On: The Clothing of Rock and Roll.* New York: Abbeville Press.

Jonsson, Hjorleifur, and Nora Taylor. 2003. "National Colours: Ethnic Minorities in Vietnamese Public Imagery." In *Re-Orienting Fashion: The Globalization of Asian Dress,* ed. S. Niessen, A.M. Leshkowich, and C. Jones 159–37. Oxford: Berg.

Joseph, Nathan. 1986. *Uniforms and Nonuniforms.* New York: Greenwood.

Kaur, Jasbir. 2003.Review of *The Sari,* by Mukulika Banjerjee and Daniel Miller. *Fashion Theory* 7 (3/4): 415–18.

Kawamura, Yunika. 2004. *The Japanese Revolution in Paris Fashion.* Oxford: Berg.

Kawamura, Yunika. 2005. *Fashion-ology: An Introduction to Fashion Studies.* Oxford: Berg.

Kawamura, Yunika. 2006. "Placing Tokyo on the Fashion Map: From Catwalk to Streetstyle." In *Fashion's*

*World Cities,* ed. C. Breward and D. Gilbert 55–68. Oxford: Berg.

Keenan, Brigid. 1977. *The Women We Wanted to Look Like.* London: Macmillan.

Kelly, Ian. 2006. *Beau Brummell: The Ultimate Man of Style.* New York: Free Press.

Kenko, Y. 1967. *"The Tsurezureguse of Kenko" or Essays in Idleness.* Trans. D. Keene. New York: Columbia University Press.

Kennett, Frances. 1975. *History of Perfume.* London: Harrap.

Kent, Tony, and Riva Berman Brown. 2006. "Erotic Retailing in the UK (1963–2003)." *Journal of Management History* 12 (2): 199–211.

Khan, Naseem. 1992. "Asian Women's Dress: From Burqah to Bloggs—Changing Clothes for Changing Times." In *Chic Thrills: A Fashion Reader,* ed. J. Ash and E. Wilson 61–74. London: Pandora.

Kinsella, Sharon. 2002. "What's Behind the Fetishism of Japanese School Uniforms?" *Fashion Theory* 6 (2): 215–38.

Kirk, Malcolm, and Andrew Strathern. 1987. *Man as Art.* Berlin: Taco.

Kitchen, Leanne. 2008. "Bullish in a China Shop." *Qantas: The Australian Way,* August: 92–100.

Klein, Naomi. 2000. *No Logo.* London: Flamingo.

Kroeber, Alfred. 1919. "On the Principle of Order in Civilization as Exemplified by Changes in Fashion." *American Anthropologist* 21: 235–63.

Kroeber, Alfred, and Jane Richardson. 1940. "Three Centuries of Women's Dress Fashions." *Anthropological Records,* 5.

Kunz, Jean Lock. 1996. "From Maoism to *Elle*: The Impact of Political Ideology on Fashion Trends in China." *International Sociology* 11 (3): 317–35.

Langley, William. 2004a. "Bright New Star." *Australian Woman's Weekly,* August: 38–46.

Langley, William. 2004b. "The Grandmother of Punk." *Australian Woman's Weekly,* November: 102–8.

Langley, William. 2004c. "Princess Masako: Prisoner in Her Own Palace." *Australian Woman's Weekly,* July: 62–68.

Langley, William 2005. "The Fall of a Supermodel." *Australian Woman's Weekly,* November: 62–66.

Langley, William 2007. "Mary, Mary Quite Contrary." *Australian Woman's Weekly,* May: 44–50.

Laver, James. 1937. *Taste and Fashion: From the French Revolution to the Present Day.* London: Harrap.

Laver, James. 1966. *Dress; How and Why Fashions in Men's and Women's Clothes have changed during the Past Few Hundred Years.* London: John Murray.

Laver, James. 1969. *Modesty in Dress: An Inquiry into the Fundamentals of Fashion.* London: Heinemann.

Laver, James. 1995. *Costume and Fashion.* Rev. ed. London: Thames and Hudson.

Lee, Suzanne. 2005. *Fashioning the Future: Tomorrow's Wardrobe.* London: Thames and Hudson.

Lehnert, Gertrud. 2000. *A History of Fashion in the 20th Century.* Cologne: Könemann.

Leopold, Ellen. 1992. "The Manufacture of the Fashion System." In *Chic Thrills: A Fashion Reader,* ed. J. Ash and E. Wilson 101–17. London: Pandora Press.

Leventon, Melissa. 2005. *Artwear: Fashion and Anti-fashion.* London: Thames and Hudson.

Lévi-Strauss, Claude. 2004. "The Two Faces of Red." In Akiko Fukai, *Fashion in Colors* 21. New York: Assouline.

Li, Xiaoping. 1998. "Fashioning the Body in Post-Mao China." In *Consuming Fashion: Adorning the Transnational Body,* ed. A. Bryden and S. Niessen 71–89. Oxford: Berg.

Lipovestsky, Giles. 1994. *The Empire of Fashion: Dressing Modern Democracy.* Princeton, NJ: Princeton University Press.

Lloyd, Valerie. 1986. *The Art of Photographic Covers.* London: Octopus Books.

Lobenthal, Joel. 1990. *Radical Rags: Fashions of the Sixties.* New York: Abbeville Press.

Locher-Scholten, Elsbeth. 1997. "Summer Dresses and Canned Food: European Women and Western

Lifestyles in the Indies, 1900–1942." In *Outward Appearances: Dressing State and Society in Indonesia,* ed. H. Schulte Nordholt 151–80. Leiden: KITLV Press.

Lunn, Jacqueline. 2003. "Anyone for Tennis?" *Sydney Morning Herald,* (August 2–3): 9.

Lurie, Alison. 1992. *The Language of Clothes.* London: Bloomsbury.

Lynch, Annette. 1995. "Hmong American New Year's Dress: The Display of Ethnicity." In *Dress and Ethnicity: Change across Space and Time,* ed. J. Eicher 255–68. Oxford: Berg.

Lynton, Linda, and Sanjay Singh. 1995. *The Sari.* London: Thames and Hudson.

Mackrell, Alice. 2005. *Fashion and Art: The Impact of Art on Fashion and Fashion on Art.* London: Batsford.

MacMaster, Neil, and Toni Lewis. 1998. "Orientalism: From Unveiling to Hyperveiling." *Journal of European Studies* 28 (1–2): 121–35.

Mansel, Philip. 2005. *Dressed to Rule: Royal and Court Costume from Louis XIV to Elizabeth II.* New Haven, CT: Yale University Press.

Marsh, Graham, and Paul Trynka. 2002. *Denim: From Cowboys to Catwalks: A Visual History of the World's Most Legendary Fabric.* London: Aurum Press.

Martin, Richard. 1999. *Fashion and Cubism.* New York: Metropolitan Museum of Art.

Mauss, Marcel. 1973. "Techniques of the Body." *Economy and Society* 2 (1): 70–87.

Mauss, Marcel. 1985. "A Category of the Human Mind: The Notion of Person: The Notion of Self." In *The Category of Person,* ed. M. Carrithers, S. Collins, and S. Lukes 1–25. Cambridge: Cambridge University Press.

Maynard, Margaret. 1994a. *Fashioned from Penury. Dress as Cultural Practice in Colonial Australia.* Cambridge: Cambridge University Press.

Maynard, Margaret. 1994b. "'A Good Deal Too Good for the Bush': Women and the Experience of Dress in Queensland." In *On the Edge: Women's Experiences of Queensland,* ed. G. Reekie 51–65. St. Lucia, Australia: Queensland University Press.

Maynard, Margaret. 2001. *Out of Line: Australian Women and Style.* Sydney, Australia: University of New South Wales Press.

Maynard, Margaret. 2004. *Dress and Globalization.* Manchester, UK: Manchester University Press.

McCann, Edwina. 2007. "Down to Business." *Wish Magazine,* August: 18–23.

McCracken, Grant. 1982. "Rank and Two Aspects of Dress in Elizabethan England." *Culture* 11 (2): 53–62.

McCracken, Grant. 1985. "Dress Colour at the Court of Elizabeth I: An Essay in Historical Anthropology." *Canadian Review of Sociology and Anthropology* 22 (4): 515–33.

McCracken, Grant. 1988. *Culture and Consumption: New Approaches to the Symbolic Character of Consumer Goods and Activities.* Bloomington: Indiana University Press.

McDermott, Catherine. 1999. *Vivienne Westwood.* London: Carlton.

McDowell, Colin. 1997. *The Man of Fashion: Peacock Males and Perfect Gentlemen.* London: Thames and Hudson.

McFedries Paul. 2002. *Word spy.* Available at: http://www.wordspy.com/words/metrosexual.asp

McRobbie, Angela, ed. 1989. *Zoot Suits and Second-Hand Dresses.* Basingstoke, UK: Macmillan.

McVeigh, Brian. 2000. *Wearing Ideology: State, Schooling and Self-Presentation in Japan.* Oxford: Berg.

Meacham, Steve. 2004. "Naval Gazing." *Sydney Morning Herald* (May 29). Available at: http://www.smh.com.au/articles/2004/05/28/1085641697729.html

Mead, Arthur. 2007. "Made in China." In *The Fashion Reader,* ed. L. Welters and A. Lillethun 419–24. Oxford: Berg.

Meagher, David. 2008. "Fabulous Fabrizio." *Wish Magazine,* May: 50–2.

Mendes, Valerie, and Amy de la Haye. 1999. *20th Century Fashion.* London: Thames and Hudson.

Metropolitan Museum of Art, New York. 1983. *Yves Saint Laurent.* London: Thames and Hudson.

Miller, Daniel. 2004. "The Little Black Dress Is the Solution, but What Is the Problem?" In *Elusive Consumption,* ed. K. Ekström and H. Brembeck 113–27. Oxford: Berg.

Mingxin, Bao, and Lu Lijun. 2008. "A Brief History of Chinese Fashion Design." In *China Design Now,* ed. Z. Hongxing and L. Parker 106–9. London: V&A Publications..

Mitchell, Louise. 1997. *Stepping Out: Three Centuries of Shoes.* Sydney, Australia: Powerhouse.

Mitchell, Louise, ed. 2005. *The Cutting Edge: Fashion from Japan.* Sydney, Australia: Powerhouse.

Miyake Design Studio. 1978. *Issey Miyake: East Meets West.* Tokyo: Heibonsha.

Molnar, Andrea. 1998. "Transformations in the Use of Traditional Textiles of Ngada (Western Flores, Eastern Indonesia): Commercialization, Fashion and Ethnicity." In *Consuming Fashion: Adorning the Transnational Body,* ed. A. Bryden and S. Niessen 39–56. Oxford: Berg:

Mort, Frank. 1996. *Cultures and Consumption: Masculinity and Social Space in the Late 20th Century.* London: Routledge.

Mulvagh, Jane. 2005. "Punk." In *Icons of Fashion: The 20th Century*, ed. G. Buxbaum 120–21. Munich: Prestel Verlag.

National Drug Strategy Network. 1997. "Clinton Condemns 'Heroin Chic' in Fashion Industry Following *New York Times* Story." Available at: http://www.ndsn.org/july97/chic.html

National Gallery of Victoria. 2008. *Black in Fashion: From Mourning to Night.* Melbourne: National Gallery of Victoria.

Niessen, Sandra. 2003. "Three Scenarios from Batak Clothing History: Designing Participation in the Global Fashion Trajectory." In *Re-Orienting Fashion: The Globalization of Asian Dress,* ed. S. Niessen, A.M. Leshkowich, and C. Jones 49–78. Oxford: Berg.

Norton, John. 1997. "Faith and Fashion in Turkey." In *Languages of Dress in the Middle East,* ed. N. Lindisfarne-Tapper and B. Ingham 149–77. Richmond, Surrey, UK: Curzon Press.

Noyes, Dorothy, and Regina Bendix. 1998. "Introduction: In Modern Dress: Costuming the European Social Body, 17th–20th Centuries." *Journal of American Folklore* 111 (440): 107–14.

O'Hara Callan, Georgina. 2002. *Thames and Hudson Dictionary of Fashion and Fashion Designers.* London: Thames and Hudson.

O'Mahony, Marie, and Sarah Braddock. 2002. *Sportstech: Revolutionary Fabrics, Fashion and Design.* London: Thames and Hudson.

Okely, Judith. 1993. "Privileged, Schooled and Finished: Boarding Education for Girls." In *Defining Women: The Nature of Women in Society,* ed. S. Ardener 93–122. Oxford: Berg.

Otto, Ton, and Robert Verloop. 1996. "The Asaro Mudmen: Local Property, Public Culture?" *Contemporary Pacific* 8: 349–86.

Packer, William. 1985. *The Art of Vogue Covers, 1909–1940.* London: Octopus Books.

Palmer, Alexandra. 2001. *Couture and Commerce: The Transatlantic Fashion Trade in the 1950s.* Toronto: UBC Press.

Parkins, Wendy, ed. 2002. *Fashioning the Body Politic: Dress, Gender, Citizenship.* Oxford: Berg.

Pattison, Angela, and Nigel Cawthorne. 1997. *A Century of Shoes: Icons of Style in the 20th Century.* Gordon, New South Wales, Australia: Universal International.

Paulicelli, Eugenia. 2002. "Fashion, the Politics of Style and National Identity in Pre-fascist and Fascist Italy." In *Material Strategies: Dress and Gender in Historical Perspective,* ed. B. Burman and C. Turbin 167–89. Oxford: Blackwell.

Pavia, Fabienne. 1995/1996. *The World of Perfume.* New York: Knickerbocker Press.

Perkin, Corrie. 2008. "Undimmed Attraction of the Dark Side." *Australian* (February 27). Available at: http://www.theaustralian.news.com.au/story/0,25197,23280386-5010800,00.html

Polan, Brenda. 2006. "Fashion Journalism." In *The Fashion Handbook,* ed. T. Jackson and D. Shaw 154–71. London: Routledge.

Polhemus, Ted. 1994. *Street Style: From Sidewalk to Catwalk.* London: Thames and Hudson.

Polhemus, Ted. 2007. "Trickle Down, Bubble Up." In *The Fashion Reader,* ed. L. Welters and A. Lillethun 327–31. Oxford: Berg.

Polhemus, Ted, and Lyn Proctor. 1984. *Pop Styles.* London: Vermilion.

Postrel, V. 2003. *The Substance of Style: How the Rise of Aesthetic Value Is Remaking Commerce, Culture, and Consciousness.* New York: Harper Collins.

Pratt, Lucy, and Linda Woolley. 1998. *Shoes.* London: V&A Publications.

Puwar, Nirmal. 2002. "Multicultural Fashion … Stirrings of Another Sense of Aesthetics and Memory." *Feminist Review* 71: 63–87.

Quan, Dick. 2008. "Buying Time." *Wish Magazine,* June: 28–33.

Quataert, Donald. 1997. "Clothing Laws, State, and Society in the Ottoman Empire, 1720–1829." *International Journal of Middle East Studies* 29 (3): 403–425.

Quick, Harriet. 1997. *Catwalking: A History of the Fashion Model.* London: Hamlyn.

Quinn, Bradley. 2001. *Chinese Style: The Art of Living.* London: Conran Octopus.

Quinn, Bradley. 2002. *Techno Fashion.* Oxford: Berg.

Quinn, Bradley. 2003a. *The Fashion of Architecture.* Oxford: Berg.

Quinn, Bradley. 2003b. *Scandinavian Style.* London: Conran Octopus.

Rabine, Leslie, and Susan Kaiser. 2006. "Sewing Machines and Dream Machines in Los Angeles and San Francisco: The Case of the Blue Jean." In *Fashion's World Cities,* ed. C. Breward and D. Gilbert 235–49. Oxford: Berg.

Radcliffe-Brown, Alfred. 1922. *The Andaman Islanders.* Cambridge: Cambridge University Press.

Rantisi, Norma. 2006. "How New York Stole Modern Fashion." In *Fashion's World Cities,* ed. C. Breward and D. Gilbert 109–22. Oxford: Berg.

Reid, Anthony. 1988. *Southeast Asia in the Age of Commerce, 1450–1680.* Vol. 1. New Haven, CT: Yale University Press.

Reinach, Simona Segre. 2005. "China and Italy: Fast Fashion versus Prèt-à-Porter: Towards a New Culture of Fashion." *Fashion Theory* 9 (1): 50–6.

Reinach, Simona Segre. 2006. "Milan: The City of Prêt-à-Porter in a World of Fast Fashion." In *Fashion's World Cities,* ed. C. Breward and D. Gilbert 123–35. Oxford: Berg.

Richardson, Catherine, ed. 2004. *Clothing Culture, 1350–1650.* Aldershot, UK: Ashgate.

Richemont. nd. "L'horologerie européenne en Chine: Watches and Wonders." Available at: http:/www.worldtempus.com/wt/1/6791/.

Richie, Donald. 1999. *Tokyo: A View of the City.* London: Topographics, Reaktion Books.

Richie, Donald. 2003. *The Image Factory: Fads and Fashion in Japan.* London: Reaktion Books.

Roberts, Claire, ed. 1997. *Evolution and Revolution: Chinese Dress, 1700s–1990s.* Sydney, Australia: Powerhouse.

Robinson, Julian. 1986. *The Fine Art of Fashion Illustration.* Kensington, New South Wales, Australia: Bay Books.

Rocamora, Agnès. 2006. "Paris, Capitale de la Mode: Representing the Fashion City in the Media." In *Fashion's World Cities,* ed. C. Breward and D. Gilbert 43–54. Oxford: Berg.

Roche, Daniel. 1996. *The Culture of Clothing: Dress and Fashion in the Ancient Regime.* Cambridge: Cambridge University Press and Editions de la Maison des Sciences de l'Homme.

Roche, Daniel. 2000. "Clothing and Appearances." *A History of Everyday Things: The Birth of Consumption in France, 1600–1800.* Cambridge: Cambridge University Press. 193–220.

Rosen, Maggie. 2004. "Sex, Rags and Rock n' Roll." April 2. Available at: http://www.iafrica.com

Ruhlen, Rebecca. 2003. "Korean Alterations: Nationalism, Social Consciousness, and "Traditional" Clothing." In *Re-Orienting Fashion: The Globalization of Asian Dress,* ed. S. Niessen, A.M. Leshkowich, and C. Jones 117–38. Oxford: Berg.

Rushton, Prue. 2002. "Cause Celebs." *Weekend Australian Magazine* (May 25–26): 40–42.

Rutherford, Judith, and Jackie Menzies. 2004. *Celestial Silks: Chinese Religious and Court Textiles.* Sydney, Australia: Art Gallery of New South Wales.

Sainderichin, Ginette. 1999. *Kenzo.* London: Thames and Hudson.

Salvemini, Lorella Pagnucco. 2002. *United Colors: The Benetton Campaigns.* London: Scriptum Editions.

Sapir, Edward. 1931. "Fashion." *Encyclopedia of the Social Sciences.* Vol. 6. New York: Macmillan.

Schiaparelli, Elsa. 2007. *Shocking Life: The Autobiography of Elsa Schiaparelli.* New York: Harry N. Abrams.

Schmid, Beate Dorothea. 1999. "T-Shirts, Jeans, and Leather Jacket." In *Icons of Fashion: The 20th Century,* ed. G. Buxbaum 76–77. Munich: Prestel Verlag.

Schneider, Jane. 1978. "Peacocks and Penguins: The Political Economy of European Cloth and Colors." *American Ethnologist* 5 (3): 413–47.

Schulte Nordholt, Henk. 1997b. Introduction. In *Outward Appearances: Dressing State and Society in Indonesia,* ed. H. Schulte Nordholt 1–37. Leiden: KITLV Press.

Schulte Nordholt, Henk, ed. 1997a. *Outward Appearances: Dressing State and Society in Indonesia.* Leiden: KITLV Press.

Schwarz, Ronald. 1979. "Uncovering the Secret Vice: Toward an Anthropology of Clothing and Adornment." In *The Fabrics of Culture,* ed. J. Cordwell and R. Schwarz 23–45. The Hague: Mouton.

Scott, Georgia. 2003. *Headwraps: A Global Journey.* New York: Public Affairs.

Sekimoto, Teruo. 1997. "Uniforms and Concrete Walls: Dressing the Village Under the New Order in the 1970s and 1980s." In *Outward Appearances: Dressing State and Society in Indonesia,* ed. H. Schulte Nordholt 307–38. Leiden: KITLV Press.

Semmelhack, Elizabeth. 2006. "A Delicate Balance: Women Power and High Heels." In *Shoes: A History from Sandals to Sneakers,* ed. G. Riello and P. McNeil 224–49. Oxford: Berg.

Simmel, Georg. 1904. "Fashion." Reprint. *American Journal of Sociology* 62 (1957): 541–58.

Sims, Joshua. 1999. *Rock/Fashion.* London: Octopus.

Sinclair, John. 1973. *Wigmen of New Guinea.* Milton: Jacaranda Press.

Skov, Lise. 2003. "Fashion-Nation: A Japanese Globalization Experience and a Hong Kong Dilemma." In *Re-Orienting Fashion: The Globalization of Asian Dress,* ed. S. Niessen, A.M. Leshkowich, and C. Jones 215–42. Oxford: Berg.

Smedley, Elliott. 2000. "Escaping to Reality: Fashion Photography in the 1990s." In *Fashion Cultures: Theories, Explorations and Analysis,* ed. S. Bruzzi and P. Church Gibson 143–56. London: Routledge.

Smith, Deborah. 2004. "Your Extreme Makeover Starts Here—Tame the Slang and Drop the Twang." *Sydney Morning Herald* (May 15–16): 10.

Smith, Thomas Spence. 1974. "Aestheticism and Social Structure: Style and Social Network in the Dandy Life." *American Sociological Review* 39 (5): 725–43.

Soh, Chung-Hee. 1992. "Skirts, Trousers, or *Hanbok?* The Politics of Image Making Among Korean Women Legislators." *Women's Studies International Forum* 15 (3): 375–384.

Sproles, George. 1985. "Behavioral Science Theories of Fashion." In *The Psychology of Fashion,* ed. M. Solomon 55–69. Lexington, MA: D.C. Heath Lexington Books.

Stafford, Andy. 2006. "Afterword. Clothes, Fashion and System in the Writings of Roland Barthes: 'Something Out of Nothing.'" In *The Language of Fashion.* R. Barthes 118–66. Sydney, Australia: Power.

Stanfill, Sonnet. 2006. "Curating the Fashion City: New York Fashion at the V&A." In *Fashion's World Cities,* ed. C. Breward and D. Gilbert 68–88.Oxford: Berg.

Stanfill, Sonnet. 2007. *New York Fashion.* New York: Harry N. Abrams.

Stearns, Peter. 2001. *Consumerism in World History: The Global Transformation of Desire.* London: Routledge.

Steele, Valerie. 1988. *Paris Fashion: A Cultural History.* Oxford: Oxford University Press.

Steele, Valerie. 1998. *Shoes: A Lexicon of Style.* London: Scriptum Editions.

Steele, Valerie. 2001. "'Style in Revolt': Hussein Chalayan, Alexander McQueen and Vivienne Westwood." In *Radical Fashion,* ed. C. Wilcox 46–53. London: V&A Publications.

Steele, Valerie. 2001. *The Red Dress.* New York: Rizzoli International.

Steele, Valerie. 2003. *Fashion: Italian Style.* New Haven, CT: Yale University Press.

Steele, Valerie. 2006. "Shoes and the Erotic Imagination." In *Shoes: A History from Sandals to Sneakers,* ed. G. Riello and P. McNeil 250–70. Oxford: Berg.

Steele, Valerie. 2007. *The Black Dress.* New York: Collins Desi.

Steele, Valerie, and John Major, eds. 1999. *China Chic: East Meets West.* New Haven, CT: Yale University Press.

Storey, Tessa. 2004. "Clothing Courtesans: Fabrics, Signals, and Experiences." In *Clothing Culture, 1350–1650,* ed. C. Richardson 95–107. Aldershot, UK: Ashgate.

Storr, Merl. 2003. *Latex and Lingerie: Shopping for Pleasure at Ann Summers.* Oxford: Berg.

Strathern, Andrew. 1987. "Dress, Decoration, and Art in New Guinea." In *Man as Art,* ed. M. Kirk and A. Strathern 10–17. Berlin: Taco.

Strathern, Marilyn. 1979. "The Self in Self-Decoration." *Oceania* 48: 241–57.

Styles, John. 2008. "Time Piece: Working Men and Watches." *History Today* 58 (1): 44–50.

Suga, Masami. 1995. "Exotic West to Exotic Japan: Revival of Japanese Tradition in Modern Japan." In *Dress and Ethnicity: Change Across Space and Time,* ed. J. Eicher 95–116. Oxford: Berg..

Sullivan, James. 2006. *Jeans: A Cultural History of an American Icon.* New York: Gotham Books.

*Sydney Morning Herald*. 2004. "Punk's Princess of Future Shock." Available at: http://www.smh.com.au/articles/2004/07/12/1089484295900/html

*Sydney Morning Herald*. 2007. "Model Earnings." Available at: http://www.smh.com.au/news/people/model-earnings/2007/07/19/1184559923678/html?s_cid=rss_aosmh

Symons, Sandra. 1983. "Australian Essence." *Mode,* August/September: np.

Szeto, Naomi Yin-Yin. 1997. "Hong Kong Style: The Evolution of the Cheungsam." In *Evolution and Revolution: Chinese Dress, 1700s–1990s,* ed. C. Roberts 54–64. Sydney, Australia: Powerhouse.

Taher, Abul. 2006. "Enter Moss, the 'Anorexic Aphrodite.'" *Australian* (February 6): 16.

Tanner, Lindsey. 2007. "Bringing Them to Heel." *Canberra Times*: 3.

Taylor, Jean. 1997. "Costume and Gender in Colonial Java, 1800–1940." In *Outward Appearances: Dressing State and Society in Indonesia,* ed. H. Schulte Nordholt 85–116. Leiden: KITLV Press.

Taylor, Lou. 1983. *Mourning Dress: A Costume and Social History.* London: George Allen and Unwin.

Taylor, Lou. 2002. *The Study of Dress History.* Manchester, UK: Manchester University Press.

Teas, Kenneth R., and Sanjeev Agarwal. 2000. "The Effects of Extrinsic Product Cues on Consumers' Perceptions of Quality, Sacrifice and Value." *Journal of the Academy of Marketing Science* 28 (2): 278–90.

Thomas, Dana. 2007. *Deluxe: How Luxury Lost Its Lustre.* London: Allen Lane.

Todtri. 2002. *Fragrance and Fashion.* New York: Todtri.

Troy, Nancy. 2003. *Couture Culture: A Study in Modern Art and Fashion.* Cambridge, MA: MIT Press.

Tulloch, Carol. 1998. "'Out of Many, One People': The Relativity of Dress, Race and Ethnicity to Jamaica, 1880–1907." *Fashion Theory* 2 (4): 359–82.

Turner, Bryan. 1991. "The Discourse of Diet." In *The Body: Social Process and Cultural Theory,* ed. M. Featherstone, M. Hepworth, and B. Turner 157–69. London: Sage.

2456.com. 2008. "Spain and Germany Seek to Optimize Sizing Systems." Available at: http://textile.2456.com/eng/marketnews/details.asp?inewsiid=4&inid=70665&ptid=545&e=1

Vainshtein, Olga. 2006. "Mapping Moscow Fashion: Spaces and Spectacles of Consumption." In *Fashion's World Cities,* ed. C. Breward, and D. Gilbert 135–58. Oxford: Berg.

van Dijk, Kees. 1997. "Sarongs, Jubbahs, and Trousers." In *Outward Appearances,* ed. H. Schulte Nordholt 39–84. Leiden: KITLV Press.

Veillon, Dominique. 2002. *Fashion under the Occupation.* Oxford: Berg.

Velblen, Thorstein. 1899. *The Theory of the Leisure Class.* New York: Macmillan.

Vergani, Guido, ed. 2006. *Fashion Dictionary.* New York: Baldi Castoldi Dalai.

von Falke, Jacob. 1881. *Costümgeschichte der Culturvoeller.* Stuttgart: Spemann.

Wagner, Christopher. 2006. "Boys Sailor Suits." Available at: http://histclo.com/style/suit/sailor/sailors.html

Wax, Murray. 1957. "Themes in Cosmetics and Grooming." *American Journal of Sociology* 62 (6): 588–93.

Webb, Bill. 2006. "Fashion Retailing." In *The Fashion Handbook,* ed. T. Jackson and D. Shaw 104–31. London: Routledge.

Weber, Caroline. 2006. *Queen of Fashion: What Marie Antoinette Wore to the Revolution.* London: Aurum Press.

Welters, Linda. 2007. "Introduction: Fashion in the Media." In *The Fashion Reader,* ed. L. Welters and A. Lillethun 275–77. Oxford: Berg,

Welters, Linda, and Patricia Cunningham, eds. 2005. *Twentieth-Century American Fashion.* Oxford: Berg.

Weston-Thomas, Pauline. nd. "Chambre Syndicale Fashion History." Available at: http://www.fashion-era.com/chambre_syndicale.htm

White, Nicola. 2000. *Reconstructing Italian Fashion: America and the Development of the Italian Fashion Industry.* Oxford: Berg.

White, Palmer. 1986. *Elsa Schiaparelli: Empress of Paris Fashion.* London: Aurum Press.

Whitfield, Danielle. 2008. "The Luxury of Woe." In *Black in Fashion: From Mourning to Night,* ed. National Gallery of Victoria 26–37. Melbourne, Australia: National Gallery of Victoria.

Wigley, Mark. 2003. *White Walls, Designer Dresses: The Fashioning of Modern Architecture.* Cambridge, MA: MIT Press.

Wilcox, Claire, ed. 2001. *Radical Fashion.* London: V&A Publications.

Wilcox, Claire. 2004. *Vivienne Westwood.* London: V&A Publications.

Wilcox, Claire, ed. 2007. *The Golden Age of Couture: Paris and London, 1947–57.* London: V&A Publications.

Williams, Raymond. 1977. *Keywords.* London: Fontana.

Wilson, Elizabeth. 1985. *Adorned in Dreams: Fashion and Modernity.* London: Virago.

Wilson, Verity. 1986. *Chinese Dress.* London: Victoria and Albert Museum.

Wolf, Arthur. 1970. "Chinese Kinship and Mourning Dress." In *Family and Kinship in Chinese Society,* ed. M. Freedman 189–207. Stanford, CA: Stanford University Press.

Wong, Gloria. 2006. "The Magic of Issue-Based Projects for Fashion Design." In *Generation Mode,* ed. S. Anna and E. Gronbach 95–107. Ostfildern-Ruit: Hatje Cantz Verlag.

Woodward, Sophie. 2002. "Making Fashion Material." *Journal of Material Culture* 7 (3): 345–53.

Wright, Lee. 2007. "Objectifying Gender: The Stiletto Heel." In *Fashion Theory: A Reader,* ed. M. Barnard 197–207. London: Routledge.

Yamani, Mai. 1997. "Changing the Habits of a Lifetime: The Adaptation of Hejazi Dress to the New Social Order." In *Languages of Dress in the Middle East,* ed. N. Lindisfarne-Tapper and B. Ingham 55–66. Richmond, Surrey, UK: Curzon Press.

Ye, Sang. 1997. "From Rags to Revolution: Behind the Seams of Social Change." In *Evolution and Revolution: Chinese Dress, 1700s–1990s,* ed. C. Roberts 40–52. Sydney, Australia: Powerhouse.

# index

Page numbers in *italic* indicate illustrations.